Turkey and European Integration

Turkey and European Integration examines the important issue of Turkey's relationship with Europe, emphasising the importance of Turkey's internal dynamics in the context of the debates on Europeanisation and convergence.

The authors focus on the interaction between domestic factors such as economic policy, business community preferences, political culture and identity politics on the one hand, and Turkey's Europeanisation trajectory on the other. They analyse not only the impact of the domestic factors on Turkey's integration with Europe, but also the extent to which Europeanisation – including compliance with EU accession criteria – have led to change and resistance in Turkish visions of state–society relations, economic and political governance, and democratic change. With this unique approach, the book addresses a large set of issues that remain in the blind spot of the EU–Turkey literature that treats EU–Turkey relations merely as a 'foreign' or 'external' policy issue for either party.

This book provides an up-to-date analysis of public opinion, economic governance, religion, democratisation, citizenship and domestic–international linkages with a view to highlighting Turkey's convergence to and divergence from the EU in the wake of the Helsinki summit decision that confirmed Turkey's candidate status. It should be of interest to all students and researchers of Turkish and European politics and political economy.

Mehmet Uğur is Jean Monnet Reader in political economy at the University of Greenwich, UK. **Nergis Canefe** is assistant professor of political science at York University, Canada.

Europe and the nation state
Edited by Michael Burgess and Lee Miles
Centre for European Union Studies, University of Hull

This series explores the complex relationship between nation states and European integration and the political, social, economic and policy implications of this interaction. The series examines issues such as:

- the impact of the EU on the politics and policy-making of the nation-state and vice versa
- the effects of expansion of the EU on individual nation states in Europe
- the relationship between the EU and non-European nation states.

Turkey and European Integration

Accession prospects and issues

Edited by
Mehmet Uğur and Nergis Canefe

Routledge
Taylor & Francis Group

LONDON AND NEW YORK

First published 2004 by Routledge
11 New Fetter Lane, London EC4P 4EE

Simultaneously published in the USA and Canada
by Routledge
29 West 35th Street, New York, NY 10001

Routledge is an imprint of the Taylor & Francis Group

Typeset in Baskerville by Wearset Ltd, Boldon, Tyne and Wear
Printed and bound in Great Britain by MPG Books Ltd, Bodmin

British Library Cataloguing in Publication Data
A catalogue record for this book is available from the British Library

Library of Congress Cataloging in Publication Data
A catalog record for this book has been requested

ISBN 0-415-32656-7

We dedicate this book to our families

Contents

Illustrations

Figures

Tables

Contributors

Serap Atan is a PhD candidate at the Free University of Brussels, Faculty of Social, Political and Economic Sciences. Her thesis is entitled 'Turkish peak business organisations and the Europeanisation of the domestic structures in Turkey: meeting the membership conditionality'. Currently, she works as researcher for the Turkish Industrialists' and Businessmen's Association (TUSIAD) Representation to the EU and UNICE in Brussels.

Gamze Avcı is currently a Postdoctoral Fellow at the Department of Turkish Studies at Leiden University in the Netherlands. She received her MA in Political Science from the University of Georgia (USA), her MSc degree in European Politics and Policy from the London School of Economics and her PhD in Political Science from the University of Georgia in 1997. Her work has appeared in journals such as the *European Foreign Affairs Review, European Journal of Political Research* and *European Journal of Migration and Law*.

Nergis Canefe is assistant professor at the Department of Political Science, York University, Canada. She received her doctorate in the area of Social and Political Thought (York, Canada) and worked as a postdoctoral fellow at the Institute of Historical Research, University of London (1998–2000), and the European Institute at the London School of Economics (2000–2002). Her main research interests are theories of citizenship, ethics of nationalism in South-Eastern Europe, Turkish social and political thought, refugee and migration studies including diasporic identities, and long-term legacies of war and forced migration. She has published articles in the journals *Citizenship Studies, Rethinking History, Refuge, Southeast European Society and Politics,* and *Turkish Studies,* and has several contributions in edited volumes. She is the co-editor of the present volume.

Ali Çarkoğlu is currently associate professor at the Faculty of Arts and Sciences in Sabancı University, Istanbul. His research interests include voting behaviour, political parties, public opinion, and popular bases of foreign policy and support for EU membership. His publications have appeared in various edited volumes as well as refereed journals. He recently co-edited with Barry Rubin the *Turkish Studies* Special Issue: *Turkey and the European Union: Domestic Politics, Economic Integration and International Dynamics* (2003).

Burhanettin Duran is associate professor of political science at the International Relations Department of Sakarya University, Turkey. He has completed his PhD thesis in 2001 on the transformation of Islamist political thought in Turkey from 1908 to 1960. His research interests include Islamism, Turkish political thought and Turkish foreign policy. He has published and presented a number of papers on Islamist intellectuals, the Islamist discourse of civilisation and the Islamist approach to ethnic coexistence.

Mine Eder is an associate professor at Boğaziçi University, Department of Political Science and International Relations, Istanbul, Turkey. She received her PhD from the University of Virginia, where she specialised in the political economy of newly industrialising countries. She is the co-author *of Political Economy of Regional Cooperation in the Middle East* (1998) and has written extensively on regionalism, populism, and the comparative political economy of Turkey.

Effie Fokas is a doctoral candidate at the London School of Economics and a research fellow at the Hellenic Foundation for European and Foreign Policy (ELIAMEP). Her research areas include the relationship between religion and nationalism; the role of religion in national–EU relations; and church activity in national welfare provision. She is currently co-editing a text entitled 'Euro-Islam at the Turn of the Millennium: Present Conditions and Future Perspectives' (forthcoming).

E. Fuat Keyman is associate professor of international relations at Koç University, Istanbul. His current research interests include globalisation and democratisation, citizenship issues, the role of civil society organisations in the democratisation process, and contemporary Turkish politics. He is the author of *Turkey and Radical Democracy* (in Turkish, 2000) and co-editor of 'Challenges to Citizenship in a Globalizing World' (forthcoming).

Ziya Öniş is professor of international relations at Koç University, Istanbul. His current research interests include the role of civil society organisations in the democratisation process, Turkey–EU relations, as well as the political economy of financial globalisation and emerging market crises. He is the author of *State and Market: The Political Economy of Turkey in Comparative Perspective* (1998) and co-editor of 'Turkey's Economy in Crisis' (forthcoming).

Jonathan Sugden was Amnesty International (AI) researcher on Turkey, Greece and Cyprus from 1990 to 1999. Since 1999 he has worked in the same capacity for Human Rights Watch (HRW). He has produced a large number of reports and action documentation on Turkey's human rights record. His most recent report was on internally displaced people of Turkey, which is entitled *Displaced and Disregarded: Turkey's Failing Village Return Program* (2002).

Mehmet Uğur is Jean Monnet Reader in the political economy of European integration at the University of Greenwich, London. His research interests include theories of regional integration, EU external economic relations, EU–Turkey relations, globalisation–regional integration linkages and regional public goods. His publications have appeared in a number of edited volumes and refereed journals. He is the author of *The European Union and Turkey: An Anchor/Credibility Dilemma* (1999), which has also been translated into Turkish.

Abbreviations

AKP	*Adalet ve Kalkınma Partisi* (Justice and Development Party)
ANAP	*Anavatan Partisi* (Motherland Party)
AP	Additional Protocol; Accession Partnership
c.i.f.	cost, insurance and freight
CBRT	Central Bank of the Republic of Turkey
CEECs	Central and East European countries
CEEP	European Centre of Enterprises with Public Participation and of Enterprises of General Economic Interest
CHP	*Cumhuriyet Halk Partisi* (Republican People's Party)
CPeI	Corruption Perceptions Index
CPI	consumer price inflation
CPT	Committee for the Prevention of Torture
CU	customs union
DEHAP	*Demokratik Halk Partisi* (Democratic People's Party)
DEP	Democracy Party
DHKP-C	Revolutionary People's Liberation Party-Front
DISK	Confederation of Progressive Trade Unions
DP	*Demokrat Parti* (Democratic Party)
DSP	*Demokratik Sol Parti* (Democratic Left Party)
DYP	*Doğru Yol Partisi* (True Path Party)
ECHR	European Court of Human Rights
EEC	European Economic Community
EESC	European Economic and Social Committee
EMS	European Monetary System
EP	European Parliament
ESC	Economic and Social Council
ESDI	European Security and Defence Initiative
ETUC	European Trade Unions Confederation
EU	European Union
FDI	foreign direct investment
FP	*Fazilet Partisi* (Virtue Party)
GDP	gross domestic product
GNP	gross national product

GP	*Genç Parti* (Young Party)
HADEP	*Halkın Demokrasi Partisi* (People's Democracy Party)
IBDA-C	Islamic Raiders of the Big East-Front
IEF	Index of Economic Freedom
IKV	*İktisadi Kalkınma Vakfı* (Economic Development Foundation)
IMF	International Monetary Fund
ISI	import-substituting industrialisation
ISO	Istanbul Chamber of Industry
ITP	Istanbul Chamber of Commerce
JCC	Joint Consultative Committee
KOSGEB	Small and Medium Industry Development Organisation
MEKSA	Foundation for Professional Formation and Small trade
MEP	Member of the European Parliament
MGK	National Security Party
MHP	*Milliyetçi Haraket Partisi* (Nationalist Action Party)
MSP	National Salvation Party
MUSIAD	Association of Independent Industrialists and Businessmen
NATO	North Atlantic Treaty Organization
NGO	non-governmental organization
NPAA	National Programme for the Adoption of the *Acquis*
NSC	National Security Council
OECD	Organisation for Economic Cooperation and Development
PBO	peak business organisation
PKK	*Partiya Karkaren Kurdistan* (Kurdistan Workers' Party)
PSBR	public-sector borrowing requirement
RP	*Refah Partisi* (Welfare Party)
RRF	Rapid Reaction Force
SEE	state economic enterprise
SMEs	small and medium-sized enterprises
SP	*Saadet Partisi* (Felicity Party)
TESEV	*Türkiye Ekonomik ve Sosyal Etüdler Vakfı* (Turkish Economic and Social Studies Foundation
TESK	Confederation of Turkish Craftsmen and Small Traders
TGNA	Turkish Grand National Assembly
TIKB	Turkish Revolutionary Communist Union
TIKKO	Turkish Liberation Army of Peasants and Workers
TISK	Turkish Confederation of Employers' Associations
TMMOB	Union of Turkish Architects and Engineers
TNRC	Turkish Republic of Northern Cyprus
TOBB	Union of Chambers of Commerce, Industry, Maritime Commerce and Commodity Exchanges of Turkey
TUSIAD	*Türk Sanayicileri ve İşadamları Derneği* (Turkish Industrialists' and Businessmen's Association)
TZOB	Union of Turkish Chambers of Agriculture

UEAPME	Association of Crafts and Small and Medium-Sized Enterprises of the European Union
UNICE	Union of Industrial and Employer's Confederation of Europe
WPI	wholesale price inflation
YTP	*Yeni Türkiye Partisi* (New Turkey Party)

Preface

The publication of this edited volume of twelve essays on Turkey and European integration coincides with a new crossroads in the evolution of the European Union (EU). The imminent epoch-making enlargement of the EU from its current fifteen member states to twenty-five in May 2004 heralds a new era in the building of Europe. But this widely-acclaimed achievement that signals the rediscovery and revitalisation of Europe, and furnishes the basis for great optimism about its future in world politics, leaves open the question of Turkish membership. What constitutes a momentous occasion for the EU also has colossal implications for Turkey.

Turkey remains, for the moment, an outsider in the new European family of nation states. In this edited collection of essays, the editors, Nergis Canefe and Mehmet Uğur, have used this unprecedented enlargement as a unique opportunity to reassess and reappraise Turkey's relationship to the EU and European integration. Their project, however, is very different from previous contributions to the mainstream literature. In this book there is a deliberate attempt to move away from the traditional paradigm for studying Turkey–EU relations that Canefe and Uğur construe as largely one-dimensional. Instead they have decided to look at these relations from an unusual set of perspectives. Their dynamic approach is one that deflects the eye away from traditional concerns about the obstacles to Turkish membership of the EU and utilises a different framework of analysis that includes the following broad features: public opinion; economic governance; religion; and international–domestic interactions. Together these four separate sections combine to produce a new line of enquiry that goes beyond the familiar negative preconceptions and preoccupations of Turkish membership.

Canefe and Uğur have assembled a collection of essays that takes into account the EU's new crossroads and Turkey's potential relationship to it. In short, the book seeks to analyse and reflect upon Turkey's complex relationship with the new EU from two principal standpoints: the contemporary pressures, directions and priorities specific to the EU; and the ever-changing perceptions of the Turkish state, society and economy. In order to do this, the volume is structured in a way that points up the historical background and the changing socio-political context that together explain how Turkish society and elites perceive the EU. It is a complex set of perceptions in which both subject and object are in constant flux.

The upshot of this Turkish awareness of the new EU – its open-ended possibilities and real limitations – is something that was not anticipated by many observers and has therefore gone largely unnoticed in the mainstream literature. This is the existence of a kind of subtle reciprocal relationship that prompts Turkey to look again at its own sense of itself. And reflection leads to reaction – a process of conscious redefinition – bringing into play with Turkish visions of self, society, progress, justice and stability. There is, then, a highly complex and sophisticated set of relations between Turkey and European integration that is essentially multidimensional. The book tries to capture this complexity by conceptualising Turkey and European integration as a kind of prism through which Turks are able to see their relations with Europe – and especially with the EU – as constitutive of their own identity. Canefe and Uğur claim that it is in this peculiar way that Turkish people perceive the treatment of their membership of the EU as an indication of how others see them and will treat them in the future.

The gist of this collection of essays suggests that previous contributions to the debate about Turkey and European integration have overlooked significant changes in the ownership of the EU membership project in Turkey. The constellation of forces that currently favour membership and the structure of those that oppose it reveal a monumental fault-line between the state and civil society together with a rupture within the Turkish state itself. The overall impact, at least in the short-term, is one of a series of tension-laden compromises between the pro- and anti-EU forces in society, the Turkish government and the EU's weak commitment to integrate Turkey. This triangular set of interactions will shape the nature of the continuing debate about the future of Turkey and European integration.

Michael Burgess
University of Hull

Acknowledgements

The editors would like to thank the University Association for Contemporary European Studies (UACES) for their financial support towards the cost of holding a conference in which the findings of this book were discussed.

1 Turkey and European integration

Introduction

Nergis Canefe and Mehmet Uğur

The majority of the contributors to this volume met at Heidelberg, Germany, at a special session on Turkey–European Union (EU) relations at the European Society for International Studies Association Meeting in 2001. There, we reached the agreement that available debates on this issue were not satisfactory for answering the kinds of questions we were asking. The studies conducted so far had mainly been concerned with either what injustices were committed by the Union against Turkey, or what major deficiencies or preoccupations Turkey exhibited (which were mostly defined as related to its culture and its 'developing country' status) that were then inhibiting its accession to the EU. The aim of the editors of and contributors to this book is to open a new line of inquiry in the field of Turkey–EU relations that goes beyond these concerns and that can provide clues about actual prospects, local dynamics and frames of change.

Nevertheless, this book and its distinct vision regarding Turkey–EU relations did not come into being in a vacuum. The late 1980s and the 1990s witnessed a renewed and wide-ranging debate on both the future and the limits of Europe (Warleigh, 2002; Kurzer, 2001; Peterson and Bomberg, 1999; Eichengreen and Frieden, 1998; Williams, 1994). In this context, although the focus was almost exclusively on 'eastern enlargement' – that is, the costs and benefits of the inclusion of Central and East European countries (CEECs) – we learned a lot from the way successive waves of enlargement were thought about. True, the respective frames of analysis were set in such a way that the desire and commitment of the CEECs to join the EU was almost taken for granted. Therefore, calculations and estimates were made on the basis of what Europe would gain or lose if there were full accession, semi-inclusion limited to economic complementarity, or no or delayed accession. Still, the debate, especially with respect to the eastern enlargement, created several offshoots, which then became essential for understanding what Europe and Europeanisation stand for. For instance, the need to devise a new kind of relationship between the member states in a larger Union, issues concerning flexibility and its applications, the meaning and merits of the subsidiarity principle, the necessity of partial or full transfer of national sovereignty in select areas of policy-making and implementation, and the limits of a common legal framework were all articulated in connection with the questioning of where the Union ends (Baldwin and Brunetti, 2001; Goetz and Hix, 2001; Neunreiteher and Wiener, 2000; Westlake, 1998; Weidenfeld, 1997; Cesarani and Fulbrook, 1996). Concomitantly, as the original, pre-Eastern enlargement Union was the embodiment of a series of political compromises, the question arose as to whether the subsequent form of the Union will also be so after the enlargement (Neumann, 1998). The *acquis*, in this regard, seems to have provided the perfect solution. The current desire to create a European Constitution is an attempt with a similar purpose.

At this point, it is important to make a note of the nature of the main motive behind the reform measures that were undertaken in the CEECs during the enlargement process. In the CEECs, the accession criteria have served and continue to serve the purpose of convergence towards Western European norms of governance and rules of conduct, aiming at full integration into the latter's political and socio-economic frame. As a result, the majority of the CEECs managed to fight recession and other socio-economic problems associated with the near-total transformation that their societies went through. By 1994, by and large almost all CEECs had secured economic and political stability. Among the CEECs, there were more successful cases of adaptation, the Czech Republic being the prime example. However, virtually all of them fulfilled and even exceeded Western European expectations in economic and political areas. It is true that inflation rates in the CEECs remain relatively higher than in the EU countries, high unemployment rates remain as a threat despite job-creation and retraining schemes, and privatisation efforts have not yet succeeded in coming to terms with enduring legacies of the communist rule in the region. Yet the big picture is that there has been a significant increase in exports to Western Europe and beyond, as well as in direct foreign investment flows, combined with already developed infrastructural facilities, and an educated *and* cheap labour force. Another important indicator suggestive of convergent adjustment of the CEECs is the increase in the proportion that the service and tourism sectors contribute to their GNPs, and a marked decrease in the proportion contributed by agriculture. This is despite the fact that groups such as Polish farmers continue to argue for entitlement to traditional subsidies associated with the Common Agricultural Policy.

Problems such as slow and inefficient public administration, remaining legal uncertainties, gaps in the conduct of human – and, in particular, minority – rights, and deficiencies in the banking, insurance and loan sectors still need to be addressed. Similarly, rules of fair competition need to be internalised, exchange rates have to be stabilised, and a stable mechanism for the scrutiny of subsidies and structural funds need to be put in place. These additional or further measures, however, appear much more achievable when there is relatively unwavering public support for joining the EU and when relevant sectors of the CEECs are in favour of, or at least are not adverse to, wholesome economic and political restructuring. Also, in the area of politics, the development and unhindered functioning of party systems, trade unions, civil society organisations and independent media, and the conducting of regular and free elections at local, regional and national levels, indicate consolidation of democratic governance. The situation of the Roma population as well as of other minorities, in this context, appears to be an exception rather than the rule, which nonetheless requires the full attention of relevant governments such as that of Slovakia. In summary, in the majority of the prescribed areas, CEECs have performed well in terms of converging towards the European Union. Equally importantly, in areas that remain controversial or troublesome, they appear to be in continual cooperation and accept the guidelines provided by the EU for political action and economic reforms.

The one remaining area of contention, which was also the major concern of the Amsterdam process of 1997, is that of adjusting the EU institutions to the enlarged EU so that effective decision-making and implementation strategies could be secured despite the Union's changed composition (Westlake, 1998). On the one hand, this requires cooperation by the new members and their full commitment to the *acquis*. On the other hand, the original member states of the EU must continue to feel a 'special responsibility' towards CEECs. Otherwise, the desire for an enlarged and thus stronger and more influential Union could not lead to long-lasting and determining effects across the continent. One of the key measures to guarantee the smooth functioning of the integration process at the EU level is that of the cohesion policy. Cohesion is commonly defined as a way of reducing economic disparities by way of distribution from richer to poorer countries until such time as a certain degree of welfare convergence is achieved. Yet we believe that the political motive behind this policy is also important. In other words, transfer of funds through the implementation of the policy also provides a foundation upon which communities and nation-states are bound together through mutual obligations and expectations. The demonstrated commitment of the CEECs to the European project and the willingness of the EU member states to extend the cohesion policy to the CEECs can form the background for a relatively stable relationship in terms of establishing an institutionalised and multi-faceted supra-national partnership.

So far, the reasons for the establishment of such a mutuality have been sought in three areas: long-term economic benefits, regional security combined with claims for global hegemony, and cultural compatibility. Of these three, although it is not listed among the CEECs for various reasons, Turkey complies with all, some or none, depending on the way the problem is defined and how the vantage point is set. For us, this phenomenon in itself constitutes a problem. Therefore, instead of trying to identify which camp to belong to, in this volume we chose to discuss the reasons for and implications of this instability of analysis regarding Turkey–EU relations. As the contributions to the book discuss in detail, there seems to be a major lack of focus and a consequent break in the flow of reasoning in terms of why or why not, and how or how not, Turkey can, could or should acquire full membership of the EU. This, we posit, could be best diagnosed as the lack of in-depth understanding of the historical background and of the changing socio-political dynamics of how Turkish society and elites relate to the EU.

A crucial case that demonstrates our point is that of the Republican project and the Kemalist elite in Turkey. If we set our task as defining a steady historical trajectory that justifies Turkey's request for full membership of the EU, the main element of it is commonly identified as the Republican drive towards Westernisation-cum-modernisation. And yet, in Turkey, *tour de force* Westernisation as a project eventually faced failure in many areas, and with debilitating consequences. This has become particularly manifest since the 1980 military coup. What emerged in post-1980 Turkish history was a multiplicity of 'other' actors – who were traditionally regarded as unlikely candidates for supporting EU membership – claiming ownership over Turkey's Europeanisation project. The definition of the project itself also underwent substantial changes. For these reasons, if we insisted on confining our analysis to a fixed model of pro-EU actors and discourses, we would have failed to recognise both the dimensions of change and the actual prospects for accession.

In summary, the most distinguishing feature of the present work on Turkey–EU relations is its problematisation of the existing paradigms and its questioning of the reasons behind the current deadlock of analysis. There are two main sources of influence that guided us in undertaking such a demanding task. The first relates to the European debate on what the Union stands for, how it can continue to exist and function effectively despite its changing composition and growing size, and where its limits might lie. The second is, as mentioned earlier, the tradition of historically conscious analysis of the dynamics of societal, economical and political change in Turkey. As the Union gradually began to embrace a new form of flexible governance and an agreement was reached that a rigid institutional structure would not carry the weight of a wider Union, achieving a more democratic, legitimate and effective polity became the new focus. This process of thinking anew about what Europe could be rather than what it is also paved the way for devising ways of achieving deeper and wider convergence for ensuring the smooth functioning of the Union during the actual enlargement process. Our desire in producing the present work has been to identify the extent to which the intra-EU debate has been and could be reciprocated in Turkey, albeit with a changed focus that brings Turkish visions of self, society, progress, justice and stability to the centre.

There are numerous volumes on Turkey's long and cumbersome relationship with the EU, published in Turkish and for Turkish readers (Somuncuoğlu, 2002; Bulaç, 2001; Karluk, 1996). We will not cite these here. Suffice it to say that these by and large define the traditional paradigm for studying Turkey–EU relations summarised in the introductory paragraph of this chapter. Instead, here we will limit ourselves to a select number of works published in English, circulated among a mixed audience and representative of the main trends in this field of analysis. We will also refrain from referring to topical articles written by a heterogeneous body of scholars who focus on Turkey–EU relations in terms of current affairs rather than as their main field of analysis (Teitelbaum amd Martin, 2003).

One of the works often cited in terms of a comparative analysis of CEECs and Turkey is that of Togan and Balasubramanyan (2001). This is a comparative study of Central and Eastern European economies and the Turkish economy that focuses on the implications of EU enlargement in the area of economic performance. The contributors discuss the creation of legal infrastructures that encourage entrepreneurial initiatives, fair competition and the full operation of market forces, and boost investor confidence. They also assess the benefits of following fiscal and monetary policies recommended by the World Bank and other financial institutions, coupled with appropriate competition, trade and foreign investment policies in the region of which Turkey forms part. In that, their endeavour is complementary to that of numerous reports produced by the World Bank during the 1980s and 1990s on the potential benefits and costs of the EU's eastern enlargement. The downside of this complementarity, however, is the rather limited scope of analysis.

A possible remedy to this approach was produced by Mehmet Uğur in his work *The European Union and Turkey: An Anchor/Credibility Dilemma* (1999). Uğur's work exemplifies the search for an analytical framework rather than a symptomatic analysis of Turkey–EU relations. He not only identifies the deficiencies of existing theories of European integration, but also proposes a new model for understanding supranational integration using the Turkish example as a case study. In order to do so, he identifies societal assertiveness and transparency in the area of policy-making and implementation as independent variables that can help us predict policy outcomes. In this regard, he suggests that to understand the process of integration and accession, it is necessary to problematise the extent to which the EU can act as an incentive provider for reforms and change as well as a body capable of sanctions. In this framework, Uğur looks at the EU's own failings in its commitments to the Turkish candidacy, but does not underline these as the main set of obstacles in Turkey–EU relations. Instead, he treats them as one side of the equation (the anchor side), the other side being Turkey's commitment and ability to convergence reforms (the credibility side). Uğur's analysis is built upon strong empirical foundations that pay attention to the state–society interface in Turkey, the implications of state–society interactions for policy design and implementation, and the institutional dynamics of the EU itself. His work does not include references to the post-Cold War factors that may have affected the EU's commitment to Turkey's membership, or to the changing profiles of both economic and political actors in post-Özal Turkey. This is so since he regards these issues as incidental or context specific rather than of determinative nature.

Meltem Müftüler-Baç's line of work (Müftüler, 1992; Müftüler-Baç, 1997, 2000; Müftüler-Baç and McLaren, 2003), on the other hand, is recognised for its strength in identifying the context-specific political dynamics in the shaping of Turkey–EU relations. Müftüler-Baç successfully traces the development of Turkey's often difficult relationship with the EU. In doing so, she identifies two main areas of puzzlement that make it difficult for outside observers to make definitive judgements about Turkey: its political system and its identity. She proposes that Turkey's future in the EU will be determined along the interplay of these two factors, and their restructuring according to the criteria of membership of the EU. Müftüler-Baç's general conclusion on this issue is that Turkey's political system has serious shortcomings that act and may continue to act as obstacles to the country's inclusion in the EU. These are not limited to human and minority rights concerns or the Cyprus problem. However, especially in her later work, she is also convinced that there is room for substantial reforms in the system and that there is an emerging political will to carry out those reforms at the public as well as state levels. She identifies the EU as an important factor in the promotion of democracy in Turkey and thus suggests that the EU has fulfilled its traditional role in the context of candidacy for EU membership. However, she contends that the EU made a strategic mistake when it started accession negotiations with countries such as Bulgaria and Slovakia, which have no better a democratic profile than does Turkey. By doing so, the EU damaged its image and credibility as an unbiased moderator. With Europeanness increasingly defined in terms of commitments to values and their practice endorsed by the Union, this loss of credibility is bad news in the post-Cold War era, and especially in the face of renewed US hegemony.

Chris Rumford is another well-recognised student of Turkey–EU relations. His articles on the subject examine both the internal and the external dynamics of the membership and criteria adaptation issues (Rumford, 2000, 2001). His approach, in this regard, is a hybrid one and offers the many benefits of multi-perspectival examination. However, his emphasis is more on making sense of historical developments and the evolution of the relationship rather than situating it in a larger analytical framework. Ziya Öniş's line of work on Turkey–EU relations, in comparison, is more analytical than descriptive. His emphasis is on the comparative dimensions of the Turkish case (Öniş, 2000, 2001).

Ali Çarkoğlu and Barry Rubin's edited book is the most recent attempt in bringing together variant lines of inquiry and is yet another attempt to move beyond the traditional paradigm of European Studies in Turkey. The editors identify the question of European Union membership as being one of Turkey's most important foreign policy problems as well as a very potent domestic issue. They make the key observation that '[d]ozens of countries in the last century have joined many international organisations without this issue becoming a focal point of their identity' (Çarkoğlu and Rubin, 2003: 1). Hence the need to understand the extraordinary Turkish engagement with and the 'mythical proportions' of the Turkish debate on Europeanness, European identity and membership in the Union. Their collection thus embodies, first and foremost, the questioning of the assumption that Turkey's full membership would guarantee the country's irrevocable acceptance as a 'Western state'.

Another critical question the contributors to the book keep in mind in addressing various aspects of Turkey–EU relations is the following: why does EU membership mean the endorsement of the 'civilised' as opposed to the 'barbaric' or 'oriental' nature of Turkish society? The core argument of the collection emerges as the following. As Turks tend to see their relations with Europe – in particular with the EU – as constitutive of their own identity, they perceive the treatment of their potential membership of the EU as an indication of how others see them and will treat them in the future. As such, Turkey–EU relations give rise to great strain in Turkish society, not only due to the expected economic costs or benefits but also due to an endemic identity crisis. Needless to say, the contours of this debate somewhat changed with the entry of proponents of political Islam into the scene as a pro-EU political force. The evaluation of Turkey's EU membership thus shifted ground from endorsement of Turkey's worthiness to the identification of openings for the production of a greater democratic space and the establishment of a just model of governance. The contributors to Çarkoğlu and Rubin's volume cover all of the above-mentioned aspects of Turkey's relations with Europe, including strategic and defence-related concerns, immigration-related issues, the Cyprus problem, human rights, Turkish attitudes towards the EU including intellectual traditions and views of Turkish parliamentarians, as well as Turkish perceptions of the membership criteria.

In this respect, our volume continues from where Çarkoğlu and Rubin's joint endeavour left off. Our intention, therefore, is not to map out Turkish responses to Turkey's EU membership. It is to build upon this already existent literature around the specific problematic of what actual convergence could bring forth, what the real prospects for full membership are and what they are dependent upon, and what EU-style Europeanisation in the Turkish context has meant and could mean in the future. In other words, we make a concerted effort to decouple the question of Turkey's membership of the EU from Turkish perceptions of what Europeans think of Turkey and the debate around whether Turks are or should be treated as Europeans. As such, our treatment of Turkey–EU relations has parallels with the debate on emergent Balkan identities and redefinitions of the Balkans as a new space that is neither Europe nor outside of Europe.

In the larger context of the debates referred to in this chapter, this book examines the internal processes that have affected Turkey's relations with the EU and are highly likely to affect the country's future in an integrated Europe (i.e. what would change in Turkey if Turkey's membership became a reality). In this volume, we strive to pay attention to issues that generally remain in the blind spot of the literature on Turkey's relationship with the EU, particularly in the branch treating this relation merely as a 'foreign' or 'external' policy issue. Specifically, we look at domestic factors such as economic policy design, preferences of the business community, political culture, religion, identity politics, nationalism, populism and public opinion – which have so far been overlooked, addressed only inadequately, or at best addressed in piecemeal fashion.

The contributions to the book are organised according to the cautious conviction that, heuristically, it is possible to treat domestic factors as *independent* variables and Turkey's European Union membership trajectory as a *dependent* variable in analysing Turkey–EU relations. This is related to our previously indicated concern about the extent to which one can decouple Turkish images of the EU (and European images of Turkey) from what actually takes place on the ground. We insert the qualifier 'cautious' here, as the totality of the contributions also indicates that internal developments in Turkey can be directly affected by the very phenomenon of candidature for entry to the EU. In this context, we define Europeanisation as the extent to which Turkish policy choices and dominant ideological trends correlate with the set of standards embodied in the EU project (the *acquis*, policy coordination, the Copenhagen criteria, etc.). Thus, we knowingly limit ourselves to a specific, institutionalised variant of the 'Europeanisation' concept, one that does not prioritise the historical and geographical dimensions usually paramount in related debates. The Turkish state and polity are, in contradistinction, used as overarching concepts that accommodate both actors and structures relevant to the specific issue(s) examined in each chapter.

Given this overall framework, the contributors address a combination of themes. What do we mean by 'Europeanisation' in specific policy contexts and what does it imply at both the design and the implementation levels? What are the characteristics of the specific Turkish context in terms of economic, political, social and cultural parameters at hand? What are the alternative paradigms to the compatibility/incompatibility debate in terms of assessing Turkey's domestic attributes and its prospects for integration with the EU? What concepts best explain the interaction between Turkey's domestic attributes and Europeanisation or closer integration? To what extent are concepts such as 'sovereignty', 'discretion', 'credibility', 'domestic ownership' and 'adaptation' useful in understanding Turkey's prospects *vis-à-vis* the EU? In addition, contributors to this volume address the question of whether the problems encountered in Turkey's relations with Europe are due to structural differences between the EU and Turkey; or whether they are due to factors such as 'trained incapacity' exhibited by policy-makers, 'path dependence' in Turkish politics, and 'the discourse of instrumental adaptation' at the societal level. In sum, we aim to shed light on the issue of the root causes of the complications experienced in Turkey's relations with the EU. These include, but are not limited to, *structural* obstacles to Europeanisation *per se* as well as the way in which public, business, political and civic actors react to the implementation of and compliance with the accession criteria on the basis of short-term considerations. At the same time, we attempt to understand whether these causes are destined to marginalise the country in an integrated Europe.

As such, this volume provides students of both Turkey's political economy and the European Union with assessments of the role of business organisations, economic policy preferences, ideologies, identity politics and public opinion in determining successive Turkish governments' approach to reforms *on par* with EU membership. A pivotal concern that binds the different chapters together is that of explaining the long-standing coexistence of pro-modernisation, pro-EU official declarations on the one hand, and recurrent policy reversals and resistance to change on the other. By paying direct attention to the dynamics that have induced pragmatism in ideology, policy and identity formation, we strive to provide a model for understanding the rather unusual phenomenon of convergence reforms being endorsed by religious and nationalist parties traditionally considered hostile to the European project. Some chapters also discuss the way in which variables concerning domestic Turkish politics and policy-making practices may have undesirable effects on Turkey's ability to benefit from EU membership in the future. Note too that in a volume of this kind, it is inevitable that the contributors will take a historical view of the issues they address, However, by and large, the book focuses on developments in the 1990s.

The debate in this volume is organised into four separate parts. Part I is titled 'Public opinion on EU membership' and includes a single chapter, by Ali Çarkoğlu. Part II is titled 'Economic governance and EU membership' and includes chapters by Mine Eder, Mehmet Uğur and Serap Altan. Part III is titled 'Religion and EU membership' and contains chapters by Burhanettin Duran and Effie Fokas. The final section is titled 'International–domestic interactions' and includes contributions by Gamze Avcı, Nergis Canefe, Ziya Öniş, E. Fuat Keyman and Jonathan Sugden.

In his chapter on societal perceptions of Turkey's EU membership, Ali Çarkoğlu examines the popular bases of resistance to EU membership among the Turkish voters. He uses data from a nationwide representative survey conducted just prior to the passage of the EU adjustment package in the summer of 2002 and after the November 2002 elections. Çarkoğlu diagnoses that religious devotion and democratic values are all significant attitudinal bases for preferences concerning EU membership. Meanwhile, the so-called sensitive issues related to minority rights in the country do seem to be significant, but their significance depends on the leadership impact which appears critical in shaping support for EU membership. On the basis of survey findings, Çarkoğlu provides an evaluation of the future development of resistance to and activism for EU membership.

Mine Eder's chapter, Chapter 3, examines the effects of populism as a barrier to integration with the EU. It starts with the assertion that of the Copenhagen criteria, the political dimension (namely, the stability of institutions guaranteeing democracy, human rights, the rule of law, and respect for and protection of minority rights) has always attracted primary attention in Turkey–EU relations. Important as these are, however, Eder suggests that we should also have a closer look at the economic criteria, which call for 'the existence of a functioning market economy' as well as 'a capacity to cope with competitive pressures and market forces within the Union'. She then asks the daring question of how realistic it is for the EU to expect its prospective members to undertake political and economic reforms simultaneously. In other words, can the new members consolidate their democracy and improve their market positions at the same time? Focusing particularly on the legacies of Turkish populism, this chapter underlines the difficult, paradoxical nature of simultaneous reforms. Eder suggests that the pro-market reforms required by the Copenhagen criteria may not be sufficient to overcome populism as a source of policy failure. In fact, pro-market reforms may well coexist with and provide a fertile ground for populism. Can neo-liberal economic reforms be compatible with populism? Can populist pressures be resisted? How and why does populism undermine the democratic process? How and why does populism emerge as both an economic and a political barrier to EU membership? Eder's contribution seeks answers to these questions through the study of Turkish populism and Turkey's prospective accession to the EU.

Mehmet Uğur's contribution in Chapter 4 on the link between economic mismanagement and Turkey's troubled relations with the EU examines the causes and consequences of economic policy divergence between Turkey and the EU. Uğur develops and substantiates two arguments. First, economic policy divergence between Turkey and the EU is the outcome of the discretion and rent-seeking that characterise Turkey's policy-making process. Second, economic policy divergence has persisted despite liberalising reforms of the 1980s and has reduced the credibility of

Turkey's commitment to integration with the EU. Uğur's findings suggest that Turkey's exclusion from the current wave of enlargement was largely predictable and that political economy factors internal to Turkey are significant variables that have determined this predictable outcome.

Serap Atan's chapter on the Europeanisation of Turkish peak business organisations (PBOs) presents evidence on their activities in Brussels, and thus draws attention to a recent and unexplored field of analysis in Turkey–EU relations. Atan sheds light on the inclusive nature of the EU-level interest intermediation system and the complex transnational dynamics of the accession process. Furthermore, with reference to the literature on Europeanisation in EU countries, she elaborates on Turkish PBOs' interaction with the EU governance system and the reform process in Turkey. Atan suggests that awareness of the 'Europeanisation' of Turkish PBOs would improve our understanding of the transformation dynamics of domestic structures in Turkey. Consequently, it would contribute to the assessment of Turkey's capacity to meet the EU accession criteria. Finally, Atan draws attention to the fact that future analysis of policy convergence towards the *acquis communautaire* would also require an understanding of the sectoral business organisations' evolution in parallel to Turkey's process of integration with the EU.

In Chapter 6, Burhanettin Duran examines the *Islamist* redefinitions of European and Islamic identities in Turkey with reference to the discourses of Islamist parties and writers. He argues that the February 28 process (i.e. the process that started with the military's ultimatum against Islamic influence in Turkish politics) brought about significant changes in the Turkish Islamist conceptualisations of Europe and democracy. As a consequence, the leading elements within Turkish Islamism left their anti-European discourses behind and began to support Turkey's integration into Europe, although there still remains a strong anti-European current among many Islamist writers. According to Duran, this change of mind can be related to the Islamist conviction that the process of transition to the EU is likely to force the Turkish political system to undertake significant democratic reforms that will make the Kemalist ideology less repressive and intrusive. Duran concludes that the Islamist support for Turkey's integration with EU can contribute to the Europeanisation of Turkey, but at the same time it necessitates a redefinition of what is 'European'.

Effie Fokas's contribution, in Chapter 7, on the role of the Islamist movement in Turkey–EU relations is complementary to Duran's chapter. However, her main point of emphasis differs. Fokas argues that tensions between secularist and Islamist trends in Turkey have strongly marked Republican Turkish politics and society. The very policies that secularist elites have pursued in the name of Westernisation and Europeanisation – including limitations posed on the Islamist movement in Turkey – are now considered by many, even within EU circles, as impediments to Turkish membership of the European Union. The author goes further to suggest that there is now a lively debate in Turkey over which issue constitutes the greater barrier to Turkey–EU relations: Islamism, or the Turkish version of secularism. Her contribution thus examines the complex dimensions of secularist–Islamist tensions in Turkey, including an in-depth study of one climax in these tensions and interview research with members of Turkish elites on contemporary Islamism. Fokas concludes with a brief consideration of Turkey–EU relations under the current Islamic-oriented government of Turkey.

In Fuat Keyman and Ziya Öniş's contribution (Chapter 8), Turkey–EU relations in the post-Helsinki era are investigated in a multi-dimensional and reciprocal manner. In the post-Helsinki era, which includes the critical Copenhagen summit of December 2002, these authors argue that the EU has played a crucial role in inducing Turkey to transform its state-centric polity in the direction of a more democratic, economically stable and pluralistic entity. Accordingly, recent improvements in Turkey's democratic order, although still incomplete, would have been inconceivable, at least at such a rapid pace, in the absence of a powerful EU anchor. At the same time, however, Keyman and Öniş point out that the possible incorporation of Turkey has also presented a serious challenge to the 'New Europe' itself. In this context, Turkey constitutes an important test case for the New Europe and its future not only on cultural but also on geopolitical grounds. Keyman and Öniş thus suggest that the decision to include or exclude Turkey from the New Europe is a decision that the EU should take not only with reference to an essentially inwardly-oriented integration project, but also in terms of its role in a drastically changing international order.

Gamze Avcı's contribution (Chapter 9) on the relationship between Turkish political parties and the EU discourse in the post-Helsinki period examines the extent to which this interaction can be regarded as a case of Europeanisation. Avcı suggests that political parties could be used as an important explanatory variable in EU–Turkish relations. In this context, she first maps party political attitudes in Turkey since the Helsinki summit. Her research is guided by the question of when, how and why parties of government move towards or away from Euro-scepticism. The empirical dimension of her work is based on four Turkish parties that have been in the two governments since 1999. Avcı concludes that parties frequently perceive and use 'Europeanisation' as an 'opportunity structure'. As a result, party political choices have – depending on the choices made – constrained, accelerated or hampered the process of Turkish accession to the EU.

Chapter 10 by Nergis Canefe, on the limits of convergence between Republican and EU-level, post-national citizenship conventions, is built upon the assertion that there is an identifiable blind spot in the current Turkish debate on what the post-national and primarily European model has to offer. Canefe does not subscribe to the view that EU citizenship is an instrumental mechanism in the service of the creation of a solidified pan-European identity. Instead, she argues for studying European citizenship as a 'fragmented' practice that can be segmented into separate yet interrelated components, which may have validity in contexts other than the EU. However, her emphasis is on the normative and consensual characteristics of the EU trajectory of citizenship rather than on how the fragments could be utilised for reaching specific ends. Canefe further argues that procedural adaptations and sharing of supranational resources to guarantee the restructuring of the Republican Turkish citizenship convention appear to have an unidentified core. In the Turkish case, she thus identifies a rather problem-laden Habermasian reading of 'correct' political conduct as the remedy for the ills of the relations in Turkish society and politics. These gaps, pertaining to the exploration of what normative foundations the much-admired European model rest upon, could make the Turkish readings of post-national citizenship of limited applicability. In her view, 'convergence' to the European trajectory requires more than sweeping legal reforms dictated by the accession process, or adherence to the rights discourse in an attempt to erode the state-centric understanding of politics.

Jonathan Sugden's contribution (Chapter 11) is an examination of Turkey's human rights record in the light of the country's EU candidacy. Sugden asks whether the supposed benefits of prospective integration within the EU have provided any leverage for the implementation of the long list of overdue human rights reforms. Specifically, he examines the interaction between Turkey's human rights record from the mid-1990s and its European orientation with a view to assessing the extent to which European pressure has been influential in engendering change. He reaches the conclusion that throughout the 1990s, a distant and merely hypothetical prospect of membership was not sufficient to bring about concrete results. Even in 1999, when the EU gave Turkey candidacy status, and a real chance of membership, Sugden argues that accomplished reforms remained mainly cosmetic. In fact, it was not until 2001, when public opinion and strong interest groups realised that government inaction was threatening to throw the opportunity away, that substantial measures were taken by the Ecevit and Gül/Erdoğan governments. Sugden concludes his analysis with an overall evaluation of the scope for human rights reforms in Turkey under external pressure.

Overall, this book marks a territory that has been largely uncharted so far, either in the context of EU accession and enlargement processes, or in the specific context of studies on Turkish society and political economy. Despite its title, this is not a collection that provides ready-made answers to the question of Turkey's accession prospects, nor is it a direct engagement in the assessment of obstacles to Turkey's EU membership. Although the contributors discuss these issues in detail, their work is more about the relationships between EU-level and national-level politics and policy-making, and in its totality the book's vantage point is that of how this relationship looks from within Turkey. In this sense, it does serve the originally set purpose of producing a distinct kind of analysis that both challenges and enlarges the contours of the debate on candidacy for and membership in the European Union.

References

Baldwin, R. and A. Brunetti (eds) (2001), *Economic Impact of EU Membership on Entrants*, Boston: Kluwer.

Bulaç, Ali (2001), *Avrupa Birliği ve Türkiye* (The European Union and Turkey), Istanbul: Zaman.

Cesarani, D. and M. Fulbrook (eds) (1996), *Citizenship, Nationality and Migration in Europe*, London: Routledge.

Çarkoğlu, A. and B. Rubin (eds) (2003), *Turkey and the European Union: Domestic Politics, Economic Integration and International Dynamics*, London: Frank Cass.

Eichengreen, Barry and Jeffrey Frieden (1998), *Forging an Integrated Europe*, Ann Arbor: University of Michigan Press.

Goetz, Klaus H. and Simon Hix (eds) (2001), *Europeanised Politics? European Integration and National Political Systems*, London: Frank Cass.

Karluk, Rıdvan (1996), *Avrupa Birliği ve Türkiye* (The European Union and Turkey), Istanbul: Istanbul Menkul Kıymetler Borsası Yayınları.

Kurzer, Paulette (2001), *Markets and Moral Regulations: Cultural Change in European Union*, Cambridge: Cambridge University Press.

Müftüler, Meltem (1992), 'Impact of external factors on internal transformation: Turkish structural adjustment process and the European Community', unpublished PhD dissertation, University of Michigan.

Müftüler-Baç, Meltem (1997), *Turkey's Relations with a Changing Europe*, Manchester: Manchester University Press.

Müftüler-Baç, Meltem (2000), 'The impact of the European Union on Turkish politics', *East European Quarterly*, vol. 34, no. 2, pp. 159–180.

Müftüler-Baç, Meltem and Lauren M. McLaren (2003), 'Turkish parliamentarians' perspectives on Turkey's relations with the European Union', in Ali Çarkoğlu and Barry Rubin (eds), *Turkey and the European Union: Domestic Politics, Economic Integration and International Dynamics*, London: Frank Cass, pp. 195–218.

Neumann, Ivor (1998), 'European identity, EU expansion and integration/exclusion nexus', *Alternatives*, vol. 23, no. 3, pp. 397–416.

Neunreiteher, Karlheinz and Antje Wiener (eds) (2000), *European Integration after Amsterdam: Institutional Dynamics and Prospects for Democracy*, Oxford: Oxford University Press.

Öniş, Ziya (2000), 'Luxemburg, Helsinki and beyond: towards an interpretation of recent Turkey–EU relations', *Government and Opposition*, vol. 35, no. 4, pp. 463–483.

Öniş, Ziya (2001), 'An awkward partnership: Turkey's relations with the European Union in comparative-historical perspective', *Journal of European Integration History*, vol. 7, no. 1, pp. 105–119.

Peterson, John and Elizabeth Bomberg (1999), *Decision-Making in the European Union*, Basingstoke, UK: Macmillan.

Rumford, Christopher (2000), 'From Luxemburg to Helsinki: Turkey, the politics of EU enlargement and prospects for accession', *Contemporary Politics*, vol. 17, no. 4, pp. 331–343.

Rumford, Christopher (2001), 'Human Rights and Democratisation in Turkey in the Context of EU Candidature', *Journal of European Area Studies*, vol. 9, no. 1, pp. 93–106.

Somuncuoğlu, Sadi (2002), *Avrupa Birliği: Bitmeyen Yol* (The European Union: An Unending Journey), Istanbul: Ötüken Neşriyat.

Teitalbaum, Michael S. and Philip Martin (2003) 'Is Turkey ready for Europe?', *Foreign Affairs*, vol. 82, no. 3, pp. 97–110.

Togan, S. and Balasubramanyan, T. S. (2001), *Turkey and Central and Eastern European Countries in Transition*, New York: St Martin's Press.

Uğur, Mehmet (1999), *The European Union and Turkey: An Anchor/Credibility Dilemma*, Aldershot, UK: Ashgate.

Warleigh, Alex (2002), *Flexible Integration:. Which Model for the European Union?* London and New York: Sheffield Academic Press.

Weidenfeld, Werner (ed.) (1997), *A New Ostpolitik: Strategies for a United Europe*, Gütersloh: Bertelsmann Foundation.

Westlake, Martin (ed.) (1998), *The European Union beyond Amsterdam: New Concepts of European Integration*, London: Routledge.

Williams, Allan (1994), *The European Community: The Contradictions of Integration*, Oxford: Blackwell.

Part I

Public opinion and EU membership

2 Societal perceptions of Turkey's EU membership

Causes and consequences of support for EU membership

Ali Çarkoğlu

Introduction

For many Turks who were waiting anxiously for the crowning jewel of the Turkish modernisation project in the form of a full commitment to European Union (EU) membership, time was passing too slowly prior to the summer of 2002. Despite massive support for EU membership in the country, the political elite were obviously dragging their feet. Necessary adjustments in the legal and political system were being left almost untouched. Europhile Turks often had the feeling that the country was sitting on bridges that link the Anatolian Peninsula to Europe, refusing to take the necessary steps towards Europe and only trying to catch whatever 'strategic fishes' passed by in the streams of the Straits.

Then time seemed to have started flying at a dizzying speed. The health condition of the then Prime Minister, Bülent Ecevit, quickly turned into a catalyst for transformation of the political system. Prominent parliamentarians from Ecevit's Democratic Left Party (*Demokratik Sol Parti*, DSP), including his Deputy Prime Minister, Hüsamettin Özkan, and the Minister of Foreign Affairs, İsmail Cem, resigned from their posts and their party. Thinking that Kemal Derviş, 'imported' from the World Bank to run the crisis-hit Turkish economy in 2001, would also join them in their efforts, they formed the New Turkey Party (*Yeni Türkiye Partisi*, YTP). The three-party coalition government of the DSP – the Nationalist Action Party (*Milliyetçi Hareket Partisi*, MHP) and the Motherland Party (*Anavatan Partisi*, ANAP) – had in the process lost its majority in Parliament. The country was on its way towards the early election that Derviş had hinted at in spring 2002. All polls showed at the time that the pro-Islamist Justice and Development Party (*Adalet ve Kalkınma Partisi*, AKP) was heading for major victory. In the event, Derviş never joined the YTP, but instead went to the Republican People's Party (*Cumhuriyet Halk Partisi*, CHP) which at the time seemed more likely to survive the coming election if not actually to win it.

The most unexpected development came with the passage of a comprehensive legislative adjustment package brought to the agenda of the outgoing parliament that had already taken the decision to hold an early election. This package included many controversial elements ranging from abolition of the death penalty to the teaching of and broadcasting in native languages other than Turkish – that is, effectively lifting the ban on the use of Kurdish in broadcasting and education. The whole country seemed to be determined to change not only its legal but also its social and political framework to adjust to the EU.

Europe then was in deep summer recess and did not fully appreciate the radical nature of the changes adopted by a parliament that admittedly had committed political suicide. The Commission remained from the very beginning highly sceptical about the implementation of the laws passed by the parliament and seemed to be waiting to see what kind of government would emerge out of the approaching elections.

The elections of November 2002 led to the ousting of all parties of the incumbent coalition government from Parliament. Compared to the 1999 election, the coalition partners – the DSP, MHP and ANAP – lost about 39 percentage points of electoral support. Nor did the two major opposition parties – the pro-Islamist Felicity Party (*Saadet Partisi*, SP), which suffered a loss of 12.9 percentage points, and Çiller's centre-right True Path Party (*Doğru Yol Partisi*, DYP), which lost 2.5 percentage points – perform much better, and they remained outside Parliament. The collapse of the centrist parties brought the populist Young Party (*Genç Parti*, GP) to the Turkish electoral scene. With the help of financial backing from its leader, Cem Uzan, a business tycoon of blemished success, the GP was able to attract about 7 per cent of voters, mainly from the centrist parties. Apart from the AKP and the centre-left CHP, the only other opposition party to gain votes relative to its 1999 level of support was the ethnic Kurdish Democratic People's Party (*Demokratik Halk Partisi*, DEHAP).

The elections brought yet another pro-Islamist party to power with an overwhelming majority in Parliament. The rise in support for the pro-Islamist AKP of Tayyip Erdoğan marks the progression of electoral collapse of the centrist politics. The left-leaning CHP is the only other party that was able to pass the 10 per cent electoral threshold and gain seats in Parliament.[1] However, this complete overhaul of the Turkish Parliament did not mean that parties that supported EU membership had lost the elections and now anti-European parties are in power. The winners of the elections of November 2002 seem committed to the Turkish modernisation project and to integration with Europe. Yet this commitment was also marked by significant reluctance, owing to the complex requirements of EU membership and their implications for domestic and foreign policy. Resolution of the Cyprus conflict, reduction of the military's role in the Turkish polity, alleviation of human rights violations, and implementation of minority rights in education and broadcasting all continued to pose a great challenge to the Turkish political system.

The AKP came to power primarily on the promise of economic relief for the masses. Its leaders were aware of the fact that its core constituency was not too eager and willing to embrace the cause of EU membership. They thus had not committed themselves too firmly on this issue, and instead focused on populist economic relief, promises of modernisation and on democratisation issues, linking them to EU membership only as a matter of convenience. Yet the AKP's most memorable policy stance came not on the domestic economic front but rather on the European front. This gave the AKP leadership an opportunity to ride on the wave of the party's electoral victory when there was no credible anti-European party on the political scene, and to seek a windfall gain at the Copenhagen summit of December 2002.

However, their gamble did not fully pay off. For strategic and domestic political reasons, no satisfactorily close date for accession negotiations could be obtained at the Copenhagen summit. Optimistically, however, pending a number of interim assessments, membership negotiations could start by December 2004. For optimists, such a clear process of development once again reaffirms the irreversible progression of Turkey's membership bid. For pessimists, this signifies yet another unfulfilled expectation of Turkey, and uncertainties continue to linger on the shaky economic horizon of the country as it faces a military conflict developing on its Iraqi borders.

Time began to pass slowly on the European front once again in the months immediately after the Copenhagen summit. With the passage of the August 2002 package, the Euro-sceptic forces seemed to have lost the first round of the battle for EU membership. Ironically, the AKP, the potential bastion of popular resistance, spearheaded the onslaught for an early delivery of victory for the Europhiles. Its failure in this attempt caused the AKP government to prefer to forget about the disillusionment of Copenhagen. Conveniently, Turkish domestic and foreign policies were simmering with the heat of the Iraq war. However, the newly surfacing cleavage around the issue of EU membership touches on many sensitivities concerning intangible national pride and more concrete issues related to national sovereignty, minority and human rights, the death penalty, the status and impact of the military in Turkish politics, the regulation of religious freedoms, and the restructuring of the Turkish economy and public administration system. Hence, the reappearance of the EU discussion as a dominant issue on the Turkish agenda and the acceleration of events, as they once again reached 'rocket speed' a short time later, is unavoidable. Despite this seasonal speed in EU-geared developments, the potential for a Euro-sceptic or Europhile direction for the country remains uncertain. In order to grasp the bent of this speedy journey, a necessary source of information is the inclinations and attitudinal characteristics of resistance to membership among the Turkish public at large.

Among the multitude of factors that shape Turkey's association with EU, public opinion about membership gives form, intensity and legitimacy to the direction of the relations.[2] Below, I focus on this roller-coaster development of EU–Turkey relations from the perspective of the mass public. I first concentrate on the development of popular support base for EU membership and related issues with reference to public opinion polls from 1996 and 1998 and using data from four representative nationwide polls between November 2001 and February 2003. Next, I discuss the so-called sensitive issues of minority rights in the country in the context of EU membership and provide a multivariate statistical analysis of the support for EU membership, followed by a series of interpretations and commentary for their implications concerning EU–Turkey relations.

2.1 Support for EU membership: observations on trends and causes

Despite the fact that relations between Turkey and the EU date back to 1959, there has been very little academic discussion concerning the mass support for this relationship. Here, I examine nationwide trends in support of EU membership since 1996.[3]

Two surveys, conducted in 1996 and 1998 respectively, asked the respondents whether they 'would like Turkey to be a member of the EU' (Erder, 1996, 1999). Starting in November 2001, a similar question was used in four consecutive survey analyses in which I took part. Each of these four surveys used the same wording and asked whether the respondent 'would vote in favour of EU membership if a referendum were to take place in Turkey'. Figure 2.1 summarises the trends observed since 1996. The first observation is from March–April 1996, about three months prior to the Dublin summit where Turkey not only was warned that it must observe the highest human rights standards but also was urged to use its influence to seek a solution in Cyprus in accordance with UN Security Council resolutions (Erdemli, 2003: 6). A bare majority, about 55 per cent of respondants, were found to support EU membership in spring 1996.

About a year and a half later, the European Council excluded Turkey from its list of formal candidates at the Luxembourg summit of December 1997, to which Turkey responded by suspending its dialogue with the EU. At the same summit, the Republic of Cyprus was allowed to start accession negotiations. Turkey declared in response that it would go ahead with plans to integrate Northern Cyprus with mainland Turkey. Tensions peaked during 1998 and much of 1999. However, public support for EU membership was found to have significantly increased, up to about 62 per cent, by May 1998. About a year and a half later, in December 1999, EU–Turkey relations were once again normalised at the Helsinki summit, at which Turkey was recognised as an official candidate for membership.

The friendly and cooperative atmosphere in the aftermath of the Helsinki summit resulted in agreement over the Accession Partnership for Turkey in December 2000 – just prior to the Nice summit, at which the European Council welcomed Turkey's progress in implementing its

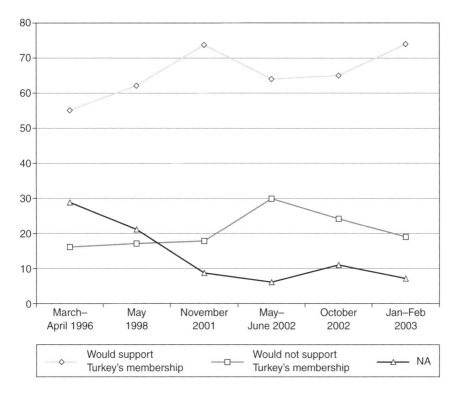

Figure 2.1 Development of public opinion support for EU membership, 1996–2003.

pre-accession strategy and requested the submission of its programme for adoption of the *acquis*. In March 2001, the Council of Ministers adopted an EU–Turkey Accession Partnership that set the short- and medium-term measures necessary to ensure Turkey's fulfilment of membership criteria followed by the adoption of the National Programme for the Adoption of the *Acquis* (NPAA) by the Turkish government. As such, a road map for legal and policy adaptations necessary for EU membership was set. In accordance with this plan, on 3 October 2001 the Turkish Parliament adopted 34 amendments to the Constitution necessary to meet the Copenhagen criteria. Thereafter, the November 2001 results showed a clearly improved public image for the relationship, with nearly 75 per cent of those questioned being in support of Turkey's EU membership.

The Laeken summit of December 2001 also took place in quite a positive atmosphere, and the Council extended its appreciation of the recent constitutional amendments. However, by the Seville summit of June 2002, the domestic scene had changed considerably. In February 2002, European Commission Representative Karen Fogg's personal e-mail account was hacked into and her private exchanges were published in a selective and manipulative manner. The messages were manipulated in such a way as to create an image of Fogg, and others who were in contact with her, as traitors who were on EU pay, working against Turkey's national interests.[4] At a time when the Turkish Parliament and intellectual circles were debating the necessity of and the strategy for handling the impending adjustments to achieve the Copenhagen criteria, this e-mail hacking and the discussion that developed around Fogg's e-mail messages generated a nationalist reaction.[5] The period also coincided with the start of bilateral talks on Cyprus. In Turkey there was growing concern about the need to resolve the conflict on the island. The issue was being extensively debated in the media, and the public were being exposed to novel views and information. Karen Fogg's e-mail messages were also used to discredit advocates of the idea of a solution in Cyprus and led to the accusation that Fogg had been interfering in the internal affairs of the Turkish Republic of Northern Cyprus (TRNC) (Çarkoğlu and Kirişci, 2003).[6]

Our results show that as a result of this media campaign, public support for membership had significantly fallen, to about its 1998 level of around 65 per cent. From the perspective of public support, all the gains in favour of EU membership since May 1998 had been lost, and the recent rapprochement between Turkey and the EU was effectively neutralised from the perspective of mobilising public support. Nevertheless, as I will elaborate in further detail, even at this point, where anti-European forces were at their peak and the campaign against the EU, through personal attacks on Fogg, was having its full impact on the public at large, the nature of public support was such that it still commanded a clear majority in favour of EU membership in almost all public opinion surveys. On issues concerning the use of languages other than Turkish in education and broadcasting, as well as abolition of the death penalty, public preferences were mildly sceptical towards the Copenhagen criteria. The latter might be due to the fact that anti-European circles linked abolition of the death penalty with the case of Abdullah Öcalan – the imprisoned ex-leader of the Kurdistan Workers' Party (PKK). Their vengeful argument was that Öcalan would go unpunished if the lifting of the death penalty were approved by Parliament.

The surprise passage of the EU adjustment package in early August 2002, and the election campaign that took full force in its aftermath, does not seem to have had much impact on the level of public support in favour of EU membership. Our October 2002 results show an almost unchanged level of support at around 65 per cent. Our latest results, from mid-January to early February 2003, also clearly show that the normalisation of the political environment in the aftermath of the election has increased the level of support back to its 2001 level of about 75 per cent. It seems that the failure of the AKP government to receive a firm date for the start of negotiations in Copenhagen did not adversely affect public opinion. However, it remains to be seen whether this high level of support is reflected among the AKP's constituency.

An overall feature of the developments in support of public opinion for EU membership over the past seven years is that the percentage of 'don't knows' has steadily fallen. This indicates the level of alertness of the mass public to the issue of EU membership. Not only have the people shown their clear support for EU membership, with levels above 60 per cent in favour since 1998, but also they seem to be increasingly attentive to this issue and willing to express steadily increasing preference concerning EU membership.

I now want to focus more closely on the period May–June 2002 and underline the characteristics of support for the EU – especially with respect to the so-called sensitive issues such as the lifting of the death penalty and the ban on the use of native languages other than Turkish in education and broadcasting.[7] Next, I will offer a short evaluation of the salience of EU-related issues and the passage of the adjustment package through Parliament in early August during the election campaign of 2002. Lastly, I will present a comparative evaluation of support for EU membership prior to the elections of November 2002.

2.2 'Sensitive issues' and support for EU membership

An important feature of public opinion concerning EU membership and related issues is that respondents' knowledge concerning these issues is very limited. People do accept and declare that they are not knowledgeable on these issues. Second, given the low level of knowledge, people's preferences on these issues are very much context dependent. Because we were aware of the difficulties of eliciting people's preferences concerning issues that are sensitive but about which the respondents know very little, questions on these issues were asked in a number of different contexts. As a result, we obtained varying (i.e. context-dependent) responses to questions involving the so-called sensitive issues.

Figure 2.2 below shows the self-evaluations of the respondents regarding their level of knowledge concerning accession criteria that need to be satisfied by all candidate countries, such as Turkey. We see that 56.2 per cent of the respondents chose to mark absolutely the lowest possible level of knowledge on our scale. Those who consider themselves knowledgeable (6–10 on our scale) comprise only 14 per cent of the sample.

In order to contextualise these sensitive issues first within a general framework and then more specifically within the current Turkish political context, we initially listed a number of rights and freedoms and asked the respondents whether these should exist at all times under all conditions and for all people; or whether they could be restricted, depending on the context and conditions prevailing at a given time. We then reminded the respondents that there are certain changes that Turkey has to implement in order to become a member of the EU. Subsequently, we asked to what degree they agree with the statements put to

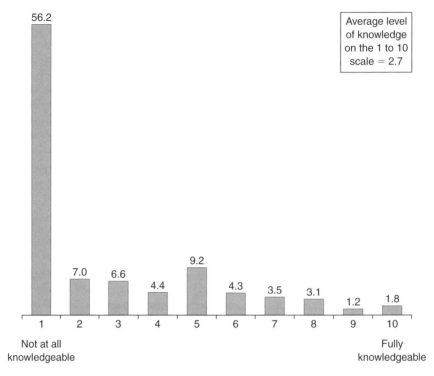

Figure 2.2 Knowledge about the Copenhagen criteria, May–June 2002.

them. Table 2.1 summarises the results obtained for the evaluations of basic rights and freedoms.

Although more than 73 per cent indicate their support for all rights and freedoms, for some freedoms, such as freedom of expression and the freedom to use one's native language, about a quarter of the sample indicated that they feel these can be restricted, depending on the time, conditions and context. The reasons for such restrictions were not questioned in detail. Nor do we know whether this result is simply an observation reflecting the conditions the country has found itself in or whether it shows positive approval for such restrictions. However, the pattern that arises shows the relative sensitivities of Turkish voters concerning their basic rights and freedoms. The least questionable of these appeared to be freedom of conscience and religion, followed by the right to free communication. For the right to be free from torture, we observed about 16 per cent indicating that this right could be restricted depending on time and conditions. For freedom of expression and use of one's native language, we again observed that respondents were worried about the implications for the Kurdish issue and remained more inclined to accept restrictions. These responses provide significant clues about the 'sensitive issues' that

Table 2.1 Evaluation of basic rights and freedoms

Question: Should the following rights and freedoms exist at all times, under all conditions and for all people or could they be restricted, dependent on the context and conditions prevailing at a given time?

	Answer 1[a]	*Answer 2*[b]	N.A./N.O.[c]
Freedom of expression	73.8	25.0	1.2
Freedom to use one's native language	73.6	25.2	1.2
Freedom of conscience and religion	90.3	8.5	1.2
Right to equal treatment and protection of the law	91.5	7.1	1.4
Right to be free of torture	82.9	16.0	1.1
Right to free communication	85.3	12.9	1.8

Notes
a Should be present at all times, under all conditions and for all people.
b Could be restricted, dependent on the context and conditions prevailing at a given time.
c N.A./N.O.: No answer/no opinion.

are prevalent among the electorate at large, and could constitute a basis for manipulation and distortion by the nationalist circles opposed to Turkey's EU membership.

The results obtained change quite substantially when the respondents were reminded of the EU conditionality under the Copenhagen criteria (Table 2.2). This time, the respondents were asked to rate their degree of agreement with the statements provided from 1 (do not agree at all) to 10 (fully agree). The distribution of support for these most general statements reveals a predominantly bimodal pattern. With respect to the abolition of the death penalty and the use of native languages in education and broadcasting, about 35 per cent indicated total disagreement, while about 25 per cent indicated full agreement. The only exception to this trend is the statement concerning freedom of thought and expression: nearly 57 per cent indicated that they fully agree with this statement. In total, 85 per cent of the respondents are closer to the full agreement side, up from 74 per cent in Table 2.1.

Here, I use the fractionalisation index of Rae (1967) as a measure of the degree of dispersion along the 1 to 10 scale. With a uniform distribution of 10 per cent of the respondents choosing each one of the ten scale points, the index reaches its maximum of 0.9. We see that even for the case of freedom of thought and expression, there is a large degree of disagreement among the sample respondents, reflected in a sizeable index value. The degree of disagreement increases even further for the remaining three statements and reaches a maximum for the case of lifting of the laws that impede broadcasting in citizens' own native languages.

However, most significantly, contextualising the issues within EU membership and Copenhagen criteria, we observe that support falls

Table 2.2 'Sensitive issues': first-round evaluations (distribution of responses along a 1–10 scale)

	Does not agree at all	2	3	4	5	6	7	8	9	Fully agrees	Doesn't agree (1–5)	Agrees (6–10)	Fractionalisation[a]
Creation of the necessary conditions for freedom of thought and expression	3.6	1.2	1.4	1.1	6.1	3.8	6.2	11.1	7.0	56.8	13.5	84.9	0.65
Lifting of the death penalty for all crimes and for everyone	38.2	8.0	3.2	1.9	8.0	2.5	3.6	6.0	3.2	24.8	59.3	40.1	0.77
Lifting of the laws that impede citizens being educated in their own native languages	34.2	7.3	4.0	1.5	7.4	3.3	4.7	6.2	3.9	26.5	54.3	44.6	0.79
Lifting of the laws that impede broadcasting in citizens' own native languages	32.5	8.1	3.7	2.1	8.0	3.5	4.7	6.1	3.8	26.3	54.3	44.4	0.80

Note

[a] The fractionalization index (F) is calculated by using distribution of support along the 1–10 scale ($i = 1 \ldots 10$ points) in the following formula: $F = [1 - \Sigma_N$ (Selectors %)^2]. F varies between 0 and 1. It reaches a minimum of 0 when one option on the scale is selected by all. As the number of options receiving relatively small shares of selections increases, the index will approach 1. In the case of 1–10 scale, if a uniform distribution appears with 10% choosing each one of the options available, ten maximum fractionalisation occurs with 0.9. See Rae (1967) for a discussion of the fractionalisation index.

significantly to around 40 per cent, while in the most general context (Table 2.1) we had a support level of about 74 per cent for use of one's native language.

When we look at the same answers across different subgroups of the sample (Table 2.3), we obtain several patterns that are worthy of note. Unlike in previous tables, here subgroups' degree of agreement is reported as the average derived from responses along a 1 to 10 scale. For example, those respondents who report that they can speak Kurdish have a mean agreement of 7.9 out of 10 with the lifting of the laws that impede education in native languages, while those who cannot speak Kurdish have a mean agreement of only 4.7. We note that on 'sensitive issues' there is no significant difference between men and women. However, while age does not affect the first argument, that concerning the conditions for freedom of thought and expression, it does have a significant impact on assessment of arguments concerning the death penalty and languages. As people get older, they are less inclined to agree with the statements given. In contrast, formal education is effective in shaping preferences concerning all these four statements. The overall trend is that as people become more educated, they tend to adopt a relatively more liberal and cooperative attitude and thus tend to agree with the adjustments along the Copenhagen criteria.

Dwelling type does not have a significant impact on responses to any of the four types of statement. Compared to respondents from relatively better off neighbourhoods, those from shanty town neighbourhoods do not have a different tendency to evaluate the statements given. However, as one moves into rural areas, the degree of support for the last two statements – those concerning the use of native languages in education and broadcasting – seems to drop. Again, increasing socio-economic status increases the level of agreements with all statements except that concerning lifting of the laws that prevent citizens being educated in their own native languages.

Knowledge of Kurdish and being a People's Democracy Party (HADEP) voter significantly increase the tendency to agree with the statements concerning the 'sensitive issues'. This is hardly surprising, since the statements all concern provision of more liberal legal rights to Kurdish-speakers in the country. Finally, differences across party constituencies also appear to be significant. ANAP voters tend to cluster around the overall averages of agreement for all statements except for that on broadcasting rights; they tend to be on average more liberal in support of lifting of the ban. Looking at other party constituencies with a similar logic, we see that CHP and DSP constituencies tend to be on the liberal side of the issues, being more supportive of the Copenhagen criteria adjustments. On the other hand, the DYP's, MHP's, and, to some degree, SP's constituencies are on the conservative side, being on average less supportive of the statements. The pro-Islamist SP and AKP

Table 2.3 Mean degree of agreement with statements on 'sensitive issues' across different groups (1–10 scale)

		Creation of the necessary conditions for freedom of thought and expression	Lifting of the death penalty for all crimes and for everyone	Lifting of the laws that impede citizens being educated in their own native languages	Lifting of the laws that impede broadcasting in own native languages
Sex	Male	8.4	4.8	5.1	5.2
	Female	8.5	4.8	5.2	5.1
Age	18–24	8.4	5.4	5.6	5.5
	25–34	8.6	4.8	5.2	5.2
	35–44	8.4	4.8	5.3	5.4
	45–54	8.4	4.3	4.6	4.7
	55+	8.4	4.3	4.2	4.4
Education	No formal schooling	8.7	5.1	5.8	5.7
	Primary + Junior high	8.2	4.4	4.7	4.7
	High school	8.6	5.2	5.4	5.4
	University +	9.0	5.5	5.6	6.3
Dwelling type	Shanty town	8.5	4.9	5.3	5.2
	Non-shanty town middle range	8.4	4.7	5.0	5.1
	Non-shanty town luxurious	8.5	5.2	5.4	5.7
Urban–rural	Province centre	8.5	4.8	5.3	5.3
	District centre	8.4	5.0	5.2	5.3
	Village	8.4	4.7	4.9	4.8
Socio-economic status	Low	8.3	4.7	5.2	5.1
	Middle	8.5	4.6	5.0	5.0
	High	8.9	5.7	5.4	5.9
Knowledge of Kurdish	No	8.4	4.4	4.7	4.7
	Yes	8.7	7.0	7.9	8.1
Party preference	ANAP	8.6	5.3	5.5	5.7
	CHP	8.9	6.0	5.3	5.7
	DSP	8.9	5.8	5.4	5.4
	DYP	8.2	4.1	4.5	4.2
	SP	7.6	4.0	5.3	5.2
	MHP	8.1	4.0	4.1	4.1
	HADEP	8.9	9.2	9.0	8.8
	AKP	8.3	3.8	5.0	5.0
Nationalist attitudes	Low	9.0	6.8	7.1	7.2
	Middle	8.4	4.7	5.0	5.1
	High	8.2	4.3	4.7	4.7
Euro-scepticism	Low	8.4	5.9	6.2	6.4
	Middle	8.3	5.2	5.3	5.3
	High	8.6	4.2	5.0	5.1
Pro-EU attitudes	Low	7.5	3.5	4.3	4.2
	Middle	8.4	5.0	5.4	5.4
	High	9.2	6.0	6.1	6.4
Religiousness	Low	8.6	5.7	5.2	5.4
	Middle	8.4	4.7	5.3	5.4
	High	8.4	4.3	5.0	5.1
Anti-democratic attitudes	Low	8.7	5.2	5.6	5.7
	Middle	8.0	4.1	4.3	4.3
	High	7.1	4.9	4.9	4.8
	Total	8.5	4.8	5.1	5.1

constituencies are on average more supportive of the creation of the necessary conditions for freedom of thought and expression, but they tend to be on the conservative side when it comes to the death penalty and use of native languages.

Attitudinal groups reflecting nationalist, Euro-sceptic, religious and anti-democratic positions are also quite successful in differentiating support levels for the Copenhagen adjustments. As would be expected, those with Euro-sceptic attitudes tend to be less supportive of the statements put, while holders of pro-EU attitudes tend to be more supportive. A devoutly religious outlook is most significant in determining attitudes concerning the death penalty. Surprisingly, the more religious groups tend to be less supportive of the lifting of the death penalty, reflecting seemingly a general conservatism rather than purely religious beliefs.

Following the general contextualisation of the 'sensitive issues', the respondents were presented with the same statements, together with explicit reference to the Copenhagen criteria for EU membership. In all cases, we tried to discover what the reactions to the legal and policy adjustments would be if the reform in question were the last hurdle facing Turkey's EU membership. We then asked whether the respondent would support the legal changes or not. By so doing, we aimed first at underlining the importance and urgency of the issue at hand, and second, at obtaining the last-resort resistance of the respondents facing the prospect of EU membership.

Table 2.4 summarises these results. One striking observation is that, with respect to all the 'sensitive issues', a clear majority of the total respondents are against the Copenhagen adjustments. For the case of the lifting of the death penalty, the margin against the lifting of the death penalty is quite narrow, with about 54 per cent against and about 43 per cent in favour of abolition. For those who were against the lifting of the death penalty, one further question was asked: whether they would approve the lifting of the death penalty if, instead, a tougher and fully implemented life imprisonment without any form of remission were to be put in place.

This second question seems to have tilted the balance in favour of those who would accept the lifting of the death penalty. In other words, among the 53.7 per cent of those against the lifting of the death penalty, about 34.3 per cent change their positions, adding about 18.4 percentage points to the 43.3 per cent who support the abolition in the first question. Then, the level of support reaches 61.7 per cent – which suggest a comfortable margin of approval, but not an overwhelming majority. In short, even if the lifting of the death penalty were to be the last hurdle preventing Turkey's membership of the EU, respondents do not seem to be overwhelmingly in support of such a policy change. From a different perspective, it seems that EU membership does not provide enough of an incentive for the respondents to change their policy preferences.

Similar observations can be made on the lifting of the laws that limit the use of languages other than Turkish in broadcasting or those that

Table 2.4 'Sensitive issues': second-round contextualisation of questions

	Approves	Does not approve	N.A./N.O.[a]
Would you approve lifting of the death penalty for all crimes and for all people if it were to be the only remaining condition to be fulfilled by Turkey before its EU membership?	43.3	53.7	3.0
(If disapproves of the first death penalty question) Would you approve lifting of death penalty if instead a tougher and fully implemented life imprisonment without any concessions were to be put in place?	34.3	62.1	3.7
Would you approve lifting of the laws that limit use of native languages other than Turkish, such as Kurdish, in radio and TV broadcasting if it were to be the only remaining condition to be fulfilled by Turkey before its EU membership?	38.9	56.2	4.9
Would you approve lifting of the laws that ban learning of native languages other than Turkish, such as Kurdish, in private language courses if it were to be the only remaining condition to be fulfilled by Turkey before its EU membership?	37.3	57.7	5.0

Note
a NA/NO: No answer/no opinion.

limit education in such languages. Majorities in excess of 55 per cent do not approve of such changes, which would benefit those Turkish citizens who speak Kurdish dialects. However, from an optimistic perspective, such a legislative arrangement that would directly benefit a minority group enjoys sizeable support, in excess of 35 per cent.

Several patterns emerge from the preceding analysis. First and foremost, despite strong overall support for basic rights and freedoms in the country, when questions are contextualised within EU–Turkey relations and the Copenhagen criteria, and when respondents are reminded of the implications for the Kurdish minority, support for the expansion of the right to use one's native language in education and broadcasting drops significantly and remains confined to a strict minority of the electorate. The second pattern observed is that for the case of the lifting of death penalty, an opportunity is present for the pro-EU forces. If people are presented with a strict application of life imprisonment without parole, those opposed to the lifting of the death penalty remain in a minority.

From the perspective of Turkish electoral politics, the significance of the passage of the Copenhagen adjustment package through Parliament should now be clearer. Having taken an early election decision soon after a major economic crisis, the coalition partners as well as the opposition parties in Parliament were facing a serious threat of opposition from the electorate, which could have been exploited by the AKP and CHP, which were not represented in Parliament at the time of the reforms in August 2002. Extending the minority language rights and delivering the adjustment package at the last minute might have left an image of acting under EU pressure. The coalition leadership would have taken the risk of pressing for the reform package only if the salience of EU membership had been high enough – that is, only if the prospect of EU membership, which was strengthened by the reform package, had been an electoral asset. Then, the question to be answered is the following: to what extent was EU membership a salient issue in the minds of the electorate prior to November 2002 elections even though EU supporters were clearly in a majority among supporters of all parties?

2.3 Salience of EU-related issues

In October 2002, just prior to the elections on 3 November, and again in January and February 2003, a few months after the election, we conducted two surveys in a panel design to study the voting decisions of the Turkish electorate.[8] In these studies, we asked a series of questions that could help us determine the salience of EU membership and related issues prior to the general election.

Table 2.5 shows the summary answers given to the most important problem Turkey faces within an open-ended question format. I added up the answers indicating the most important and the second most important problems Turkey faces, and calculated the shares of problems among all answers given for both surveys. We observe that economic problems occupy the top three slots among answers in both pre- and post-election surveys. As expected, with the forming of the AKP's single-party government, political instability and uncertainty has significantly dropped as a proportion of answers. With a war on the horizon in Iraq, nearly 12 per cent of the respondents placed war in Iraq as the most important problem facing the country, ranking it fourth on the list. Most significantly for our purposes, EU and related foreign policy issues occupy the most important problem in the minds of only about 1 per cent of the electorate. No significant change is observed with respect to EU and related foreign policy issues in the aftermath of the elections. We are accordingly led to believe that despite the heated debates in early August and just prior to the Copenhagen summit in December 2002, the electorate continued to see EU and related foreign policy issues as of minor importance for the country compared to other issues on the agenda.

In both pre- and post-election surveys, the respondents were asked whether or not they remembered the reforms contained in the EU adjustment package of 3 August 2002. Table 2.6 shows that before the elections

Table 2.5 Most important problems of the country

	October 2002	Jan.–Feb. 2003
Unemployment	29.7	28.3
Economic instability and crisis	27.1	27.1
Inflation	19.6	18.7
Political instability/uncertainty	7.4	2.9
Education	4.4	3.4
Corruption–bribery	3.4	1.9
Health–social security	2.3	2.1
Conflict in Iraq war	1.2	11.6
EU-related and foreign policy	0.6	1.0
Others	4.4	3.1
Total	100	100

Source: Çarkoğlu *et al.* (2003).

on 3 November 2002, the proportion of those who remembered what the adjustment package was, was about 25 per cent. About two to three months after the elections, on the other hand, the proportion of those who remembered what the August package was about had dropped to about 17 per cent.

Those who claimed to remember the contents and nature of this package were asked to list the reforms. The answers to this question were obtained in an open-ended format, so whatever the respondents told the interviewers was noted. The answers show us that, while in the pre-election context about 75 per cent gave an acceptable answer about the amendments, in the post-election survey the proportion of acceptable answers fell to about 55 per cent. In other words, about six months after the passage of the package only about 9 per cent (55 per cent of the 17 per cent) of the electorate seemed to remember what it was really about. Clearly, these answers show that only a small minority of the electorate did remember the August reform package in detail, and the size of this minority became even smaller with the passage of time. Even the then hotly debated issues of abolishing the death penalty and broadcasting/education in native languages other than Turkish were remembered by only about 5 per cent (27.5 per cent of the 17 per cent) of the respondents in the aftermath of the elections – down from about 13 per cent (51.8 per cent of the 24.6 per cent). All this suggests that the salience of the adjustment package for the electorate was quite low.

One important reason for such an abrupt decline of attention to and salience of EU and related issues might be the failure of the political elite to push these issues forcefully and in a consistent and coherent manner during the election campaign. Although a comprehensive analysis of the November 2002 election campaign is not presently available, my reading of the election manifestos of both the AKP and the CHP provides some

Table 2.6 Salience of EU issues

Q: *Do you remember the issues contained in the EU adjustment package passed by Parliament on 3 August 2002?*

	October 2002	Jan.–Feb. 2003
Remembers	24.6	17.0
Does not remember	74.2	81.9
No Answer	1.2	1.2

Q: *Could you tell us what the issues were?* (Question put only to those who remember the issues.)

	October 2002	Jan.–Feb. 2003
Lifting of the death penalty	41.3	20.1
Broadcasting and education in native languages	10.5	7.4
Human rights	14.4	21.4
Freedom of thought	3.9	4.3
Minority foundations	3.0	1.3
Other	26.9	45.4

Source: Çarkoğlu *et al.* (2003).

support for this argument.[9] The AKP's election manifesto does not have the EU at its centre but rather uses the EU for linking different issues. Specifically, the AKP's focus on the EU is shaped around the obvious foreign policy discussions on Cyprus and Turkish–Greek relations. The CHP's emphasis is more on the membership aspect of the debate. However, in a similar fashion to the AKP's argumentation, the CHP manifesto intricately linked EU issues to a large number of policy areas.

Another reason for the falling away of attention paid to, and salience of, EU-related issues could be the emergence of a major populist/nationalist threat from the Young Party (GP) and the Nationalist Action Party (MHP) (see Çarkoğlu, 2003). Both these parties' constituencies were in favour of EU membership. However, their elite ideology was staunchly nationalist in the case of the MHP or populist in the case of the GP; and both were highly anti-European in their rhetoric and policy stands. Although both the GP and the MHP failed to mobilise sizeable constituencies against the EU, they nevertheless were successful in deterring the other major parties, especially the two likely winners (the AKP and CHP), from being proactive on the EU front.

As a result of these factors, the EU cause remained abandoned in the election campaigns.

> [N]either CHP facing GP, nor AKP facing MHP in their core constituencies in coastal or central Anatolian provinces respectively, could afford to push EU related issues beyond the mere subtle linkage

to various reform debates. In consequence, the anti-European front was not confronted publicly in any public debate and the two largest parties kept the EU issues at low salience. At the same time, the eurosceptic front was conveniently kept divided into smaller party constituencies thus helping to waste their representation by keeping them out of the parliament for being below the ten percent threshold.

(Çarkoğlu, 2003: 192)

2.4 A multivariate analysis of support for EU membership in Turkey

The analysis hitherto opens up a number of interesting questions concerning the determinants of the Turkish electorate's support for EU membership. The first question concerns the impact of the so-called sensitive issues on support for EU membership. The second concerns the impact of leadership in guiding mass support for EU membership. Are people who tend to agree with the legal changes that aim to fulfil the Copenhagen criteria significantly more likely to support EU membership? How does the perceived EU support of the leaders, political elites or the Turkish people at large affect an individual's likelihood of supporting Turkey's EU membership?

A comprehensive analysis of the determinants of EU support among the Turkish voters can be found in Çarkoğlu (2003). Here, I use the same dataset and variables as a basis for addressing the two sets of questions on the impact of leadership and 'sensitive issues'. Doing so will give us an extensive model with a larger number of relevant variables, and we will also be able to make a comparative assessment of the impact of these new factors on the support for EU membership.[10]

Table 2.7 reports the results of a binary logistic regression using the referendum question as the dependent variable, which is coded as 1 for those who indicated that they would vote for Turkey's full membership of the EU and 0 for those who would vote against it. The dependent variable is specified as a binary dummy variable and thus violates the assumptions of conventional regression methods. I accordingly use a binary logit specification.[11] The estimated model involves a number of dummy variables as well as usual interval ratio variables. It is therefore necessary to note the reference category that is grasped by the model's constant term, which is the joint complement of all dummy variables in the equation. It represents women with no formal schooling who do not know Kurdish and who live in urban, metropolitan areas. These women are also undecided about their party of choice, they just managed to make ends meet or were able to make savings in the past year, and are optimistic about their families' economic conditions over the next year.

We observe that the constant term has a negative sign, implying that these women have a bias against voting in favour of Turkey's full membership of the EU. The results in Table 2.7 are similar to those presented in Çarkoğlu (2003), although there are a number of significant differences. Once again we see that party choice variables are all insignificant, this time without any exception. When the impacts of attitudinal, demographic and other variables are controlled for, party choice is not significant in explaining support for EU membership in a referendum.

Attitudinal indicators discussed in detail in Çarkoğlu (2003) appear once again to be the most influential of all variables in the model. Surprisingly, once new variables concerning leadership and sensitive issues are taken into account, the degree of Euro-scepticism ceases to have a significant negative impact, while pro-EU attitudes continue to have a significant positive impact on the likelihood of voting in support of EU membership. More specifically, as an individual's pro-EU attitudes increases by one standard deviation in the factor scores, then the probability of being supportive of Turkey's EU membership increases by 40 per cent (exp (β) = 1.4). Similarly, as an individual becomes more religious or more in support of anti-democratic assertions, that individual's likelihood of being supportive of EU membership declines. In odds ratio terms, the odds of being supportive of Turkey's EU membership as opposed to being against it drops by 23 per cent (exp (β) = 0.77) for one standard deviation increase of religiousness. The same odds of being supportive of EU membership fall by 19 per cent (exp (β) = 0.81) for one standard deviation increase of anti-democratic attitudes. In other words, religiousness has a larger impact on the odds of being supportive of EU membership than anti-democratic attitudes.

Nationalistic/patriotic attitudes once again have an insignificant impact in a multivariate setting on the odds of being supportive of EU membership. This might again be a reflection of the fact that in measuring this complex phenomenon of nationalist/patriotic attitudes, patriotism rather than nationalism dominates the measurement. Being patriots rather than nationalists, Turkish voters are thus not significantly more negatively predisposed against the EU.

Besides pro-EU attitudes, evaluations of individuals concerning the impact of EU membership on their personal lives have one of the largest positive impacts on those individuals' decisions concerning EU membership. As individuals become more convinced that they will personally benefit from membership, they tend to support EU membership in a referendum setting. A unit increase on this 1 to 10 scale of evaluation of the impact of EU membership on personal lives increases the odds of being supportive of EU membership by 46 per cent (exp (β) = 1.46).

Again surprisingly, respondents' age is positively associated with support for EU membership. An additional year of age leads to a 2 per cent increased likelihood of being an EU supporter as opposed to a non-supporter. As a result, compared to an 18-year-old voter, someone who is 48 years old is nearly 48.3 per cent ($e^{0.02 \times 20}$ = 1.483) more likely to be a

Table 2.7 Determinants of support for EU membership in a referendum

	β	S.E.	Wald	Sig.	Exp (β)
Constant	−2.62	0.64	16.59	0.00	
Political preferences					
ANAP	0.39	0.49	0.66	0.42	1.48
CHP	0.06	0.36	0.03	0.87	1.06
DSP	0.13	0.48	0.08	0.78	1.14
DYP	−0.02	0.38	0.00	0.97	0.98
SP	−0.67	0.57	1.39	0.24	0.51
MHP	−0.07	0.39	0.03	0.86	0.93
HADEP	−0.31	0.50	0.38	0.54	0.74
AKP	0.20	0.31	0.40	0.53	1.22
Not going to cast a vote	0.14	0.38	0.14	0.71	1.15
Will vote for none of the presently available parties	−0.08	0.30	0.08	0.78	0.92
Will vote for other, smaller parties	−0.44	0.47	0.86	0.35	0.65
Attitudinal indicators					
Nationalist/patriotic attitudes	−0.01	0.09	0.01	0.94	0.99
Euro-scepticism	−0.08	0.08	0.94	0.33	0.92
Pro-EU attitudes	0.34[a]	0.09	13.55	0.00	1.40
Religiousness	−0.26[a]	0.09	7.93	0.00	0.77
Anti-democratic attitudes	−0.21[a]	0.08	6.02	0.01	0.81
Not satisfied with the way Turkish democracy works	0.34	0.26	1.71	0.19	1.40
Evaluation of the way personal life will change in case Turkey becomes a member of the EU	0.38[a]	0.03	118.45	0.00	1.46
Evaluation of the possibility that Turkey becomes a full member of the EU over the next 10 years	0.03	0.03	1.33	0.25	1.03
Perceived willingness for EU membership of different groups (General populace)	0.59[a]	0.09	45.35	0.00	1.80
Perceived willingness for EU membership of different groups (elites)	0.14[b]	0.08	3.55	0.06	1.15
Perceived willingness for EU membership of different party leaders (pro-EU leaders)	−0.04	0.07	0.35	0.56	0.96
Perceived willingness for EU membership of different party leaders (anti-EU leaders)	0.13[b]	0.08	3.08	0.08	1.14
Various demographic indicators					
Age	0.02	0.01	9.74	0.00	1.02
Male	−0.03	0.16	0.05	0.82	0.97
Knows Kurdish	0.42[b]	0.26	2.68	0.10	1.53
Living in a rural area	−0.16	0.18	0.81	0.37	0.85
Number of adults working in the household	−0.05	0.07	0.56	0.46	0.95

Table 2.7 Continued

	β	S.E.	Wald	Sig.	Exp (β)
Cluster 1	−0.45[b]	0.25	3.16	0.08	0.64
Cluster 2	−0.49[a]	0.20	5.82	0.02	0.61
Cluster 4	0.17	0.31	0.31	0.58	1.19
Cluster 5	−0.40[a]	0.22	3.29	0.07	0.67
Primary + junior school graduate	0.46	0.35	1.70	0.19	1.58
High school graduate	0.57	0.40	2.08	0.15	1.77
University + graduate	0.88[b]	0.47	3.52	0.06	2.42
Economic wellbeing and expectations					
Socio-economic status	−0.07	0.11	0.41	0.52	0.93
Pessimistic expectations for the family's economic situation over the next 1 year	−0.17	0.15	1.36	0.24	0.84
Condition of family's economic situation over the past year)had to take loans or used past savings	0.17	0.15	1.42	0.23	1.19
Sensitive issues					
Dummy for those who would support lifting of the death penalty if this were the only stumbling block facing Turkey's membership of the EU	0.21	0.17	1.64	0.20	1.24
Dummy for those who would support lifting of the ban on the use of native languages other thanTurkish, such as Kurdish, in radio and TV broadcasting if this were the only stumbling block facing Turkey's membership of the EU	−0.23	0.21	1.28	0.26	0.79
Dummy for those who would support lifting of the ban on the teaching of native languages other than Turkish, like Kurdish, in private courses if this were the only stumbling block facing Turkey's membership of the EU	−0.08	0.21	0.16	0.68	0.92

	Predicted		
	Y to EU	N to EU	%
Observed (Y)es to EU	882	94	90
Observed (N)o to EU	198	270	58
Cox and Snell *R*-square = 0.33			
Nagelkerke *R*-square = 0.46	Overall		80

Notes
a $p < 0.05$; b $p < 0.1$
B: Logistic regression coefficients.
S.E.: Standard error of the estimated coefficients.
The observed values are for those individuals who support EU membership in their answers to our referendum question. The predicted values are the outcome of the reported logistic regression. Those individuals for which our model predicts a likelihood larger than 50 per cent are classified as supporting membership of the EU; others are classified as non-supportive.
Cluster 3 is a reference category. Therefore, it is incorporated in the constant term.

supporter of EU membership if all other variables are held constant. Although knowing Kurdish has something of a positive influence over the EU vote, it is significant only at the 10 per cent confidence interval. However, even at that level of significance we observe that knowing Kurdish increases the odds ratio by a factor of 1.53.

The urban–rural divide does not seem to be significant, either. As to the level of education, we observe that being a university graduate raises the odds of being supportive of EU membership by 2.42. The fact that lower levels of education do not have a significantly different impact on the odds of being an EU supporter is surprising. Only when a respondent has gone through a university education does he or she become more likely to be a supporter of EU membership; lower levels of education have little effects.

The respondents' geographical location has a significant effect on their tendency to support membership of the EU.[12] After controlling for the impact of other variables, respondents from Cluster 2 of the inner Aegean region, together with some Black Sea and south-eastern provinces, continue to remain significantly below the rest of the country in their tendency to support EU membership. Individuals in all remaining clusters have a relatively higher tendency to support EU membership. The proportion of those supporting EU membership falls to about 61 per cent of those who do not support EU membership (exp (β) = 0.61). It is also worthy of note that after we controlled for their nationalist/patriotic and anti-democratic attitudes, together with their Euro-scepticism and other demographic characteristics, only individuals in Cluster 2 are likely to be against EU membership compared to the rest of the country. The decision on whether to vote for EU membership in a referendum setting does not seem to be influenced by socio-economic status, or by retrospective or prospective evaluations of economic conditions.

The newly introduced variables concerning the 'sensitive issues' (the lifting of the death penalty, and education and broadcasting in native languages other than Turkish) do not seem to exert any significant influence on the likelihood of being supportive of Turkey's EU membership. In other words, knowing an individual's evaluation of these 'sensitive issues' does not add significantly to our model's classification of that individual as supportive or otherwise of Turkey's membership of the EU. However, perceived acceptance of EU membership mostly varies significantly among different groups. As the perceived acceptance of EU membership on the part of government officials, workers, peasants, students, small and medium merchants and the Turkish population at large increases, we observe a significant increase in the respondents' likelihood of being supportive of EU membership. One standard deviation increase in this composite factor of perceived willingness for EU membership on the part of the general populace increases the odds ratio of being supportive of EU membership by 80 per cent (exp (β) = 1.80). Similarly, increased perceived willingness on the part of the elite circles in the banking and business sectors, politicians and the military leads to an increase in the likelihood of being supportive of EU membership of about 15 per cent $(\exp (\beta) = 1.15)$.

What is interesting is that the probability of a respondent's support for EU membership is not affected by that respondent's perception of an increase in the disposition of the pro-EU politicians in favour of EU membership. However, as the perceived disposition of the anti-EU politicians in favour of EU membership increases, the respondents' likelihood of support for EU membership increases significantly. A unit increase in this composite factor of perceived disposition in favour of EU membership by anti-EU camp leaders led to a 14 per cent $(\exp (\beta) = 1.14)$ increase in the chance of being in favour of membership.

All in all, the multivariate model predicts 80 per cent of the vote correctly. However, while the model correctly predicts 90 per cent of the observed support for EU membership, only 58 per cent of the observed declarations of intention to vote against EU membership are correctly predicted.

Conclusions

The results of the analysis above complement the results previously obtained with the same dataset collected in May–June 2002. There exists very little if any significant difference between different party constituencies when it comes to supporting or being against Turkey's membership of the EU. Among the general attitudinal bases of resistance to EU membership, religiousness and anti-democratic attitudes – together with Euroscepticism – form the sources of resistance to EU membership. As Turkish voters' expectations from membership grow, their tendency to support membership also grows significantly. Finally, geography and the generation gap are among the factors that inhibit consensus on EU membership.

From a policy perspective, the so-called sensitive issues that can easily be used by those groups and parties that choose to oppose EU membership do not form a significant stumbling block to the creation of support for EU membership. These issues are certainly candidates for public expressions of anti-EU rhetoric. Therefore, they are being conveniently exploited within a nationalistic, Euro-sceptic and religious rhetoric so as to make them more palatable to a largely EU-supportive Turkish public. However, after other attitudinal factors such as religiousness, democratic values and Euro-scepticism, together with various demographic variables, have been taken into account, the impact of sensitive issues on support for EU membership ceases to be significant.

The above analysis also demonstrates how the choice of rhetoric may significantly change the level of support for or antagonsim towards policy modifications necessary for compliance with the Copenhagen criteria. One reason for such fragility of EU support and manipulations of the anti-European camp is the apparent lack of information about the EU membership process and policy requirements necessary for full membership. Accordingly, despite mass public support for EU membership, the polarised elite resistance to membership may find ample opportunities for manipulating the public agenda. However, attempts to shrink the mass support for EU by providing misinformation to the public and strategically shaping the rhetoric around the 'sensitive issues', especially concerning the cultural rights of those citizens of Kurdish origin and abolition of the death penalty, do not lead to a significant reduction in likelihood of support for EU membership. This is a major reason for optimism concerning the future of mass support for EU membership in Turkey. Short-run, manipulative issue linkages to EU membership do not seem to be effective. Longer-run tendencies reflected in attitudinal characteristics of the respondents such as their democratic values, their religiousness, their age and ethnicity, and their education level are more important determinants.

Given these findings, leadership and public relations campaigns in favour of EU membership may be highly effective. As people perceive that the general populace is becoming more supportive of EU membership, their tendency to support EU membership also increases. Especially important in this respect is the finding that as the perceived willingness of formerly anti-EU party leaders for EU membership increases, the respondents' own willingness to support EU membership also increases. The catch here is that as the perceived willingness decreases among leaders of the anti-EU camp, it correspondingly reduces the respondents' willingness to support EU membership. So the key here is to counterbalance such leaders' anti-EU rhetoric with equal effectiveness.

The discussion in this chapter concerning the salience of EU membership and related issues is also directly linked to the issue of advocacy for EU membership by the political elite. The historical gamble by the centrist parties in passing the EU adjustment package in August 2002 did not yield an electoral pay-off, primarily because of the low salience these issues occupied in the minds of the voters. The pro-EU forces failed to shape the agenda of the November 2002 election around EU membership and the social and political transformation this necessitates. *Ex post facto*, the pro-EU forces leave the impression of being intimidated by the anti-EU camp on the grounds that the 'sensitive issues' might work against them in the election. The results presented here suggest, however, that such a detrimental impact from the 'sensitive issues' was never effectively binding.

Looking into the future, the threat from the anti-EU camp will continue on the basis of, once again, 'sensitive issues'. To counteract such resistance, a concerted effort and coordinated leadership are needed, especially to gain support from Turkish youth, a large sector that dominates the electoral scene in the country, especially in the critical regions of EU resistance in the central Anatolian provinces.

Looking at Turkey and its relations with the EU, oscillations between the 'fast' and 'slow' passage of time is likely to continue. For the anti-EU camp, time is more like an express train that is moving too rapidly towards membership, especially after the passage of the August 2002 adjustment package. For the Europhiles, however, time passes slowly, and the domestic resistance to membership renders the process increasingly slow. Despite hurdles and roadblocks, however, the process is still moving. Like the evaluations of the speed of time, appraisals of the swiftness of this process will depend on who actually judges it.

Notes

1 The CHP remained about 14 percentage points below the AKP, at around 20 per cent of the vote.
2 Robert Putnam's (1988) account of the dual nature of the foreign policy-making forms the theoretical background to this claim. Following many earlier claims, Putnam analytically asserts that intricate sets of relations between the diplomatic negotiators (Level I) and the grass-roots interactions between non-official players such as businesses, NGOs and other civil society groups (Level II) shape foreign policy. See also Evans *et al.* (1993).
3 For two provincial survey results that focus on support for EU membership, see Esmer (1997).
4 A selection of these messages was compiled by Perinçek (2002).
5 Bağcı (2002) argues that hacking into Karen Fogg's e-mail messages is part and parcel of an effort to hinder the adoption of reforms that would open the way for Turkey's eventual accession to the EU. In the media, there were also commentators who took a critical view of the hacking. See Yılmaz (2002).
6 For coverage of these e-mail messages from the perspective of the problem in Cyprus, see Ismail and Yusuf (2002).
7 The May–June survey was undertaken by a team of scholars including the author, Refik Erzan, Kermal Kirişci and Hakam Yılmaz. The Turkish Economic and Social Studies Foundation (Türkiye Ekonomik ve Sosyal Etüdler Vakfı–TESEV) funded the survey. For details see <http://www.tesev.org.tr/eng>.
8 The pre-election study that forms the basis of these results is a nationwide survey of the population of voting age in October 2002 that included 2,028 face-to-face interviews in 33 provinces. Districts, streets and building numbers in the 33 provinces where the interviews were carried out were randomly selected by computer. The expected margin of error is ±2.2 at the 95 per cent confidence level. Field research was conducted by the Frekans Research Company during the period 10–25 October. The project carried out by the author, Üstün Ergüder and Ersin Kalaycıoğlu was funded by Sabancı University and the Turkish Economic and Social Studies Foundation (TESEV).
9 See AKP (2002) and CHP (2002).
10 Dummy variables are created to evaluate the impact of 'sensitive issues'. Perceived willingness variables are obtained by a factor analysis of evaluations on a 1 (totally against) to 10 (very willing) scale of perceived willingness for EU membership on the part of different groups and party leaders. Four dimensions explaining 55 per cent of total variation are derived. The first dimension captures the perceived willingness for EU membership for the general populace including civil servants, workers, peasants, the Turkish population at large, and small merchants. The second represents pro-EU leaders such as

Deniz Baykal of the CHP, Bülent Ecevit of the DSP, Mesut Yılmaz of the ANAP, Tansu Çiller of the DYP, Mehmet Ali Bayar of the DTP and Murat Bozlak of HADEP. The third captures the perceived willingness for EU membership by elites such as bankers, owners of big holding companies, politicians and the army. The fourth dimension captures anti-EU leaders such as Tayyip Erdoğan of the AKP, Recai Kutan of the SP and Devlet Bahçeli of the MHP. The fact that Erdoğan appears in this dimension together with Bahçeli is only a reflection of the perceptions of the respondents and the perceived closeness of the AKP leadership to that of the MHP.

11 See Aldrich and Nelson (1984), Demaris (1992) and Long (1997) for accessible reviews of the methods used here.

12 The Turkish provinces are divided into five clusters according to their socio-economic characteristics and political preferences. Cluster 1 comprises the coastal provinces of the Black Sea, Marmara and Aegean regions. Cluster 2 comprises mostly inner Aegean and some Black Sea and south-eastern provinces. The metropolitan provinces form Cluster 3. Cluster 4 comprises the south-eastern provinces. Finally, the provinces of central and eastern Anatolia constitute Cluster 5. A detailed map of these five clusters can be found in Çarkoğlu (2003).

References

AKP (2002), *Herşey Türkiye İçin* (Everything Is for Turkey) [election manifesto], available at http://www.akparti.org.tr/.

Aldrich, John H. and Forrest D. Nelson (1984), *Linear Probability, Logit and Probit Models*, London: Sage.

Bağcı, Hüseyin (2002), 'Karen Fogg: victim or scapegoat?', *Turkish News*, 18 February, available at www.foreignpolicy.org.tr.

Çarkoğlu, Ali (2003), 'Who wants full membership? Characteristics of the Turkish public support for EU membership', *Turkish Studies*, vol. 4, no. 1 (Spring), pp. 171–194.

Çarkoğlu, Ali and Kemal Kirişci (2003), 'Two-level diplomatic games: the role of public opinion in Greek-Turkish relations', unpublished manuscript.

Çarkoğlu, Ali, Üstün Ergüder and Ersin Kalaycıoğlu (2003), 'Turkish election study – 2002', unpublished manuscript in preparation.

CHP (2002), *Güzel Günler Göreceğiz!* (We'll See Good Days!) [election manifesto], available at http://secim2002.chp.org.tr/bildirge.asp.

Demaris, Alfred (1992), *Logit Modelling, Practical Applications*, London: Sage.

Erdemli, Özgül (2003), 'Chronology: Turkey's relations with the EU', *Turkish Studies*, vol. 4, no. 1 (Spring), pp. 4–8.

Erder, Necat (1996), *Türkiye'de Siyasi Parti Seçmenlerinin Nitelikleri, Kimlikleri ve Eğilimleri* (Characteristics of Political Party Constituencies, Their Identities and Tendencies in Turkey), Istanbul: Boyut Matbaacılık. (A TÜSES – Turkish Social Economic and Political Studies Foundation – Publication.)

Erder, Necat (1999), *Türkiye'de Siyasi Parti Seçmenleri ve Toplum Düzeni* (Political Party Constituencies and Social Order in Turkey), Istanbul: Boyut Matbaacılık. (A TÜSES – Turkish Social Economic and Political Studies Foundation – Publication.)

Esmer, Y. (1997), 'Türk kamuoyu ve Avrupa' (Turkish public opinion and Europe), in *Türkiye Avrupa Birliğinin Neresinde? Gümrük Birliği Anlaşmasının*

Düşündürdükleri (Where Is Turkey in Europe? Thoughts on Customs Union with the EU), Istanbul: Ayraç Yayınevi, pp. 124–135.

Evans, Peter B., Harold K. Jacobson and Robert D. Putnam (eds) (1993), *Double-Edged Diplomacy: International Bargaining and Domestic Politics*, Berkeley and Los Angeles: University of California Press.

İsmail, S. and H. M. Yusuf (2002), *AB Karen Fogg ve Kıbrıs AB'nin KKTC Üzerinde Bitmeyen Oyunları Karen Fogg'un Hedefi: Denktaş* (The EU, Karen Fogg and Cyprus, the EU's Unending Games over the Turkish Republic of Northern Cyprus, Karen Fogg's Target: Denktaş), Istanbul: Akdeniz Haber Ajansı Yayınları.

Long, J. Scott (1997), *Regression Models for Categorical and Limited Dependent Variables*, London: Sage.

Perinçek, Doğu (2002), *Karen Fogg'un E-Postaları* (E-mail Messages of Karen Fogg), Istanbul: Kaynak Yayınları.

Putnam, Robert (1988) 'Diplomacy and domestic politics: the logic of two-level games', *International Organisation*, vol. 42, no. 3, pp. 427–460.

Rae, Douglas (1967), *The Political Consequences of Electoral Laws*, New Haven, CT: Yale University Press.

Yılmaz, Mehmet (2002), 'Alaturka bir casusluk Öyküsü (An *à la turc* spygame story)', *Milliyet*, 12 February.

Part II

Economic governance and EU membership

3 Populism as a barrier to integration with the EU
Rethinking the Copenhagen criteria

Mine Eder

Introduction

Among the Copenhagen criteria, the political dimension (namely, the stability of institutions guaranteeing democracy, human rights, the rule of law, and respect for and protection of minority rights) has always attracted primary attention in Turkey–EU relations. Equally important, however, are the economic criteria, which call for 'the existence of a functioning market economy' as well as 'a capacity to cope with competitive pressures and market forces within the Union'. But how realistic is it for the EU to expect its prospective members to undertake political and economic reforms simultaneously? Can the new members consolidate their democracy and improve their market positions at the same time?

Focusing particularly on the legacies of Turkish populism, this chapter underlines the difficult, paradoxical nature of simultaneous reforms. It suggests that pro-market reforms required by the Copenhagen criteria may not be sufficient to overcome populism as a source of policy failure. In fact, pro-market reforms may well coexist with and provide a fertile ground for populism. Can neoliberal economic reforms be compatible with populism? Can populist pressures be resisted? How and why does populism undermine the democratic process? How and why does populism emerge as both an economic and a political barrier to EU membership? This chapter seeks answers to these questions through study of Turkish populism and Turkey's prospective accession to the EU.

3.1 Defining populism

Defining populism is an arduous task, as the concept has acquired new meanings and its usage has expanded so as to include almost any political movement that appeals to the populace. In addition, there seems to be populism for every taste, ranging from urban or agrarian populism to populism from below or above.[1] This wide canvass has led some scholars to call for the elimination of the concept from the terminology of social science (Roxborough, 1984; Quintero, 1980).

As Roberts (1995) and Weyland (1996) point out, however, it is still possible to utilize the concept of populism without falling into the trap of what Sartori (1970, 1984) called conceptual stretching – namely, distorting the concept when it does not fit the case under examination (Collier and Mahon, 1993). Furthermore, Latin America's recurrent encounter with populism has generated a significant and even coherent literature (see, for instance, Laclau, 1977; Mendes, 1977; Quintero, 1980; Germani, 1978; Stein, 1980). It is thus premature to write the epitaph of populism. But a fundamental question remains: how can we associate the concept with more than one socio-political context without singling out one or two of its characteristics in an *ad hoc* and teleological manner?

Inter alios, Ianni (1980) has suggested that populism corresponded to a specific transition phase in Latin America in the 1930s: the transition from a traditional agrarian society to an industrial one. Following the breakdown of oligarchic rule, they argued, populism created room for the integration of the newly emerging urban working and middle classes into the political process. The formation of multi-class, cross-cutting coalitions and their incorporation into the political system was also closely associated with urbanization and import-substituting industrialization (ISI) (Vilas, 1992). Despite the appeal of this structural approach that links populism with ISI, *coalitional* analysis is too narrow and static to be generalized into other cases. More importantly, it does not envision a post-ISI populism and cannot explain why and how populism can survive various socio-economic conditions.

A similar definitional problem emerges when populism is equated with a set of redistributive economic policies. These policies include, but are not limited to, Keynesian strategies of running budget deficits to stimulate domestic demand, nominal wage increases and price controls to effect income distribution, and exchange rate controls (Dornbusch and Edwards, 1990). This *economistic* definition is useful, as it rightly identifies economic inequality and associated social discontent as fundamental reasons behind populism. However, it still remains inadequate as it fails to recognize that inflationary wage increases or deficit spending might not actually be necessary in mobilizing popular support (Roberts, 1995: 86). Clientelism or other economic instruments such as selective and targeted distribution of state funds, creating discretionary funds for the poor without significant macroeconomic redistribution, can be just as effective. Furthermore, such an approach does not allow for the coexistence of populism and neoliberal economic policies that emphasize fiscal discipline and tight monetary policies. Finally, this approach is reductionist, as it ignores the political and ideological dimensions of populism (Cardoso and Helwege, 1991; Knight, 1998).

No definition of populism can be complete without taking into account the political and ideological strategies and the institutional features associated with populist politics. In fact, populism's best-known and earliest definition includes these factors. DiTella (1965) characterized populism as 'a political movement, which enjoys the support of the masses and is supported by sectors upholding an anti-status quo ideology.' In his analysis of Latin American populism, Laclau (1977) argued that populism is essentially an ideological discursive struggle between 'the people' and 'the power bloc', and populist movements are essentially processes of 'hegemonic rebalancing within the power bloc'. Mouzelis (1985) added an organizational dimension to Laclau's definition and suggested that populism is an anti-elitist and anti-establishment ideology. In this definition, populism goes well beyond clientelism – that is, the exchange of favours for votes. In populism, Mouzelis argued, the decision-making is much more centralized than in clientelism, but mass mobilization still bypasses and/or undermines strong intermediaries between the state and society. Hence, *de-institutionalization of political authority and weakening of representative institutions such as political parties and legislatures* emerge as fundamental characteristics of populism. In that sense, there are direct linkages between the often charismatic leader and the masses.

The political dimension of populism becomes more apparent when it is contrasted with the concept of democracy. Theoretically, the relationship between populism and democracy has always been ambiguous (Canovan, 1999; Urbinati, 1998). Nevertheless, populism can be seen as an effective instrument of democracy in integrating lower classes into the political process and addressing their social discontent. Referring to the American origins of the term, Michael Kazin (1995: 2) argues that populism can be a democratic way to counterbalance the composition of forces holding political power within a democratic society. Emphasizing the mobilizational nature of populism, Laclau (1977: 182–190) also reached a similar conclusion and argued that a counter-hegemonic political discourse can always emerge against the power bloc.

However, as Oxhorn (1998: 212) rightly points out, 'social reform and political incorporation of the lower classes in Latin America have not been the result of grassroots pressures but more often the consequence of authoritarian efforts at cooptation and regime institutionalization'. The top-down nature of mobilization, or what Oxhorn called 'controlled inclusion', undermines the quality of the democratic process. Direct links between the leader and the masses – the bypassing of intermediary institutions – impede the formation of an autonomous, non-state-dependent civil society, which is a fundamental pillar of any given democracy. In short, populism circumvents the deliberative process and searches for ways to shorten, if not eliminate, the democratic process. De-institutionalization and reliance on top-down mobilization rather than independent formation of civil society suggest that populism can be conceived as a major impediment to democracy.

Hence, neither a purely economistic, ideological, institutional nor a pure political definition is enough to capture the multi-dimensionality of populism. Since populism emerges in so many different contexts and in so many different forms, no single ideological framework, no single set of economic policies or institutional feature can fully explain its characteristics and its transformation. Nevertheless, three main features of populism appear to survive all these different economic and political contexts. First, all populisms, in one form or another, include top-down mobilization that circumvents all institutional channels between the state and civil society. Second, the coalitional profile of which societal groups and sectors are mobilized can change significantly. Finally, all populisms, despite their wide range of eclectic ideological instruments, utilize an anti-elitist and anti-establishment discourse. As discussed in the next section, these characteristics have remained constant throughout the transformation of populism in Turkey.

3.2 Populism: the birth defect of Turkey's democracy

As in many other developing countries, populism continues to be the 'birth defect' of Turkey's democracy. Turkish populism has survived three military interventions, numerous boom-and-bust cycles in the economy, and a large number of ideologically different governments and parties. More importantly, Turkish populism has coexisted with different economic development programmes, including the state-sponsored rural development policies of the Democratic Party (*Demokrat Parti*, DP) in the 1950s, and the import substitution of the 1960–1979 period. Most recently, populism has also survived the liberalization reforms that started in 1980 and were maintained in the 1990s.

This new breed of populism, widely known as 'neoliberal populism', differs from its predecessors (Weyland, 1996, 1999). The main difference is that it coexists with neoliberal policies, which are supposed to deliver improved economic efficiency as well as a better quality of governance. Yet as we know from the cases of Alberto Fujimori in Peru, Fernando Collor in Brazil (1990–1992), Carlos Menem in Argentina (1989–1999) and Carlos Salinas in Mexico (1988–1994), neoliberal policies have long existed side by side with populist strategies. As Bresser Pereira *et al.* (1993: 208) explain,

> Since the neoliberal strategy entails significant social costs, reforms tend to be initiated from above and launched by surprise, independent of public opinion and without the participation of organized political forces.... The political style of implementation tends to be autocratic: governments seek to demobilize their supporters rather than compromise the reform program through public consultation.... [The] autocratic policy-style ... tends to undermine representative institutions, to personalize politics and to generate a climate in which politics becomes reduced to quick fixes or to a

search for redemption. Even if neoliberal reform packages make good economics, they are likely to generate voodoo politics.

These findings are supported by Evans (1995), who establishes that neoliberalism, which has long been thought as being totally against rent-seeking behaviour and redistributive pressures on 'predatory' states, can be totally compatible with the main aspects of populism.[2]

According to some proponents of the Washington consensus (see, for example, Sachs, 1990), the scarcity of foreign exchange, huge budget deficits due to immense fiscal expansion, coupled with capital flight and inflationary pressures, which are all associated with populist policies, usually lead to inevitable and often reluctant acceptance of International Monetary Fund (IMF) stabilization programmes. The 'stopgo' nature of stabilization and structural reform programmes typical in most Latin American countries as well as Turkey suggests, however, that a reverse argument is equally plausible. IMF stabilization programmes and rapid neoliberal restructuring systematically collapsed and were followed by the return of economic populism and redistributive strategies. Such outcomes suggest that the essential characteristics of populism have remained strong throughout the stabilization programmes and/or the neoliberal reform agenda, which has reinforced and perpetuated the existing populist legacies in a given regime. In short, 'populist tendencies could arise *within* – rather than *against* – a neoliberal project' (Roberts, 1995: 83).

Exploring the 'unexpected affinities' between neoliberalism and populism (Weyland, 1996) is particularly important for understanding Turkey's European trajectory, for three reasons. First, Turkey's lingering populism in the midst of neoliberal reforms raises serious questions about the often-assumed symbiosis between economic liberalization and democratization. The Turkish case provides further evidence that neoliberal technocrats suppress and/or circumvent mechanisms of accountability, and weaken institutional links between society and the state for the sake of 'efficient' economic decision-making. Therefore, accountability and representation, two fundamental pillars of any given democracy, are systematically undermined. Second, if indeed there is this affinity, we might have to rethink the feasibility of fulfilling the Copenhagen criteria, which envisage simultaneous market reforms and democratization. In fact, Turkey's populism might even survive in the aftermath of the country's EU membership. Finally, the fact that populism has survived neoliberal reforms also suggests that explanations for the longevity of populism must be sought beyond pure economic policies and development models. The persistence of populism under different economic development models and strategies suggests that a more comprehensive analysis is required. Such analysis must take into account the degree of institutionalization in a given society and the capacity of the state to withstand capture.

In the following sections, the chapter provides an overview of how populism has survived significant transformations in Turkey's political economy. Indeed, during the period 1930–1980, populist strategies and patronage politics remained constant despite significant changes such as state-led industrialization, transition to a multi-party system, as well as a shift towards ISI. More interestingly, populism has survived significant liberalization of the economy in the aftermath of the 1980s. Populism in both periods has also systematically undermined Turkey's accession bid towards the EU, creating policy oscillations, short-termism, arbitrary and wasteful expenditure of state resources for legitimacy and patronage purposes, and significant macroeconomic instability – all of which are incompatible with converging towards the EU.

3.3 Turkish populism and EU–Turkey relations, 1930–1980

In broadest terms, Turkey's economic transformation can be divided into four periods: *étatisme*, when the state was heavily involved in the economy as an investor in infrastructure, a regulator as well as a major producer and employer (1930–1950); rural modernization (1950–1959); the ISI regime (1960–1979); and liberalization (post-1980).

What is remarkable in the country's economic history, however, is that none of these transformations has actually been complete. Turkey's nation-building project, coupled with top-down modernization efforts in the 1930–1950 period, meant that bureaucratization and state-building occurred long before democratization (for elaboration of this point, see Sunar, 1990, 1994a). Although the Kemalist state was largely elitist, backed by a military-bureaucratic elite, the single-party regime was still populist. Indeed, Kemalist populism had all the essential elements of populism: mobilization of the masses was very much couched within the nation- and republic-building project (hence the term 'Jacobin populism'); it lacked institutional patterns linking society and the state, but had instead a charismatic leader with a modernizing mission; and it had an ideological rhetoric that appealed to the masses without ever including them politically or economically. This degree of exclusion led Sunar (1994b: 100) to call Kemalist populism, 'populism without incorporation'.

In contrast, transition to a multi-party system in 1950 and the DP's rise to power provided the first example of relatively inclusionary populism. By appealing to the values of the 'people', the DP was able to mobilize the rural sectors as well as the nascent proto-industrial bourgeoisie against the established state elite. Furthermore, the DP pursued private-sector development and first introduced liberal principles such as the liberalisation of trade and legislation permitting foreign direct investment (FDI). But extensive state intervention into the economy through infrastructure investments and the expansion of state economic enterprises (SEEs) remained unchanged.

Once again, however, mobilization of the popular sectors against the bureaucratic elite was not from below. None of the petit bourgeois groups (e.g. the middle peasantry, the urban self-employed, and those in the informal sector) was mobilized independently. The DP claimed legitimacy on the grounds that it speaks for 'the people', that it represented the democratic sovereign, not sectional, interests. Yet with its leader-centred party structure and clientelistic ties to the rural sector, the DP remained quite elitist. As Urbinati (1998: 113) explains,

> The populist strategy has become a practice of inflaming anti-elite passions in order to castigate its critics and make *them* into enemies of equality and common people. The actual scenario, however, is that of a new born oligarchy (*homines novi*) profiting from popular dissatisfaction and actual subjection in order to penetrate the ruling class.

Indeed, the DP's populist strategy ended up by merely replacing one political elite with another. With its anti-establishment rhetoric and its challenge against the modernizing, bureaucratic and military elite, the *homines novi* of the DP were a newly empowered, culturally liberated petty bourgeoisie.

The DP government engaged in significantly redistributive strategies to push for rapid agrarian development. The DP's appeal to the small peasantry to ensure popular support and the party's willingness to use extensive state resources for agricultural price subsidies and inflationist incentive packages were the fundamental reasons behind Turkey's first macroeconomic crisis. This crisis also marked Turkey's first encounter with the IMF and IMF stabilization programmes. Uncontrolled expansion and fiscal indiscipline made adjustment inevitable, and highlighted the limits to patronage and the model of state-financed agrarian development. In that sense, the DP's populism confirmed the conventional wisdom that populist cycles usually end with stabilization programmes, which are considered a panacea for ending populism.

Yet the abrupt and dramatic end to the DP's populism came through the 1960 military coup, not through the IMF programmes. The military coup of 1960 marked the return of the bureaucratic elite with a vengeance and ushered in a new governing coalition consisting of the military, the bureaucracy and the increasingly powerful urban middle class. On the economic front, the 1960–1979 period witnessed the return of full-fledged *étatisme*. State-sponsored ISI, planned industrialization, domestic market-oriented production, protectionism, etc. marked a significant, albeit slow, transformation of Turkey's economy from a strictly agrarian to an increasingly (pre-)industrial one. Urbanization and rapid industrialization (there was annual growth of around 9 per cent throughout the 1960s) also paved the way for a new type of populism, usually referred to as 'classical populism' in Latin American literature.

The 1960–1979 period was also tumultuous in terms of Turkey–EU ties.

Turkey applied for an association agreement with what was then the European Economic Community (EEC) in 1959, only a few months after Greece. Long rounds of talks had led to the Ankara Agreement in 1963, which made Turkey an 'associate member'. What is most surprising, however, is that this agreement has hardly been discussed by the public and by different sectors. The weak organizational capacity of agriculture and industry as well as the unions, coupled with the absence of sufficient detail concerning the agreement, largely accounts for this silence (Tekeli and İlkin, 1993a: 205–212). The fact that neither the First Five-Year Plan (1963–1967) nor the Second Five-Year Plan (1968–1972) discussed the Ankara Agreement and its impact on Turkey's economy also indicates that the agreement was largely ignored by subsequent governments, the bureaucracy and the public. In short, the post-Ankara Agreement period was already a testimony to the non-consulting, non-inclusive, excessively centralized decision-making in the Turkish polity, which, as mentioned on p. 57, is a central feature of populism.

But it was really following the Additional Protocol (AP) and its aftermath that Turkey's populist tendencies began to take a toll on Turkey–EU ties. The request to revise the AP only two years after it was signed, for instance, was largely explained by the incompatibility of overall import substitution strategies and the trade liberalization associated with the AP. Finally having discovered the relevance of AP in preparing for the Third Five-Year Plan (1973–1977), the State Planning Organization began to argue that the AP was a barrier to ISI. This was not surprising, because the Justice Party and the Republican People's Party, despite intense ideological polarization, actually saw ISI as crucial for dispensing state patronage to their respective constituencies. Unstable coalition governments also allowed fringe parties such as the National Salvation Party (MSP) and the Nationalist Action Party (MHP) to have a disproportionate voice in economic policy-making (Uğur, 1999: 94).

Furthermore, ISI meant that there would be excessive protection of import-competing industries, significant portions of which were already state economic enterprises (SEEs). Adjusting to the trade liberalization required by the AP would have meant significant restructuring of the SEEs as well. Yet the SEEs have long been the pool of political patronage; governments have systematically used them to distribute rents to their party loyalists. In effect, elimination of these state privileges would have been political suicide.

Ironically, even the supporters of the AP, such as the big industrialists and various chambers of commerce (with the exception of the Eskişehir Chamber of Commerce, which represents small to medium-sized enterprises and has systematically argued for longer adjustment periods so as to survive EU competition), have largely made their support conditional on continuing state subsidies and support. Vehbi Koç, the head of the largest conglomerate in Turkey at the time, listed several demands of the state.

These included privileges such as state guarantees for imports and stable exchange rates, state guidance and support on certain strategic sectors, and, most interestingly, the stabilizing of wage increases through state intermediation (cited in Tekeli and İlkin, 1993b: 101).

Against this background of entrenched ISI interests, systematic demands for state patronage and particularistic privileges, and the vulnerability of the political parties to such pressures, the Turkish government first decided on the unilateral suspension of the AP in 1978, followed by the mutual freezing of relations for five years starting in 1979. These policy reversals created serious credibility problems in terms of Turkey's commitment to the EU and in effect permanently scarred Turkey–EU ties in the subsequent years (Uğur, 1999: 55–85).

The military coup in 1980 created yet another estrangement leading to a new freezing of associational ties. Meanwhile, the acceptance of Greece into full membership and Greece's subsequent vetoes began to create yet another hurdle in Turkey's relations with Europe. Though none of these developments can solely be attributed to Turkey's persistent populism, it is clear that short-termism, macroeconomic instabilities, failed developmental goals and uncertainty, which are often by-products of populism, have largely contributed to the oscillating nature of Turkey–EU ties.

3.4 Neoliberal populism in the 1980s and 1990s

Perhaps the most interesting and unexpected populist cycle in Turkey started in the post-1980 period. The authoritarian military regime during the period 1980–1983 reflects a typical aftermath of ISI exhaustion and an abrupt end to the classical populism discussed in the previous section. The government, whose economic team was led by Turgut Özal (the Deputy Prime Minister, who later became Prime Minister and President), began implementing a typical IMF package agreed upon on 24 January 1980.[3] Elimination of price controls including controls over interest rates, foreign exchange rate reforms, liberalization of trade and foreign direct investment, and the privatization of the SEEs were main elements of this package. Such policy changes indeed represented a stark contrast with the long-standing import substitution policies that the government had followed prior to 1980. It was argued that *étatisme* – that is, significant state intervention in the economy so as to secure economic growth – was finally dead. (For various interpretations of this era, see Öniş and Webb, 1994; Heper, 1991; Nas and Odekon, 1988; and Krueger, 1995.) According to the policy mission statements of the Motherland Party, which won the first elections after the end of the military regime in 1983, Turkey aimed at applying a typical IMF stabilization programme (Öniş, 1991).

Despite considerable setbacks (such as the mini-crisis of 1987, the crisis of 1994, the 1999 recession, and finally the financial crises of November 2000 and February 2001), the transformation of the Turkish economy from an ISI-based development model to an open, liberal economy has been remarkable. What had started during the Özal years as a major adjustment programme continued throughout the major coalition governments of the 1990s. For better or worse, the Turkish adjustment has accomplished a major reorientation of the economy. The financial markets were opened internationally and developed in depth. Substantial trade liberalization also occurred, particularly in the aftermath of Turkey's entry into a customs union with the EU in 1996.

What is paradoxical about the Özal years in the 1980s and coalition governments in the 1990s, however, is that populism has survived the neoliberal economic policies described here. In fact, the neoliberal strategies appear to have fostered populism, which reflected the following features: (i) de-institutionalization; (ii) patronage politics; and (iii) charismatic leadership. The following subsections will examine these features with a view to setting the stage for assessing the impact of neoliberal populism on EU–Turkey relations.

3.4.1 De-institutionalization and weakening of representative institutions

Weyland (1996: 16) states that

> Neopopulists and neoliberals . . . display surprising similarities in their efforts to centralize power and enact policy in an autocratic manner. Both apply a top-down state-centred approach that concentrates an enormous amount of influence in a political leader and his close aides.

This is in fact what happened in the Turkish case. As Buğra (1994: 264) succinctly argues,

> These attempts at the restructuring of the economy did not lead to the retreat of the state, an objective which was stressed as major component of the official ideology of the state. There was a reorganisation of the state apparatus, which brought about a centralisation of decision-making by enlarging the powers of the executive branch and of the Prime Minister in particular. The legislative as well as the legal and bureaucratic institutions were undermined throughout the process, but this did not imply in any way a decline in the significance of the state for business activity. The state remained – perhaps more significantly than in any other period in the Republican era – the central focus of the Turkish businessmen concerns.

One implication was increased scope for discretionary allocations in the economy. As Waterbury (1992: 128) has indicated, Özal's version of liberalism has promoted the survival of the fittest in the export sector *and* entitlements elsewhere. This discretion was made both feasible and necessary by the new Constitution, which enabled the Prime Minister to create extra-budgetary funds such as Mass Housing and Public Transportation Funds. In addition, the flow of public investments remained very high. A significant portion of these investments came to be disbursed through extra-budgetary funds, the total number of which ranged from 96 to 134 and the total assets of which stood at $3.5 to $5.7 billion in 1987–1988 (Waterbury, 1992: 134).[4] In 1990, the revenues from extra-budgetary funds actually constituted approximately 60 per cent of Turkey's consolidated budget revenues (Oyan, 1991: 125).

Decrees were another strategy for circumventing the democratic process in the post-1980 period. A total of 629 governmental decrees with the power of law have been passed. The overwhelming majority were passed during the Özal years and involved economic restructuring. These decrees were justified by citing the need for efficiency and speedy governance. This was in line with the work of Leaman (1999: 99), who quotes the Argentine deputy Cesar Arias, who, speaking of a Menem proposal for reform, stated: 'Putting it through our constitutional machine, no one knows how long it will take to resolve. Therefore, the executive is obliged to resolve these matters by means of decree. We have made more transformations than other governments because of decrees.' Decrees were also significant for coalition governments with weak mandates and razor-thin majorities. This may explain, for instance, the insistence of the 1999–2003 coalition government, made up of the Democratic Left Party (DSP), the Nationalist Action Party (MHP) and the Motherland Party (ANAP) on the use of decrees and the return of 16 decrees from the constitutional court.[5]

The third indicator of de-institutionalisation was the increased role of the technocratic elite, which is alleged to have a value-free social engineering approach. Describing the predominance of engineers within the political elite, Göle (1994: 218) states that 'engineers substitute a technocratic approach for an ideological one and claim that, as agents of science and rationality, it is only they who have access to the objective knowledge, or the key to truth'.

This collusion between economic liberalization and technocratic policy-making becomes even more evident in the frequent IMF programmes that coalition governments tried to implement in the aftermath of Turkey's 1994 financial crisis. For example, the economic reform package of 5 April 1994 (which included a typical IMF package with a 38.8 per cent devaluation, radical privatization targets, severe budget cuts and additional taxes) was announced with the hope of receiving the 'green light' from the IMF. None of measures in the package was discussed in public. Instead, they were presented as unpleasant but necessary decisions that the government had to take.

The seventeenth IMF package that the DSP–MHP–ANAP coalition

introduced in May 1999 provided yet another example of centralized decision-making. The anti-inflationary programme, which involved a series of austerity measures and strict monetary policy, was introduced without debate despite the fact that it led to a 6 per cent decline in GDP in 1999. The failure of the 1999 programme in February 2001 and the coalition government's decision to bring one of the World Bank's vice-presidents, Kemal Derviş, as an 'economic tsar' to solve the liquidity and foreign exchange crisis, also exemplified arbitrariness and exclusionary patterns of decision-making.[6]

Even though Derviş and his team regularly consulted with (or reported to) the cabinet and the coalition leaders, the severity of the financial crisis increased the temptation to circumvent some of the liberal democratic procedures and even overlook some of the constitutional constraints, as was the case with legal changes allowing the privatization of Turkish Telecom and the amendment of the banking laws.[7] Also, other legal changes associated with the IMF conditions were rushed through Parliament and reflected the preference for a technocratic/elitist policy style (*Finansal Forum*, 8–15 May 2001). Parliament was largely reduced to rubber-stamping. The Economic and Social Council, established in 1999 in a semi-corporatist fashion with representatives from business and labour organizations, has also failed to achieve its purpose and engages only in limited deliberations, often justified by the urgent need for reform.

This chapter does not address the question of whether IMF programmes, regional agreements, or economic liberalization *per se* generate such anti-democratic tendencies. What is important to note, however, is that neoliberal reforms may make good economics, but they are also highly likely to generate 'voodoo politics'. IMF programmes and trade liberalization, even Turkey's presumed EU membership, have been presented as mechanisms that would introduce market efficiency and put an end to populism. In fact, the conditionality imposed by sponsors of the reforms has been presented as a mechanism that would lock in the reforms and make them irreversible. As noted earlier, however, the technocratic and elitist decision-making through which the reforms have been undertaken may in fact perpetuate populism – especially through its de-institutionalising effects.

3.4.2 Lingering patronage politics

Populist politics involves an 'interclass alliance based on strong political leadership; a Manichean and moralistic discourse that divides society into *el pueblo* and the oligarchy'; and 'clientelist networks that guarantee access to state resources' (De la Torre, 1998: 87). To a large extent, the shift to neoliberal economic policies in Turkey has failed to change this picture, and in some cases has even created new avenues for further patronage.

What neoliberal policies did was to place fiscal constraints on widespread redistribution, depending on the severity of the financial crisis itself. What lingered, however, was patronage politics involving targeted, particularistic clientelism, which can easily coexist with neoliberalism.

For instance, even though Özal's strategies worsened the income levels of workers and farmers, the rapid rise of the informal economy and the willingness of the government to overlook bribery (hence the famous motto of Turgut Özal: 'My civil servant knows what to do!') created alternative avenues to mediate increasing inequality. So instead of attracting those from the lower middle classes and the workers (as the ISI populists often did), neoliberal populists sought support in the new urban para-classes that depended on informal sectors as well as new small to medium-sized entrepreneurs who were eager to exploit market opportunities but highly reluctant to pay taxes or social insurance contributions.

More importantly, economic liberalization and export-led growth in the 1980s largely failed to restructure state–society relations in Turkey. In essence, Turkey's liberalization did not result in the transforming of the behaviour of the economic groups that had long relied on import substitution policies. Some of the industrial conglomerates of the 1960s and 1970s began to shift towards exports, largely thanks to the extraordinary conditions of the post-coup era such as the frozen wages as well as generous export incentives. Özal's economic programme ended up creating an alternative, but equally rent-seeking, export elite. This new rent-seeking elite of exporters created yet another cleavage between big industrialists and exporters (Arat, 1991). Just like their predecessors, they relied on state patronage such as export incentives, tax breaks and credits leading to 'fictitious' exports (Waldner, 1999).

Side payments across various interest groups such as subsidies for agricultural elites and industrial incentives for various industrial groups – for example, the lowering of import tariffs on certain goods – were all crucial for building various large electoral coalitions for successive governments in the 1980s and 1990s. Democratic pressures and electoral concerns increased the need for more side payments and the extension of state patronage (Waterbury, 1992). Hence, increased state spending and growing public deficits characterized the 1980s and particularly the 1990s. Centre-right coalitions led by Özal after 1987 as well as the first Süleyman Demirel-led (1991–1993) and later Tansu Çiller-led (1993–1995) True Path Party coalitions with the Social Democrats distributed these payments to their constituencies. These constituencies included the farmers in the case of Çiller's True Path Party and the urban workers in the case of the Republican People's Party (see Cizre Sakallıoğlu, 1996; Cizre-Sakallıoğlu and Yeldan, 2000). Increasing support for the new Anatolian business community and small to medium-sized enterprises during the time of the True Path and Welfare Party coalition (July 1996–June 1997), and the increase in support prices for tea during the Motherland Party-led coalition government between 1997 and 1999, constituted the most publicized examples of side payments. Even in the case of the Welfare Party, whose party linkages were allegedly based on a more ideological and programmatic platform, similar patronage politics was pursued *vis-à-vis* small to medium-sized enterprises (see Heper and Keyman, 1998; Kamrava, 1998; Ayata, 1996; Gülalp, 2001). Hence, instead of dealing with painful, long-term reforms with uncertain political outcomes, politicians have continued with the existing patronage patterns. Growing political fragmentation within Parliament and the logic of coalition governments combined to generate populist policies as each party tried to use state resources for its own constituencies.

However, populist strategies are not simply a result of political calculations and electoral concerns on the part of a government. They are also a result of persistent pursuit of particularistic interests by a variety of actors from business associations to unions and various societal groups. In her study of the Turkish Industrialists' and Businessmen's Association (TUSIAD), Buğra (1994: 164) describes vividly how these particularistic ties actually work in state–business relations:

> He who explains his case to the Prime Minister or the Minister concerned solves his problem. You go to Işın Çelebi (one of the ministers responsible for the economy), you cry on his shoulders and he says 'O.K. I'll find you the necessary funds.' When the Central Bank says that the funds are not available, the Minister orders the transfer of funds from one budget to the other. This leads to interferences at all levels of the bureaucratic process. And, of course, you are a very happy person because your problem is solved. You tell everyone what a nice, understanding person the Minister is, and how nicely he has solved your problem. But the institutions cannot function under these circumstances.

The expectation of populist policies and selective patronage mechanisms, then, has been just as problematic, indicating the double-edged nature of populism.

3.4.3 Charisma, leadership and the language of anti-politics and anti-elitism

Turkish political parties have relied on their charismatic and anti-elitist leaders. Post-1980 neoliberal reforms have not necessarily changed this combination. While Özal has targeted the ISI-dependent elite, Demirel has always projected himself as the 'father' of the people against special interests. In fact, Demirel can be considered as the epitome of neoliberal populist leadership, with the use of 'common man' language and mass appeal while engaging in the worst form of nepotism and small patronage networks (Arat, 2002). Erkaban and his Welfare Party have used the slogan of 'just order' to attack the 'rentier' elite, which they saw as benefiting from growing public debt through high-interest government bonds. In the 1999 elections campaign, even Mesut Yılmaz and the ANAP, which are often associated with patronage politics, adopted the 'voice of the silent majority' as their election campaign motto.

The MHP's rise to power in the 1999 elections and its 'new' presentation of the party as the 'new centre-right' was a testimony to a new populist coalition in the making. The MHP also couched its language in terms of a 'fight against the vestiges of special interests'. Even the collapse of the 1999 anti-inflation programme in the aftermath of the financial crisis of February 2001 was attributed to an ambiguous 'inflation lobby', referring largely to banks, brokers and other financial institutions that have long financed the spiralling government debt. Similarly, Tayyip Erdoğan, the leader of the Justice and Development Party (AKP), which came to power with a landslide electoral victory in November 2002, always projected himself as the 'man of the street' or as having grown up in a rough neighbourhood of Istanbul, namely Kasımpaşa.

Another major feature of Turkish political parties that has also survived during the neoliberal era is the absence of internal party democracy and the emphasis on leadership rather than participation and consultation. Short of a sudden death or someone moving up to become President, leadership change has been extremely rare. 'Arranging' the party delegates through distributing party patronage, particularly prior to party congresses, and limiting and manipulating party membership have been the norm (Çarkoğlu *et al.*, 2002). This has not only made it almost impossible for alternative leaders to emerge but also severely limited grassroots political participation.

Depoliticisation and a language of anti-politics have always been part of the neoliberal agenda, which defends the need to separate economics and politics for the sake of efficacy. In fact, as Boron (1996: 309) suggests, subordination of politics to the technical economic logic of neoliberalism has produced a 'satanizing discourse' that holds the state responsible for all misfortunes and mishaps. The establishment of presumably independent regulatory boards since the mid-1990s – such as the Telecommunications Board, the Competition Board and the Banking Supervisory and Regulatory Board – provides a good example of this language of anti-politics. The neoliberal argument behind these boards has been to establish technocratic policy-making and to limit the political influence of governments on economic decision-making. Initial observations on the structure and the performance of these boards suggest, however, that they have become new institutional agents of old-style patronage politics. In addition, the weakness and the fragmented nature of the institutional and legal framework for these boards have created serious legitimacy questions (Zenginobuz, 2002; TUSIAD, 2002). In effect, in the absence of a coherent institutional environment, the neoliberal discourse of insulating economic decision-making from political influence created new avenues for populism and patronage.

Meanwhile, as Cizre-Sakallıoğlu and Yeldan (2000: 495) explain,

> this quest for neoliberal mandate has meant a convergence of economic policies both on the left and right, so the informed political debate in the public sphere is retarded by the absence of ideas, values, objectives as bases for conciliation and integration – which is after all, what politics is all about.

Indeed, with the exception of some fringe parties on the right and on the left, most political parties, including social democratic alternatives such as the Republican People's Party, have come up with very similar economic programmes that in effect take economic decision-making out of the political realm. Needless to say, this is fertile ground for populism: most crucial decisions are taken without any public input, and depoliticisation eliminates any legitimation or accountability problems that governments might otherwise face.

3.5 Interaction between neoliberal populism and EU–Turkey relations, 1980–2000

If indeed populism and neoliberalism can coexist, what does this mean for Turkey's prospects for membership and compliance with the Copenhagen criteria? The account presented here suggests that Turkey faces serious dilemmas and challenges in meeting the Copenhagen economic and political criteria simultaneously. If, in the process of economic reforms, the decision-making process creates the risk of undermining participatory and deliberative democracy; if urgent market reforms to establish a 'functioning' market economy involve short-cutting the political process, then undertaking market reforms may also lock in a populist, low-grade democracy.

Part of the difficulty is that the EU's own project and strategies are also changing from a Keynesian one, emphasizing integration and cohesion, to a neoliberal one with emphasis on deregulating markets in the face of growing global competition. This is particularly true in the post-Maastricht era, when meeting the convergence criteria for the single currency has overwhelmed concerns of equity, and social policies (Bohle, 2002; Gill, 1998). This shift has inevitably influenced EU's enlargement process and the associated conditionality for accession known as the Copenhagen criteria. The core of the EU's economic agenda for enlargement has become increasingly neoliberal, emphasizing privatization, overall retreat of the state's involvement in the economy, and further liberalization of trade. Despite the immense variety of economic systems within the EU, ranging from the 'Anglo-Saxon' model to 'Rheinish' social market economies, to the Latin-style economies of Southern Europe, the progress reports on candidate countries have presented a uniform set of expectations based on the Anglo-Saxon recipe (Albert, 1991; Rhodes and van Apeldoorn, 1998; Eder, 2003).

Turkey's progress reports prepared by the EU Commission very much reflect this trend. These reports predominantly focus on neoliberal recipes such as privatization and price and trade liberalization, which have been on Turkey's economic agenda as a result of IMF stand-by agreements.[8] Yet as discussed above, the existence of IMF stabilization programmes and neoliberalism has not brought the end of populism. On the contrary, there are elements in this neoliberal agenda that complement and reinforce populist legacies. This technocratic policy-making and increased use of decrees instead of parliamentary procedures continue to impede democratic institutions and undermine the importance of the legislative process. However limited, selective patronage appears to survive fiscal austerities, and the political realm appears to shrink more and more as politics and the state become equated with corruption. In short, the most common elements of populism – the appeal to the masses, the lack of institutionalization, the continuing importance of leaders rather than institutions, lingering patronage ties as well as extremely centralized, technocratic policy-making – have all survived IMF adjustment programmes and neoliberal pressures.

Turkey's failure to meet the economic and political conditions of membership, however, cannot be attributed solely to the 'neoliberalization' of the Copenhagen economic criteria and to what appear to be its internally conflicting goals. As noted, populism throughout the 1960s and 1970s systematically undermined Turkey's prospects for convergence with the EU. The new breed of neoliberal populism in the post-1980 period has continued to constrain Turkey's membership prospects and has induced Turkey to circumcise the Copenhagen criteria (which has affected Turkey's chances of accession). This process was most evident during the negotiation of and the implementation of the customs union (CU) agreement with the EU.

The negotiations provided an example of technocratic and centralized decision-making. The agreement was significant in terms of the degree of trade liberalization and its impact on Turkey's various industrial sectors. It reduced the nominal rate of protection against EU imports from 10.2 per cent to 1.4 per cent and brought down the overall rate against third countries to 6.9 per cent.[9] Yet once again, CU negotiations were largely conducted by the State Planning Organization and the Ministry of Foreign Affairs. Although the State Planning Organization wanted to seek the views of interest groups and take its time in the negotiations, the Department of Foreign Affairs, largely influenced by the governing coalition's insistence, rushed the agreement through. Most of the interest group organizations, both winners and losers, found out about what was being negotiated in the agreement only *after* the agreement had been approved. As a result, institutional channels for government–industry dialogue on the agreement remained limited (Eder, 1999, 2001; Tekeli and İlkin, 2000).[10]

The implementation of the CU agreement has also been extremely slow. The 2001 Progress report (EU Commission, 2001: 49) observes, for instance, that

> According to the Decision 1/95 of the EC–Turkey Association Council on implementing the final phase of the Customs Union, Turkey undertook to adopt Community legislation relating to the removal of technical barriers to trade by the end of 2000. . . . However, Turkey has not been able to meet its obligation under Decision 1/95. The transitional arrangements have expired by the end of 2000 while a substantial part of the *acquis* remains to be transposed and implemented in Turkey. Although industrial goods largely circulate freely within the Customs Union territory, the number of non-tariff barriers has in practice increased during 2001. This distorts trade and prevents the Customs Union from being used to its full potential.

As of mid-2003, issues such as standardization, the preparation and implementation of technical legislation on products, and the independent and effective functioning of the Competition Authority still remain problematic. Even though talks have begun to extend the CU into agriculture and services, no significant progress has been made.

The slow, stop–go nature of the CU's implementation reflects typical patronage-based politics. From the very start, the CU has been a victim of political posturing and calculations. A governing coalition of the True Path Party and the Republican People's Party (June 1993–March 1996) undertook the bargaining over, and completion of, the CU agreement with the EU. Moderate opposition came from the major opposition party on the right, the Motherland Party, even though it was Turgut Özal, the party's founder, who had initiated Turkey's application to the EU in 1987. (The same party's leader, Mesut Yılmaz, later became the Deputy Prime Minister responsible for EU affairs in another coalition government, which was in power between April 1999 and November 2002.) The most visible and consistent source of opposition was the Islamist Welfare Party (RP), which saw membership as incompatible with the country's national interest, as well as its religious/cultural heritage.[11] Necmettin Erbakan, then the leader of the RP, who became Prime Minister two months after the CU went into effect, suggested during his election campaign that once in office, his party would seek renegotiation of the agreement. Erbakan later retracted this statement, but these events showed the political fragility and reversibility of the CU (Uğur, 1999: 79).

Patronage politics was also evident with regard to TUSIAD's approach to the customs union. TUSIAD represents the interests of large conglomerates in Turkey, and largely supported the customs union. The group is also known for its secularist and Western orientation. Its four hundred members are largely those companies that either have formed an alliance with foreign partners or were already competing with their European counterparts.

As was the case in the discussions over the AP, however, there was some opposition even among TUSIAD's members. The companies in the automotive industry were initially rather lukewarm towards the CU agreement, particularly fearing that the Turkish market would be open to European used cars. The industry, which has long epitomized the ISI period in Turkey, restructured in the 1980s and increased its partnership with European and Japanese multinationals such as Renault, Fiat and Toyota. Ironically, it was these European partners who also opposed the complete liberalization of the automotive market in Turkey. Some of the support for the Motherland Party's opposition to the CU came precisely from such companies, which had long relied on import substitution policies and had thereby avoided fierce competition from their European counterparts. In effect, Özal's liberal reforms have transformed state–business ties considerably, but reliance on government support has remained largely unchanged (Buğra, 1994; Waldner, 1999). Finally, a 20-year exemption for used cars was granted, silencing much of this opposition. Only when the specific benefits were 'granted' and patronage was used could some of the business groups support the CU agreement.

The way in which the Customs Union was 'sold' to the public also reflected familiar populist themes. In domestic debates, instead of the agreement being characterized as involving technocratic negotiation between industry groups and business associations, the nature of the agreement was brought to an entirely different plane: to one that emphasized issues of Islamic fundamentalism and human rights. In short, instead of negotiating the terms of trade liberalization, the nature of escape clauses, the implementation of the competition and intellectual property legislation, the governing parties transformed the discussion into a 'discourse of civilization' and repackaged the entire issue as Turkey becoming part of 'the West' (Tekeli and İlkin, 2000: 420–425, 514–528). This 'secularism card' obfuscated the economic nature of the agreement and provided fertile ground for populism. The possible negative effects – short-term adjustment costs of the agreement, particularly in the absence of full membership – were all brushed aside and the public debate was 'sanitized' to focus on the rise of Islamic fundamentalism.

Hence, Turkey–EU relations within the context of the CU reflect the typical neoliberal populist elements of the Turkish political economy: circumventing institutions, lingering patronage politics and hallowing out economics from the political and public debate. Not surprisingly, the results have been disappointing. Trade liberalization under the CU agreement occurred as an end in itself, not as part of a development strategy. While there has been a reduction of tariffs, the regulatory aspects of this liberalization have lagged behind. In effect, Turkey's neoliberal populism since the 1980s has largely prevented the state from coupling its liberalization strategies not only to investment and productivity growth, but also to an adequate regulatory and institutional framework.

Yet it is investment that is key for economic growth in the long run. As Dani Rodrik (1996: 16) has aptly put it,

> What drives economic growth in practice is a process whereby capacity expansion and profitability of private investment feed on each other.... Governments have to be imaginative in devising investment strategies that exploit their country's resources and capabilities, while respecting administrative and budgetary constraints. A useful starting point is to acknowledge that openness is a part of a development strategy, it is not a substitute for one.

The fundamental question that needs to be asked in facing the challenge of meeting the Copenhagen criteria, then, is not simply how much liberalization *per se*, but how private investment and economic growth can be increased through membership and how the necessary institutional environment can be improved.

Conclusion

Empirically, the starting point of this chapter was selective examples of populism in Latin America. Many of the 'unexpected affinities' between neoliberalism and populism observed in Latin America – such as appeal to the informal sectors of society, a technocratic and exclusionary policy-making style, adverse relations with vested interests – all hold true for the Turkish case in the 1980s and 1990s. The Turkish case also underscores that with an overdeveloped state, underdeveloped class structures and state-dependent civil society groups, it is extremely difficult to undertake market reforms and democratisation at the same time. Neoliberal populism may indeed be the most problematic barrier to Turkey's EU membership, trapping the country into a low-grade and 'delegative' democracy and in effect defeating the very purpose of the political Copenhagen criteria. At first glance, the prospects appear rather bleak. The growing emphasis on neoliberal rather than social aspects of the Copenhagen economic criteria in the enlargement process has not helped Turkey's accession bid, as the neoliberal reforms have been accompanied by populism.

Furthermore, Turkey- EU ties, as was the case in the Additional Protocol and customs union agreements, appear to reflect rather than solve the two fundamental problems of Turkey's political economy:(i) a suboptimal liberalization experience that remained far short of producing radical reforms and ending populist policies, but also failed to mediate the side effects of its liberalization through an investment and growth strategy; and (ii) a patronage-based politics, which made long-term planning and institutionalization impossible. This picture also suggests that Turkish populism could persist even after EU membership, this time marginalizing Turkey within the EU.

Can the EU-related economic and political reforms eventually end patronage politics and policy reversals in Turkey? Clearly, neither the customs union nor Turkey–EU ties will be sufficient to address populism and the deeply rooted problems in Turkey's political economy. Yet there is also room for optimism. Latin America's experience with neoliberal populism, particularly the case of Collor in Brazil, and more recently Fujimori in Peru, suggests that patronage politics based on selective distribution of resources and top-down mobilization of the masses also have its limits. Indeed, the EU offers a priceless opportunity for governments to 'lock in' their reforms and to increase their credibility. The extent to which Turkey can resolve these dilemmas and challenges will depend on the ability of successive governments to balance the neoliberal and social economic strategies. Those governments coupling the liberalization agenda with a growth/investment strategy, developing the necessary regulatory and institutional framework and making use of the EU within that context, will be the most likely to succeed.

Even more importantly, however, governments and societal actors will all need to recognize that unless populist strategies and patronage politics (including its neoliberal version) finally come to an end, Turkey may never fully integrate with the EU. If populism is a virus that spreads easily among fragile democracies, then recognizing its new forms, adaptations and mutations, and coming up with new and realistic institutional solutions to limit, if not end, populism, is ever more crucial. Only then perhaps can Turkey overcome its Sisyphus predicament and finally become a fully integrated member of the EU.

Notes

1 That is why Peter Wiles (1969: 166) writes, 'To each his own definition of populism according to the academic axe he grinds.'
2 Roberts (1995: 102) demonstrates, for instance, that in Peru, autocratic neoliberal policy-making embodies the core political and sociological aspects of populism.
3 The argument that authoritarian governments are better at implementing neoliberal reform programmes and can take decisions that lead to radical

income redistribution without fear of reprisal from the public is not new (Foxley, 1983).

4　Though most of these extra-budgetary funds have been eliminated with the customs union, such funds, which appear as 'special revenues and funds' in the Budget, still constituted 11 per cent of the total national revenues in 1999 (*Finansal Forum*, 14 November 2000).

5　Note that this is not necessarily a developing country phenomenon. In describing Thatcherism and the New Right, Hall (1985: 117) argues, for instance, that 'an anti-statist strategy is not one which refuses to operate through the state; it is one which conceives a much more limited role, and which advances through the attempt, ideologically, to *represent itself* as anti-statist for the purposes of populist mobilization. This highly contradictory strategy which we have in fact seen in operation under Thatcherism: simultaneously dismantling the welfare state, "anti-statist" in its ideological self representation *and* highly state centrist and dirigiste in many of its strategic operation will inflect politics in new ways and have real political effects.'

6　For details, see www.treasury.gov.tr.

7　In the case of banking law reforms, some articles are sure to be contested in the Constitutional Court.

8　In contrast to IMF conditionality, however, EU conditionality has not brought definite, immediate and quantifiable benefits. IMF conditionality meant money flow to help the country get out of crises, whereas CU benefits, for instance, remained small and EU adjustment money was never delivered. (For elaboration of this point, see Eder, 2003).

9　http://www.foreigntrade.gov.tr.

10　Given the uncertainty of the outcome of the CU agreement and how exactly it will affect the Turkish economy, the governing coalition could also avoid a major dilemma. Only as a result of the realization of the agreement could the government gain the prestige and credibility it needs in order to carry out further reforms, yet if the terms of the deal were to become the centre of public debate, the government could not rely on economic interest groups to support it (see Eder, 2001).

11　Welfare Party *election manifesto*, p. 29.

References

Albert, Michel (1991), *Capitalisme contre capitalisme*, Paris: Éditions du Seuil.

Arat, Yeşim (1991), 'Politics and big business: Janus-faced link to the state', in M. Heper (ed.), *Strong State and Economic Interest Groups: The Post-1980 Turkish Experience*, New York and Berlin: Walter de Gruyter, pp. 135–149.

Arat, Yeşim (2002), 'Süleyman Demirel: national will and beyond', in Metin Heper and Sabri Sayarı (eds), *Political Leaders and Democracy in Turkey*, Boulder, CO, and New York: Lexington Books, pp. 87–107.

Ayata, Sencer (1996), 'Patronage, party and state: the politicization of Islam in Turkey', *Middle East Journal*, vol. 50, no. 1, pp. 40–57.

Bohle, Dorothee (2002), 'The ties that bind the new Europe: neoliberal restructuring and transnational actors in the deepening and widening of the European Union', paper presented at Workshop 4, 'Enlargement and European Governance', ECPR Joint Session workshops, Turin, 22–27 March.

Boron, Atilis A. (1996), 'Governability and democracy in Latin America', *Social Justice*, vol. 23, no. 1–2, pp. 303–338.

Bresser Pereira, Carlos Luiz, Jose Maria Maravall and Adam Przeworski (1993), *Economic Reforms in New Democracies: A Social Democratic Approach*, Cambridge: Cambridge University Press.

Buğra, Ayşe (1994), *State and Business in Modern Turkey: A Comparative Study*, Albany, NY: State University of New York Press.

Canovan, Margaret (1999), 'Trust the people! Populism and the two faces of democracy', *Political Studies*, vol. 47, no. 1, pp. 2–16.

Cardoso, Eliana and Ann Helwege (1991), 'Populism, profligacy and redistribution', in R. Dornbusch and S. Edward (eds), *The Macroeconomics of Populism in Latin America*, Chicago: University of Chicago Press, pp. 45–77.

Çarkoğlu, Ali, Tarhan Erdem, Ömer Faruk Gençkaya and Mehmet Kabasakal (2002), *Siyasal Partilerde Reform* (Reform in Political Parties), Istanbul: TESEV Publications.

Cizre-Sakallıoğlu, Ümit (1996), 'Liberalism, democracy and the Turkish centre-right: the identity crisis of the True Path Party', *Middle Eastern Studies*, vol. 32, no. 2, pp. 142–162.

Cizre-Sakallıoğlu, Ümit and Erinç Yeldan (2000), 'Politics, society and financial liberalization: Turkey in the 1990s', *Development and Change*, vol. 31, no. 2, pp. 481–508.

Collier, David and James Mahon (1993), 'Conceptual stretching revisited', *American Political Science Review*, vol. 87, no. 2, pp. 845–855.

De la Torre, Carlos (1998), 'Populist redemption and the unfinished democratization of Latin America', *Constellations*, vol. 5, no. 1, pp. 85–95.

DiTella, Torcuato S. (1965), 'Populism and reform in Latin America', in Claudio Veliz (ed.), *Obstacles to Change in Latin America*, London: Oxford University Press.

Dornbusch, Rüdiger and Sebastian Edwards (1990), 'Macroeconomics of populism in Latin America', *Journal of Development Economics*, vol. 32, no. 1, pp. 247–277.

Eder, Mine (1999), 'Becoming Western: Turkey and the European Union', in Wil Hout and Jean Grugel (eds), *Regionalism across the North–South Divide: State Strategies and Globalization*, London: Routledge, pp. 79–95.

Eder, Mine (2001), 'Deeper concessions and rising barriers to entry: new regionalism for Turkey and Mexico', *Studies in Comparative International Development*, vol. 36, no. 3, pp. 29–57.

Eder, Mine (2003), 'Implementing the economic criteria of EU membership: how difficult is it for Turkey?', *Turkish Studies*, vol. 4, no. 1, pp. 219–244.

EU Commission (2001), *Regular Report from the Commission on Turkey's Progress towards Accession*, Brussels: EU Commission.

Evans, Peter (1995), *Embedded Autonomy: State and Industrial Transformation*, Princeton, NJ: Princeton University Press.

Foxley, Alejandro (1983), *Latin American Experiments in Neoconservative Economics*, Berkeley: University of California Press.

Germani, Gino (1978), *Authoritarianism, Facism and National Populism*, New Brunswick, NJ: Transaction.

Gill, Stephen (1998), 'European governance and new constitutionalism: economic and monetary union and alternatives to disciplinary neoliberalism in Europe', *New Political Economy*, vol. 3, no. 1, pp. 1–22.

Göle, Nilüfer (1994), 'Engineers: technocratic democracy', in Metin Heper, Ayşe Öncü and Heinz Kramer (eds), *Turkey and the West: Changing Political and Cultural Identities*, London: I. B. Tauris, pp. 199–219.

Gülalp, Haldun (2001), 'Political identity in Turkey: globalization and political Islam: the social bases of Turkey's Welfare Party', *International Journal of Middle East Studies*, vol. 33, no. 3, pp. 433–449.

Hall, Stuart (1985), 'Authoritarian populism: a reply to Jessop *et al.*', *New Left Review*, no. 151 (May–June), pp. 115–125.

Heper, Metin (ed.) (1991), *Strong State and Economic Interest Groups: The Post-1980 Turkish Experience*, Berlin and New York: Walter de Gruyter.

Heper, Metin and Fuat Keyman (1998), 'Double-faced state: political patronage and the consolidation of democracy in Turkey', *Middle Eastern Studies*, vol. 34, no. 4, pp. 259–277.

Ianni, Octavio (1980), *A formaçao do estado populista na América Latina*, Mexico DF: Ediciones.

Kamrava, Mehran (1998), 'Pseudo-democratic politics and populist possibilities: the rise and demise of Turkey's Refah Party', *British Journal of Middle Eastern Studies*, vol. 25, no. 2, pp. 275–301.

Kazin, Michael (1995) *The Populist Passion: An American History*, New York: Basic Books.

Knight, Alan (1998), 'Populism and neo-populism in Latin America, especially Mexico', *Journal of Latin American Studies*, vol. 30, no. 2, pp. 223–248.

Krueger, Anne O. (1995), *Trade Policies and Developing Countries*, Washington, DC: Brookings Institution.

Laclau, Ernesto (1977), *Politics and Ideology in Marxist Theory*, London: New Left Books.

Leaman, David (1999), 'Populist liberalism as dominant ideology: competing ideas and democracy in post-authoritarian Argentina, 1989–1995', *Studies in Comparative International Development*, vol. 34, no. 3, pp. 98–118.

Mendes, Candido (1977), *Beyond Populism*, Albany: State University of New York Press.

Mouzelis, Nicos (1985) 'On the concept of populism: populist and clientelistic modes of incorporatism in semi-peripheral polities', *Politics and Society*, vol. 14, no. 3, pp. 329–348.

Nas, Tevfik F. and Mehmet Odekon (eds) (1988), *Liberalization and the Turkish Economy*, New York: Greenwood.

Öniş, Ziya (1991), 'Political economy of Turkey in the 1980s: anatomy of unorthodox liberalism', in M. Heper (ed.), *Strong State and Economic Interest Groups: The Post-1980 Turkish Experience*, Berlin and New York: Walter de Gruyter, pp. 27–40.

Öniş, Ziya and Steven B. Webb (1994), 'Turkey: democratization and adjustment from above' in Steven B. Webb and Stephan Haggard (eds), *Voting for Reform*. Oxford: Oxford University Press, pp. 128–185.

Oxhorn, Philip (1998), 'The social foundations of Latin America's recurrent populism: problems of popular sector class formation and collective action', *Journal of Historical Sociology*, vol. 11, no. 2, pp. 212–246.

Oyan, Oğuz (1991), *Türkiye'de Maliye ve Fon Politikaları: Alternatif Yönelişler* (Turkey's Fiscal and Fund Policies: Alternative Trends), Ankara: Adım Yayıncılık.

Quintero, Rafael (1980), *El mito del populismo en el Ecuador* (The Myth of Populism in Ecuador), Quito: FLASCO.

Rhodes, M and Bastiaan van Apeldoorn (1998), 'Capitalism unbound? The transformation of European corporate governance', *Journal of European Public Policy*, vol. 5, no. 3, pp. 406–427.

Roberts, Kenneth (1995), 'Neorealism and the transformation of populism in Latin America', *World Politics*, vol. 48 (October), pp. 82–116.

Rodrik, Dani (1996) *The New Global Economy and Developing Countries: Making Openness Work*, Policy Essay 24, Washington, DC: Overseas Development Council.

Roxborough, Ian (1984), 'Unity and diversity in Latin American history', *Journal of Latin American Studies*, vol. 16, no. 2, pp. 1–26.

Sachs, Jeffrey (1990), *Social Conflict and Populist Policies in Latin America*, San Francisco: ICS Press.

Sartori, Giovanni (1970), 'Concept misformation in comparative politics', *American Political Science Review*, vol. 64, no. 4, pp. 1033–1053.

Sartori, Giovanni (ed.) (1984), *Social Science Concepts*, Beverly Hills, CA: Sage.

Stein, Steve (1980), *Populism in Peru*, Wisconsin: Wisconsin University Press.

Sunar, İlkay (1990), 'Populism and patronage: the Demokrat Party and its legacy in Turkey', *Il Politico*, anno V, pp. 745–757.

Sunar, İlkay (1994a), 'State, society and democracy in Turkey', Bogazici University Research Paper ISS/POLS 94-04, Istanbul: Bebek.

Sunar, İlkay (1994b) 'The politics of state interventionism in populist Egypt and Turkey', in Ayşe Öncü, Çağlar Keyder and Sadd Eddin Ibrahim (eds), *Developmentalism and Beyond: Society and Politics in Egypt and Turkey*, Cairo: American University in Cairo Press, pp. 94–111.

Tekeli, İlhan and Selim İlkin (1993a), *Türkiye ve Avrupa Topluluğu: Ulus Devleti Aşma Çabasındaki Avrupa'ya Türkiye'nin Yaklaşımı 1* (Turkey and the EC: Turkey's Approach to Europe Attempting to Transcend the Nation-State 1), Ankara: Ümit Yayıncılık.

Tekeli, İlhan and Selim İlkin (1993b), *Türkiye ve Avrupa Topluluğu: Ulus Devleti Aşma Çabasındaki Avrupa'ya Türkiye'nin Yaklaşımı 2* (Turkey and the EC: Turkey's Approach to Europe Attempting to Transcend the Nation-State 2), Ankara: Ümit Yayıncılık.

Tekeli, İlhan and Selim İlkin (2000), *Türkiye ve Avrupa Birliği: Ulus Devleti Aşma Çabasındaki Avrupa'ya Türkiye'nin Yaklaşımı* (Turkey and the EU: Turkey's Approach to Europe Attempting to Transcend the Nation-State 3), Ankara: Ümit Yayıncılık.

TUSIAD (2002) *Bağımsız Düzenleyici Kurumlar ve Türkiye Uygulaması* (Independent Regulatory Institutions and Turkish Application), Publication no. 2002-12/349.

Uğur, Mehmet (1999) *The European Union and Turkey: An Anchor/Credibility Dilemma*, Aldershot, UK: Ashgate.

Urbinati, Nadia (1998), 'Democracy and populism' *Castellations*, vol. 5, no. 1, pp. 110–124.

Vilas, Carlos M. (1992), 'Latin American populism: a structural approach', *Science and Society*, vol. 56, no. 4, pp. 389–421.

Waldner, David (1999), S*tate Building and Late Development*, Ithaca, NY: Cornell University Press.

Waterbury, John (1992), 'Export-led growth and center-right coalition in Turkey', *Comparative Politics*, vol. 24, no. 3, pp. 127–145.

Weyland, Kurt (1996), 'Neopopulism and neoliberalism in Latin America: unexpected affinities', *Studies in Comparative International Development*, vol. 31, no. 3, pp. 3–31.

Weyland, Kurt (1999), 'Neoliberal populism in Latin America and Eastern Europe', *Comparative Politics*, vol. 31, no. 4, pp. 379–402.

Wiles, Peter (1969), 'A syndrome not a doctrine', in Ghita Ianescu and Ernest Gellner (eds), *Populism: Its Meaning and National Characteristics*, New York: Macmillan, pp. 166–180.

Zenginobuz, Ünal E. (2002), 'Political economy of independent regulatory authorities: some observations on the case of Turkey', unpublished article.

4 Economic mismanagement and Turkey's troubled relations with the EU

Is there a link?

Mehmet Uğur

Introduction

The current debate on Turkey's relations with the European Union (EU) tends to focus on socio-political determinants of the crises that have recurred since Turkey's membership application in 1987. This is understandable, because there is indeed a significant degree of divergence between EU and Turkish socio-political structures and orientations. One needs only to recall that Turkey has to undertake short- to medium-term reforms in no fewer than 32 policy areas in order to satisfy the political range of the Copenhagen criteria. These reform requirements were specified in the EU's Accession Partnership document and Turkey had to spell them out somewhat reluctantly in its National Programme for the Adoption of the *Acquis* (NPAA). Because most of these reforms constitute highly sensitive issues for Turkey, it is natural that they have acquired a certain degree of prominence in public as well as academic debates. Yet there are equally significant indicators of economic policy divergence between Turkey and the EU. In fact, there are 85 short- to medium-term economic reform areas specified in the Accession Partnership as opposed to 32 areas for political reform (EU Council, 2001). Economic policy divergence, however, is either ignored or mentioned only in passing as an issue of secondary importance. This tendency has been evident at all major turning points in Turkey–EU relations – including the customs union decision of 1995. Part of the reason for this anomaly is the assumption that Turkey is well placed to satisfy the Copenhagen economic criteria, given the post-1980 liberalisation efforts. The other reason is the assumption that economic policy divergence between Turkey and the EU is bound to disappear (or diminish) as Turkey implements the structural reforms required by international financial institutions – especially the International Monetary Fund (IMF) and the World Bank.

This chapter aims to address the imbalance by focusing on the causes and consequences of economic policy divergence between Turkey and the EU. The chapter develops and substantiates two central arguments. First, economic policy divergence between Turkey and the EU is the outcome of the discretion and rent-seeking that characterise Turkey's economic policy-making process. Second, the persistence of economic policy divergence between Turkey and the EU has reduced the credibility of Turkey's commitment to integration with the EU. Put together, these arguments suggest that Turkey's initial exclusion from the Eastern enlargement was largely predictable and that political economy factors internal to Turkey constitute significant variables that have determined this predictable outcome.

To pursue these arguments, the chapter is organised as follows. In section 4.1, I will examine Turkey's economic policy choices in the 1980s. The aim here is to demonstrate how liberalisation coexisted with discretion and rent-seeking, and how this symbiotic relationship drove a wedge between Turkish and European economic policies despite the rhetoric to the contrary. In section 4.2, I will focus mainly on macroeconomic policy outcomes observed in the 1990s and on their implications for EU–Turkey relations. Here, I will demonstrate that the legacy of the preceding period had provided perverse incentives for economic actors and paved the way for macroeconomic instability. Macroeconomic instability has not only prevented Turkey from realising its growth potential, but also exacerbated the credibility problem that haunted Turkey–EU relations for four decades. Section 4.3 provides a comparative assessment of Turkey's economic policy environment relative to ten Central and East European countries (CEECs). It will be demonstrated that Turkey scores less satisfactorily than most of the CEECs, with the exception of Bulgaria and Romania. Finally, the conclusions will highlight the main findings and ascertain the extent to which Turkey's economic policy choices in the 1990s contributed to its exclusion from the most recent round of enlargement.

4.1 Liberalisation: a free hand for the government?

Research on the Turkish state's involvement in the economy reflects a high degree of consensus. Since the 1930s, the state has acted not only as a regulator and planner, but also as a significant producer and employer. In the 1960s, the public sector produced more than half of the industrial output and undertook about 50 per cent of total investment. Despite foreign exchange shortages and liberalisation reforms, this pattern remained the norm throughout the 1970s and 1980s. Even during the first half of the 1980s, the Turkish state remained a significant source of fixed capital formation. (On the state's role in the 1960s and 1970s, see Land, 1970; Krueger, 1974; Boratav, 1982; and Tezel, 1986. For the 1980s, see Uçtum, 1992.) This heavy state involvement in the economy has been branded as *devletçilik* (*étatisme*).

The consequences of *étatisme* have been discussed widely in the academic literature as well as reports by international organisations. (OECD,

1987/1988; Rodrik, 1990; Öniş and Riedel, 1993). One consequence of *étatisme* was the high level of discretion it conferred on public policy-makers in general and economic policy-makers in particular. This was encouraged by the state's control on significant economic resources, which could be used by the government of the day to maximise electoral support. Discretion was also necessary because the policy-maker had to strike a balance between the interests of the public sector and the objective of encouraging private entrepreneurship via under-priced intermediate and/or consumer goods that would help in keeping production costs and/or wage levels relatively low. The second consequence of *étatisme* was the incentives it provided for rent-seeking. Rent-seeking was encouraged because private economic actors realised that they could exchange political support for privileged access to economic resources and employment opportunities controlled by the state. At the same time, rent-seeking was necessary because private economic actors had to balance the risks instigated by discretionary policies with side payments from the state (Uğur, 1999: 59–67).

The third consequence of *étatisme* was the adverse effect it had on Turkey–EU relations. Given the import substitution strategy that characterised *étatisme* since its inception in the 1930s, Turkey was unable to comply with the gradual tariff removal envisaged in the Additional Protocol (AP) of 1973. From 1973 to 1987, Turkey reduced its tariffs on industrial products only twice: once in 1973 and once in 1976. These reductions represented 20 per cent of the tariff phasing-out applicable to products in the 12-year list and only 10 per cent of that applicable to products in the 22-year list. As far as adoption of the common external tariff was concerned, Turkey did not undertake any of the required adjustments until 1988. The link between *étatisme* and the problematic Turkey–EU relations was acknowledged even by the State Planning Organisation, which stated in 1972 that the AP was incompatible with Turkey's import substitution strategy (Uğur, 1999: 91; Tekeli and İlkin, 1993: 124–140).

Étatisme ran into a serious crisis by the late 1970s. The crisis was characterised by a deep recession, galloping inflation and a severe shortage of foreign exchange – consequences that had been predicted well in advance by the critics. To get out of the crisis, the centre-right government of the day adopted a package of devaluation and liberalisation in line with IMF prescriptions – the so-called 24 January 1980 decisions. While devaluation tackled the over-valuation of the Turkish lira, liberalisation removed the ceiling on interest rates and the prices of public-sector goods. The aim was to increase the significance of price signals for resource allocation, stimulate foreign demand for Turkish exports, and pave the way for export-led growth instead of import substitution.

The next steps in the programme involved external liberalisation. In May 1981, the fixed exchange rate policy was abandoned in favour of managed floating. In 1984, Turkish citizens were granted the right to open foreign exchange deposit accounts in Turkish banks, and current account transactions were liberalised. In 1989, the government introduced capital account convertibility. So, by the end of the 1980s, there was little restriction on inward and outward financial transactions by either residents or non-residents.

The liberalisation programme led to impressive improvements in Turkey's macroeconomic performance. The export/GDP ratio increased from 4.1 per cent in 1980 to 13.3 per cent in 1988. The external balance was reversed from a deficit of 7 per cent of GDP in 1980 to a 1 per cent surplus in 1988. Consumer price inflation fell from 110 per cent in 1980 to 30 per cent in 1987, while the public-sector borrowing requirement as a percentage of GDP was brought down to single digits from 1981 onwards (Ertuğrul and Selçuk, 2001: 8, 12; Akyüz and Boratav, 2002: 3). International organisations monitoring Turkey's economic policy and performance were generous in their praise (see OECD, 1987/1988). Some students of Turkey–EU relations, on the other hand, suggested that the economic reforms of the 1980s aimed to facilitate Turkey's integration into the EU. They even argued that reform recommendations by the IMF and OECD played only a complementary role, with the ultimate aim being compliance with EU standards (Müftüler, 1995).

Yet it is possible to view the liberalisation reforms of the 1980s from a totally different angle. My contention is that these reforms paved the way not only for macroeconomic instability in the 1990s, but also for Turkey's divergence from the emerging macroeconomic policy trends in the EU. These adverse consequences were due not to liberalisation *per se*, but to the fact that liberalisation was introduced within an institutional environment marked by two deficiencies: (i) excessive discretion enjoyed by policy-makers; and (ii) a pervasive rent-seeking culture among private economic actors. Indicators of excessive discretion and pervasive rent-seeking are listed in Table 4.1.

The combination of excessive discretion and pervasive rent-seeking was bound to reduce Turkish policy-makers' willingness and ability to subscribe to rules that would tie their hands – irrespective of whether these rules were internal or external. Binding rules were undesirable because they would imply an end to the policy-maker's ability to exercise discretion. As the scope for discretion declines, the policy-maker would suffer not only a loss of status but also a decline in his or her ability to secure economic or political gains. Even if policy-makers could be envisaged as social planners trying to maximise societal welfare, they might not be able to introduce the necessary rules because of private economic actors' stake in the existing culture of discretion. In other words, resistance to binding rules was highly likely to come not only from the government but also from Turkish society.

The evidence in Table 4.1 demonstrates that each discretionary practice tends to generate a matching rent-seeking strategy by private

Table 4.1 Selected indicators of discretion and rent-seeking in Turkey, 1980s

Indicators of discretion in economic policy	Indicators of rent-seeking
1 Frequent use of **governmental decrees** for the purpose of economic regulation. Approximately 600 decrees were passed in the 1980s. These decrees enter into force before parliamentary approval.	1 **Intensive lobbying** by economic actors of bureaucrats drafting the decrees in order to influence the final outcome. **Corrupt relationship** between private economic actors and bureaucrats working on relatively low salaries.
2 Heavy reliance on **extra-budgetary funds** as sources of revenue and avenues for expenditure. First established in 1984, these special funds are not subject to budgetary control. Their revenue in 1987 was equal to 4 per cent of the gross national income (GNP).	2 Emergence of extra-budgetary funds as **powerful interest groups**. Ability to insulate themselves against downturns in the economy. Bureaucratic expansion, with few or no budget constraints or accountability.
3 **Non-transparent** and **generous state-aid** regime. At the investment stage, incentives can amount to 77 and 109 per cent of project costs in developed and underdeveloped regions, respectively. At the operation stage, incentives can amount to 57 and 104 per cent. Most aid funding is not included in the budget. There is no upper limit for individual firms.	3 Emergence of **moral hazard**, whereby investors minimise the risk of investment and/or maximise the benefits of exit (bankruptcy) at the expense of the taxpayer. Investors are enabled to regard state aid as compensation for risks emanating from macroeconomic instability. Hence, support for stabilisation is weakened.
4 **Discretionary surcharges** on imports. The aim was to generate revenue for extra-budgetary funds and increase the rate of protection. For example, in 1988 customs revenue was 3.4 per cent of the CIF value of imports. When all surcharges are included, the figure rises to 12.2 per cent.	4 Producers' ability to demand (and secure) **tailor-made protection**. Strategic alliance between extra-budgetary funds and import-competing industries. Strengthening of reluctance to restructure with a view to withstanding competition in the EU market.
5 **Decree-based** export subsidies. These included tax rebates; direct subsidies; exemptions from corporation tax; exemption from customs duties on imported raw materials. Permission to retain up to 30 per cent of foreign exchange earnings.	5 Emergence of essentially uncompetitive **export lobbies**. **Artificial rents** for competitive exporters. In 1987, tax rebates amounted to 5 per cent of the total value of exports and direct subsidies were equal to 20 per cent of export value for major export items such as textiles and clothing. Frequent scandals concerning fictitious exports.
6 Managed floating, which was used to engineer real depreciation. Central bank dependence that enabled the government to monetise budget deficits.	6 Intensive lobbying of the central bank to maintain **real depreciation** of the Turkish lira. **Weak central bank control** on private banks holding government bonds.

Sources: Information compiled from European Commission (1989), Sayıştay (2000) and elsewhere.

economic actors. This is not surprising, because discretion encourages rent-seeking behaviour whereas the latter requires further discretion. As discretion increases, private economic actors are induced to engage in rent-seeking in order to secure parochial gains or to minimise the risks generated by the discretionary economic policy itself. On the other hand, increased rent-seeking requires that the policy-maker has a high degree of freedom that enables him or her to satisfy particularistic demands. This symbiotic relationship was observable not only in areas traditionally open to such interaction (such as trade policy), but also in other areas such as fiscal and monetary policies that, at least in OECD countries, had become more rule based.

What was more striking, however, was the fact that the discretionary and increased rent-seeking practices listed in Table 4.1 emerged and became entrenched during the period of liberalisation reforms. The liberalisation reforms of the 1980s ended the import substitution strategy of the preceding decades and the types of government intervention associated with it. Yet these reforms were compromised by a sequencing problem: liberalisation was introduced before the rules of the game, which had generated discretion and rent-seeking in the past, were changed. It was thought (or advised by the IMF) that liberalisation reforms would exert pressure on both government and private economic actors to develop and embrace new rules and institutions. Such expectations, however, were unrealistic because liberalisation created not only new rent-seeking demands in the face of increased risks, but also new financing opportunities that would enable the government to engage in 'innovative' discretion. In fact, the government emerged as an 'aggressive' market player, drawing initially on the domestic and later on foreign capital markets to borrow and hand out patronage.

This was just the opposite of what a standard IMF-sponsored stabilisation package would expect. The central assumption of IMF-sponsored stabilisation programmes is that internal and external liberalisation will reduce the scope for discretion and rent-seeking as market discipline is factored in. The problem with such assumptions is well known: why should policy-makers and/or private economic actors subscribe to such a package in a *credible* manner, knowing that liberalisation would eventually put an end to the *ancien régime* that had delivered parochial economic and/or political gains in the past? Or the question can be posed differently: could liberalisation, within an environment marked with extensive discretion and rent-seeking, generate perverse incentives conducive to further discretion and rent-seeking?

The existing evidence on the Turkish experience suggests that there was indeed a symbiotic relationship between the liberalisations reforms of the 1980s and the discretion/rent-seeking environment depicted in Table 4.1. For example, the liberalisation of interest rates in the early 1980s led to intense inter-bank competition for deposits and encouraged the emergence of non-bank financial intermediaries. Although savings deposits increased as a result, interest rate liberalisation also encouraged the entry of high-risk/high-return financial intermediaries who caused Turkey's first financial crisis in the early 1980s. The government of the day banned the activities of non-bank financial intermediaries, but left the banking system almost untouched. Failure to reform the banking system was underpinned by discretion and rent-seeking. As the existence of large state-owned banks induced policy-makers to take a lenient approach, private banks were enabled to escape restructuring as they argued that a level playing field was necessary for them to compete with the state-owned banks.

Indicators of the symbiotic relationship were observable in trade policy too. Following the current account convertibility measures taken in 1984, the Turkish government resorted to 'innovative' discretionary practices in order to accommodate the rent-seeking demands of both export-oriented and import-competing industries. As trade liberalisation increased the risk for import-competing industries, the Turkish government introduced a wide range of sector- or product-specific surcharges on imports. As indicated in Table 4.1, by 1988 these surcharges accounted for 8.8 per cent of the c.i.f. value of imports. In addition, the average rate of protection (measured as the proportion of tariff revenue and import surcharges to the value of imports) increased from 6.7 per cent in 1981 to 12.2 per cent in 1988. Similarly, export promotion schemes proliferated – leading the European Commission to complain that export subsidies to some sectors had reached 10 per cent of the value of exports to the EU (European Commission, 1989: 18–19, 87).

A third indicator of the symbiotic relationship between liberalisation and discretion/rent-seeking can be seen in the central bank's accommodating stance towards government and private-sector demands. Despite the disinflation component of the liberalisation package, central bank credits accounted for 30–60 per cent of the government's short-term borrowing between 1981 and 1988 – with the exception of 1983, when government borrowing was low but the share of central bank credits was 288 per cent. (CBRT, various years). In addition, the central bank kept the Turkish lira undervalued, leading to a real depreciation of 40 per cent between 1981 and 1988 (Ertuğrul and Selçuk, 2001). This result reflected a clear reluctance to use the exchange rate as a nominal anchor that would dampen inflationary expectations.

The final indicator of the symbiotic relationship that will be examined here concerns the liberalisation of capital account transactions. It is true that capital account liberalisation, together with interest rate liberalisation, was introduced in order to encourage the deepening of the financial markets. However, in an environment characterised by a high degree of discretion and fiscal indiscipline, capital account liberalisation could serve other purposes too. One such purpose was the external financing of budget deficits. Both Akyüz and Boratav (2002: 3) and Ertuğrul and Selçuk (2001: 12) indicate that such considerations were important in the timing of capital account liberalisation. The government of the day introduced capital account liberalisation in 1989, mainly to be able to finance a populist programme that had been adopted after heavy losses in the local elections of 1987 (Boratav and Yeldan, 2001). External borrowing considerations were also evident from the reversal in exchange rate policy: the central bank engineered a real appreciation of 22 per cent in 1989 in order to reduce the domestic currency equivalent of foreign credits.

What is more relevant for the purpose of this chapter is the implications of this symbiotic relationship for Turkey–EU relations. One implication has been the wedge driven between Turkish macroeconomic policies and those adopted by EU member states. The stylised facts about monetary and fiscal policies in EU member states in the 1980s are well known. Keynesian demand-management policies were abandoned within a short period of time, beginning with the change of government in the United Kingdom in 1979 and culminating with the conversion of the socialist French government from 'Keynesianism in one country' to supply-side policies in 1983. As demand management was abandoned, monetary policy was introduced with the intention of achieving a low inflation target. To increase the credibility of the anti-inflationary policy, central bank independence was either introduced or strengthened across EU member states. In addition, fixed exchange rates were presented (and sometimes picked up by some member states such as Italy) as additional nominal anchors that would tie the government's hands (see, for example, Giavazzi and Pagano, 1988).

As a result, inflation in members of the European Monetary System (EMS) fell from 8.8 per cent in 1977 to 3.8 per cent in 1990. In fact, disinflation was the norm in non-EMS countries too, with non-EMS inflation falling from 9.0 per cent to 5.4 per cent over the same period. As inflation rates fell, divergence between countries declined. Hence, the standard deviation of inflation rates fell from 4.9 per cent in 1977 to 1.5 per cent in 1990 in the EMS; and from 5.4 per cent to 2.8 per cent in non-EMS countries (Fratianni and von Hagen, 1992: 69).

Unlike monetary policy, European fiscal policies have gone through three phases of convergence. First, from the late 1970s until the mid-1980s, there was an attempt at consolidation. By the mid-1980s, government spending as a share of GDP was stabilised, and fiscal stabilisation became a convergent pattern across EU member states – with the exception of Italy and Belgium (Roubini and Sachs, 1989: 100–101). From the mid-1980s until the early 1990s, the convergent pattern was towards a slight increase in government expenditure as a share of GDP. This was mainly due to monetary and exchange rate discipline imposed by the EMS – which left fiscal policy as the only instrument for stabilisation. Yet from the mid-1990s onwards, we witness a new phase of convergence towards lower spending as well as budget deficits – mainly as a result of the Maastricht criteria imposed during the transition to monetary union.

In comparison, what are the facts about Turkey's macroeconomic policy choices? The prominent aspect of Turkey's macroeconomic policy in the 1980s was the lack of any serious and credible attempt at stabilisation. In fact, Turkey has been the only developing country that combined liberalisation of trade in goods and in the financial markets with lack of stabilisation for nearly two decades. That is why Turkey's case has been described as 'liberalisation without stabilisation' (Snowden, 1996). The other aspect is that monetary policy was geared towards 'monetising' central government deficits as well as the deficits of the state-owned economic enterprises until the mid-1980s. As a result, inflation in Turkey increased from 30 per cent in 1982 to 77 per cent in 1988, reaching tits highest level, 106 per cent, in 1994 (Dibooğlu and Kibritçioğlu, 2001: 24).

Lax monetary policy was accompanied by fiscal indiscipline. The ratio of debt to GNP increased from 45 per cent in 1984 to 56 per cent in 1988 (World Bank, 1990: 32). In contrast to the move towards fixed exchange rates in the EU, Turkey followed a managed floating regime. The currency was allowed to depreciate in real terms with a view to encouraging exports. This policy not only was in conflict with the move towards monetary integration in Europe, but was exacerbating Turkey's external debt burden too (Rodrik, 1990).

The other legacy of the 1980s was the reluctance to commit credibly to EU membership – both at the governmental and at the societal levels. This was the outcome in equilibrium, irrespective of the rhetoric or policy announcements to the contrary. For example, the architect and executor of the liberalisation reforms, Turgut Özal, declared on the eve of Turkey's application for EU membership in 1987 that 'the aim of economic liberalisation programme and our reforms was to facilitate our integration in the European Community as a full member' (quoted in Müftüler, 1995: 85). How can we accept this announcement as credible when the evidence clearly suggests that Özal was also responsible for the introduction of discretionary and non-transparent policy instruments (including extrabudgetary funds, selective import duties and export subsidies, etc.) that were incompatible with a rule-based economic policy in general and EU rules in particular? As I demonstrated in an earlier work, Turkey's declared commitment to integration was not credible throughout the 1980s, despite the rhetoric to the contrary (Uğur, 1999).

4.2 Further divergence from the EU in the 1990s: a predictable harvest

The combination of liberalisation and discretion/rent-seeking examined above led to disastrous consequences in the 1990s. As Turkey became more integrated into the world economy, high levels of discretion and rent-seeking led to three financial crises: in 1994, 2000 and 2001. Because of the recessions that followed each crises, average annual GDP growth from 1990 to 2001 remained at 3 per cent, depriving Turkey of the opportunity to narrow the development gap with the EU. In addition, macroeconomic instability and poor quality of governance discouraged foreign direct investment (FDI). Total FDI inflows over the 1993–1998 period amounted only to 2.7 per cent of Turkey's GDP in 1998, whereas the ratio was 34.2 per cent in Hungary, 25.9 per cent in the Czech Republic and 19.2 per cent in Poland. In terms of stocks, the FDI stock/GDP ratio for 1998 was 3.8 per cent in Turkey, but 12.1 per cent in the CEECs (Lowendahl and Ertugal-Lowendahl, 2001: 10–11).

The implications for Turkey–EU relations were no less negative. After the rejection of Turkey's application for membership in 1989, Turkey–EU relations deteriorated in relative terms. While the CEECs upgraded their relations with the EU, Turkey became marginalized. This was partly due to the EU's reluctance to accept Turkey as a member and partly due to lack of commitment to integration within Turkey. The lack of commitment has been underpinned by Turkish policy-makers' preference for discretion rather than rules in economic policy. In addition, the macroeconomic instability caused by these preferences reduced the credibility of any attempt at accelerating Turkey's integration with the EU.

The macroeconomic instability that plagued Turkey over the 1990s had both fiscal and monetary causes. As far as fiscal policy is concerned, Atiyas and Sayın (1997) confirm that the high level of discretion that existed in the 1980s reached new heights in the 1990s. This high level of discretion led to budgetary fragmentation, which was reflected in the emergence of extra-budgetary funds and off-budget quasi-fiscal activities (Sayıştay, 2000). Although some of the extra-budgetary funds were incorporated into the budget in 1993, the World Bank (2001) reports that extra-budgetary fund expenditures still amounted to 10 per cent of Turkish GNP in 1999. On the other hand, Atiyas and Sayın (1997) state that quasi-fiscal activities amounted to approximately 10 per cent of GNP in mid-1990s and benefited rent-seekers organised around the distributive policies of the government.

Because of the heavy reliance on extra-budgetary arrangements, there has always been a significant discrepancy between total budget deficits and total borrowing. Total net borrowing from 1971 to 1999 was more than twice the total budget deficits recorded over the same period. While recorded budget deficits amounted to US$109 billion, total net borrowing amounted to US$225 billion – leaving a discrepancy of US$116 billion (Sayistay, 2000: 12). This result was due to debts incurred for financing off-budget expenditures. What is also clear from Table 4.2 below is the fact that the origins of this discrepancy date back to the second half of the 1980s, when the pro-liberalisation government enjoyed a comfortable majority.

Table 4.2 Discrepancy between Turkey's public-sector borrowing requirements (PSBR) and net borrowing (NB), 1980–1999

	1980	1985	1986	1988	1990	1995	1996	1997	1998	1999
PSBR/GNP (%)	8.8	3.6	3.7	4.8	7.4	5.2	9.0	7.9	10.1	14.3
NB/GNP (%)	10.2	9.2	14.2	14.6	6.6	9.9	13.3	9.2	12.1	13.8

Source: Sayıştay (2000: 160–162).

It is possible that sometimes either public-sector borrowing requirement (PSBR) and budget deficits or PSBR and net borrowing figures do not tally because of time lags between receipts and expenditures or between borrowing and disbursement. However, if the discrepancy always involves net borrowing overshooting and if the extent of overshooting is about twice the amount of the apparent PSBR, the only explanation is that the government was consistently undertaking expenditure commitments that exceeded the commitments recorded in the budget. As a result, Turkey accumulated an 'invisible' public debt that amounted to 7 per cent of GNP in 1996 and 18 per cent in 1999 (Sayıştay, 2000: 49).

The non-transparent and discretionary budgetary process provided ample scope for moral hazard in public and private economic decisions. For example, the procurement law encourages the submission of under-priced proposals but fails to limit cost escalation subsequent to project awards. This practice generates a selection bias that favours unsophisticated bidders and reduces the efficiency of investment projects (World Bank, 2001). Another moral hazard concerns military spending. Defence expenditures in Turkey are not subject to full parliamentary control. Defence expenditures are examined by the Parliamentary Budget and Planning Commission, which meets behind closed doors and approves the expenditures in total rather than on the basis of item-by-item scrutiny. According to estimates by Günlük-Şenesen (2002), military expenditures accounted for 14–18 per cent of non-interest government expenditures and have been insulated against the business cycle. Therefore, it is not surprising that wages and maintenance costs (indicators of over-manning and poor-quality equipment) make up 78 per cent of defence expenditures.

Yet the most evident indication of moral hazard is the so-called duty losses of public enterprises, especially public banks. Public banks are required to provide subsidised credits to farmers as well as small businesses, in return for a government guarantee that covers any losses incurred. The guarantee takes the form of converting duty losses into government debt, the interest on which is set to cover losses accumulated each year. In effect, the banks were provided with an automatic bail-out and became increasingly willing to distribute patronage, as instructed by the politicians. As a result, the *stock* of unpaid duty losses increased from

US$1 billion in 1993 to US$19 billion in 1999. The annual *flow* of duty losses also increased from 1 per cent of GNP in 1993 to 8 per cent of GNP in 1999 (International Monetary Fund, 2000: 13).

The discretion inherent in Turkey's fiscal system led not only to an explosion in the extent of the public debt by the end of the 1990s, but also to gross incompatibility between Turkish and EU/OECD practices. The incompatibility is striking across a range of comparison criteria. First, the Turkish budgetary process is marked by perverse incentives that encourage budgetary fragmentation. Perverse incentives are generated by heavy and multi-layered *ex ante* control coupled with ineffective *ex post* control on spending agencies. Therefore, the government as an entity and individual ministries have been induced to engineer off-budget revenues and expenditures in order to escape the *ex ante* control. This has been a significant cause of budgetary fragmentation and has driven Turkey away from the trend towards reducing budgetary fragmentation in mature democracies in general and in EU countries in particular.

Second, budget negotiations in Turkey lacked credibility in the eyes of spending agencies. Although the formal budget process begins in June, budget ceilings for spending agencies are not communicated until very late in the budgetary process. Last-minute negotiations between budgetary authorities and spending ministries generally result in top-down imposition of ceilings that may or may not tally with the bottom-up demands (World Bank, 2001: v). This is just the opposite of the practice in most OECD and EU countries, where the emphasis is on flexibility during budget preparation but effective accountability and control during the spending phase.

Third, Turkey is one of the few OECD countries that do not use a multi-annual budget framework. The budget focuses on the 12 months corresponding to the budget year and 'makes no attempt to anticipate the consequences of current decisions for subsequent years' (World Bank, 2001: v). Although the investment budget has a multi-annual perspective, the World Bank states that future estimations are unreliable, owing to uncertainties associated with high inflation. In addition, there is no verifiable linkage between the investment budget and the current budget. The only linkage between the two over the 1990s was the gradual crowding out of investment expenditures as interest payments on existing debt started to account for about 30–40 per cent the government expenditures. As a result, investment expenditures fell from 10 per cent of GNP in 1990 to 5 per cent in 1999. Divergence from European standards was also evident in monetary policy, which had been dominated by fiscal considerations until the 2001 crisis.

One indicator of fiscal dominance is the extent to which public-sector financing requirements have been monetised. According to the IMF (2000), the government's large financing requirements would have led to an explosion in the debt/GNP ratio earlier than 2001 had the deficits not been monetised through higher inflation rates. In other words, the central bank has been accommodating fiscal policy by preaching disinflation but doing very little to disinflate. It is true that this accommodating monetary policy did not lead to chronic hyperinflation, as was the case in some Latin American countries. However, this was a result of the private-sector demand for base money rather than a success of monetary policy *per se.* According to the IMF (2000: 16–17), the demand for base money tended to fall at a slower pace in Turkey than in other countries that eventually experienced hyperinflation. As a result, hyperinflation was avoided while at the same time high inflation enabled the government to extract *seignorage* (inflation tax) equalling 2.7 per cent of GNP over the 1987–1998 period.

Another indicator of fiscal dominance is pointed out by Napolitano and Montagnoli (2001), who examine the link between policy credibility and the persistence of inflation in Turkey from 1990 to 2000. These authors establish a significant loss of monetary policy credibility before two crises in 1994 and 2000. The loss of credibility in 1994 was due to two events that were directly linked to fiscal policy. The first event was the central bank's failure to announce a monetary programme in 1993, owing to its inability to control the financing needs of the public sector (Emir *et al.,* 2000). The second event concerned the Treasury's attempt to lower the interest rates on government securities at the end of 1993 and the beginning of 1994. As the banking system declined to purchase the securities at low interest rates, the Treasury resorted to central bank credits under the short-term advances (STA) facility. In the last three months of 1993, STA credits amounted to 30 per cent of the central bank reserves, which stood at an all-time high (Özatay, 1999: 24). Therefore, liquidity increased, and increased liquidity prompted portfolio investors to expect a depreciation of the Turkish lira. As expectations were revised, foreign portfolio investors began to withdraw their funds, which led to the 1994 crisis.

The central bank again found itself helpless when faced with the crisis of November 2000 – less than a year after the IMF-sponsored stabilisation programme had been adopted in December 1999. Partly because of IMF backing and partly as a result of excessively high real interest rates (at more than 30 per cent above inflation), the Turkish lira became overvalued. Overvaluation and high real interest rates, coupled with massive borrowing by the Treasury and by private banks, led to massive inflows of short-term capital. As of November 2000, net capital inflows amounted to US$15.2 billion. More than one-third of these inflows (US$5.7 billion) was accounted for by public-sector borrowing (Akyüz and Boratav, 2002: 14). As reserves increased, owing to capital inflows, the central bank had to decide between letting the liquidity increase and sterilising the impact of capital inflows. Initially it decided in favour of sterilisation. However, when capital outflows began, it had to increase liquidity. Otherwise, interest rates would have increased even further and public debt servicing – which accounted for 50 per cent of government expenditures – would have become even more costly. In addition, the banking system held large open positions in foreign exchange and was threatened with collapse when foreign creditors refused to roll over their contracts. The central bank was faced with the classical dilemma: either sticking to its monetary policy rule (which then involved a pegged exchange rate as an anchor); or injecting liquidity to prevent a major financial crisis. It decided in favour of the latter, losing the credibility that it had begun to build during the course of the year.

Fiscal dominance deprived Turkey of the opportunity to disinflate at relatively low output and employment costs. For example, Dibooğlu and Kibritçioğlu (2001) report that Turkish inflation has been driven by aggregate demand disturbances while output has been driven by aggregate supply disturbances over the 1980–2000 period. Hoon Lim and Papi (1997) support this finding by reporting that over the 1975–1995 period, monetary variables played a significant role in determining inflation in Turkey. Finally, Leigh and Rossi (2002b), as well as Napolitano and Montagnoli (2001), demonstrate that Turkish inflation has been essentially a monetary phenomenon and that its persistence has tended to increase when the credibility of the monetary policy was undermined. These findings suggest that a credible anti-inflationary policy would not have necessarily led to substantial output losses in Turkey.

Another study by Leigh and Rossi (2002a) not only confirms the findings already mentioned, but also sheds light on the link between Turkish inflation and exchange rate policy. As indicated above, and in contrast with the trend in the EU, Turkey has refrained from using the exchange rate as a nominal anchor for monetary policy. The only exception was the brief period between December 1999 and February 2001. Even then, however, the commitment to fixed exchange rates was questionable: Turkish policy-makers and the IMF confirmed the difficulty of committing to a fixed exchange rate by devising an escape route through a widening fluctuation band over time. This was in contrast to most CEECs, which set their eyes on meeting the requirements of the Exchange Rate Mechanism II (ERM II) after EU membership and opted for pegged regimes or currency boards.

This lack (or impossibility) of commitment to fixed exchange rates took place against a background where the effect of exchange rate on domestic inflation was very high. Again according to Leigh and Rossi (2002a), the exchange rate pass-through in Turkey was both quicker and higher than in other developing countries. Exchange rate shocks explain 40 per cent of wholesale price inflation (WPI) and 30 per cent of consumer price inflation (CPI) in Turkey. Given that 20 per cent of CPI is also explained by movements in WPI, the exchange rate pass-through on CPI is 38 per cent. This is much higher than, for example, in Brazil, where the pass-through is 22 per cent, or Thailand, where it is 25 per cent. Possible explanations for the higher pass-through in Turkey include persistent inflationary expectations (which induces price-setters to adjust prices quickly after depreciation); lack of a nominal anchor for monetary policy (which induces price-setters to expect that the central bank will accommodate the higher prices rather than tighten monetary policy); and oligopolistic industrial structures (which enables the wholesalers to pass the exchange rate shocks on to retailers).

This analysis enables us to derive three interim conclusions for Turkey–EU relations in the 1990s. First, the combination of 'innovative' discretion and rent-seeking that had emerged in the 1980s continued in the 1990s and led to increased divergence between Turkish and EU macroeconomic policy choices. This divergence was evident in fiscal, monetary and exchange rate policies. As economic policy divergence increased, the perceived risk of integrating Turkey increased, and EU policy-makers became increasingly able to present their reluctance to integrate Turkey as a risk-minimising strategy.

Second, the combination of discretion and rent-seeking has created ample scope for perverse incentives and moral hazard in Turkish economic policy. As a result, economic growth remained low, and, more importantly, commitment to a rule-based economic policy framework has weakened. From 1994 onwards, Turkey adopted a number of stabilisation programmes, but the commitment to stabilisation was so weak that each programme had to be abandoned within one to two years after its adoption. For example, the stabilisation programme of 1994 was abandoned in 1995; a stabilisation programme that started in 1998 was abandoned in 1999 partly as a result of election considerations and partly owing to the earthquake; and the stabilisation programme of December 1999 had to be revamped in the face of the crisis of February 2001. All these failures were due to 'policy shocks' – with the possible exception of the failure in 1999, which was also affected by external shocks such as the earthquake or the Russian financial crisis of 1998. Given these policy reversals, it was unrealistic to expect Turkey to adhere to rules that would ensure compliance with the economic range of the Copenhagen criteria – namely, the existence of a functioning market economy and ability to withstand competitive pressure in the EU market.

Finally, the combination of discretion and rent-seeking has also reduced the attractiveness of EU membership as an arrangement that could help break the vicious circle of discretion/rent-seeking and repeated economic crises. Indeed, Turkish policy-makers, with the exception of Kemal Derviş, who was brought in from the World Bank to lend credibility to the stabilisation programme after the February 2001 crisis, have never considered the EU as a possible anchor that would enhance the credibility of the stabilisation programmes. On the contrary, they turned a blind eye to macroeconomic policy developments in the EU, ignored the manner in which Greece eventually had to accept EU discipline in 1995 after a long period of experimenting with populism, and remained stuck to counter-productive accusations that the EU was discriminating against Turkey. As we shall see in the next section, however, these policy failures did nothing but reduce the probability of EU membership, as Turkey was overtaken by CEECs in the race for integration.

4.3 Turkey versus CEECs: commitment makes a difference

A regular argument put forward by Turkish policy-makers as well as some students of Turkey–EU relations has been that the EU has become increasingly reluctant to integrate Turkey after the systemic change brought about by the end of the Cold War (Eralp, 1993; Aybet and Müftüler-Baç, 2000). It is not possible to take issue with this argument, given the aim of this chapter and space limitations. Yet it is possible to demonstrate that, in terms of economic policy choices, Turkey has done little to counter-balance EU reluctance. In what follows, I will present some evidence suggesting that Turkey has become gradually less capable of satisfying the economic criteria for membership, while the CEECs have moved up the score board.

As was indicated in the previous section, one economic criterion for membership is the existence of a functioning market economy. This criterion includes the following components: liberalisation of the goods market; free entry into and exit from the market; a well-developed financial system; an enforceable legal system and property rights; and macroeconomic stability. In the 1990s, Turkey could legitimately claim to have satisfied only one sub-criterion: liberalisation of the goods market. The extent to which the remaining sub-criteria were met is questionable. As demonstrated in section 4.2, macroeconomic instability was the norm in the 1990s. In addition, the impact of discretion/rent-seeking on the legal system was negative, leading to oligopolistic company structures and poor-quality corporate governance. Finally, the Turkish banking sector and capital markets recorded significant developments in the 1990s, but the capital market remained shallow and the weakness of the banking system was always a handicap. Therefore, it was not surprising to observe that Turkey's scores on the 'Index of Economic Freedom' (IEF) have deteriorated from 1995 onwards – as can be seen in Table 4.3.

The IEF is defined as a measure of the 'absence of government coercion or constraint on the production, distribution, or consumption of goods and services beyond the extent necessary . . . to protect and maintain liberty itself' (Beach and O'Driscoll, 2003). I do not suggest that the IEF is necessarily a reliable indicator of the existence of a market economy as prescribed by the Copenhagen criteria. Nor do I suggest that the IEF is free of ideological baggage. Yet I do propose to use it as an indicator of relative performance by Turkey and the CEECs , for two reasons. First, the

Table 4.3 Country scores on the Economic Freedom Index, 1995–2003

	1995	1996	1997	1998	1999	2000	2001	2002	2003
Estonia	2.40	2.50	2.50	2.30	2.35	2.20	2.05	1.80	1.80
Lithuania	n.a.	3.45	3.10	3.00	3.00	3.05	2.90	2.35	2.35
Latvia	n.a.	3.05	2.95	2.85	2.75	2.65	2.65	2.50	2.45
Czech Republic	2.20	2.20	2.20	2.35	2.20	2.20	2.20	2.40	2.50
Hungary	3.00	3.00	3.00	3.00	2.95	2.55	2.55	2.40	2.65
Slovenia	n.a.	3.50	3.30	3.00	2.90	3.00	2.90	3.10	2.85
Poland	3.30	3.10	3.10	2.90	2.80	2.80	2.75	2.70	2.90
Slovak Republic	2.80	3.00	3.05	3.15	3.10	3.00	2.85	2.90	2.90
Bulgaria	3.50	3.50	3.60	3.65	3.50	3.40	3.30	3.40	3.35
Turkey	2.80	2.90	2.70	2.60	2.80	2.75	2.90	3.35	3.50
Romania	3.60	3.65	3.40	3.30	3.30	3.30	3.65	3.70	3.75

Source: Heritage Foundation (2003: various pages)

Key:
Score of 1.95 or less: full economic freedom.
Score of 2.00–2.95: mostly free.
Score of 3.00–3.05: mostly unfree.
Score of 4 or above: repressed economy.

IEF is based on a uniform methodology for all countries involved. Second, it captures the effect of missing institutional and regulatory variables that the Copenhagen conditionality requires. Therefore, the IEF scores can be taken as suggestive indicators of the extent to which Turkey's performance has deteriorated while the performance of the CEECs (with the exception of Bulgaria and Romania) improved between 1995 and 2003. In fact, by 2003 Turkey's performance had fallen even below that of Bulgaria. Because the index incorporates policy/institutional variables (corruption, barriers to trade, fiscal burden, rule of law, regulatory burdens, black market activities, etc.) that reflect the extent to which a market economy exists, the results in Table 4.3 suggest that Turkey has been becoming less able to satisfy the economic criteria for membership, whereas eight CEECs (though not Bulgaria and Romania) have been demonstrating progress in terms of meeting the criteria.

Another conclusion that can be derived from Table 4.3 relates to the debate on whether or not Turkey's exclusion from the eastern enlargement could be justified on economic grounds. The evidence in Table 4.3 suggests that Turkey's exclusion, at the Luxembourg summit of 1997, cannot be justified on economic grounds. In 1997, when the EU declared the CEECs to be candidates and excluded Turkey, most of the CEECs (excluding Estonia and the Czech Republic) were behind Turkey on the 'IEF'. In that sense, the evidence in Table 4.3 justifies the argument that the EU, in 1997, did discriminate against Turkey – at least so far as economic criteria were concerned. That is why I was one of those who criticised the Luxembourg summit decision of 1997 as unjustified and counterproductive (Uğur, 2003). Yet one cannot invest too heavily in the 'discrimination' argument for two reasons.

First, the EU has always stated that Turkey 'has many of the characteristics of a market economy' and should be able to 'cope with competitive pressure' within the EU market, provided that 'macroeconomic stability is attained' and 'legal and structural reforms' are carried out (see, for example, European Commission, 2000: 22). In other words, the sticking point was macroeconomic instability and the lack of progress in legal/structural reforms. The evidence in Table 4.3 suggests that the Commission's proviso was not misplaced. Indeed, as Turkey continued to be plagued with macroeconomic instability, and structural/legal reforms were not forthcoming, its performance on the 'IEF' has deteriorated from 1999 onwards. Therefore, it can be argued that Turkey's policy failures have provided *ex post* justification for the EU's discrimination – which, in the light of the 'IEF' scores after 1999, could be presented as a forward-looking, risk-minimising decision.

Second, the 'discrimination' argument also overlooks the fact that almost all candidate countries, unlike Turkey, had demonstrated a clear commitment to macroeconomic stability and convergence towards EU policies. Exchange rate policy was one policy area where the contrast was evident. While Turkey maintained managed floating, seven candidate countries (excluding the Czech Republic, Romania and Slovenia) had adopted a pegged exchange rate against the euro or a basket of currencies including the euro; or had a currency board arrangement anchored on the deutschmark (DM). The majority of these fixed exchange rate arrangements dated back to the 1992–1994 period, well before the Luxembourg summit of 1997 at which the CEECs were granted candidate status (see Temprano-Arroyo and Feldman, 1998). In addition, by 1997 all CEECs had introduced policy independence for their central banks, whereas the Turkish central bank was legally bound to determine monetary policy jointly with the government.

Turkey's reluctance or inability to introduce a fixed exchange rate policy and central bank independence may well have been dictated by economic 'realities' of the 1990s. For example, the experiment with a crawling peg in 2000 proved a disaster within a year – mainly because of capital outflows induced by economic policy failures. In addition, central bank independence was highly likely to remain on paper, given Turkey's persistent fiscal deficits and escalating public debt. However, this unfavourable macroeconomic environment has been essentially a cumulative result of discretion/rent-seeking practices rather than exogenous factors. Therefore, it only proves the argument that Turkey's policy choices in the 1990s were a major obstacle to a rule-based macroeconomic policy. In addition, it also proves that a credible commitment matters – not only in terms of stabilisation, but also in terms of convergence towards EU policies. While Turkey has become increasingly vulnerable to frequent economic crises and forfeited the benefits of using the EU membership target as a catalyst for reform, the CEECs have benefited on both counts.

It must be added that the difference between Turkey and the CEECs reflected in the IEF scores is confirmed by the results of other ranking exercises that are less ideologically laden and use different methodologies. For example, the Corruption Perceptions Index (CPeI) of Transparency International (2002) accords Turkey a rank of 64, suggesting that in 2002 the Turkish public policy framework was perceived to be more corrupt than that of any CEEC except Romania (see Table 4.4). The interesting aspect of the CPeI is that it is a composite index constructed on the basis of 15 different indices developed by the World Bank, rating agencies, audit institutions and universities. Although not all the constituent indices were available for all countries listed in Table 4.4 the ranking of each country is determined by information from at least seven indices.

Tables 4.3 and 4.4 also enable us to state that there is a strong correlation between Turkey's 2002 score on the IEF (Table 4.3, column 2), its rankings on the CPeI (Table 4.4, Rank 1) and its ranking on the growth competitiveness index (Table 4.4, Rank 2). In other words, information processed by three different institutions delivers a unanimous verdict that places Turkey consistently below nine CEECs, the exception being Romania. Given that these indices have been compiled by different institutions and with different methodologies, one can safely conclude that Turkey's overall standing *vis-à-vis* CEECs is subject to a minimal risk of bias or methodological idiosyncrasy. The correlation also holds when we include ranking on the public institutions index (Table 4.4, Rank 4) and the macroeconomic environment index (Table 4.4, Rank 5).

Interestingly, however, the correlation is weaker when the 2002 IEF score is compared with rankings on 2002 indices of microeconomic performance. As can be seen from Table 4.4, Turkey's ranking on various indices of microeconomic performance is consistently better than its ranking on indices of macroeconomic/institutional environment. In addition, Turkey performs better than not only Romania but also Bulgaria. This evidence suggests that Turkey's poor ranking on the IEF (Table 4.3, column 2) and the growth competitiveness index (Table 4.4, Rank 2) is determined by macroeconomic policy and macroinstitutional variables rather than micro-level variables such as company strategies (Table 4.4, Rank 6) or microeconomic business environment (Table 4.4, Rank 7), which are known to be influenced by macro-level variables.

Nevertheless, the evidence examined above suggests that in 2002 Turkey still had a long way to go to catch up even with the microeconomic scores of eight CEECs that had embraced the market economy only after 1989. As can be seen from Table 4.4, even in terms of microeconomic environment,

Table 4.4 Country ranking, 2002: Turkey versus CEECs

	Rank 1	Rank 2	Rank 3	Rank 4	Rank 5	Rank 6	Rank 7
Slovenia	27	28	27	23	50	26	27
Estonia	29	26	30	28	46	36	28
Hungary	33	29	28	30	49	29	29
Lithuania	36	36	40	36	45	39	39
Poland	45	51	46	61	54	46	45
Bulgaria	45	62	68	47	75	72	63
Czech Republic	52	40	34	50	59	34	34
Latvia	52	44	45	52	55	48	42
Slovak Republic	52	49	42	53	64	43	40
Turkey	64	69	54	63	78	56	55
Romania	77	66	67	67	58	69	64

Sources: Rank 1: Transparency International (2002); Ranks 2–7: World Economic Forum (2003).

Notes
Higher rank indicates poorer performance.
Rank 1: ranking on the corruption perception index.
Rank 2: ranking on the growth competitiveness index.
Rank 3: ranking on the microeconomic competitiveness index.
Rank 4: ranking on the public institutions index.
Rank 5: ranking on the macroeconomic environment index.
Rank 6: company operations and strategy ranking.
Rank 7: quality of the microeconomic business environment ranking.

Turkey is eight to ten places below Poland despite the fact that Poland is the lowest-performing member of the CEECs that were accepted for EU membership in 2002. This divergence is not surprising, because macroeconomic and macro-institutional variables have significant effects on microeconomic performance. It is also interesting because it reflects the extent to which the microeconomic environment in the CEECs has improved now that destructive effects of the transition are over.

Conclusions

One conclusion that can be derived from the preceding paragraphs is that Turkey's liberalisation efforts in the 1980s have been over-sold. This chapter examines the over-selling only with respect to declared aims, which included macroeconomic efficiency/stability and convergence with emerging EU norms in economic policy. On both counts, and particularly from the mid-1980s onwards, the liberalisation reforms have produced totally opposite outcomes. Not only has Turkey become the least stable economy in Europe, but it has also diverged from the emerging trends in European macroeconomic policies – especially from the trends towards intra-European fixed exchange rate arrangements, fiscal discipline and anti-inflationary monetary policies. Irrespective of whether or not these policies are desirable in and for themselves, Turkey's divergence from these policies was evident and provided significant signals as to its inability to commit itself in a *credible* manner to integration with the EU.

The second conclusion that can be derived from the analysis above is that Turkey's divergence from the EU was in sharp contrast to the convergence of the CEECs. True, as Öniş (2003) has indicated, Turkey's relatively poor performance may be partly related to 'asymmetric incentives' caused by its exclusion from the eastern enlargement that began in 1997. However, the analysis presented in this chapter also suggests that the CEECs' commitment to adopting EU standards had been evident well before 1997. Some of the macroeconomic policy reforms had been introduced as early as 1994. Therefore, and irrespective of the criticism that can be levelled against the EU's failure to act as an effective anchor for Turkish policy reform, the risk associated with Turkey's integration has increased while the risk associated with the integration of the CEECs has diminished.

As a result, Turkey's exclusion from the recent enlargement has become a predictable outcome even for those in favour of Turkey's EU membership. What is more telling, however, is the fact that this predictable outcome was an *endogenous* choice for Turkish policy-makers as well as economic actors. In other words, the delay in Turkey's integration has been an outcome of the maximising behaviour of Turkish politicians and economic actors, given the rules of the game that characterised the decision-making environment in Turkey. The analysis presented here suggests that these rules of the game provided ample scope for and necessitated a high degree of discretion and rent-seeking. Liberalisation was expected to reduce discretion/rent-seeking, but it produced just the opposite outcome because of incorrect sequencing – that is, because liberalisation was introduced before the establishment of new rules and institutions that would check discretion/rent-seeking.

The third conclusion is that until the late 1990s, Turkish policy announcements in favour of EU membership (made by the government or economic actors) lacked credibility for two reasons. First, announcements in favour of EU membership were overshadowed by continuing discretion/rent-seeking, which raised question marks about the extent to which Turkish policy-makers and economic actors were prepared to tie their hands by adherence to EU rules. Second, discretion/rent-seeking has been conducive to macroeconomic instability and increased the risks of integrating Turkey, as perceived by the EU as well as Turkish policy-makers. Put differently, macroeconomic instability has become a major source of uncertainty about the extent to which the Turkish economy could withstand the competitive pressures in the EU market.

The fourth conclusion is that the policy environment characterised by discretion and rent-seeking may well have become unsustainable in Turkey. One reason is that this policy environment has led to depressing results in terms of economic growth. Despite its huge potential in terms of natural resources and human capital, Turkey's income per-capita for 2002 (adjusted for purchasing parity) was still lower than that in all the CEECs except Bulgaria and Romania. The other reason is that the policy environment has been conducive to recurrent and more frequent economic crises, with detrimental effects not only on growth but also on FDI flows into Turkey. For these reasons, the *ancien régime* has led to intense public discontent with the policy environment itself as well as its policy outcomes. Against this background, EU membership is now perceived by the Turkish public as a paradigm shift that would open new avenues for economic development as well as better governance.

The final comment to be made here is of a more speculative nature. Would compliance with the Copenhagen criteria and eventual EU membership necessarily guarantee better economic performance and higher governance quality in Turkey? The analysis above does not allow us to provide a direct answer to this question. However, an indirect answer can be attempted by emphasising two points. First, the Copenhagen criteria have been designed to reduce the risk for existing EU members and institutions of integrating relatively less developed and less stable countries. As such, they are not necessarily designed to address the development needs of the candidate countries, including Turkey. Second, candidate countries can use the Copenhagen conditionality as a commitment device that would reduce resistance to economic and political reform. Although the Copenhagen conditionality is not designed to guarantee faster economic growth and cannot necessarily ensure better governance, it may well provide a starting point for a candidate country such as Turkey to break with past policies that produced undesirable outcomes.

Note

I would like to thank Ferda Halıcıoğlu, Nergis Canefe and Ziya Öniş for their helpful comments and suggestions.

References

Akyüz, Y. and K. Boratav (2002), 'The making of the Turkish financial crisis', paper submitted to PERI, University of Massachusetts Conference on Financialization of the Global Economy, 7–9 December 2002, Amherst, MA.

Atiyas, İ. and Ş. Sayın (1997), *Siyasi Sorumluluk, Yönetsel Sorumluluk ve Bütçe Sistemi: Bir Yeniden Yapılanma Önerisine Doğru* (Political Accountability, Administrative Accountability and the Budgetary System: Towards a Restructuring Proposal), Istanbul: TESEV.

Aybet, G. and M. Müftüler-Baç (2000), 'Transformations in security and identity after the Cold War: Turkey's problematic relations with Europe', *International Journal*, vol. 50, no. 4, pp. 567–582.

Beach, W. W. and G. P. O'Driscoll, Jr (2003), 'Explaining the factors of the index of economic freedom', available at http://www.heritage.org/research/features/index/2003/chapters/Chapter5.html (accessed May 2003).

Boratav, K. (1982), *Türkiye'de Devletçilik* (Étatisme in Turkey), Ankara: Savaş Yayınevi.

Boratav, K. and E. Yeldan (2001), 'Turkey, 1980–2000: financial liberalisation, macroeconomic instability and patterns of distribution', mimeo, CEPA, New School, December.

CBRT (various years), Central Bank of the Republic of Turkey, *Annual Reports*, Ankara.

Dibooğlu, S. and A. Kibritçioğlu (2001), 'Inflation, output, and stabilisation in a high inflation economy: Turkey, 1980–2000', Working Paper no. 01-0112, Office of Research, University of Illinois at Urbana-Champaign.

Emir, O. Y., A. Karasoy and K. Kunter (2000), 'Monetary policy reaction functions in Turkey', Discussion Paper, Central Bank of the Republic of Turkey (October).

Eralp, A. (1993), 'Turkey and the European Community in the changing post-war international system', in C. Balkır and A. M. Williams (eds), *Turkey and Europe*, London: Pinter, pp. 24–44.

Ertuğrul, A. and F. Selçuk (2001), 'A brief account of the Turkish economy, 1980–2000', *Russian and East European Finance and Trade*, vol. 37, no. 6, pp. 6–30.

EU Council (2001), 'Council decision of 8 March 2001 on the principles, priorities, intermediate objectives and conditions contained in the Accession Partnership with the Republic of Turkey', *Official Journal*, no. L85, pp. 13–23.

European Commission (1989), *The Turkish Economy: Structure and Developments*, SEC (89) 2290/final, Brussels.

European Commission (2000), *2000 Regular Report on Turkey's Progress towards Accession*, Brussels: European Commission 8 November.

Fratianni, M. and J. von Hagen (1992), *The European Monetary System and European Monetary Union*, Oxford: Westview Press.

Giavazzi, F. and M. Pagano (1988), 'The advantage of tying one's hands: EMS discipline and central bank credibility', *European Economic Review*, vol. 32, pp. 1055–1082.

Günlük-Şenesen, G. (2002), *Türkiye'de Savunma Harcamaları ve Ekonomik Etkileri* (Turkish Defence Expenditures and Their Economic Impacts), Istanbul, TESEV.

Heritage Foundation (2003), *2003 Index of Economic Freedom*, available at http://cf.heritage.org/index/pastScores.cfm (accessed May 2003).

Hoon Lim, C. and L. Papi (1997), 'An econometric analysis of the determinants of inflation in Turkey', IMF European I Department Working Paper no. WP/97/170.

IMF (2000), *Turkey: Selected Issues and Statistical Appendix*, Report no. 00/14, Washington, DC: IMF.

Krueger, A. O. (1974), *Turkey: Foreign Trade Regimes and Economic Development*, Princeton, NJ: Columbia University Press.

Land, J. W. (1970), *The Role of Government in the Economic Development of Turkey, 1923–63*, Houston: Rice University.

Leigh, D. and M. Rossi (2002a), 'Exchange rate pass-through in Turkey', IMF Working Paper, no. WP/02/204.

Leigh, D. and M. Rossi (2002b), 'Leading indicators of growth and inflation in Turkey', IMF Working Paper, no. WP/02/231.

Lowendahl, H. and Ertugal-Lowendahl, E. (2001), 'Turkey's performance in attracting foreign direct investment: implications of EU enlargement', European Network of Economic Policy Research Institutes, Working Paper no. 8, November.

Müftüler, M. (1995), 'Turkish economic liberalisation and European integration', *Middle Eastern Studies*, vol. 31, no. 1, pp. 85–98.

Napolitano, O. and A. Montagnoli (2001), 'Inflation persistence and credibility in Turkey during the nineties', manuscript, Brunel University, UK.

OECD (1987/1988), *OECD Economic Survey: Turkey*, Paris: OECD.

Öniş, Z. (2003), 'Domestic politics, international norms and challenges to the state: Turkey–EU relations in the post-Helsinki era', *Turkish Studies*, vol. 4, no. 1, pp. 9–35.

Öniş, Z. and Riedel, J. (1993), *Economic Crisis and Long Term Growth in Turkey*, Washington, DC: World Bank.

Özatay, F. (1999), 'Populist policies and the role of economic institutions in the performance of the Turkish economy', *Yapı Kredi Economic Review*, vol. 10, no. 1, pp. 13–25.

Rodrik, D. (1990), 'Some policy dilemmas in Turkish macroeconomic management', in T. Aricanli and D. Rodrik (eds), *The Political Economy of Turkey: Debt Adjustment and Sustainability*, New York: St Martin's.

Roubini, N. and J. Sachs (1989), 'Government spending and budget deficits in the industrial countries', *Economic Policy*, no. 8 (April), pp. 100–132.

Sayıştay (2000), *2000 Yılı Raporu (Fiscal Report for Year 2000)*, available at http://www.sayistay.gov.tr (accessed April 2003).

Snowden, P. N. (1996), 'Financial reform in Turkey since 1980: liberalisation without stabilisation', in S. Togan and V. N. Balasubramanyan (eds), *The Economy of Turkey since Liberalisation*, Basingstoke, UK: Macmillan, pp. 67–87.

Tekeli, İ. and S. İlkin (1993), *Türkiye ve Avrupa Topluluğu: Ulus Devletini Aşma Çabasındaki Avrupa'ya Türkiye'nin Yaklaşımı II* (Turkey and the European Community: Turkey's Approach to Europe Attempting to Transcend the Nation-State II), Ankara: Ümit Yayıncılık.

Temprano-Arroyo, H. and R. A. Feldman (1998), 'Selected transition and Mediterranean countries: an institutional primer on EMU and EU relations', IMF European I Department, Working Paper no. WP/98/82, Washington, DC: IMF.

Tezel, Y. S. (1986), *Cumhuriyet Döneminin İktisadi Tarihi* (Economic History of the Republican Era), Ankara: Yurt Yayınları.

Transparency International (2002), 'Corruption Perceptions Index 2002', http://www.transparency.org (accessed May 2003).

Uçtum, M. (1992), 'The effects of liberalisation on traded and non-traded goods sectors: the case of Turkey', in F. N. Tevfik and M. Odekon (eds), *Economics and Politics of Turkish Liberalisation*, Bethlehem, PA: Lehigh University Press, pp. 143–154.

Uğur, M. (1999), *The European Union and Turkey: An Anchor/Credibility Dilemma*, Aldershot, UK: Ashgate.

Uğur, M. (2003), 'Testing time in EU–Turkey relations: the road to Copenhagen and beyond', *Journal of Southern Europe and the Balkans*, vol. 5, no. 2, pp. 161–178.

World Bank (1990), *Turkey: Debt Management and Borrowing Strategy under Macroeconomic Adjustment*, Report no. 7732-TU, Washington, DC: World Bank.

World Bank (2001), *Turkey: Public Expenditures and Institutional Review – Reforming Budgetary Institutions for Effective Government*, Report no. 22530, Washington, DC: World Bank.

World Economic Forum (2003), Global Competitiveness Report 2002–2003, available at http://www.weforum.org/site/homepublic.nsf/Content (accessed May 2003).

5 Europeanisation of Turkish peak business organisations and Turkey–EU relations

Serap Atan

Introduction

This chapter will examine the Europeanisation of peak business organisations (PBOs)[1] in Turkey and its possible consequences for Turkey's integration with the EU. For analytical purposes, we define the concept of Europeanisation as

> processes of (a) construction, (b) diffusion and (c) institutionalisation of formal and informal rules, procedures, policy paradigms, styles, 'ways of doing things' and shared beliefs and norms which are first defined and consolidated in the making of EU decisions and then incorporated in the logic of domestic discourse, identities, political structures and public policies.
>
> (Radaelli, 2000: 4)

Therefore, the concept refers to a large-scale transformation at the national level that impinges upon domestic structures as well as public policies. In this definition, domestic structures, as objects of Europeanisation, are different from policies. They represent the 'political structures, structures of representation and cleavages, cognitive and normative structures' (Radaelli, 2000: 4). Incidentally, these structural characteristics are rather more resistant to change than public policies. Nevertheless, the literature on Europeanisation shows that the business organisations in EU member states undergo a remarkable transformation.

Streeck (1987) demonstrates that the integration process has affected 'the socio-economic environment in which interest associations act, [their] formal organization, and [their] institutional target structure' (cited in Lehmkuhl, 2000: 3). Also, Green Cowles (2001) argues that business–government relations – that is, understanding of governance at national level – are transformed by the effect of the EU integration process. In this respect, the Europeanisation process enhances the significance of business actors in policy analysis. The EU institutional and legal framework progressively acts upon national regimes in candidate countries too. This framework brings pressure on national business organisations to adapt to new policy structures and actors, and offers them considerable opportunities to improve their organisational structures and capacity to intervene in national policy-making. Therefore, within the context of the EU accession process, we might question the role of the PBOs at particular cases of contemporary policy changes in Turkey.

The EU accession process has had various consequences for national business organisations in candidate countries. These depend on the history of national interest politics and the characteristics of the accession process in each candidate country. Hence, the most immediate effect for the Central and East European Countries (CEECs) has been the restructuring of the associational system[2] (Draus, 2001) and the recognition of business organisations' legitimacy as policy actors (Pérez-Solórzano Borragán, 2002). In Turkey, the enlargement process has not caused a dramatic restructuring of the associational system since interest groups politics has been inherent in the national political system (Bianchi, 1984). Nevertheless, we observe that interaction with EU-level policy-making has somehow shaped the negotiating patterns of Turkish PBOs and their interventions in the national reform process. Therefore, it is interesting to question to what extent this trend could affect Turkey's progress in fulfilling the economic and political criteria for accession.[3]

Specifically, my aim here is to test the argument that there exists a significant relationship between the Europeanisation of Turkish PBOs and the current democratic reform process geared towards compliance with accession criteria. I detect that Europeanisation has emerged at a particular political conjuncture in Turkey, one that challenged the government's traditional predominance in setting the policy agenda. This political conjuncture is underpinned by the current internal political instability and the convergence requirements of the accession process, both of which render Turkish governments more receptive to support and inputs from private policy actors.

The chapter will proceed as follows. In section 5.1, we will examine the dynamics of Europeanisation in Turkish PBOs until the Helsinki summit decision of December 1999. On the one hand, we will look at the evolution of PBOs' interests in the context of Turkey–EU relations. On the other hand, we will examine the mechanisms through which PBOs have pursued their interests within the Turkey–EU association regime as well as through EU-level governance structures. I demonstrate that the association regime, set up in 1963, has evolved as an instrument of only limited economic policy convergence between Turkey and the EU – mainly in trade-related matters.[4] Therefore, traditional lines of business–government relations have persisted and PBO inputs into Turkey–EU relations have remained limited. However, after the Luxembourg summit decision of December 1997, Turkey was faced with the risk of exclusion from the current wave of enlargement. This was mainly due to Turkey's failure to meet the Copenhagen criteria – especially those related to the political domain. Therefore, traditional lines of business–government relations began to give way to a new style of PBO involvement in the making of public policy as the business community started to contemplate the risk of Turkey's exclusion while CEECs were on the way towards accession.

In the second section, we explore the significance of PBO discourse on the adoption of EU rules and norms. I maintain that this discourse is noteworthy in shaping the public debate over the model of national development strategies. We will recall here the progressive convergence of the discourse adopted by big business in Turkey, which is pro-Western, and that adopted by the traditionalist small business ('Anatolian Tigers'). Consequently, we argue that in so far as they are socialised in the EU governance system, Turkish PBOs acquire new resources to promote a European model of political, social and economic development strategy. This, in turn, determines their contribution to the national reform process aimed at fulfilling the accession criteria. To test the hypothesis, I refer to two specific cases: the latest constitutional amendments addressing the deficiencies of the democratic regime, and the establishment of an Economic and Social Council (ESC) in Turkey.

My concluding remarks emphasise the significance of the EU accession process in influencing Turkish PBOs' characteristics (policy agenda and strategy, internal structures, and coalition-building capacity) as well as the conditions defining their role and capacity in their relations with the government. The findings suggest that a causal relationship exists between the Europeanisation of PBOs and their mediating role in Turkey's transformation towards EU membership. In addition, the PBO discourse advocating a European political, economic and social model has contributed to shaping the policy agenda towards compliance with the accession criteria.

5.1 The emergence of PBOs as new actors in Turkey–EU relations

Studies of Turkey–EU relations document the Turkish state's leadership role in the establishment of an association regime with the European Community in 1963. The government of the time did not bring the issue to the Turkish Grand National Assembly (TGNA); nor did it open a general public debate on the costs and benefits of association. However, the initiative enjoyed overall support from the TGNA as well as the business community as a confirmation of the country's European vocation. The Association Agreement had foreseen the opening of channels of dialogue beyond governmental actors – mainly between the European Parliamentary Assembly (currently the European Parliament) and the European Economic and Social Committee (EESC) on the one hand and their Turkish counterparts on the other (Association Agreement, article

27). During the preparatory phase of the association, only members of the TGNA and the European Parliament set up a permanent dialogue forum – namely, the Joint Parliamentary Committee. It was not until 1995 that Turkish social partners and other professional organisations could form a Joint Consultative Committee (JCC)[5] with their EU counterparts within the EESC. This body guarantees business associations formal access to the Association Council, which is the main institutional locus of the association regime.[6]

The immediate reaction of Turkish PBOs towards the association regime was the establishment of the Economic Development Foundation (IKV),[7] with the aim of being better informed about the consequences of this unusual economic partnership. The PBOs' interest in Turkey's integration with the EU emerged at a time when the functional cleavage between national commercial and industrial interests began to take shape. Overall, until the establishment of the customs union in 1996, the attitude of business organisations towards the EU was mainly patterned in accordance with their position *vis-à-vis* the national development strategies and the implications of transition to an open market economy. In fact, the national development strategy, based on import substitution, was implemented without any reference to the policy priorities implied by the association regime. This situation persisted for a long time, until 1980, when the Turkish market was liberalised and integration with the world economy became the main objective of government policy.

The cleavage between commercial and industrial interests, intensified by rapid industrialisation policies, shaped the associational system in Turkey during the 1960s and 1970s. Thus, the leadership of the Union of Chambers of Commerce, Industry, Maritime Commerce and Commodity Exchanges of Turkey (TOBB) in both the commercial and the industrial sectors was seriously undermined in the 1970s. More independent organisational channels were formed at this period, namely 'the Union of Chambers of Industry, a loose and informal coalition within TOBB itself, the Turkish Confederation of Employers Associations (TISK), and the Turkish Industrialists and Businessmen's Association (TUSIAD)' (Bianchi, 1984: 259). As representatives of the fastest-growing sector of the economy and willing to compete on the foreign markets, the large manufacturers that founded TUSIAD in 1971 became keen advocates of integration with the EU. The accession process to the EU was defined not only as 'a project of modernisation', but also as an embodiment of the organisation's cultural vision towards Western society.

During the 1980s, Turkey's relations with the EU gained a new dimension with the submission of an application for membership. Once again the government had taken the initiative without seeking the support of the TGNA or public opinion. Although there appeared to be general public support for the membership target, divergences emerged between large entrepreneurs and small and medium-sized enterprises (SMEs) over membership requirements. The European Commission's negative opinion concerning Turkey's application made it evident that, the prospect of Turkey–EU relations would thereafter be dependent on Turkey's success in tackling political questions such as human rights and democratisation. In response to that opinion, TOBB, representing mainly SMEs, urged the government to reconsider relations with the EU and to explore the possibility of developing links with neighbouring countries sharing common cultural ties with Turkey. TUSIAD, representing mainly the large entrepreneurs, openly criticised the government for failing to grasp the close link between a liberal economy and a liberal political regime (Eralp, 1990: 251–252). As a result, the national debate on the membership gained an ideological dimension.

Following Turkey's formal application for membership to the EU, two PBOs, namely TISK and TUSIAD, became members of the Union of Industrial and Employers' Confederation of Europe (UNICE).[8] This showed Turkish PBOs' interest in strengthening their presence *vis-à-vis* EU institutions and developing closer relations with the European business community. In fact, until the late 1980s only a TOBB liaison office existed in Brussels. Moreover, only a small group of business organisations, especially sectoral organisations, were members of EU level business organizations.[9] In addition to financial constraints, Turkish business organisations' limited interest was due to their insufficient knowledge of EU matters and the perception that the issue was outside their field of activity (Ayberk and Boduroğlu, 1990: 227–230). TOBB had become an associate member of the Association of European Chambers of Commerce and Industry (Eurochambres)[10] at the beginning of the 1980s. Since then, its European Affairs department has specialised in the management of programmes in which Turkish chambers of commerce participate. The membership of Eurochambres is particularly important to increase the capacity of chambers of commerce to deal with EU policies, programmes and projects. Within this context, Eurochambres helps its members to deliver a better-quality service to the business community and encourages them to undertake joint actions.

The negotiations over the customs union decision between Turkey and the EU marked a turning point in Turkish PBOs' interests in EU affairs. After the European Commission's unfavourable response to Turkey's membership application, the government presented the customs union as a last chance to guarantee Turkey's right of membership. Therefore, PBOs became engaged in an unprecedented effort to seek the collaboration of the European business community in gaining the approval of the European Parliament for a Turkey–EU customs union. At the same time, they increased their pressure on the Turkish government to ensure that they were consulted on negotiations with the EU. Obviously, the most important actors of this lobbying campaign towards the members of the European Parliament were the large entrepreneurs who had developed important business links with European companies. Along with this mobilisation, TUSIAD insisted that 'economic diplomacy' should be set up as a means to shape the external policies according to the national economic interests. This new concept was thereafter used to legitimise TUSIAD's engagement in Turkey–EU relations.[11] The efforts of TUSIAD in favour of EU membership culminated with the opening of a representative office in Brussels.[12] By this initiative, the organisation aimed to strengthen its presence within UNICE as well as its representation towards the EU institutions.

In parallel to its efforts to follow the 'organizational structures and the working principles' of its Western counterparts (TUSIAD, 1994: 38), TUSIAD adapted its internal structure to UNICE's organisational scheme. The significance of UNICE membership has been enhanced since the establishment of an EU-level social dialogue mechanism in the Maastricht Treaty.[13] As a first-level social partner, UNICE shares with the European Trade Unions Confederation (ETUC) and European Centre of Enterprises with Public Participation and of Enterprises of General Economic Interest (CEEP) the right to initiate EU legislation in social and employment policies. Therefore, despite the absence of such a mechanism at national level, TUSIAD and TISK became part of a governance structure guaranteeing the formal participation of PBOs in policy-making. In addition, UNICE members are business organisations qualified by their independence from the state, and their voluntary membership basis. In that respect, UNICE membership also contributed to the debate on the definition of PBOs' structures and roles in Turkey.[14]

The customs union also marked a turning point for the representation of Turkish SMEs and craftsmen at the EU level. Together with the Foundation for Professional Formation and Small Trade (MEKSA), the Small and Medium Industry Development Organisation (KOSGEB) and the Union of Turkish Craftsmen and Tradesmen Credit Cooperatives (TESKOMB), the Confederation of Turkish Craftsmen and Small Traders (TESK) opened a representative office in Brussels and became an associate member of the Association of Crafts and Small and Medium-Sized Enterprises of the European Union (UEAPME)[15] in 1994. The Brussels office provided a valuable source of information for Turkish SMEs and craftsmen about EU policies and programmes. Furthermore, through UEAPME, TESK aims to contribute to Turkey's harmonisation with EU policies on enterprise and SMEs. In the aftermath of the customs union, the Brussels office also lobbied actively to stop the European Parliament vetoing Turkey's involvement in the EU's education and training programmes.

Until the establishment of the customs union in 1996, however, the PBOs lacked a visionary strategy towards the association regime between Turkey and the EU. Despite the explicit target of the Association Agreement to open the Turkish economy to the European market, protectionist trends persisted in national economic policies until the 1980s. The main concern for national business community was to face the radical economic policy shift of the 1980s. The programme of 24 January 1980 was drafted as a result of the 'recognition of Turkey's constraints and of the revision expected in its policy stance by external creditors (World Bank, IMF)' (Kazgan, 1993: 71). Although the programme has put an end to Turkey's state-controlled inward-looking economic policy, during the mid-1980s the government failed to resist the distributional pressure of the export-oriented economic policy regime. Consequently, it turned to populism, which is a legacy of the former protectionist economic regime.

Traditionally, '[the] Turkish state has appeared as the major source of uncertainty that characterised the socio-economic and political context of business activity' (Buğra, 1998: 523). The structural basis of government–business relations in Turkey weakened the PBOs *vis-à-vis* their members. The Turkish state considered interest organisations as potential sources of conflict and therefore preferred to develop corporate relations with semi-official chambers based on obligatory membership. It also preferred to allocate public resources to the business community on a selective rather than a collective basis. The unwillingness of coalition governments of the 1990s to confront the short-term costs of the adjustment policies under electoral constraints provided a favourable environment for the continuity of clientelistic relations[16] between politicians and business.

This traditional policy style had significant effects on policy-making so far as compliance with the Association Agreement provisions, especially the customs union, was concerned. The Turkish business community was preoccupied with the immediate effect of tariff reductions on sensitive sectors, such as the automotive sector, pharmaceuticals, iron and steel, and paper. Hence, sectoral organisations and the business community were engaged in harsh negotiations with the government to protect themselves from the consequences of the new customs regime. The policy-makers had to find ways of compensating the sectors likely to lose out because the Turkish business community exploited the government's short-sighted policy style 'to present their private losses as social losses which the state must internalise' (Uğur, 1999: 59). Given this pattern of government–business relations, PBOs have remained essentially irrelevant in the implementation of the association regime.[17]

The issue of the political Copenhagen criteria was not perceived as a serious threat to the prospect of membership until the Luxembourg summit decision of December 1997, which blurred Turkey's perspective in the enlargement process. The Turkish government considered the summit's conclusions discriminatory and stated that the political criteria with 'concealed intentions' were unacceptable for Turkey (Ministry of Foreign Affairs, 1997). It declared that bilateral relations would progress depending on the EU's efforts to respect its commitments towards Turkey.

As a result, the Turkish business community, especially large entrepreneurs, voiced their serious concern about the possible isolation of Turkey as compared with the CEECs. It was increasingly felt that the CEECs would constitute an essential rival for Turkey in attracting foreign direct investment (FDI). While the customs union could not attract the flow of FDI towards Turkey, the share of FDI in CEECs' GNP increased to a considerable level during the pre-accession period.

After 1997, Turkish PBOs, TUSIAD in particular, continued strengthening their ties with their European counterparts with and through whom they lobbied EU institutions and governments in favour of Turkey's EU membership. In this context, TUSIAD campaigned through UNICE for the European business community's endorsement of Turkey's candidacy. Before both the Helsinki (December 1999) and the Copenhagen (December 2002) summits, TUSIAD visited EU capitals in collaboration with UNICE member federations whose members have important business links with Turkey and are members of TUSIAD. Furthermore, UNICE position papers on enlargement expressed European business support for the membership perspective of Turkey. In Turkey, TUSIAD urged the government to take the necessary steps to accomplish its reform process, without which the country was losing its negotiating power in the international arena. At the national level, the organisation conveyed its messages through direct contacts with the government and parliamentarians or by addressing itself to the public at large through its publications and the media.

The publication of a comprehensive report on democratisation in Turkey (Tanör, 1997) was a significant example of the public campaigns led by TUSIAD. Through seminars and publications, TUSIAD fostered public debate on the serious political issues listed in that report. In this context, academics, parliamentarians and businesspeople came together to discuss different approaches to the political reform process.[18] Under its policy committees and working groups,[19] TUSIAD tried to enhance the participation of its members in the organisation's agenda-setting and principal activities. TUSIAD's Parliamentary Affairs Committee has become an important unit that scrutinised the committee work within the Turkish National Assembly and conveyed TUSIAD's position on related issues to relevant ministers and deputies. Furthermore, TUSIAD's Ankara office was established after the Helsinki summit, in order to strengthen and accelerate the involvement of TUSIAD within the domestic decision-making processes (TUSIAD, 2000: 40). As a consequence, and despite the traditional hesitation of the public authorities to cooperate with the voluntary business associations, TUSIAD has become an important interlocutor for the policy-makers in the legislative reform process.

Moreover, Turkish business, workers and professional organisations continued their dialogue with their European partners through the JCC. After the Luxembourg summit, the parties issued a common declaration in favour of strengthening Turkey–EU relations. (Joint Consultative Committee, 1998; Işık, 2001: 164) Progressively, Turkish organisations represented in the JCC became familiar with the ways in which European public and private actors interact at both the EU and the member state level. In a break with the traditional policy style in Turkey, where a formal platform for consultation between private and public actors was lacking, they have started to socialise within the EU, where the economic and social organisations actively participate in policy-making. This experience has led them to take the initiative to put pressure on the Turkish government to set up a formal and efficient dialogue with economic and social actors. Such a process accelerated the creation of the Economic and Social Council (ESC), which has emerged as a means of coordinating industrial relations in European countries and of enabling the social partners to participate in the policy debate and decision-making.

The approval of Turkey's candidate status at the Helsinki summit (December 1999) formally confirmed the country's obligation to fulfil the Copenhagen political criteria in order to start the accession negotiations. In accordance with the pre-accession strategy, the EU Council of Ministers approved an Accession Partnership (AP) for Turkey, which is a road map for the reform process towards the fulfilment of the Copenhagen criteria. In response, the National Programme for the Adoption of the *Acquis* (NPAA) presented the Turkish government's programme, setting the short- and medium-term priorities of the AP within a time frame. Despite apparent reluctance, the government's commitment through NPAA gave fresh impetus to Turkey's reform process, especially in dealing with the democratic deficit. Yet Turkey remains the only candidate country that has failed to start accession negotiations with the EU, because of non-compliance with the Copenhagen political criteria. In that sense, the Helsinki decision rendered the cost of delaying the reforms clearer for both the business community and the public at large.

5.2 From limited economic policy convergence to transformation of domestic structures

Until the end of the 1990s, economic policy convergence was the principal objective of the association regime between Turkey and EU. However, the formal recognition of Turkey's candidacy in 1999 triggered a new debate over the compatibility of Turkey's political structures and norms with EU membership. Fulfilling the Copenhagen political criteria for accession requires comprehensive policy convergence with the EU, which implies a deep transformation of domestic structures. In addition, the process challenges the dominant understanding and norms about democracy, human rights and the rule of law in the country. From an institutionalist analytical perspective, Europeanisation as the incorporation of new rules and norms into domestic structures can occur if there exists a certain degree of compatibility between the new norms and the 'collectively shared understanding and meaning structure' at the national level.

The institutionalist approach foresees that, in this case, 'actors are more open to learning and persuasion' (Börzel and Risse, 2000: 11). For Turkey, the accession criteria challenge the most entrenched values of national political regime and identity, such as the state's role in economic and social life, the role of the army in politics, and the definition of minorities' rights. We might, then, expect resistance to change, on the basis of the perceived need to preserve the regime's identity and integrity. However, the same approach predicts that 'radical and rapid transformations are likely ... under special conditions' characterised by crisis and external pressure (Olsen, 1996: 253). While these factors could increase the probability of profound change, they might not be sufficient without a certain level of agency by the government, the opposition parties or Turkish society.

The recent reform process in Turkey seems to confirm this hypothesis. During the period of unstable coalition governments in the 1990s, the domestic political system was affected by a combination of policy failures and external shocks that resulted in severe economic crises. Furthermore, the unrest in south-east Turkey and the resurgence of political Islam exacerbated the security concerns of the state. These events increased the cost of reforming the 1980 Constitution, even though it was considered a source of democratic deficit in Turkey. Nevertheless, after the Helsinki summit at the end of 1999 a spectacular reform movement was started by one of the most incongruous coalition governments in Turkish political history. Turkey's exclusion from the enlargement process in 1997 and the arrest of the Kurdistan Workers' Party's (PKK) leader during the minority government rule of the Democratic Left Party (DSP) were important factors in the electoral victory of the coalition partners DSP and the Nationalist Action Party (MHP) in the April 1999 elections. The pro-European Motherland Party (MP) remained the smaller partner within this coalition.

As argued earlier, political instability and electoral concerns prevented the government from mobilising serious resources for long-term reform initiatives. Also, the frustration in Turkish public opinion about the country's membership prospects made it difficult for governments to justify any move to adopt EU norms. I argue, therefore, that given the serious incompatibility of EU norms, social pressure becomes an important factor to explain the degree and the direction of reforms towards fulfilling the accession criteria. While Turkish civil society is traditionally weak *vis-à-vis* the state, Turkish PBOs appear as significant actors to challenge the government's policy agenda. Familiarisation with the EU-level governance system has provided them with additional resources to act upon the domestic agenda-setting process. Obviously, governments' efficiency concerns in delivering economic welfare also enhance their responsiveness to business demands in modern societies.

The following cases highlight the role of private actors, notably the PBOs, in recent reforms. I suggest that although the Europeanisation process had not fundamentally changed business–government relations in policy-making, it affected PBOs' approach to issues in their new socio-economic environment. We examine two steps in the recent reform process in Turkey: (i) improvement of the democratic standards; and (ii) establishment of the ESC.

5.2.1 Improving democratic standards

After the Helsinki summit, the pre-accession strategy made a qualitative difference to the Turkish reform process. The democratic deficit of the national regime began to be perceived as an urgent problem to be addressed by the government. PBOs, TUSIAD in particular, aimed to address Turkish society's concerns about Turkey's membership process in order to foster public support for political reforms. TUSIAD's report on democratisation (Tanör, 1997) in 1997 was the first and the boldest step reflecting business commitment to the adoption of European norms. The organisation emphasised the interdependence of economic and political liberalisation and claimed that 'all Turkish citizens and all institutions representing the civil society are obliged to strive towards the improvement and internalisation of democracy'.[20] Clearly, TUSIAD needed to legitimise its stance *vis-à-vis* both the public and its own members to promoting the democratisation in Turkey.

There has been a long-lasting confrontation between the old and young generations of TUSIAD members, starting from the first critical stance of Ömer Dinçkök[21] towards the government on democratic standards, until the publication of the report on democratisation (Buğra, 1995, 1998). Europeanisation shaped the priorities and the style of TUSIAD's attitude in favour of the vision of its young-generation leaders and led the organisation to be proactive on the political reform process. Gradually, TUSIAD reports and opinions became a valuable source of information for the European Commission officials by which to assess the government's performance in the reform process. Together with its increasing prestige in EU policy-making circles, the development of its internal structure allowed the organisation to become a non-negligible partner in the national reform process. Consequently, TUSIAD's discourse and actions urging compliance with the accession criteria set a serious constraint on the government's policy agenda.

After being elected in a Euro-sceptical political environment, the DSP–MHP–ANAP coalition was confronted by an urgent policy agenda prescribed by the EU pre-accession strategy. A spectacular reform process from 1999 led to a series of constitutional amendments even in the most sensitive issues such as the death penalty, the right to education in mother tongue, and the composition and role of the National Security Council (NSC). Despite its parliamentary majority, the current Justice and Development Party (AKP) government, elected in November 2002, is not in a stronger position to implement the reform agenda. The secular state elite[22] and the public are highly sceptical about the party's pro-Islamic origins. To legitimise its untested government (supported by 34 per cent of the electorate), the AKP certainly needs to address the perception of threat to the secular regime and tackle the issues of compliance with the accession criteria by 2004.[23] In view of this background, the support of pro-Western business representatives in Turkey and European policy-makers certainly becomes crucial for the government.[24]

In the aftermath of the elections, several EU officials expressed their satisfaction with the AKP's commitment to fulfil the accession criteria. Furthermore, TUSIAD declared that five years after its publication, its famous democratisation report has served its purpose (TUSIAD, 2002), as integration with the EU has been declared and adopted as state policy by the current AKP government (Dünya, 2003). Yet it is still too early to declare triumph when uncertainty over the reform is intensified by recurrent crises, including the war in Iraq, accentuated by the government's lack of experience in war diplomacy as well as post-war politics. As regards to the PBOs' intervention in the reform process, we should mention the position of another Turkish PBO, namely the Association of Independent Industrialists and Businessmen (MUSIAD), which has remained basically aloof from the Europeanisation trend as I have identified it here. Given its constituency's support for the current AKP government, the organisation has become an important actor affecting the government's policy-agenda setting. Hence, it is important to understand the significance of the evolution of its originally Euro-sceptic position.

MUSIAD members are businesspeople, mainly from dynamic, export-oriented SMEs in Anatolian towns who became influential in the 1980s following the economic policy shift in Turkey and the worldwide reputation of the Asian capitalist model. Also called 'Anatolian Tigers' (by analogy with Asian Tigers), these businesspeople formed MUSIAD[25] in 1990 to improve their representation within the national associational system. MUSIAD appeared to be an organisation advocating a different model of economic and social development using 'a certain interpretation of Islam' to ensure the coherence of its members and 'to represent their economic interest as an integral component of an ideological mission' (Buğra, 1998: 522, 528). Advocating an East Asian development model, MUSIAD supported the Islamic Virtue Party (FP) and its coalition government with the centre-right True Path Party (DYP) in the late 1990s. That government's poor performance and the upsurge of political Islam triggered a strong reaction from Turkish business and workers' organisations (Baydur, 2000). Adopting the title of 'civil initiative', TISK, TOBB, TESK and Türk-İş (the Turkish Trade Unions Confederation) undertook an unprecedented joint action against the perceived threat to the stability of the secular regime in 1997. This joint opposition campaign constituted part of the build-up towards the National Security Council recommendations of 28 February 1997 that eventually led to the demise of the coalition government.

Since then, the pro-Islamic political tendency within the AKP, a modernist faction of the former RP, and MUSIAD have undergone a parallel evolution towards adopting a discourse emphasising the compatibility of EU membership with the 'Islamic democrat' identity of Turkish society. Initially, MUSIAD was more enthusiastic about the promotion of alternative foreign economic relations to EU membership and the customs union (MUSIAD, 1996: 18). Recently, however, the organisation has become increasingly interested in the accession process, yet underlining the importance of the country's own strategic potential in its relations with the EU (Çerçeve, 2003: 1). Moreover, the organisation, together with other business organisations, joined the 'civil society declaration' in favour of the EU membership despite the fact that it had been doubtful about the relevance of Europeanisation (Ilknur, 2002). The shift in MUSIAD discourse illustrates the change in policy-making dynamics in Turkey in parallel to the Europeanisation of the main Turkish PBOs.

An important dimension of Turkish PBOs' Europeanisation is the way they have gradually related the fulfilment of EU membership obligations to the achievements of national political and economic stability. The main motivation of PBOs' interest in the accession process is clearly the economic consequences of the process for the business sectors they represent. Nevertheless, from mid-1995 the political dimension prevailed in the debate over Turkey's EU membership aspiration. As we mentioned earlier, SMEs were initially highly sensitive towards the EU's 'far-reaching' demands concerning the national political regime. By contrast, the representatives of large business were more confident about the compatibility of Turkish democratic liberalisation with the sustainability of the liberal economy in the country. Therefore, they could defend the integration of Turkey with the EU not only in terms of the competitiveness of the economy, but also in the light of the popular aspiration towards the stability of the democratic regime in the country.

The accession process entails important short-term costs for an important part of the Turkish economy – in particular, the SMEs. Nevertheless, the mainstream debate stressing the qualitative contributions of EU membership for Turkey restricts the possibility of slowing down or reversing the reform process solely on the basis of particularistic interests. Thus, it is becoming inappropriate for MUSIAD, which basically represents a traditionalist line within domestic politics, to defend the distinctive characteristics of the national economy or political culture in opposition to adopting the EU norms. What we observe is essentially the success of a 'rhetorical action' or 'the strategic use of norm-based arguments' (Schimmelfennig, 2001: 48), which currently ties the hands of political actors who might lose from the comprehensive reform process. As long as a credible membership perspective is maintained, this normative framework might generate an important stimulation for the execution of the current reform agenda.

5.2.2   Institutionalisation of the concerted approach to policy-making

Developments in industrial relations during the 1980s in Europe led to the reorganisation and restructuring of concerted practices in collective bargaining.[26] While the dimension and level of concerted action remained diverse, more informal ways of consulting and acting in concert at the national level have become the norm. Yet restructuring of industrial relations in the candidate countries has led to the establishment of the Economic and Social Councils (ESCs). The European Commission considers the ESCs important institutional structures that can contribute to the development of sound industrial relations in candidate countries. It supports their establishment as a crucial step 'in the integration of basic values and features of the European social model'. Moreover, the European Commission believes that the tripartite process of consultation by government, employers and workers within ESCs, despite its deficiencies, has contributed to the avoidance of conflicts in the structural reform process in the CEECs (European Commission, 2002).

The establishment of the ESC in Turkey is an important development in the process of compliance with the EU *acquis* on social and unemployment policy. In addition, it affects the Turkish state's traditions and its understanding of economic and social governance. Europeanisation is an apparent factor in the establishment of the ESC in Turkey. Although the formation of a tripartite forum in industrial relations had been discussed since the 1970s, the current law[27] on the ESC has been influenced by the developments related to the accession regime between Turkey and the EU. Under the Democratisation and Restructuring Implementation Plan of 18 May 1994, the government of the day committed itself to establishing an ESC in Turkey. In fact, the first government decree in this field made explicit reference to the Association Agreement (article 27). Subsequent government decrees remained insufficient to provide a formal status for the national ESC until 2001.[28] The AP put an end to the government's discretion in preventing the institutionalisation of concerted action in economic and social policy-making by requiring a calendar for legislative work in this field.

The JCC appeared to be a crucial EU-level platform that shaped the vision of Turkish PBOs concerning concerted practices in industrial relations. The interaction between the European and the Turkish organisations within the JCC[29] has affected the dialogue between Turkish PBOs and the workers' organisations. Observing the avenues that the JCC provided for dialogue between business and workers, and the participation of economic and social organisations in policy-making in EU countries, Turkish PBOs started to intensify their demands for similar structures in Turkey. However, the PBOs' divergent interests and priorities prevented them from reaching a consensus on their strategy towards the national legislative process. Two conflicting models were tabled by these organisations, which weakened the position of peak business and workers organisations *vis-à-vis* the government's legislative work.

The JCC proposal, led by TESK and the Istanbul Chamber of Industry (ISO), was essentially based on European models and advocated a multipartite structure. It envisaged a consultative body consolidated by constitutional and legislative guarantees whereby civil participation was extended to include all categories of interests represented in the JCC, and the government's presence and authority was restricted. Identifying themselves as *de facto* members of the national ESC, these organisations also wanted it to become the formal basis of participative democracy. By contrast, the 'civil initiative'[30] group aimed to strengthen the dialogue between employers and workers as a means of tackling the consequences of recurrent economic crises, which were seen as a cause of social unrest in the country. This group had emerged as a political reaction to the government policy failure and to the perceived threat to the secular regime, but it attempted to transform this *ad hoc* cooperation into an institutionalised participation in national social and employment policy-making. In its proposal, the ESC was foreseen to be a high-level tripartite dialogue forum between the socio-economic organisations and the state.

Unable to bridge the gap between these two proposals, the ISO put forward another proposal – making explicit reference to Turkey's contractual obligation under the Association Agreement to establish a national ESC. The ISO's view was that the business group in that platform should comprise Turkish PBOs that are members of EU-level business organisations such as UNICE and Eurochambres. Although this proposal has not been accepted, it remains an important example of the way in which the vision of Turkish PBOs has been influenced by their socialisation at the EU level. Also, TUSIAD has promoted the improvement of industrial relations in Turkey to ensure the sustainability of economic competitiveness.[31] Recently, its Social Affairs Committee worked on European models and prepared TUSIAD's position concerning the formation of the ESC. The organisation urged the strengthening of this method of acting in concert with legislative guarantees, and the effective participation of autonomous civil society organisations, including academics. It defended its right to participate in the national ESC on the grounds that it is a member of UNICE, the 'highest level business organization' at EU level. In addition, as this platform is also supposed to be responsible for Turkey's relations with international organisations, namely the EU, TUSIAD argued that its exclusion would be an important weakness for the ESC (TUSIAD, 1997: 51).

The ESC still remains weak, and the government keeps its dominant position *vis-à-vis* the socio-economic actors within it. While the proponents of the 'civil initiative' (TOBB and TISK) remained confident in the capacities of the current law, the advocates of the JCC model for civil participation in the national ESC (the ISO, TESK and also DISK) believe that the law needs to be improved. The ISO Board President (also the co-chair of JCC), H. Kavi, is convinced that the evolution of organisational leadership both in Turkish business and on the workers' side would make them more open to Europeanisation. That would, in turn, gradually affect both side's positions concerning the structure and role of the ESC.[32]

While the debate on social dialogue in Turkey is not closed, Europeanisation continues to make Turkish PBOs more familiar with the concerted policy-making practices in the EU countries. Moreover, the support of the European Commission and social partners for the strengthening of both business and the workers' organisations in the candidate countries is crucial for the development of European-model industrial relations in Turkey. Therefore, the ESC case can be considered another example of how the Europeanisation of Turkish PBOs has affected business–government relations in Turkey.

Concluding remarks

The cases elaborated in this chapter show that the accession process has transformed the political and social conditions within which Turkish PBOs operate. Moreover, they demonstrate that being part of the EU policy-making network has gradually affected their characteristics. To a large extent, this is inevitable, because EU-level policy-making is a complex and unpredictable mechanism. First, it is as open to interest groups as to the politico-administrative elites of member states. Second, agenda-setting and implementation of decisions occur in a political setting of multi-level governance. Therefore, business organisations have to follow national and EU-level agendas at the same time. Third, they need to acquire a good knowledge of the decision-making mechanism in order to act at the earliest stage possible. Finally, they have to develop good contacts with European Commission officials and Members of the European Parliament, and be capable of forming coalitions with their European counterparts (Mazey and Richardson, 1993).

The accession process has reached a crucial stage, which imposes an additional constraint on the government policy agenda. The NPAA binds the Turkish government with a formal road map and timetable to fulfil the accession criteria. Henceforth, EU policy-makers, particularly the European Commission, will have a say on the entire process of transition in the national regime. Also, EU policy-makers, while assessing the

Turkish government's compliance with the accession criteria, communicate with autonomous interlocutors such as PBOs. This evolution implies an important change in Turkish domestic structures. In fact, the European political, social and economic norms are gradually becoming a benchmark for Turkish PBOs' vision concerning the domestic reform process. Also, these organisations, through socialisation within the EU policy-making process, are acquiring important resources and insights that will enable them to promote a new discourse in national policy-making. As a result, the Europeanisation of the Turkish PBOs has considerably altered the political dynamics of national policy-making.

As Greenwood argues, interest organisations 'are themselves socialised by their participation in European public affairs, they act as bearers of ideas ... and they socialise their members to the norms operating at the European level' (1997: 25). I believe that, similarly, Turkish PBOs' attitudes are being gradually shaped by EU rules and norms; thus, they are becoming significant agents in persuading their members and the public of the compatibility of the EU accession criteria with national norms and values. Hence, they provide major impetus for public pressure on the government's policy agenda to execute key structural reforms. This, in turn, is a crucial force driving the policy-makers to carry out their contractual obligations to fulfil the accession criteria. Although this peculiar social pressure seems to give a boost to the national reform process, its sustainability clearly depends on the government's capacity to develop and implement a coherent strategy.

Actually, the distribution of the structural adjustment costs associated with EU membership and the government's responsiveness to public pressure are highly likely to affect the pace of reforms. In this context, MUSIAD's appeals to the government seem to represent a distributional pressure mainly from an SME perspective, though one coloured with a pro-Islamic discourse. MUSIAD is an organisation that remained outside the Europeanisation trend. Therefore, it would be understandable were it to be opposed to the mainstream reform process. We have observed, however, that the current normative framework promoted by the Europeanised Turkish PBOs constrains MUSIAD, like any other socio-economic group, to defend its particularistic interests *vis-à-vis* the government. In addition, the experience of 1997 limits the current government's responsiveness to MUSIAD its likely conservative appeal because of the sensitivity to any compromise affecting the stability of the secular regime. Nevertheless, any loosening of the pressure from the EU might trigger the rise of wider particularistic demands on the government. If the prospect of membership is blurred or left uncertain, alternative normative discourses might prevail and justify a new rhetorical action. This development could challenge the momentum of reforms despite the aspirations of the Turkish public to enjoy a genuinely democratic society.

In this chapter, we examined some examples of the causality between the progressive integration of Turkish PBOs' to EU governance and their changing role in the domestic reform process. In this respect, we maintained that TUSIAD, by adopting UNICE's organisational structure, could efficiently use input from the EU to strengthen its lobbying strategy in Turkey. As to its advocacy to improve national democratic standards, its commitment was already clear, given the stance of its younger-generation leaders towards government policies. However, increased interaction with European business through UNICE enhanced the legitimacy of the organisation's proactive role in the promotion of democratisation in Turkey. Furthermore, the JCC enhanced Turkish PBOs' consciousness concerning social reconciliation and the institutionalisation of concerted action in social and economic policy-making. In addition, the more that Turkish sectoral business organisations became Europeanised,[33] the more significant they become in analysing the policy convergence towards the adoption of the EU *acquis*. They should, therefore, be taken into consideration in the assessment of the legal harmonisation process, especially after the opening of the accession negotiations with the EU. PBOs will also remain important actors for alleviating conflicts of interest among the business community during the adoption of the single market *acquis*.

Notes

The views expressed in this chapter are those of the author and do not necessarily represent those of the Turkish Industry and Business Association (TUSIAD).

1 Peak business associations (PBOs) are defined as 'sector-unspecific (that is, intersectoral, general, "horizontal", comprehensive, encompassing or inclusive, according to linguistic preferences) forms of interest organizations' (Lanzalaco, 1992: 174). The term 'PBOs' is preferred in this chapter to avoid any confusion arising from the legal status of the business interest groups – that is, whether they are associations, federations, confederations or unions.

2 '"[A]ssociational system" in the context of the analysis on the peak business organization is "the universe of all business interest associations representing the common general, cross sector interests of capitalists in a given (national, subnational of transnational) system"' (Lanzalaco, 1992: 204)

3 'Accession criteria' and 'the Copenhagen criteria' will be used interchangeably in the chapter. They are as follows: being a stable democracy that respects human rights, the rule of law and the protection of minorities; having a functioning market economy; and adopting the common rules and policies that make up the body of EU law.

4 The Association Agreement established an association regime with a framework for the transitional arrangements for Turkey to move from a protectionist to an open economy. The provisions of this agreement, in particular the establishment of a customs union regime with the EU, necessitate policy convergence between the parties in areas such as external trade regime, intellectual and industrial property, and competition policies.

5 The JCC brings together 18 bodies representing economic and social interest organisations of the EU and Turkey. The Turkish delegation on the JCC for 2000–2002 included the following: Group I, employers: TOBB (represented by the Istanbul Chamber of Industry (ISO), the Istanbul Chamber of Commerce

(ITO), the Economic Development Foundation (IKV) and the Turkish Bankers Union; TISK; Group II, workers' confederations: three major trade union confederations, namely Türk-İs, Hak-İs and DISK; Group III, other interests: the Union of Turkish Chambers of Agriculture (TZOB); the Confederation of Turkish Craftsmen and Small Traders (TESK), the Turkish Bar Association; changing members: the Union of Turkish Architects and Engineers (TMMOB); the Turkish Industrial Relations Association; and the Turkish Consumers' Association.

6 The recommendations of the JCC are submitted to the Association Council, which is the executive and policy-making body within the association regime.

7 The IKV was founded by the Istanbul Chamber of Commerce and the Istanbul Chamber of Industry in 1965.

8 Founded in 1958, UNICE represents national federations of European PBOs. It has 35 members and 4 observers from 28 European countries. Five policy committees and 60 working groups support its work. http://www.unice.org.

9 Also, the Turkish workers' confederations DISK and Türk-İs became members of ETUC in 1986.

10 Founded in 1958, Eurochambres represents more than 1,600 chambers of commerce and industry, most of them with public law status, and their national organisations in 40 countries. It represents over 15 million businesses, of which 95 per cent are SMEs. http://www.eurochambres.be.

11 'Conscious of the importance of the economic diplomacy activities for the future of Turkey, we believe that the businessmen should become the country's open face to the world' (Kayhan, 1998). Muharrem Kayhan was President of the TUSIAD Board in 1997–1998.

12 The TUSIAD Permanent Delegate in Brussels represents TISK *vis-à-vis* the EU and UNICE.

13 The Maastricht Treaty institutionally recognised the social dialogue at EU level. This allows social partners to negotiate European-level agreements that can be transposed into EU law. The Commission should also consult the social partners on the possible direction of its legal initiatives and the content of its actual proposals. This mechanism has been incorporated into the Amsterdam Treaty (Article 138–139).

14 In his answer to Osman Arolat's article in the newspaper *Dünya* entitled 'Is TUSIAD living an identity crisis?' (19 October 1996), Halis Komili (then Chairman of the TUSIAD Board) argued that there was no conflict between Turkish business representations to the EU by TOBB, IKV and TUSIAD, because each organisation has its own legitimate functions and they are all 'useful but different'. In this respect he stressed the characteristics of UNICE membership (letter, 23 October 1996).

15 Founded in 1979, UEAPME has 75 member organisations from national cross-sectoral federations, European branch federations and associate members. Across Europe it represents 10 million enterprises with nearly 50 million employees. http://www.ueapme.com.

16 'These relations are based on an elaborate set of loyalties (regional, social, personal and interest based) linking politicians to businessmen' (Leander, 1994: 17).

17 The Association Agreement envisaged a preparatory and a transitory stage to establish a customs union between the parties. The customs union is considered the final stage of harmonisation and coordination of economic policies between the parties, leading towards eventual membership.

18 See debate reports series 1 to 5 on www.tusiad.org (in Turkish).

19 Several technical working groups currently work under the Committees for:

Economic and Financial Affairs, Social Affairs, Parliamentary Affairs, Industrial Affairs, Company Affairs, External Relations, Information Society and New Technologies, and Relations with local and Professional Organisations.

20 Preamble by the TUSIAD Board: 'TÜSİAD, which is committed to the universal principles of democracy and human rights, together with the freedoms of enterprise, belief and opinion . . . strives to fortify the concepts of a democratic civil society and a secular state of law in Turkey' (Tanör 1997).

21 President of the TUSIAD Board, 1987–1988.

22 Heper distinguishes between the political and the state elite, where the latter includes ' "the intellectual-bureaucratic elite" and the military' (Heper and Keyman, 1999: 259).

23 When the EU Council will decide on the prospects for opening accession negotiations with Turkey.

24 One of the current policy advisers to the Prime Minister, who is one of the founders of AKP, is a TUSIAD member.

25 The 2,100 members of MUSIAD represent 10,000 firms. However, their contribution to the national value added is 23 per cent, that to exports is US$2.5 billion and their sales volume is US$5 billion. TUSIAD's 471 members represent 1,300 firms. Their contribution to value added is 47 per cent, that to exports is US$15.5 billion and their sales volume is US$69.6 billion (Sabah, 2002).

26 Treu (1992: 1–25) argues that structural factors, such as the changed conditions of the product market, the decline of national markets and of state powers, increased differentiation of the labour force and technological innovations, had an uneven impact in this context. This is mainly reflected in the level of centralisation, institutionalisation and the unionisation of the industrial relations systems.

27 Law no. 4641, adopted on 11 April 2001; *Official Gazette*, 21 April 2001, no. 24380.

28 On the legislative work of successive governments as well as the proposals of peak business and workers organisations, see Işık (2001).

29 See note 5.

30 With the participation of TZOB and Hak-Is (known as the workers' confederation linked to the RP), the group was called 'the initiative of seven'. However, DISK has withdrawn from the ESC proposal and from the group.

31 TUSIAD organised a seminar on social reconciliation and participation in 1992 and published reports in this field.

32 Interview in Brussels, 30 January 2003.

33 Business organisations in sectors such as textiles, chemicals and banking are already members of European-level sectoral organisations.

References

Ayberk, U. and E. Boduroğlu (1990), 'Les Groupes d'intérêt turcs face à la Communauté européenne', in U. Ayberk and D. Sidjanski (eds), *L'Europe du Sud dans la Communauté européenne: analyse comparative des groupes d'intérêt et de leur insertion dans le réseau communautaire*, Paris: Presses Universitaires de France, pp. 203–232.

Baydur, R. (2000), *Bizim Çete* (Our Gang), Ankara: Cem Ofset.

Bianchi, R. (1984), *Interest Groups and Political Development in Turkey*, Princeton, NJ: Princeton University Press.

Börzel, T. A. and T. Risse (2000), 'When Europe hits home: Europeanisation and domestic change', European Integration Online Paper, 4/15, available at http://eiop.or.at/eiop/texte/2000-015a.htm (accessed 29 October 2001).

Buğra, A. (1995), 'Cumhuriyet dönemi girişimcilik tarihi ve Yeni Demokrasi Hareketi (History of enterpreneurship in the Republican era and the New Democracy Movement)', *Toplum ve Bilim*, Spring/66: 29–46.

Buğra, A. (1998), 'Class, culture and state: an analysis of interest representation by two Turkish business associations', *International Journal of Middle East Studies*, vol. 30, pp. 521–539.

Çerçeve (2003), Special issue on the EU, *MUSIAD Quarterly Magazine*, April.

Draus, F. (2001), *Dialogue social dans les pays candidats à l'Union européenne, Rapport de synthèse*, prepared for CES, UNICE, UEAPME and CEEP, with the support of the European Commission, Brussels.

Dünya (2003), 'Meclis'ten bir buçuk ayda 15 yasa geçti (15 laws passed by the Assembly in one and a half months)', *Dünya* (Turkish daily), 20 January. http://www.dunyagazetesi.com.tr (accessed 10 January 2003).

Eralp, A. (1990), 'The politics of Turkish development strategies', in A. Finkel and N. Sirman (eds), *Turkish State, Turkish Society*, London: Routledge, pp. 219–258.

European Commission (2002), *Industrial Relations and Industrial Change*, Directorate General for Employment and Social Affairs, Directorate D, Manuscript, May.

Green Cowles, M. (2001), 'The transatlantic business dialogue and domestic business government relations', in M. Green Cowles, J. Caporaso and T. Risse (eds), *Transforming Europe: Europeanisation and Domestic Change*, New York: Cornell University Press, pp. 180–198.

Greenwood, J. (1997), *Representing Interests in the European Union*, Basingstoke, UK: Macmillan.

Heper, M. and E. F. Keyman (1999), 'Double-faced state: political patronage and the consolidation of democracy in Turkey', in S. Kedourie (ed.), *Turkey before and after Ataturk: Internal and External Affairs*, London: Frank Cass, pp. 259–277.

Işık, R. (2001), *Avrupa Birliği'ne doğru Ekonomik ve Sosyal Kararlara Katılım: Yeni bir Hukuki Düzenleme için Çalışma Metinleri* (Participation in Economic and Social Decisions towards the European Union: Draft Texts for New Legislation), Istanbul: Boyut Matbaacılık.

İlknur, N. (2002), '*AB için lobicilik dönemi*' (The era of lobbying for the EU), *Cumhuriyet*, 12 June.

Joint Consultative Committee (1998), Press release issued by the two co-chairmen at the fifth meeting of the EU–Turkey Joint Consultative Committee, Brussels: JCC, 21 January.

Kayhan, M. (1998), 'Çok sesli diplomasi' (Multi-voice diplomacy), *Görüş*, no. 36 (July–August), pp. 6–7.

Kazgan, G. (1993), 'External pressure and the new policy outlook', in C. Balkır, and A. M. Williams (eds), *Turkey and Europe*, London: Pinter, pp. 69–99.

Lanzalaco, L. (1992), 'Coping with heterogeneity: peak associations of business within and across Western European nations', in J. Greenwood, R. Grote Jürgen and K. Ronit (eds), *Organised Interests and the European Community*, London: Sage, pp. 173–205.

Leander A. (1994), '"Robin Hood" politics? Turkey probing a new model in the 1990s', Working Papers 94/9, European University Institute, Florence.

Lehmkuhl, D. (2000), '*Under stress: Europeanisation and trade association in the member* states', *European Integration Online Papers* 4/14, available at http://eiop.or.at/eiop/texte/2000-014a.htm (accessed March 2003).

Mazey, S. and J. J. Richardson (1993), 'A European policy style?', in J. J. Richardson and S. Mazey (eds), *Lobbying in the European Community*, Oxford: Oxford University Press, pp. 246–258.

Ministry of Foreign Affairs (1997), Statement of Turkish government concerning the conclusions of the Luxembourg Summit, 1 December 1997, available at http://www.mfa.gov.tr/grupa/ad/adab/luxembourg2.htm (accessed November 2002).

MUSIAD (1996), *Bulletin*, June–July.

Olsen, J. P. (1996), 'Europeanisation and nation-state dynamics', in V. Gustavsson and L. Lewin (eds), *The Future of the Nation-State: Essays on Cultural Pluralism and Political Integration*, London: Routledge, pp. 245–287.

Pérez-Solórzano Borragán, N. (2002), 'The impact of EU membership on interest politics in Central and Eastern Europe', ESRC 'One Europe or Several?' Civic Working Paper 1/2002.

Radaelli, C. M. (2000), 'Whither Europeanisation? Concept stretching and substantive change', European Integration Online Paper 4/8, available at http://eiop.or.at/eiop/texte/2000-008a.htm (accessed 21 August 2002).

Sabah (2002), 'İş dünyasının yeni sözcüleri MÜSİAD mı olacak' (Will the new voice of business be MUSIAD?), *Sabah* (Turkish daily), 5 November, available at http://emedya.sabah.com.tr/ (archive) (accessed 10 January 2003).

Schimmelfennig, F. (2001), 'The Community trap: liberal norms, rhetorical action, and the Eastern enlargement of the European Union', *International Organization* 55 (1) (winter): 47–80.

Tanör, B. (1997), *Perspectives on Democratisation in Turkey*, Istanbul: TUSIAD (20 January).

Treu, T. (1992), 'Tripartite social policy-making: an overview' in T. Treu (ed.), *Participation in Public Policy-Making: The Role of the Trade Unions and Employers' Associations*, Berlin: Walter de Gruyter, pp. 1–25

TUSIAD (1994), *Annual Report*.

TUSIAD (1997), *Annual Report*.

TUSIAD (2000), *Annual Report*.

TUSIAD (2002), 'Meclis tarihi bir görevi başardı' (The Assembly accomplished a historical task), TS/BAS/02-62 (press release, 3 August), Istanbul: TUSIAD.

Uğur, Mehmet (1999), *The European Union and Turkey: An Anchor Credibility Dilemma*, Aldershot, UK: Ashgate.

Part III

Religion and EU membership

6   Islamist redefinition(s) of European and Islamic identities in Turkey

Burhanettin Duran

Introduction

Sakallıoğlu (1998: 8) characterizes Kemalist modernization as a 'radical commitment to emulating and matching Europe' and points to the fragile synthesis it has formed with democracy. The uneasy relationship between Kemalism and democracy becomes even more fragile when faced with iden-tity politics – whether based on ethnic differences or on religious claims such as Islamism. Kemalism has traditionally viewed all quests for difference 'not as natural components of a pluralistic democracy but as sources of instability and as threats to unity and progress' (Göle, 1997: 84). The Islamist response has taken the form of a quest for a new paradigm that includes the rejection of Western civilization and the secular nationalist identity in favour of an Islamic identity and civilization. In that sense, Islamism is a project that tries to deal with challenges posed by Western modernity and its Turkish 'adop-tion' by Kemalism. As a consequence of the Islamist critique of the West and of the Kemalist reforms, Islamists in Turkey (including Islamist political parties, intellectuals and religious orders) have traditionally objected to Turkey's integration with the European Union (EU).

However, the Islamist approach towards the EU went through a major shift towards the end of the 1990s, when public support for Turkey's EU membership was becoming evident. Some Westernist circles in Turkey desire membership because they believe it would anchor Turkey in the West and reinforce secularism. Islamists, on the other hand, hope that membership will bring a liberal democratic political environment in which their demands can be met. Therefore, they have particularly called for compliance with the political Copenhagen criteria, which require stability of institutions guaranteeing democracy, the rule of law, human rights, and respect for and protection of minorities. What is notable here is that the remaining Islamist objections to Turkey's EU membership are no longer couched in essentialist terms. Ironically, the Islamist retreat from anti-Europeanism has shown that it is the nationalist sensitivities of the Kemalist elite over the issues of national security and independence that cloud their 'Occidentalist outlook' (Kösebalaban, 2002).

This chapter is based on a survey of some of the Islamist attitudes towards Turkey's EU membership in the aftermath of the military ultimatum of 28 February 1997 against the Islamist influence in Turkish politics. In Turkey, this is referred to as the February 28 Process.[1] The chapter discusses the following questions: How did Islamist parties and intellectuals perceive Europe before and after the February 28 Process? Has this process resulted in changes in the Islamist conceptualization of Europe and attitudes towards Turkey's EU membership? To what extent can these changes contribute to Turkey's integration with the EU? What are the weaknesses of and possible problems with the changes in Islamist discourses regarding European identity? These questions certainly apply to all Islamists, be they members of political parties, religious orders and communities, or intellectuals. However, here I shall focus primarily on political parties and some of the leading writers who are columnists and essayists in Islamist daily newspapers in Turkey.

It is also important to note here that I examine a diversity of opinions and interpretations rather than a single, coherent ideological position on various topics ranging from Kemalism and democracy to the EU. The main reason for taking 28 February 1997 as the demarcation line is my conviction that since that date, a change of attitude has taken place towards democracy and the EU among Islamist writers and intellectuals. In addition, these changes have important implications for Islamist evaluations of democracy and Europe in Turkey, as well as Turkey's potential for integration with Europe.

6.1 Anti-European roots of Islamism in Turkey

The notion of a European civilization as the 'other' and the critique of the Westernization project have long been central to Islamist discourse in Republican Turkey. Islamists argue that what is necessary is a 'real' understanding of European civilization in contrast to the 'imitative and unreal' image of the one presumably created by the Westernists/secularists. Having been humiliated and frustrated by Europe's 'imperialist' and 'colonial' past, Turkish Islamists tend to reject the European way of life. Central to this rejection is the denunciation of materialism and the destructive side of European civilization. Generally, in Islamist eyes, 'Europe' tends to suggest a monolithic reality, viewed as morally decadent in spite of its technological domination over nature (Kısakürek, 1959; Karakoç, 1986: 81; Özdenören, 1998: 220).

By the term 'West', Islamists refer mainly to Europe, not to the United States, which, however, can never be separated from Europe. In Europe/the West, the institutions of religion and the family, regarded in Islam as the very foundations of society, are seen as being in ruins. The moral crisis in the West/Europe is related to Christianity's defeat by secularization, which nourishes atheism and spiritual crisis. In that sense, the

European moral crisis is seen as the consequence of modernity. Islamists also often emphasize that the Ottoman Empire and Islam have been influential in the construction of the modern European identity as the 'other' for Europe (Özel, 2001a).

In general, Islamist discourses rest upon the premise that Islamic civilization is ontologically and epistemologically different from the West (Lewis, 1993). The relationship between the Islamic and Western civilizations is generally presented in terms of difference, and often in terms of polarization. A critical view of the West and its 'occidentalization' is crucial not only for rejecting Western modernity but also for redefining the Islamic way of life. Islamists' essentializing attitudes towards the concepts of the West and Islam constitute an ideological position that tries to demolish the superiority of Western modernity and positivism. To this end, Islamists have employed internal critics of the West (communitarian, postmodernist, and so on) to deconstruct the hegemony of its modernity project. Western/European modernity is defined as 'a pattern of thinking, a civilisation and a way of life' (Gürdoğan, 1995: 6), shaped by three constitutive elements: Greek reason, Roman law and Christian morality.

Traditionally, Islamists in Turkey have been negative concerning the prospects of Turkey's integration with the EU, seeing this as the last stage of the assimilation of Turkey's Islamic identity into the Christian West. In addition, EU membership has been considered a Kemalist plot to convert Turkey to Western civilization and as a solution that would prevent the growing influence of political Islam (Erbakan, 1991b). Turkish Islamists would also frequently argue that the EU had no intention whatsoever of accepting Turkey, and thus the customs union agreement would remain as an arrangement to keep Turkey on the periphery. Although some Islamist intellectuals have proposed more sophisticated conceptions of the West (Toprak, 1993: 255), even they, in the final analysis, shared these arguments. Turkey's will to be a member of the EU was by and large interpreted as the last stage of the Westernization process that began with the *Tanzimat* (Reform) Proclamation of 1839.[2] However, because Turkish history had been shaped by wars between Europeans and Muslims, there could not be a place for a Muslim Turkey either in NATO or in the EU as a Christian club (Bulaç, 1989: 85; Dilipak, 1989; Erbakan, 1991b: 35). In this vein, the Welfare Party (*Refah Partisi*, RP), as late as 1995, was voicing a powerful criticism of European civilization as a project that prefers 'might' (*kuvvet*) to 'right' (*hak*). It argued that capitalism will fade away just as communism did, leaving space for the Just Order (*Adil Düzen*) (Erbakan, 1991a). This line of thinking concluded that 'the history of mankind is the struggle between two civilizations: the one that prefers "power" (Western civilization) and the other that prefers "right" (Islamic civilization)' (Erbakan, 1991a: 16–17; and see also Erbakan, 1995; Yavuz, 1997). Of course, victory belongs to Islamic civilization. In that sense, there is a fundamentalist and essentialist commonality between Erbakan's discourse of civilization and Samuel Huntington's (1993) clash of civilizations.

In this context, the RP redefined Turkish national identity not only with reference to Islamic civilization but also in opposition to its European counterpart. In other words, the RP line considered Turkey's membership of the European Community to be the last stage of the imitative Westernization movement that began with the *Tanzimat*. Erbakan, the leader of the party, was sure that the Turks are not European and must strive for the establishment of an Islamic union rather than to be part of the European Community (Erbakan, 1991b: 29, 35).

During the process that started with the military's ultimatum of 28 February 1997, it seems that these Islamist arguments have lost much of their relevance among Islamist politicians and writers. Paralleling this development, the sincerity of the Kemalist elite regarding its 75-year-old desire to be part of Europe has increasingly been questioned – first when the EU decided to exclude Turkey from the eastern enlargement at the Luxembourg summit of December 1997, and then when the Turkish government prepared its own National Programme for the Adoption of the *Acquis* in March 2001.

6.2 The February 28 process: internalization of democratic vocabulary while criticizing Kemalism

The RP was closed down by the Turkish Constitutional Court on 16 January 1998 on charges of being the focal point of anti-secular activities. Its successor, the Virtue Party (*Fazilet Partisi*, FP), was founded by 33 former RP deputies under the leadership of Recai Kutan on 17 December 1997. Unlike their predecessors, however, FP cadres relinquished the emphasis on 'just order' and declared their support for Turkey's EU membership. By underlining issues of democratization, human rights and personal liberties, the FP came to criticize the headscarf-ban issue as a matter of human rights violation rather than as a suppression of an Islamic demand. It also called for democratization of the Turkish political system and supported Turkey's EU membership, which the National Outlook (*Milli Görüş*)[3] tradition had opposed since the early 1970s. This change of mind was directly related to the expectation that Turkey's membership of the EU would facilitate the realization of Islamist demands that had been suppressed by the secular Turkish state.

The FP consequently developed a new discourse that promoted principles such as rule of law, democracy, human rights and civil society. This new direction, to a certain extent, was the result of the lessons learned from the February 28 process. This new discourse was used to criticize anti-democratic aspects of the Turkish political regime and to seek civil societal pluralism (Groc, 2000). The RP opposed the Turkish practice of secularism and argued instead for the implementation of secularism as it existed in the Anglo-Saxon tradition. Islamists also tried to deconstruct Kemalist conceptualizations of Western ideas such as secularism, democracy and civil society with a view to opposing the exclusion of identity politics from Turkish political life.

Post-February 28, a central element in the Islamist critique of the Kemalist project has been the question of democratization and rule of law. According to Islamists, democracy must be instituted as a constitutional framework that guarantees liberties and rights – most notably, liberties regarding religious practice and freedom of thought and expression. Islamist writers have also denied the simple identification of democracy with elections, arguing that free elections are just one element of an established democracy. Instead, they argued that other notions of liberal democracy, such as the superiority of civilians over the armed forces, the supremacy of law, and the state as servant to the people, must be institutionalized in order to secure human rights and freedoms in Turkey (Koru, 1999a; Taşgetiren, 1998a).

Signs of a crucial transformation in the Islamist conceptualization of democracy can be observed in statements such as this: 'Voters demand not a representative and pacifying democracy' but rather 'a participatory, active and direct democracy' (Gürdoğan, 1998a; Bulaç, 1997a). In other words, the Islamist appeal to the values and institutions of liberal democracy as universal values – cited often with reference to Karl Popper's 'open society' – has extended itself to demands for radical democracy, recognition of differences, and direct participation.

According to Islamists, Turkish democracy, being imported from the West but unlike the Western experience, has not been established by a 'contract' and/or 'consensus' that originated from the struggle of competing powers. The continuing absence of consensus in the consolidation of Turkish democracy is attributed to the political culture and to the mentality of social engineering on the part of the modernizing elite, including the Ottoman as well as Republican elites (Ocaktan, 1997a; Koru, 1999b). The major obstacle that Islamists find regarding the consolidation of democracy is the authoritarian nature of the Kemalist modernization project.

The relative ease with which the military forced the *Refahyol* coalition government (formed by the RP and the True Path Party) to resign and the manner in which it co-opted labour and business associations against the RP itself testifies the fragile nature of the Turkish democratic experience. It also indicates the unwillingness of the Kemalist elite to permit the peripheral elements with distinct Islamic features to participate in Turkey's public space. The Kemalist mentality, with its exclusionary attitude towards Islamic (and Kurdish) demands for recognition, resulted in weak institutionalization of political parties and civil society, and in a series of crises concerning legitimacy, representation, participation and integration (Koru, 1999a; Gürdoğan, 1998a). The crises of representation and participation were manifest in the form of neglecting and distorting the national will (*milli irade*). In fact, this is not seen by Kemalists as a legitimate source of change in the basic parameters of the secular Republic. Islamists, therefore, argue that the Kemalist elite tries to mask the tensions of the regime, which emanate from the crises just mentioned, by resorting to undemocratic tools that are built into the constitutional framework of the system and into the symbols of Atatürk, republicanism and secularism (Taşgetiren, 1997a, 1998b).

The destruction of the Ottoman Sultanate through the establishment of the Republican regime in 1923 does not represent, in the eyes of Islamists, a development or a democratic opening towards what is achieved in the West. With respect to modern democratic values such as pluralism, the rule of law, social justice, freedoms and human rights, they argue that the Republic has not established good credentials since its inception in 1923. In their deconstruction of Kemalist narratives, Islamists tend to be concerned not with the type of the regime, but with its undemocratic nature. For instance, the so-called threat of '*irtica*' (religious fundamentalism) argument portrays the Turkish Republic as under constant threat from reactionary/theocratic forces. This discourse is then read as a way of establishing and maintaining ideological hegemony for a minority who do not want to lose their privileged status (Bulaç, 1997b).

Islamists claim that there has been no search for a different type of regime (other than the Republic) since 1923 in Turkey; and that they call only for democratization of the Republic (Emre, 1998a; Gürdoğan, 1998b). To open up the system and establish a democratic platform comprising oppositional parties, the Islamists argue that civil societal elements should be established – if need be, by cooperation with democratic forces in the world (Gürdoğan, 1999a). In a sense, this is the main line of retreat from the earlier Islamist demands for the Islamizing of the Turkish Republic.

Yet in the eyes of Islamist writers, after the ultimatum of 28 February, Turkish democracy is returning to the 1930s – shedding all the freedoms that religious people had obtained over the past 50 years since the end of single-party rule. In other words, the February 28 process is seen as the revitalization of the Kemalist one-party modernization model of the early Republican era. This period constitutes the most radical attempt at secularization in the history of Turkish modernization, by its insistence on keeping Islam within people's private lives, without allowing its appearance in the public arena (Bulaç, 1997c; Taşgetiren, 1997b; Aydın, 1998). As a result, the indirect military intervention on 28 February 1997 has brought into the open the discomfort that Kemalists felt with 'the Turkish nation's request for the revision of this modernization project' (Aydın, 1999).

Islamists have used the terms 'postmodern coup', 'extraordinary fascism', 'the twilight period/zone', 'McCarthyism' to describe the atmosphere of the post-February 28 period (Ocaktan, 1997b; Emre, 1998b; Taşgetiren, 1998b). They have also emphasized the 'politicization of law' and the 'capture' of the three powers of the democratic system (the legislature, the executive and the judiciary) by what is described as an 'oligarchic dictatorship' of the civil–military bureaucracy, the media and business cartels. The regime that the 'despotic powers' want to institute in Turkey is believed to share some commonalities with Third World regimes such as that of Saddam's Iraq and Assad's Syria (Taşgetiren, 1997c; Emre, 1997).

Since 1997, calls for a pluralist and participatory democracy, 'real' secularism and human rights in the Western/European sense have become the cornerstones of the Islamists' resistance to the further narrowing of the Turkish political landscape. In this context, the Copenhagen criteria are conceived as providing real possibilities for an Islamic quest to democratize the Turkish political system and problematize the Kemalist project of modernization. It is this 'rediscovery' of the West/Europe and its values that produced a space in which Islamists could articulate an anti-essentialist critique of the Kemalist modernization.

6.3 Islamist deconstruction of Kemalist 'narratives' and the EU

For Islamists, Kemalism is a modernization project that maintained the top-down tradition of the *Tanzimat* and *Islahat* reform movements. In that sense, it represents modernization from above by social engineering (Göle, 1997). In addition, it is not possible to claim that Kemalism has achieved its self-declared aim of reaching the level of modern civilization. In fact, Kemalism is stranded within a two-sided crisis built into its very nature: it is neither internalized by Turkish society nor respected by its source of inspiration, Europe (Bulaç, 1997d). What is more irritating for Islamists is that the Kemalist elite still insists on a state-led and secularizing model of modernization, while the modern world is evolving along democratic, pluralistic and participatory lines. Again according to Ali Bulaç (1997e), a well-known Islamist intellectual, Kemalist doctrine is presented with all the certainty of a grand narrative, determining what is good and bad, whereas such grand narratives are now outdated.

Another central element of the Islamist discourse is the question of civilization. From a civilizational standpoint, Islamist writers problematize the Kemalist project of civilization and criticize its attribution of universality to Western/European civilization. They are also critical of its show of political authority in terms of a 'civilizational conversion' (Göle, 1995: 21). The Kemalist attribution of universality to Western modernity – which in fact originated from specific historical and social conditions – is seen as a product of the perplexed mind that equated modernization with Westernization. Western modernization is unique to Western societies; it is not a universal project. Islamist intellectuals argue that this misperception created an ontological and epistemological rupture, resulting in an identity crisis at the civilizational level (Kaplan, 1998; Gürdoğan, 1998c). The crisis-laden nature of Turkish modernization initiated further crises of hegemony and legitimacy, which have been accompanied by the distortion of imported concepts such as secularism, democracy and the rule of law.

For Islamists, a significant obstacle to Turkey's integration with Europe is the Kemalist ideology and elites who resist democratization reforms on the grounds of national security. For that reason, Islamists have come to the conclusion that the Kemalist will to participate in European civilization is not a sincere one. The reluctance of the Kemalist elite to undertake the necessary reforms to meet the conditions for EU membership is attributed to the very nature of the Kemalist modernization project, which gives a central place to the state (Bulaç, 1997f; Koru, 1999c). Unlike the post-communist states of Eastern Europe, the Turkish state and state-supported private capital are against reducing the state's centralized administrative role, empowering local administrations, and further privatization. In addition to a free market economy, the EU declares human rights and democracy to be its basic principles. It is the Kemalist state and state-supported capital that really do not want either to accept these three principles or to modify the Turkish judicial system accordingly (Bulaç, 1999; Aydın, 2000).

The dilemma stems from the inherent conflict of the Kemalist modernization project, which envisages Westernization in spite of the West and the people (*Batı'ya ve halka rağmen Batılılaşma*). This conflict must be resolved by undertaking reforms concerning the Kurdish question and the revival of Islamic identity (Bulaç, 1997f). It is thus argued that in the case of full EU membership, Kemalist modernization will lose one of its basic characteristics (i.e. Westernization in spite of the West) and will eventually collapse (Bulaç, 2000a: 149). The Western rule of law, which gives priority to people's preferences, to human rights and to civility, is far from the present conditions of Turkey, identified with the National Security Council (MGK) and military democracy (*askeri demokrasi*) (Koru, 1999c). Again according to Bulaç (1997f), Turkey's Islamic identity does not constitute an obstacle for the process of its integration with the EU. The obstacle is the Kemalist elite, who are very intent on pushing Islamic identity out and away from the public and societal spheres.

Turkey's candidacy, as accepted at the Helsinki summit in 1999, is often seen as an irreversible process that necessitates change in the Kemalist mentality, which opposes democratization, human rights and liberalization. Among the Islamists, the necessity of change is expressed as the will of Turkish society (Koru, 1999d). The Copenhagen criteria, which call for the broadening of individual and liberal freedoms and for lessening of state intervention into cultural identities and beliefs as well as the economy, are in conflict with the February 28 process (Ocaktan, 1999). Hence, integration with the EU can be conceived as an antidote to the model of authoritarian Westernization that goes back to the *Tanzimat* period (Gürdoğan, 1999b).

Islamists in Turkey seem united in seeing the EU as a project of civilization. However, some tend to perceive Europe as a Judaeo-Christian civilization, while others conceive it to be a union based on common universal values such as democracy, multiculturalism and civil society. Given this divided Islamist conception of Europe, it is imperative to classify Islamist conceptualizations of European identity and current Islamist attitudes towards Turkey's EU membership. This will be the task of the following section.

6.4 Transformation of Islamist party tradition: from Islamism to New Islamism?

After the decision of the Turkish Constitutional Court on 22 June 2001 to ban the Virtue Party (FP) on the grounds that it was (also) a focal point for anti-secular activities, the former RP mayor of Istanbul, Recep Tayyip Erdoğan, formed the Justice and Development Party (*Adalet ve Kalkınma Partisi*, AKP). The founders of the AKP consisted of the reformist wing of the FP and some other conservative politicians. The FP's traditionalist wing, under the leadership of Recai Kutan, who remained loyal to Necmettin Erbakan, formed the Felicity Party (*Saadet Partisi*, SP).

The SP leader, Recai Kutan, stated that they openly supported Turkey's accession to the EU, and would deal with the democratization problems of Turkey without severing relations with the Islamic world. Referring to the change of mind in the National Outlook Movement (*Milli Görüş Hareketi*) regarding Turkey's EU membership, Kutan noted that they had rejected the European Economic Community and European Community in the past because at that time it was a Christian club with a monist and Eurocentric culture. But today the EU proposes a multicultural, equal, individualist political contract and union (Kutan, 2002).

From a civilizational standpoint, Kutan redefined Europe as a multireligious and multicultural unity that would contribute greatly to world peace and to the construction of a just international system. In spite of this redefinition, the supranational character of the EU would constitute a concern for Turkey's 'national independence'. Kutan (2002) also made it clear that the SP did not see EU membership as part of a modernization programme for Turkey. Although the membership process is expected to contribute to democratization in Turkey, the SP has some reservations about supporting accession to the EU. In part, these reservations are reflected in the argument that there would be no concessions from Turkey's Islamic identity and that the European identity must be redefined. The EU is expected to reshape its culture to admit a different country, the inheritor of a thousand-year-old civilization (Kutan, 2000; Bekaroğlu, 2000).

The AKP leadership, however, has been mainly concerned with establishing a new public discourse according to which democratization, accountability, civil society and the rule of law would shape the debate over the reform and restructuring of the Turkish political system. Indeed, what is striking about the AKP's discourse is that it represents a departure from the Islamism of the National Outlook Movement, which had pursued an anti-European stance from the 1970s to the 1990s. Since its foundation in August 2001, the AKP has declared its commitment to Turkey's integration into Europe. The party's representatives insist that theirs is a conservative party seeking the religious freedoms enjoyed in the West and will not follow an Islamic agenda. Erdoğan (2002b) has also indicated that his party is not based on religion and is a 'conservative democratic' political movement.

What has remained of Islamism in the AKP is its adherence to a rather vague version of the Islamic civilization discourse and the Islamist background of the party's leaders, including Tayyip Erdoğan, Abdullah Gül and Bülent Arınç. Although it has been part of the Islamist tradition in Turkish politics, particularly since the 1980s, the AKP took the important step of rejecting the ideologization of Islam. It also voiced an allegiance to the tradition of the Democrat Party of Adnan Menderes in the 1950s and the Motherland Party of Turgut Özal in the 1980s (Çarkoğlu, 2002). In one interview, Erdoğan stated the following:

> I appreciate the importance of pluralism, variety and tolerance. As a requirement of my beliefs, I have set my political ideals as democracy, freedoms, tolerance, basic human rights, secularism and political participation and I know that we have to go hand in hand with other countries of the world in furthering both technologic advance and democratic values.
>
> (Erdoğan, 2002a)

In its programme, the AKP argues for unconditional EU membership and states that Turkey will meet the political criteria without doubts or conditions. Its leader, Tayyip Erdoğan, states that Turkey has been in close relation with Europe both geographically and historically and therefore relations with Europe will remain one of Turkey's foreign policy priorities. He also indicates that 'Turkey will rapidly fulfil its obligations towards the EU, which apply to other candidate nations as well. Thus, it will prevent the agenda becoming occupied by artificial problems' (Erdoğan, 2002b).

Just after the elections of 3 November 2002, Erdoğan went on a tour of European capitals to secure a definite date for the start of accession negotiations, despite the fact that he was not (yet) the Prime Minister. In his visits, Erdoğan often argued that 'Europe will not only be giving Turkey a timetable. It will also be taking an historic decision on whether or not the EU is essentially a Christian club.' At the Copenhagen summit, the EU 'will either give Turkey a "date" for the start of the accession talks, thus embracing a "multiculturalism" that would avoid a clash of civilisations; or it will fail to give Turkey a "date" and will thus remain as a Christian club' (Erdoğan, 2002c).

On the issue of alternative options in Turkish foreign policy, Erdoğan stated that the EU is not a geography but a model that has no political alternative in promoting democratisation. Other options can be regarded only as complementary. Being part of the European model will eliminate Turkey's security problems, for the European project has emerged out of the nationalist and religious wars in Europe and has transformed the continent into a place of stability and peace by establishing democracy and human rights (Erdoğan, 2002b). These statements, unlike the traditional Islamist arguments about Europe, not only salute the achievements of the European project but also signal a full commitment to be part of it. Several times, the AKP leader stressed that EU membership is the most important element in Turkey's modernization. Turkey has successfully completed its nationalization project ignited by the 'Republic missile', he states. It now has to realize its second biggest step with the 'EU missile' to catch up with contemporary civilization. 'In a developing and globalizing world', Erdoğan views EU membership as a necessary step 'in order not to remain as a peripheral nation on the fringes of civilization and development' (Erdoğan, 2002d).

True to its commitment to EU membership, the AKP government has sent several packages of proposed reforms to Parliament for approval in order to bring Turkish law into line with EU standards. At the same time, it welcomed UN Secretary-General Kofi Annan's plan to resolve the Cyprus problem and regarded it as a negotiable proposal.

At this point, an important question comes to mind: what is the significance of the AKP discourse for Islamism? It seems that the concepts of 'Islamic state' and 'Islamic ideology' have lost their significance in the AKP discourse. This can be traced back to public debates during the presidency of Turgut Özal (1989–1993), when Islamist writers started to question the idea of an Islamic state and the ideologization of Islam around certain journals such as *Yeni Zemin* (New Ground). However, the influence of the February 28 process has been vital, to the extent that formerly Islamist politicians such as Erdoğan have abandoned the Islamist vocabulary, with the exception of the discourse concerning Islamic civilization. This new discourse is also voiced so as to appropriate the universal values of modernity, which are now seen as compatible with Islam. Yet despite the transformation theorized by Islamist writers and politicians, there still remains a strong anti-European current among Islamist circles – and it is high time to look at their discourses on Europe.

6.5 Turkish Islamist writers at the crossroads: Islamist redefinitions of Europe

On the issue of integration with Europe, Islamist writers of Turkey seem to be divided into three positions: support, denial and hesitation. Ersin Gürdoğan (1999c), who usually underlines the promising aspects of globalization, makes the most positive comment on Europe: for him, the more Turkey is excluded from Europe, the more powerful will undemocratic forces in Turkey become. In his view, the undemocratic trend, which had its origins in the single-party rule of the 1930s and had its latest peak on 28 February 1997, contradicts the deepening wave of democratization in the post-Cold War period, and therefore it is doomed to extinction. Various statements by Turkish generals on the possibility of alternatives to the EU – such as the strengthening of ties with Russia and Iran – are rejected by Gürdoğan on the grounds that there is no alternative to EU membership (2002a).

In the age of globalization, it is impossible to catch up with European political, economic and cultural standards without integration with Europe. Following this line of argument, Gürdoğan claims that Turkey's position in the world will be empowered by a new Ottomanist representation within Europe: 'Turks have always looked to Europe, not to Asia, and the Ottoman state collapsed in Paris, London and Berlin. [The revival of] the Ottoman mission will manifest itself in Brussels, Vienna and Rome ... the history of Europe is the history of the Ottomans' (2002a). In his mind, Turkey is the small homeland while Europe is the great homeland for the Anatolian people (Gürdoğan, 2002b).

This positive attitude towards integration with the EU is closely related to the belief in the strength of Islamic culture and Anatolian entrepreneurs who will carry their civilization to Europe as the conquerors of the modern age (Gürdoğan, 1999d; Koru, 2001). Being aware of the unwillingness of conservative European circles to accept Turkey's membership, Fehmi Koru (1997) also insisted that

> we should challenge the EU's tendency to isolate Turkey from the Union. Even if we are not accepted as a member of the EU, we should continue relations with Europe. Even when things go wrong with the EU, this should not be a cause to draw closer to the United States.

In this context, the traditional Islamist fear of losing one's religiousness and religious consciousness in the process of integration with Europe is rejected by a new self-perception that envisions further Islamization of Turkey within Europe. According to Mustafa Karaalioğlu (2001), Turkey's accession to the EU will not weaken its Islamic characteristics. On the contrary, it will bring its civilizational perspective to a level where Turkey could contribute to Europe. However, this self-confident approach also calls for the elimination of the anti-Islamic bias within European culture and the transformation of the European mentality in a way that recognizes plurality of religions. Indeed, the European bias against Turkey's religious and civilizational difference is identified as the most significant potential obstacle to Turkey's full membership (Karaalioğlu, 2002).

The expectation that Turkey's EU membership will increase the scope for religious freedom and religious demands is criticized by some Islamist writers who draw on world system analysis. For instance, Mustafa Özel (1999) argues that the core powers of the capitalist world system will not allow any enlargement of freedoms and human rights in peripheral and semi-peripheral countries. In this context, the possibility of Turkey's EU membership has nothing to do with freedoms but is linked to the hegemonic rivalry between the EU and the United States. The role given to Turkey within the EU meets the military needs of Europe to defend its borders in this struggle for hegemony. Similarly, İsmet Özel (1999) claims that in spite of the refined and sophisticated characteristics of today's (capitalist) imperialism, the major feature of the relationship between the centre (*metropol*) and the periphery remains unchanged.

From this perspective, Turkey is under 'deep colonization' (*deruni kolonyalizm*), in which the elites of peripheral countries are persuaded to see the imposed (world) order as a desired goal and an ideal to be achieved. Referring to Turkey's bid for EU membership, Özel also argues that an Islamic society's search for its salvation through European values is the result of that society's taste for false happiness developed under colonization. In addition, and unlike other civilizations (Mesopotamia, Egypt, China, India, the Aztec and Inca civilizations) in world history, European civilization is the only civilization that has gained its strength by challenging spirituality, nature and the idea of creation. As such, the victory of European civilization has come to mean a retreat from spirituality, nature and the Creator (Özel, 2001b).

Upon acceptance of Turkey's candidacy at the Helsinki summit, Yusuf Kaplan suggested that Turkey was given candidacy simply because of Western concerns about keeping the country under control. The rise of the Islamic presence in Turkey is regarded by Kaplan as a new civilizational vitality that will challenge Western hegemony and interests. In fact, this vitality constituted the major factor that has obliged the EU to keep silent about the February 28 process, in contrast to its sensitivity concerning issues of human rights violations and the Kurdish question. According to Kaplan, Europe is aware of the fact that Turkey's Ottoman past and geography will play a central role in the resurgence of Islamic civilization in the Middle East (Kaplan, 1999a, b). By employing postmodernist arguments, Kaplan overemphasizes the crisis of meaning, belief and freedom in Western intellectual life and draws attention to the 'destructive' aspects of Western civilization. Western culture disrupted the chain of existence and meaning by demolishing relations between humankind, nature and God. Accordingly, the only remaining option that will put an end to the selfishness, injustice and exploitation in the world is the resurgence of Islam as a political, economic and cultural actor (Kaplan, 2001).

Another *Yenişafak* writer, Akif Emre, advances the idea that the Ottoman Empire and Islam had represented the 'other' in the eyes of Europeans and contributed greatly to the construction of the European identity in the past. The author argues that even today, in spite of the pluralist, democratic and modern universal principles of the EU, this traditional European perspective influences Europe's relations with Turkey. Consequently, any possibility of Turkey's membership is tied to the necessity of making Islamic culture less visible in Turkish society (Emre, 2002).

From this critical perspective, Islamists also find a relationship between the West and the February 28 process (Taşgetiren, 2000). It is stated that Turkey is locating itself in the post-Cold War era under the umbrella of a Western security system, by adopting an anti-fundamentalist stance that replaced the fight against communism during the Cold War. However, this positioning in the orbit of the United States–Israel axis will result in the isolation of Turkey from the rest of the world. For this group of Islamist writers, the recent Kemalist depiction of political Islam as the most dangerous internal threat is tied to NATO's conceptualization of Islamic fundamentalism as the new threat to the Western world (Taşgetiren, 1997d; Emre, 1999).

The best example of the Islamist argument that disapproves of Turkey's accession to the EU is expressed by Rasim Özdenören, who argues that the membership process necessitates democratization for the Kemalists and the abandonment of Islamic demands for Muslims. It is a contradiction to combine membership with Islamic demands that are related to the application of Islamic law (Özdenören, 2000: 157). In a similar vein, some Islamists reject the idea of integration on the grounds that there is a cultural difference between Islam and Europe. According to this viewpoint, the EU is a civilization project and within this project Turkey has no place. The argument that follows emphasizes that Turkey does not have to be European to become civilized: Turkey can democratize its political system on its own terms without having to be intimidated by the European Parliament and the EU so frequently.

Given the Westernizing effects of Kemalism, it is also argued that accession to the EU will increase Turkey's alienation from the Islamic world, assimilate the Islamic identity into Western culture, and rule out the option of the re-Islamization of Turkey (Pamak, 2002). These sorts of Islamist arguments against the EU find echoes especially among the writers of the Islamist daily *Akit* (later *Vakit*), who support democratization

measures in the membership process but see some parts of the Copenhagen criteria, such as minority rights, as a second Sèvres Treaty[4]
(Karakoç, 2000; Üzmez, 2002; Özdür, 2002). Within this camp, some
Islamists are highly critical of various European politicians and parlia-
ments that lend support to Kurdish nationalism or to allegations of
Turkish genocide of the Armenians during the First World War. European
'support' for the Greek side on the question of Cyprus, or for the Armenian claims of a massacre in Ottoman Turkey, are interpreted by a leading
member of the SP, Süleyman Arif Emre (2000), as a sign of the 'European
Crusade mentality' and as a search for a re-application of the Treaty of
Sèvres.

Some Islamists, however, insist on meeting the Copenhagen criteria
even if Turkey fails to join the EU. Stemming partly from the lessons of
the February 28 process, this insistence is also partly related to the recognition that for the first time in the history of Turkish modernization,
externally imposed change meets civil societal demands within Turkey
(Bulaç, 2000b). Bulaç (2000c) enumerates two basic factors as the reasons
for the change of mind among the Islamist circles: the authoritarian atmosphere of the February 28 process and the positive change of attitude in
Europe towards Islam and Turkey.

Yet integrationist policies that aim at creating a United States of Europe
revive some deep-seated fears of assimilation into European secular
culture. This is the case even among Islamists who support the integration
project. For example, Bulaç perceives the EU as 'a totalitarian organization' that is trying to recreate the nation-state model at a regional level.
Still adhering to the idea of Islamic union as his political imagination,
Bulaç underlines the difference between Islam and the EU as religious
and cultural: religion is marginal in the secular culture of Europe, while
this can never be accepted in Islam. After mentioning the possible
achievements of democratization through the membership process, he
gives only a functionalist and pragmatic 'yes' to EU membership (Bulaç,
2002).

Conclusions: the future of Islamism in Europe

This *tour d'horizon* of Islamist positions regarding European identity in
Turkey leads us to several important conclusions. First, the February 28
process has brought some significant changes in the Islamist conceptualizations of Europe and democracy. Islamists, after seeing the Kemalist
determination not to allow any Islamist modification in the Turkish political system, have come to re-evaluate their views on Turkey's membership
of the EU. Islamist parties and significant sectors of Islamist intellectuals
have dropped their anti-European assessments concerning Turkey's
integration with the EU. They have also adopted a new discourse according to which democratization, the rule of law and the Copenhagen criteria

should shape the reform and restructuring of the Turkish political system. As a result, Turkey's endeavour to become a full member of the EU has become compatible with their aim of democratizing the Turkish political system.

Second, the Islamist support for Turkey's EU membership is based on the premise that the process of accession is likely to force the Turkish political system to undertake significant democratic reforms that will make the Kemalist ideology less repressive and intrusive. The change in Islamist perceptions of Europe and the new discourse envisaging Islamic culture as a potential factor that can enrich European identity have been reinforced by the acceptance of a compromise between Islam and democracy. In part, this is due to the recognition that closer integration with Europe constitutes the only option by which to obtain a more open and liberal Turkish political system.

Third, the Islamist support for Turkey's integration with EU can contribute to the Europeanization of Turkey, which has been one of the main tenets of Kemalism. Ironically, however, the Europeanization project poses significant challenges for both Kemalists and Islamists. On the one hand, further Europeanization – such as the recognition of ethnic and religious identities and demands – has come to mean not only the fulfilment of the Kemalist project of Europeanization, but also a decline in the power of the Kemalist elites, who regarded themselves as guardians of the Westernizing reforms. On the other hand, Europeanization may enable the Islamists to overcome the exclusionary approach of the Kemalist elite towards Islamist demands. Yet it also poses the question of whether they want Turkish identity to become part of the European identity and Turkey part of Europe. Although Islamist discourses supportive of Turkey's membership pay much attention to 'being in Europe', they pay far less attention to 'being/becoming part of Europe'.

Fourth, the process of transformation within Turkish Islamist discourses regarding their perception of Europe and EU–Turkey relations is not yet complete. As can be seen in the Islamist discourse that disapproves of Turkey's accession to the EU, identity-related aspects of Islamism are still being voiced as a dividing line between Turkey and Europe. This signifies the difficulty of carving out a space for a Turkish Islamic identity within the European identity, and the limits of the transition from an anti- to a pro-European stance. In addition, the influence of conjunctural elements such as the February 28 process and some indicators of anti-Islamic inclinations in Europe should also be incorporated into the analysis of Islamism and its approach to Turkey's membership in the EU. European silence over the non-democratic consequences of the February 28 process – such as the ban on headscarves and the closing down of Islamist political parties – is seen by some Islamists as a sign of Europe's double standards towards Islam. Unlike the Kurdish question, human rights issues regarding religious freedom have not been paid enough attention by EU institutions.

Islamist intellectuals relate this to European 'insincerity' or interpret it as a sign of Europeans' lack of regard for democratization as the basic problem of the Turkish political system. As evidence, some Islamist writers underline the negative statements of the leaders of European Christian Democratic political parties regarding Turkey's membership, who claim that the EU is based on Christian principles and that it cannot accommodate countries such as Turkey. Some sceptical Islamists have always interpreted these statements as a sign that the EU is a Christian club in which a Muslim country such as Turkey will never be accepted. However, others argue that Europe is not a monolithic unity, though they acknowledge that there are forces inside the EU that view the European project from a Western-Christian perspective.

Fifth, the new Islamist definitions of Europe – whether positive or sceptical – underline the difficulties inherent in the construction of a common European identity. The new Islamist definitions confront Europeans with the possibility that Turkey's membership may transform Islam into a means of political mobilization within the EU and that the European public space may be reshaped politically in order to meet Islamic aspirations. In one sense, this is tantamount to accepting that the issue of Muslim communities across Europe, which have adopted the vocabulary of Islamism as a means of expressing their identities and have been making demands for equal access to social, economic and cultural resources within the EU (Glavanis, 1998: 5), will have to be acknowledged within the parameters of European identity. Islamism in Turkey will challenge and complicate this process of constructing a new, common European identity that is politically viable. If Turkey is included, Islamism can no longer be considered a minority problem of multicultural Europe. Instead, it will take the form of a multicultural and multi-religious identity problem affecting all European citizens.

Finally, a significant dimension of the Islamist impasse in accepting Turkey's integration with the EU is related to the issue of Europeanization. The complication inherent in Islamists' acceptance of full membership is necessarily compounded by their demand to redefine what is 'European'. Whether as a confrontation of civilizations or as a learning process, the concept of Europeanization in Islamist discourse has always gone together with some suspicion about Europe – a tendency that has affected Islamist discourses since the Young Turks, during the Ottoman period (Deringil, 1993). In its current variant, this suspicion is justified by comparing the EU's resistance to accepting Turkey as a full member with the policy towards Central and Eastern European countries that also fail to fulfil – or at least initially did so – some of the Copenhagen criteria. According to the Islamist perception, this mindset comes, at least in part, from the Christian mentality and the anti-Turkish biases of Europe. However, the Islamist suspicion regarding European perceptions of Turkey seems to be attenuated by the fact that the EU has a long way to go in order to realize cultural integration in the aftermath of full institutional integration. Furthermore, the supra-national aspect of the EU presupposes the need to recognize multiple identities. In the case of Turkey's membership, this indeed will mean the reinforcement of diverse religions and cultures within the idea of Europeanness. To put it differently, European identity would have to be redefined to recognize the possibility of being – at the same time – Muslim, Turkish and European.

Notes

1 Starting at the end of 1996, a series of events during the Welfare Party-led coalition government culminated in a crisis for the Turkish political regime. These events included the promise to build a mosque in Taksim, Istanbul; the invitation of the leaders of religious orders to the Prime Minister's official residence; and the Jerusalem Night celebrations in the township of Sincan near Ankara. On 28 February 1997, the National Security Council made recommendations to the government about measures to be taken against the increasing anti-secular activities. These recommendations called for the limitation of the number of religious schools; the extension of compulsory education from five to eight uninterrupted years; and a close scrutiny of Islamist business associations. (For the 18 recommendations, see the *Turkish Daily News*, 3 March 1997.) This military intervention brought down the Welfare-led coalition government, and later the Welfare Party was closed down by the Turkish Constitutional Court on the grounds of its anti-secular activities.

2 With the proclamation of the *Tanzimat* in 1839, known as *Gülhane Hatt-ı Şerifi* (the Noble Edict of the Rose Garden), the Ottoman statesmen aimed to restructure the Ottoman administration and to establish the rule of law. This edict guaranteed the safety of life, honour and property of all Ottoman subjects and the equality of Muslims and non-Muslims before the law. Davison (1990: 243) argued that the *Tanzimat* was a 'seed time' in which ideas and institutions of political modernization that later came to fruition in the Turkish Republic first took root.

3 *Milli Görüş* is the name of Islamist ideology for a series of Islamist political parties established by Necmettin Erbakan and his friends; the National Order Party (1970–1972), the National Salvation Party (1972–1980), the Welfare Party (1983–1998), the Virtue Party (1998–2001) and now the Felicity Party. Indeed, the word *Milli* (national) has been used instead of Islamic.

4 The Treaty of Sèvres, signed on 10 August 1920 by the Entente powers and the Istanbul government, reduced the Ottoman Empire to a small state in northern Asia Minor. Britain and France established mandates in different parts of the Empire while creating an independent Armenia and an autonomous Kurdistan in eastern Anatolia. Eastern Thrace and İzmir were also given to Greece. The Greek military imposition of the treaty on the nationalist independence movement in Ankara resulted in a full-scale Turkish–Greek war that lasted until 1922 (Zürcher, 1993: 153).

References

Aydın, M. A. (1998), 'Devletle milletin barışması' (Reconciliation between state and nation), *Yenişafak*, 11 July.

Aydın, M. A. (1999), 'Sistem kendine güvenini kaybetti' (The system has lost its self-confidence), *Yenişafak*, 9 January.

Aydın, M. A. (2000), 'Katılım Belgesi'nin ortaya koyduğu gerçek' (The truth exposed by the Accession [Partnership] Document), *Yenişafak*, 10 December.

Bekaroğlu, M. (2002), Untitled conference speech, in K. Alpay (ed.), *Avrupa Birliği Süreci ve Müslümanlar* (The European Union Process and the Muslims), Istanbul: Özgür-der, pp. 17–19.

Bulaç, A. (1989), 'Tanzimatın temelinde İslam–kapitalizm çatışması vardır' (The essence of *Tanzimat* is the conflict between Islam and capitalism), in M. E. Gerger (ed.), *Tanzimat'tan Avrupa Topluluğu'na Türkiye* (Turkey: From *Tanzimat* to the European Union), Istanbul: İnkilab, pp. 81–87.

Bulaç, A. (1997a), 'Bazan taraf olan bertaraf olur' (Partiality sometimes brings about elimination), *Yenişafak*, 6 November.

Bulaç, A. (1997b), 'Cumhuriyette ideolojik monarşi' (Ideological monarchy in the Republic), *Yenişafak*, 29 October.

Bulaç, A. (1997c), 'Dine ve ibadete müdahale' (Interference with religion and worship), *Yenişafak*, 18 November.

Bulaç, A. (1997d), 'Türk modernleşme projesi' (The Turkish modernization project), *Yenişafak*, 23 December.

Bulaç, A. (1997e), 'Bu gerilim aşılabilir mi?' (Can this tension be overcome?), *Yenişafak*, 25 December.

Bulaç, A. (1997f), 'Türkiye ve AB' (Turkey and the EU), *Yenişafak*, 9 December.

Bulaç, A. (1999), 'AB'nin önündeki engel' (The obstacle in front of the EU), *Zaman*, 19 October.

Bulaç, A. (2000a), 'AB süreci: kimlik ve gelecek' (The EU process: identity and future), *İslami Araştırmalar*, vol. 13, no. 2, pp. 143–153.

Bulaç, A. (2000b), 'Bir hukukçu ile AB süreci' (The EU process as viewed by a lawyer), *Zaman*, 10 June.

Bulaç, A. (2000c), 'AB'yi ne kadar tanıyoruz?' (How well do we know the EU?), *Zaman*, 26 October.

Bulaç, A. (2002), Untitled conference speech, in K. Alpay (ed.), *Avrupa Birliği Süreci ve Müslümanlar* (The European Union Process and the Muslims), Istanbul: Özgür-der, pp. 41–45.

Çarkoğlu, A. (2002), 'Turkey's November 2002 elections: a new beginning?' *Meria*, vol. 6, no. 4, pp. 30–41.

Davison, R. H. (1990), *Essays in Ottoman and Turkish History, 1774–1923: The Impact of the West*, Austin: University of Texas Press.

Deringil, S. (1993), 'The Ottoman origins of Kemalist nationalism: Namık Kemal to Mustafa Kemal', *European History Quarterly*, vol. 23, pp. 165–191.

Dilipak, A. (1989), 'Tanzimat bir komplo idi' (The *Tanzimat* was a conspiracy), in M. E. Gerger (ed.), *Tanzimat'tan Avrupa Topluluğu'na Türkiye* (Turkey: From *Tanzimat* to the European Union), Istanbul: İnkilab, pp. 133–136.

Emre, A. (1997), 'Cezayir olmadı, buyurun Suriye?' (Algeria did not work, here is Syria?), *Yenişafak*, 10 June.

Emre, A. (1998a), 'Alkışla cumhuriyet olmaz (Applause does not make a republic)', *Yenişafak*, 28 October.

Emre, A. (1998b), 'Postmodern ara rejim' (A postmodern interim regime), *Yenişafak*, 28 September.

Emre, A. (1999), 'Nato'nun başörtüsü stratejisi' (NATO's headscarf strategy), *Yenişafak*, 6 May.

Emre, A. (2002), 'AB'nin "öteki"si ve Türkiye' (The EU's "other" and Turkey), *Yenişafak*, 26 September.

Emre, S. A. (2000), 'Avrupa Birliği'nin gerçek yüzü ve bizimkiler' (The European Union's true face and our fellows), *Milli Gazete*, 17 November.

Erbakan, N. (1991a), *Adil Ekonomik Düzen* (A Just Economic Order), Ankara: Semih Ofset.

Erbakan, N. (1991b), *Türkiye'nin Temel Meseleleri* (Turkey's Fundamental Problems), Ankara: Rehber.

Erbakan, N. (1995), *Adil Düzen: 21 Soru / 21 Cevap* (The Just Order: 21 Questions / 21 Answers), election booklet.

Erdoğan, R. T. (2002a), *Turkish Daily News*, 11 December.

Erdoğan, R. T. (2002b), Sabancı Üniversitesindeki konuşma (Speech at Sabanci University), 29 March, available at http://www.akparti.com.tr (accessed 1 March 2003).

Erdoğan, R. T. (2002c), *Hürriyet*, 14 November.

Erdoğan, R. T. (2002d), 'Kesinlikle AB'den yanayız' (We are definitely in favour of the EU), *Hürriyet*, 5 June.

Glavanis, M. P. (1998), 'Political Islam within Europe: a contribution to the analytical framework', *Innovation*, vol. 11, no. 4, pp. 391–410.

Göle, N. (1995), 'Authoritarian secularism and Islamist politics: the case of Turkey', in A. R. Norton (ed.), *Civil Society in the Middle East*, Leiden: E. J. Brill, pp. 17–43.

Göle, N. (1997), 'The quest for the Islamic self within the context of modernity', in Sibel Bozdoğan and Reşat Kasaba (eds), *Rethinking Modernity and National Identity in Turkey*, Seattle: University of Washington Press, pp. 81–94.

Groc, G. (2000), 'The Virtue Party: an experiment in democratic transition', in S. Yerasimos, G. Seufert and K. Vorhoff (eds), *Civil Society in the Grip of Nationalism: Studies on Political Culture in Contemporary Turkey*, Istanbul: Orient Institut, pp. 507–559.

Gürdoğan, E. N. (1995), 'Hangi İslam? Hangi entegrasyon?' (Which Islam, which integration?), *İzlenim*, vol. 20, pp. 6–12.

Gürdoğan, E. N. (1998a), 'Temsili demokrasinin sonu' (The end of representative democracy), *Yenişafak*, 9 December.

Gürdoğan, E. N. (1998b), 'Anadolu'suz cumhuriyet' (A republic without Anatolia), *Yenişafak*, 31 October.

Gürdoğan, E. N. (1998c), 'Aydın kendisiyle hesaplaşmasını bilendir' (An intellectual is one who engages in self-assessment), *Yenişafak*, 18 June.

Gürdoğan, E. N. (1999a), 'Açıklık içinde siyasi yapının yeniden yapılanması' (Restructuring the polity under openness), *Yenişafak*, 9 May.

Gürdoğan, E. N. (1999b), 'Anadolu insanının Asya'dan Avrupa'ya uzun yürüyüşü' (The long march of the Anatolian people from Asia to Europe), *Yenişafak*, 13 December.

Gürdoğan, E. N. (1999c), 'Dayatmacılığın sonu geldi' (Forceful approach runs its course), *Yenişafak*, 8 June.

Gürdoğan, E. N. (1999d), 'Türkiye'yi Avrupa Birliği'ne girişimciler taşıyacak' (The entrepreneurs will carry Turkey to the European Union), *Yenişafak*, 23 December.

Gürdoğan, E. N. (2002a), 'Avrupa Birliği'nde olmayan Türkiye Türk ve İslam dünyasında hiç olamaz' (A Turkey outside the European Union can never count in the Turkic and Islamic world), *Yenişafak*, 10 March.

Gürdoğan, E. N. (2002b), 'Türkiye küçük, Avrupa büyük vatan' (Turkey is the small, Europe is the large country), *Yenişafak*, 12 May.

Huntington, S. P. (1993), 'The clash of civilizations?', *Foreign Affairs*, vol. 72, no. 3, pp. 22–49.

Kaplan, Y. (1998), 'Yeni bir parti, yeni bir medeniyet projesi' (A new party, a new modernity project), *Yenişafak*, 22 January.

Kaplan, Y. (1999a), 'Avrupa'nın Türkiye'si, Türkiye'nin Avrupa'sı' (Europe's Turkey, Turkey's Europe), *Yenişafak*, 13 October.

Kaplan, Y. (1999b), 'Türkiye'den korkmak veya korkmamak' (To be or not to be afraid of Turkey), *Yenişafak*, 13 December.

Kaplan, Y. (2001), 'İslâm meydan okuyor' (The challenge of Islam), *Yenişafak*, 12 December.

Karaalioğlu, M. (2001), 'AB üyeliğinde ısrar etmekte ne sakınca var!' (What is wrong in insisting on EU membership!), *Yenişafak*, 14 November.

Karaalioğlu, M. (2002), 'AB üyeliği bizi dinden imandan çıkartır mı?' (Does EU membership make us non-religious, non-believers?), *Yenişafak*, 26 March.

Karakoç, A. (2000), 'Zoraki karasevdamız' (A forced love affair), *Akit*, 23 November.

Karakoç, S. (1986), *Sur*, Istanbul: Diriliş.

Kısakürek, N. F. (1959), *İdeolacya Örgüsü* (The Web of Ideology), Istanbul: Büyük Doğu.

Koru, F. (1997), 'Türkiye Avrupayı değiştirebilir' (Turkey can change Europe), *Zaman*, 14 March.

Koru, F. (1999a), 'Korkunun faydası yok' (Scare is not a way out), *Yenişafak*, 1 February.

Koru, F. (1999b), 'O ince, hassas çizgi' (That fine, delicate line), *Yenişafak*, 7 May.

Koru, F. (1999c), 'Miş gibi yapmak' (Act of pretension), *Yenişafak*, 18 February.

Koru, F. (1999d), 'Yolculuk başladı' (The journey begins), *Yenişafak*, 13 December.

Koru, F. (2001), 'Avrupa ve İslâm' (Europe and Islam), *Yenişafak*, 20 December.

Kösebalaban, H. (2002), 'Turkey's EU membership: a clash of security cultures', *Middle East Policy*, vol. 9, no. 2, pp. 131–142.

Kutan, R. (2000), 'Son gelişmeler ışığında AB–Türkiye ilişkileri' (EU–Turkey relations in the light of recent developments), *Yeni Türkiye*, vol. 35, pp. 20–31.

Kutan, R. (2002), *SP Genel Başkanı Recai Kutanın AB Konulu Çankaya Zirvesindeki Konuşma Metni* (Speech by SP Leader Reaci Kutan at the Çankaya Summit on the EU).

Lewis, B. (1993), *Islam and the West*, Oxford: Oxford University Press.

Ocaktan, M. (1997a), 'Demokrasi barometresi tehlike sınırında' (The democracy barometer is at the danger threshold), *Yenişafak*, 22 September.

Ocaktan, M. (1997b), 'Kurtarın Türkiye'yi bu ayıptan' (Save Turkey from this disgrace), *Yenişafak*, 27 October.

Ocaktan, M. (1999), 'Demokrasi ödevi' (Homework on democracy), *Yenişafak*, 13 December.

Özdenören, R. (1998) *İki Dünya* (Two Worlds), Istanbul: İz.

Özdenören, R. (2000), 'AB'ye girme sürecinde Müslümanların ve Türkiye'nin konumu' (The position of Muslims and Turkey in the transition to EU membership), *İslami Araştırmalar*, vol. 13, no. 2, pp. 155–157.

Özdür, A. (2002), 'Kolay gelsin' (*Bon travail*), *Vakit*, 17 October.

Özel, İ. (1999), 'Deruni kolonyalizm' (Deep colonialism), *Yenişafak*, 23 February.

Özel, İ. (2001a), 'Kafirdir (noktalı virgül); Kafir değil diyen de kafirdir (nokta) (Non-believer; those who object are also non-believers)', *Gerçek Hayat*, 43, 26 October.

Özel, İ. (2001b), 'Men Çi Guyem', *Gerçek Hayat*, 61, 21 December.

Özel, M. (1999), 'Kaçaklar (Elusive players)', *Yenişafak*, 23 December.

Pamak, M. (2002), Untitled conference speech, in K. Alpay (ed.), *Avrupa Birliği Süreci ve Müslümanlar* (The European Union Process and the Muslims), Istanbul: Özgür-der, pp. 53–84.

Sakallıoğlu, Ü. C. (1998), 'Rethinking the connections between Turkey's "Western" identity versus Islam', *Critique*, no. 12 (Spring), pp. 3–18.

Taşgetiren, A. (1997a), 'Dokunmanın sınırı' (The limits to irritation)', *Yenişafak*, 22 November.

Taşgetiren, A. (1997b), 'Gölgesinde ot bitirmeyen zihniyet' (A barren mentality that fails to accommodate), *Yenişafak*, 17 November.

Taşgetiren, A. (1997c), 'Suriyeleşmek' (Syrianization), *Yenişafak*, 9 August.

Taşgetiren, A. (1997d), 'Nato nanik yapabilir' (NATO may act cheekily), *Yenişafak*, 30 October.

Taşgetiren, A. (1998a), 'Simav'da başörtüsü konuşmak' (Speaking on the headscarf in Simav), *Yenişafak*, 2 November.

Taşgetiren, A. (1998b), 'Derinleşen tekelci çizgi' (A deepening monopolist line), *Yenişafak*, 9 November.

Taşgetiren, A. (2000), 'Haçlı geni' (The Crusader gene), *Yenişafak*, November 20.

Toprak, B. (1993), 'Islamist intellectuals: revolt against industry and technology', in M. Heper, A. Öncü and H. Kramer (eds), *Turkey and the West: Changing Political and Cultural Identities*, London: I. B. Tauris, pp. 237–257.

Üzmez, H. (2002), 'AB kapıları bize açılacakmış' (EU gates were supposed to be lifted), *Vakit*, 9 August.

Yavuz, M. H. (1997), 'Political Islam and the Welfare (Refah) Party in Turkey', *Comparative Politics*, October, pp. 63–82.

Zürcher, E. J. (1993), *Turkey: A Modern History*, London: I. B. Tauris.

7 The Islamist movement and Turkey–EU relations

Effie Fokas

Introduction

The most recent Turkish national elections of 2002 were surrounded by apprehension and alarm. *Le Monde* heralded the 'election test for a European Turkey'; *Hurriyet* declared, 'Turkey obliged to say goodbye to EU if AKP comes to power'; and the *Independent* reported, after the fact, that 'Turkey's voters have delivered the "wrong" result'.[1] Although Tayyip Erdoğan's Justice and Development Party (*Adalet ve Kalkınma Partisi*, AKP) campaigned on a staunchly pro-EU platform, many in Turkey question the extent to which the party indeed embraces the EU and the enhanced democracy it would entail for Turkey – *beyond*, that is, the democratic rights desired for the party itself. Among the causes of this mistrust I identify the fact that Islamists, including much of the AKP's current leadership, were strongly anti-European in the past. Among its consequences is a vicious cycle of secularist–Islamist tensions.

As Richard Tapper notes in his *Islam in Modern Turkey*, a frequently asked question is whether Islamic revival poses a political 'threat' to the survival of the modern Turkish state; conspicuously missing in scholarship, however, is 'the age-old Western fear of Islam, *now shared by many Turks*, and the rarely articulated role of this fear in determining Turkey's relation to Europe' (1994; emphasis added). I will explain in what follows how this fear has translated into efforts to limit the public role of Islam, and how, furthermore, these efforts negatively affect Turkish–EU relations. One of the climaxes of secularist–Islamist tensions in recent Turkish history is the 'February 28 process', through which the military-dominated National Security Council (NSC) gradually forced the ruling *Refah* ('Welfare') Party out of power in 1997. In my view, this process contains the roots of both the enhanced pro-European claims among Islamists in Turkey, and the perceptions that the AKP simply represents a continuation of that banned Islamist party's aims.

Thus, section 7.1 is devoted to an examination of the *Refah* Party, the February 28 process, and the legacies of the latter in the Turkish political scene. A special focus on the constraints on political Islam serves as a backdrop to the present consideration of Islamists' changed stances on Turkish membership of the European Union. In section 7.2, I concentrate on Turkish elites' own assessments of the Turkish Islamist movement. I begin by addressing secular elites' opinions on whether indeed a transformation within the movement has taken place, followed by religious-minded individuals' own explanations of their past and current attitudes to the EU. Finally, in section 7.3 I examine the Justice and Development Party in the light of the controversy surrounding its rise to power. Following a schematic assessment of the party's performance thus far, I conclude with a consideration of the present state of secularist–Islamist tensions and their effect on Turkey–EU relations.

7.1 Political Islam in Turkey: a brief account

The *Refah* Party's rise to power in 1996 was one of the greatest shocks in Turkish political history, sparking much debate over the possibility of a 'return to religion' in Turkey and an undermining of the secular republic. *Refah* shared a number of characteristics with religious movements in general.[2] We shall address two characteristics that help explain *Refah*'s appeal and rise to power, followed by two that offer insight into the radical change in perspective, within political Islamist circles, on Turkish membership of the EU.

First, religion-based political mobilisation in modern nation-states tends to be anti-systemic. This applies to *Refah* in so far as it did not share the values of the political order within which it operated (Narlı, 1999c). Many analysts explain *Refah*'s success in terms of its attraction of *protest*, rather than specifically *Islamist*, votes (Çakır, 1990; Heper, 1981). Nilufer Narlı describes the protest in terms of centre–periphery tensions (with the centre comprising military officers, senior bureaucrats, notables and secular industrialists). While rapid urbanisation in Turkey from the 1950s onwards yielded increasing social mobility of the periphery, rural poverty for the most part simply translated into urban poverty: a *new periphery* developed for the economically disadvantaged, culturally disintegrated and politically isolated (Narlı, 1999b). Thus, *Refah* reflected a 'religious' cleavage in so far as it expressed the interests of dominated actors who, in alliance with the middle classes, contested the hegemony of the ruling elites in the cultural and political field.[3]

Second (and related to the first point), religious mobilisation tends to have cross-class appeal. Islamism as represented by the *Refah* Party was a multi-class political movement that 'used class-related issues to promote a project of change in lifestyle and to establish its own version of Islamic society' (Gülalp, undated). Moreover, religious parties address collective action not through abstract religious ideas but through selective incentives, such as provision of local social services, sponsoring of economic projects, subsidising education centres, and creation of wide networks of religious publishing and broadcasting enterprises (Kalyvas, 2003). It is through such policies that *Refah* was able to secure the support and involvement especially of Turkish youth, the economically disadvantaged, and small to medium-sized entrepreneurs (Narlı, 1999b).

These points should help us understand *Refah*'s appeal and rise to power. The party had a number of strengths that other political parties lacked. These have been summarised as 'money, purpose, and an alternative vision for Turks which has not yet been tested ... perhaps *Refah*'s strongest advantage is the increasing ineffectiveness of Turkey's other political parties' (Göksel, undated). Since secular parties had failed to address the deteriorating economic conditions plaguing many Turks, the promise of the *Refah* Party was especially appealing. Furthermore, *Refah* placed on the political agenda certain critical issues that had long been neglected by other parties, such as corruption and the growing social chaos in large Turkish cities (Sayarı, 1996).

A third factor common to contemporary religion-based movements is that ideology is a poor predictor of their behaviour. As Stathis Kalyvas notes, religious movements consist of a social and political phenomenon that is far more complex than the religions to which they refer:

> While they emerge in the context of a broad societal diffusion of religious symbols, they do not just mobilize existing religious identities; they reconstruct them by blending religious, social, economic, and political concerns, by synthesizing traditional and modern appeals, and by mixing utopian millenarist messages with concrete political action. In short, these parties are not just an expression of dormant identities; they redefine these identities. In this sense, they are revolutionary and radical not just within the context of the political regimes within which they operate but ... [even] within the religious structure they claim to uphold and represent.

Accordingly, beyond political Islam's ideology, we should also consider its leadership and 'situational factors' such as the cultural, economic, political and social variables relevant at a given time (Heper, 1981; Kalyvas, 2003). For instance, in the case of *Refah*'s policies it is crucial to understand Erbakan as a *populist* leader, variously nationalistic and anti-national (Zubaida, 2000). Specifically in terms of *Refah*'s traditional anti-Europeanism, one must also note the fact that Erbakan played on disenchantment – across the political spectrum – following the Luxembourg summit's rejection of Turkey in 1997.

Finally, a fourth element of religious mobilisation is that political success depends on a party's willingness or ability to moderate. Kalyvas argues that religion-based parties often face two major decisions. First, should they modify their religious goals in order to operate within a secular and competitive political environment? Religious parties are

generally willing to moderate their policies because of a number of constraints, both electoral and non-electoral. In terms of electoral constraints,
such parties tend to moderate their anti-systemic positions in accordance
with the incentive that arises from the realisation that power is within
reach. Non-electoral constraints stem from the fact that ruling elites either
control or are closely linked to military authorities. Thus, politically successful religious parties are obliged to moderate in order to gain and
maintain ultimate power, because otherwise the military may subvert their
victory. The second decision faced by religion-based parties is *how* to moderate. This challenge often leads to a division within the party between traditionalists and modernists (Kalyvas, 2003). In the Turkish case, one can
observe both tendencies of moderation and division in *Refah's* moderation
of its anti-EU stance before and after its electoral success, and through the
split in its successor party (*Fazilet*, or the Virtue Party), between *traditionalists* and *modernisers*.[4]

The constraints facing Turkish political Islam are especially important
for the purposes of this chapter because they enable us to understand the
pro-European attitudes prevailing within its current formations. Space
limitations do not allow for a thorough analysis. Suffice it to note that
there was a primary shift in policy on Europe in the aftermath of the
December 1995 elections, when *Refah* gained a majority of the votes – but
not enough to rule on its own. Faced with this constraint, Erbakan began
modifying his rhetoric against the EU when it became clear that the
party's only chance to power was in coalition with one of the two leading
pro-European parties: Tansu Çiller's True Path Party and Mesut Yılmaz's
Motherland Party (Finkel, 1995). A second limitation on *Refah's* earlier
staunch anti-Europeanism, once in power, came as a result of combined
pressure exerted by its coalition partner (the True Path Party) and the
NSC on the government's foreign policy. Erbakan's pre-election promises
to 'tear up' the customs union with the EC, to cancel Operation Provide
Comfort[5] and to end Turkey's military arrangements with Israel were
either unfulfilled or reversed. Far greater than the restrictions on *Refah's*
foreign policy, though, were those aimed at curbing the domestic force of
Islamism through the February 28 process.

In fact, tension had mounted between the secularist elite and Erbakan
from the very beginning of the latter's term in office, specifically because
of his attempts to grant Islam a greater role in public life. Erbakan had
proposed to lift the ban on the wearing of headscarves by female civil servants in government offices. He also called for the building of mosques in
central Ankara and Istanbul in locations widely viewed as symbols of secularism (Dorsey, 1997), and for changing the working hours in government
offices during the month of Ramadan (Osman, 1997). On 28 February
1997, the NSC introduced a bill comprising 18 specific measures designed
to curb Islamic 'reactionaryism'. The NSC compelled a reluctant Erbakan
to sign the bill, thus granting it force of law. In the '28 February 1997 Dec-

laration', the NSC severely criticised the anti-secular atmosphere and asked the *Refah* government to take measures to stop the proliferation of Islamist cadres in the bureaucracy. Furthermore, the military gave a series of press briefings in which religious fundamentalism was declared the most dangerous enemy facing Turkey.

The February 28 process later came to be seen as a 'post-modern coup',[6] as it signalled the beginning of the end of *Refah* and Erbakan. More significantly, however, it marked the beginning of a long-term effort to quell the political and social strength of Islamism in Turkey. The first main stage in this process was the forced closure of the *Refah* Party and the ousting of Erbakan from political activity.[7] The second was the successor government's enactment of a series of anti-fundamentalist measures backed by the Kemalist political and military elite. The government, led by Mesut Yılmaz, began to actively investigate the Islamists, inspect student dormitories of Islamic orders, transfer Islamists holding key government posts to less significant posts, question the Islamist tendencies of some provincial and district governors, and assert control over religious foundations.

Meanwhile, Recai Kutan formed the *Fazilet* ('Virtue') Party out of the ashes of the *Refah* Party.[8] *Fazilet* embodied a concerted effort to reform political Islam. It promoted itself as pro-democratic, and conspicuously implemented this by declaring support for Turkish membership of the EU. Whether the party was sincere in its embrace of democracy is a matter of intense debate. One positive indication is the split that developed in the party between the 'traditionalists' and the 'reformists'. In spite of such developments, however, the party was closed down by the Constitutional Court in 2001, on the grounds that it was a continuation of the *Refah* Party.

Fazilet's closure, together with other NSC-led actions designed to limit Islamism in Turkish politics, may be considered further extensions of the February 28 process. A prime example is the liberal use of article 312 of the Turkish Penal Code to convict people suspected of 'reactionaryism'. The article prohibits incitement of the public to hatred, enmity or division based on racial, ethnic, religious, sect, regional or class lines. The list of those convicted for religion-related offences includes such prominent political figures as Necmettin Erkaban and Tayyip Erdoğan (while the latter was Mayor of Istanbul), but also influential social and religious leaders, such as the popular journalist, Fehmi Koru and Fethullah Gülen.[9] Another critical example is the Civil Servants Decree (a decree with the force of law) that was, according to the then Prime Minister, Bülent Ecevit, 'a legislative effort in accordance with the February 28th decisions' (*Briefing*, 14 August 2000, p. 3). This controversial decree, advanced by the NSC in August 2000, was designed to purge the Turkish bureaucracy of religious 'reactionaries' by sacking thousands of civil servants suspected of sympathising with political Islam or Kurdish separatism.[10]

7.2 Secular and religious perspectives on Turkish political Islam

I now turn to an examination of Turkish elite perspectives on the Islamist movement in Turkey. This section draws on information from over 100 interviews conducted with religious and political leaders, scholars, journalists and businessmen in Turkey throughout 2000 and 2001 (that is, before the formation of the AKP). The focus here is especially on Islamists' 'change' to pro-Europeanism, and the guiding question is whether this change may be considered genuine. I address first the perspectives of those interviewees who identify themselves as secular; these are followed by the explanations of individuals who identify themselves as religious.[11] The focus is on the range of perspectives offered by the interviewees, rather than on their individual identities (see the appendix for further details). The intent here is simply to offer insight into the mindsets of those individuals who influence the state of the secularist–Islamist tensions that are under examination in this chapter.

In view of the constraints faced by political Islam – both electoral and non-electoral – it is difficult to judge its representatives' true intentions. Many members of the secular-minded Turkish elite attribute the change in Islamists' perspective to *realpolitik*. However, opinion varies as to when the change came about and whether it can be considered genuine. Relatively few respondents see the change in Islamists' perspective as a result of a gradual and internal transformation.[12] Assessing the Islamist movement from its earliest political formations to the present, one sociologist asserts that Islamists changed slowly, becoming more secular with each successive political party: 'they saw their parties could not survive as only religion-oriented, so they began providing goods and services ... now the religion-oriented party is no longer anti-system'.[13] This view is supported by another scholar, who explains that the closer doctrinaire parties come to power, the less they can remain doctrinaire, pure and radical.

But by far the most popular interpretation of current Islamists' attitudes to the EU is that 'they learned their lesson' through the February 28 process. They 'changed overnight', argues one diplomat. According to a representative of TUSIAD (the peak organisation of the pro-EU business elite), *Refah* learned, or received, a precious lesson in 1997; 'but', he continues, 'how much of it they [those still active in politics] actually learned, or are willing to learn, or are able to apply, we don't know'.

Despite the Islamists' strong pro-European rhetoric, many interviewees doubt whether the Islamists are actually aware of what EU membership will entail, or whether they are better prepared to secure the goal of EU membership. One scholar contends that 'they haven't thought about what they need to do'. Thus, there is a strong sense that Islamists are naïve in their perspectives on the EU. The headscarf issue is frequently cited as an example, with reference to the fact that in both Germany and France, Muslims have faced limitations of their freedom to wear headscarves in schools. The view expressed here, then, is that Islamists are 'creating a myth' with regard to freedoms that may be guaranteed by EU membership.

Beyond expressions of such presumed naïveté, several respondents openly question Islamists' intentions in their current pro-European rhetoric. According to one diplomat's strict assessment, 'Islamists want Europe to soften secularism'. Religious groups are *very* pro-EU because they expect enhanced democracy and freedom there, 'but they don't want freedom. They have it in Turkey ... They want more.' This especially cynical perspective is often expressed with reference to *takiye*, a word of Arabic origin variously defined as presenting yourself as something you are not, or hiding your true identity in order to preserve yourself.

We have, then, a range of perspectives as to why the change came about and whether it is genuine. The overwhelming majority of secular-minded respondents consider the change a direct effect of the February 28 process, rather than a gradual modification of previous stances on Europe, as might come with shedding of Islamic orthodoxy or traditionalism. Likewise, most consider the change either merely tactical or simply naïve. Again, the prevalence of these sentiments among 'mainstream' Turkish elites is especially significant as it is on the basis of mistrust of Islamists' motivations that the NSC has continually pursued its strictly secularist strategy. This strategy, in turn, has been implemented through measures that are increasingly identified as anti-democratic and thus as barriers to Turkish membership of the European Union.

In the remainder of this section, I will examine Islamists' own explanations for their current pro-Europeanness. I present here the perspectives of individuals who are formally part of political Islamist movements, and other social and religious leaders who identify religion as a primary aspect of their identities. It is important to note that many of these elite figures in Turkish Islamism (including representatives from various Muslim social, political and business organisations, Muslim intellectuals,[14] journalists and scholars) admit that it is a struggle to convince their 'masses' of their opinions on Europe. Furthermore, as Peter Berger (2000: 43) notes, we must be sensitive to differences among Islamists: 'Where the political circumstances allow it, there is a lively discussion about the relationship of Islam to various modern realities, and there are sharp disagreements between individuals who are equally committed to a revitalised Islam.' This clearly applies to Turkish Islamists' stances on political Islam, and to their perspectives on Europe, as will be discussed in what follows.

Diversity of opinion is especially evident through many interviewees' explicit disassociation from *Refah* in their assessments of when and why that party changed its stance on EU membership. Several respondents support the view that political Islam changed purely as a result of electoral and other constraints. One former bureaucrat argues that 'they dropped their anti-EU stance ... in order to open more political space for themselves'. All parties more or less misuse religion, and 'the party that misused religion the most got the worst lesson. I think Turkey lived through this process and it came to an end.' Likewise, a journalist for a religious newspaper who is an influential Muslim intellectual declares, 'We believe the *Refah* Party interpreted religion wrongly. They saw democracy as a means, not an end. After 28 February, they learned the true value of democracy.' These perspectives represent a spectrum of cynicism expressed by many interviewees – much like that evident in many secularists' perspectives, but with one critical difference: indication that a sincere change *has* taken place, that 'the lesson was learned'. Of all interviewees consulted for this part of the study, only one expressed continued mistrust of political Islamists' intentions *vis-à-vis* the EU: an Alevi spokesman, who believes that

> they were against Europe, tried to establish an Islamic common market, etc., and *now*, if they have seemed to change, theirs is not a genuine change. Because in Europe and in the EU, they will have the opportunity for a much more liberal expression of their ideas and, once they come to power, they will say 'it's until here ... now we will create our own Islamic federation'.[15]

A thorough understanding of the change in Islamists' perspectives on Europe must also include reference to the explanations of the political actors themselves. According to one leading figure in the AKP, 'we now realise we will have more freedom there than in our own country'. The politician indicates his personal preference for *bilateral* relations with the EU, but, 'because democracy and human rights standards are low in Turkey, and because internal dynamism is not, and will not be, sufficient to bring about the necessary changes, we are obliged to join'. Another leading AKP figure admits that he, in line with the *Refah* Party, was against membership of the European Community/European Union because of the perceived religious prejudice coming from Europe. 'But now, especially for universal rights, human rights, democracy, freedoms, rule of law, freedom of finance, I no longer think so.' Taken together, these opinions are representative of the new pro-Europeanness within political Islam: a negative, defensive and survivalist attitude with regard to the Turkish internal political situation; a positive embrace of European democracy; and an explicit shelving of previous anti-European feeling, which was largely based on a sense of prejudice coming from Europe.

Beyond the immediate circles of political Islam as well, the impression given by most respondents is that previously held reservations about Europe have been overtaken by problems facing Turkish Muslims on the domestic front. As one journalist explains, 'The EU means for me to live my religion privately and freely. But in Turkey, people do not feel free. I feel more free as a Muslim in Germany, so how can I be anti-EU?' Another expresses his pro-EU stance as a hope of broadening the horizons of Turkish Muslims: someone who has established himself in Europe has a better position than he does because of education and opportunities. In Turkey, he declares, he has been subjected to structural violence, constrained and victimised, and thus restricted in his ability to contribute more to humanity.

These views may be interpreted as results of the February 28 process and its 'legacies', but many respondents direct us to a broader perspective, including other concurrent factors that have been crucial in determining their current pro-Europeanism. One journalist emphasises that the change is a *social process*:

> [W]e saw the realities of the world. As religious groups became increasingly active in political, economic, and social circles in Turkey and made real contact with the Turkish system, they had to leave behind the utopia in which they were living.

Speaking specifically from his personal experience in the popular and now global *Fethullah Gülen Cemaati* (*Fethullah Gülen* Community), he explains that 'they saw the US, Europe, they saw the importance of democracy in those countries and the vision of these people'. Furthermore, as a renowned Muslim intellectual explains, 'Before, the Germans – especially the Christian Democrats – were the governing part of the EU, and they see the EU as a Christian club.' However, because of the current prevalence of socialist parties in Europe, together with the fact that 'Turkey is very top in suppression of religion', Islamists have begun to see the EU as a community in which religious freedom is protected. Finally, the change in perspective also has to do with globalisation and with economics: 'we want to grow economically with Europe. Muslim business too is suppressed.' Muslims today, another scholar notes, are no longer confined to small, closed communitarian groups. Muslim businessmen travel globally and want to have a direct path into Europe. Current Islamists, he emphasises, also include intellectuals who want to have enhanced connections with Europe and all over the world, and who seek a more global rather than a local approach.

The main criticisms launched by the secular-minded elite with reference to Islamists' pro-Europeanism are that Islamists are creating a myth (especially with their expectations related to the headscarf); that Islamists are blatantly insincere and have not changed fundamentally to become more open; and that they are naïve (not really knowing, or not having really thought through, what membership entails). The heavy emphasis of these Islamist interviewees on freedoms expected with EU membership, particularly with regard to the headscarf issue, provides some evidence in support of the first criticism. With reference to the latter opinion – that no real change amongst Islamists has taken place – the views offered by two respondents could perhaps be considered to support this claim also. A popular journalist for a religious newspaper and a central political figure in both *Refah* and *Fazilet* explain in unison that a major motivation for Islamist pro-Europeanism is the expectation that EU membership will provide Islamists with the chance to spread in Europe. After noting the prevalence of Christian missionaries in Europe, the journalist states, 'but this without the benefit of a Muslim movement in Europe. Membership means many Muslims will also be in a position to affect European minds.' The politician even goes on to say:

> In fact, we think that we will dominate. First, we have a strong army. Second, Turks can work for less money, but make more money. There will be no cultural threat, and it will give us the opportunity to spread there.

It should be noted, however, that such extreme expressions are quite limited in number.

With reference to the third criticism – concerning *naïveté* with regards to EU membership – members of Islamist elites were asked whether they felt that membership might threaten Turkish Islamic values. According to a former director of *Diyanet*,[16] there are Muslim people who feel they will lose their values if Turkey enters the EU. 'But', he contends, 'this should not be, and is not, an obstacle; if you want to lose your values, even now, you can easily do so.' And as one AKP leader emphasises, the EU is secular: 'they don't get involved in your religion and religious activities. That's good. That's enough.' As for loss of Muslim identity, he posits that 'you cannot prevent something by keeping yourself out. Islam is broad, and is not against science or development. With freedom to educate oneself, you can keep your own identity.' The EU does not want us to change our religion, notes another leading figure in the AKP:

> [I]t is not one of the criteria. We as individuals can be a part of any kind of society with our belief. Turkish Muslims do not have a problem with integration, but in terms of assimilation; that becomes hard. If Europe wants to go through assimilation, there will be a problem.

But citing the example of the United Kingdom, integrated in the EU but opting out of the monetary union, he notes that 'there's no negative thinking about the UK'. Asked whether he expected 'negative thinking' from the EU towards Turkey for the latter's resistance to assimilation in some respects, the politician asserts, 'we haven't yet solved our integration problems; assimilation will come later'. This response may indeed be considered naïve by proponents of greater assimilation within the EU.

Other interviewees, however, express well-thought-out concerns about ways in which membership may jeopardise their interests as practising Muslims. For example, one journalist feels that EU membership does not present a threat to Islamic identity, but it may negatively affect Turkish family values. According to a Muslim intellectual, there will be some conflict in the sphere of religion if Turkey joins the EU: 'in Europe, religion is well established in the social sphere; in Turkey, there is a vacuum here. If Turkey enters the EU, it will be difficult to fill this vacuum.' Another respondent is much more explicit in his concerns:

> There will be problems: I am concerned about our souls, because the European way of life, sex, drugs, etc. will definitely come here. These problems are contagious, and I'm not sure that they will be controlled if they come to a society like Turkey.

Yet in spite of these reservations, each of the aforementioned interviewees promotes Turkish membership of the EU.

With reference to the question of Islamists' naïveté, also important are some interviewees' carefully measured critiques of the EU. According to one Muslim intellectual, there is a critical problem in that 'European democracy is not culturally plural. There is political pluralism, but not cultural.' If cultural pluralism cannot be established in institutional terms, he declares, 'we will be administered by Brussels, and I am very afraid of this'. The respondent disapproves of trends towards 'the standardisation of everything ... which leads people to be like social puppets. We have to keep our freedom to have critical views against the technocrats and the bureaucrats who define these standards.' Another scholar is also resistant to such domination by the EU: 'A self-confident Muslim is not afraid of interaction with Europe. But a two-way relationship must be established. Such a relationship cannot exist when Turkey feels itself to be a passive follower of Euro-centric development.' The important thing, he argues, is 'our dignity – we can't sacrifice our own values, and culture, in our relations. We would prefer dignity rather than wealth.'

The vastly diverse perspectives of Turkish Islamists preclude any simple conclusions about their current pro-European attitudes. This is the case with respect to when the change in perspective came about, what its decisive motivating factors were, and whether it can be considered genuine. Less ambiguous, though, is the fact that the tension between Turkish Islamists and secularists is itself incompatible with European norms and thus poses a significant barrier to Turkey's membership of the EU – even though this barrier cannot be identified with reference to the Copenhagen criteria. Accordingly, we return now to our starting point: the 'election test for a European Turkey'. The 'test', I contend, is not so much related to electoral outcomes, but to the cessation of the cycle of secularist–Islamist tensions. For the Islamist movement, this test entails its demonstrated respect for Turkish secularism and democratic principles, and maintenance of its much-contested pro-Europeanism.[17] The corresponding test for the secularist elites relates to their commitment to European values, which can be measured as consent to the rule of a democratically elected AKP government. Hingeing on the results of these tests is the implementation of certain reforms that are necessary for Turkey's EU membership.

7.3 The new faces of political Islam in Turkey: how Islamist are they?

The AKP's efforts to distance itself from previous, now outlawed, Islamist parties left both Turks and international observers at a loss for how to describe the party. A *Le Monde* headline clearly reflects the confusion: 'Islamiste, démocrate, conservateur, comment qualifier l'AKP?' (Bourcier, 2002). Unquestionably, the party's leadership base largely derives from earlier banned political formations. In fact, the party's chairman was himself banned from political activity when the party was first formed, for statements challenging the secular state of the Republic. But AKP leaders have consistently stated that they do not represent an Islamist movement, nor should they be described as an Islamic Party. Erdoğan himself promotes the use of the term 'conservative democrats' (Vick, 2002). Furthermore, with regard to the EU, Erdoğan declares, 'Our party is a national force which believes that there is a direct relationship between EU membership and our national interests, and which forms its policies accordingly.'[18] The newly elected government's intense diplomatic missions to the EU prior to the Copenhagen summit of December 2002 may be perceived as evidence of these policies.

Yet a great deal of mistrust remains, in Turkey and abroad, as to the party's real intentions *vis-à-vis* the secular state and the EU. Extensive attention is given in the foreign press to statements made by the party's leaders prior to the AKP's formation. The *Guardian* has published declarations made by Erdoğan while Mayor of Istanbul: 'Thank God, I am for Sharia'; 'one cannot be a secularist and a Muslim at the same time'; and 'for us, democracy is a means to an end' (Bowcott, 2002). Likewise, Abdullah Gül is reported to have said, 'Turkey should not join the European Union, we have said this from the beginning . . . look at a European city, and then look at Istanbul. It's not a Christian city' (Woollacott, 2002). Such statements led the author of this latter article to surmise that 'it is permissible to wonder how completely they have changed their minds . . . the party remains fixed in its basic aims'; namely, 'to take the society back from the foes of Islam'. 'Islamists', continues the author, 'have used Europe to take power for what we must still assume are Islamist purposes.'

Far more consequential is, of course, the mistrust facing the AKP on the domestic front – and, in particular, from the Kemalist elite. Ruşen Çakır believes there has been a real transformation in Erdoğan, 'but the problem is that that is not enough. The question is whether they [the establishment, the army] believe it or want to believe it. I think here there's no chance for him' (*Turkish Daily News*, 14 September 2002). Indeed, the tremendous challenges facing Erdoğan in his rise to the premiership may be viewed as indications that 'they' do not 'want to believe it'. According to its party programme, the AKP

> considers religion as one of the most important institutions of humanity, and secularism as a prerequisite of democracy, and an assurance of the freedom of religion and conscience ... Our Party refuses to take advantage of sacred religious values and ethnicity and to use them for political purposes.

Furthermore, Erdoğan has explicitly stated that 'In Turkey, each institution has its own role. The Turkish army is the apple of our eyes. No one is going to interfere between our army and us' (*Le Monde*, 6 November 2002: 4). Yet such statements did not suffice as assurance to a sceptical secularist establishment. In this context, the Court of Cassation's chief prosecutor brought a number of cases against Erdoğan, calling for his ban from party leadership and from participation in parliamentary elections; challenging a Diyarbakır State Court ruling clearing Erdoğan's criminal record; demanding the AKP's closure; and pursuing corruption charges against Erdoğan.[19]

Beyond these challenges, the AKP has already faced a number of 'litmus tests' in its short experience in power. Considering how, in the past, some of the strongest anti-European currents within Turkish Islamism (e.g. complaints against the exclusive 'Christian club') have arisen in response to the negative atmosphere emanating from the EU, the harsh 'anti-Turkish' statements of Giscard d'Estaing and the results of the 2002 Copenhagen summit may be regarded as significant initial tests for the AKP. The public responses of both Gül and Erdoğan in these cases merit high marks. While Giscard d'Estaing's stated opinion that Turkish entry to the EU would signal the 'end' of the latter provoked intense reactions from international observers (one view was that 'Giscard is more Le Pen than Monnet'; Georgiou, 2002), Erdoğan's response was a markedly calm reiteration that the European Union is not a Christian club (Boulton, 2002). And though the failure, at the Copenhagen summit, to secure a 2003 date for the start of EU accession negotiations was considerably more disappointing for the AKP, still the overwhelming response was reiteration of resolve to meet the Copenhagen criteria.

Another major test for the AKP, closely connected to the Copenhagen summit, is the Cyprus question. Erdoğan's relatively progressive policy on

Cyprus was well received in Brussels during discussions of Kofi Annan's UN plan for uniting the island. The Turkish military's reception of Erdoğan's policy was less positive:

> Erdoğan happens to be on a line most hardliners may not subscribe to at this point ... [he] is suspected for intending to give up Cyprus for EU accession talks which, he calculates, would prune the military's role in politics and secure his own survivability ... Erdoğan may or may not have such intentions. But the fact is he is suspected to have them.
>
> (Bekdil, 2002)

The AKP's keenness on the Annan plan verged on being considered evidence of its anti-systemic nature: in Erdoğan's own words, 'AKP's vision of Cyprus and Turkey's traditional policy on Cyprus do not overlap' (Çağatay, 2002). But it would be wrong to assume that the AKP's willingness to settle the Cyprus issue was contingent on its desired outcome for the Copenhagen summit: even after the summit, Erdoğan berated the Turkish Cypriot leader, Rauf Denktaş, for the latter's intransigence. Taking the debate to the public sphere, Erdoğan embarked on serious efforts to create a national consensus on the Cyprus issue (Smith, 2003).[20] 'But', one local observer states disappointedly,

> the National Security Council ... has lent support to Denktaş and the objections he has raised against the UN peace plan ... it is not the government that makes the decisions on this issue. If I know the Turkish military, they must have ordered Denktaş not to resolve the problem.
>
> (Ütkü, 2003)[21]

In the same vein, a *Le Monde* article notes the AKP's favourable position on the Annan plan but questions who really governs Turkey – the military or the democratically elected government (Pope, 2003). The answer, the article's author contends, is very ambiguous. Indeed, one sees a shift in Erdoğan's rhetoric on Cyprus the closer he comes to formal leadership of Turkey. Shortly after his victory in the Siirt by-elections, he declared:

> [W]e have emphasised from the outset that a solution is unavoidable in Cyprus. But we see that the problem needs more discussion. The Annan plan is neither acceptable nor unacceptable ... we want a political solution which guarantees that the Turkish Republic of Northern Cyprus will have sovereignty and enjoy equal political status.
>
> (*Turkish Daily News*, 12 March 2003)

Responsibility for the collapse of the 2002/2003 talks on solution to the Cyprus issue is clearly placed on Denktaş. But the fact that the situation was so ripe for solution, in terms of popular opinion in Northern Cyprus and in terms of the AKP's strong parliamentary majority, has led to a great deal of blame being placed on the AKP as well.

A third major, multi-faceted test for the party is its policy *vis-à-vis* the United States and on the war in Iraq. The war raised problems in three main domains: namely, the economy, national security and public opinion. The economic dimension is complicated in and of itself: while the financial losses following the last Gulf War and the slump to be expected in Turkey's tourism sector discouraged any support of the war, the large influence of US–Turkey relations on the Turkish economy, together with the substantial sums of funds promised by the United States in exchange for Turkish cooperation, suggested that full cooperation with the United States might be the lesser of two evils.[22] As the Chief of Staff, General Hilmi Özkök, emphasised, Turkey's choice was between 'bad and worse': 'if we don't participate, we submit ourselves to the same consequences of the war, but our losses will not be compensated and we will not have the right to a say in the aftermath' (*Le Monde*, 6 March 2003). The dreaded scenario for the aftermath was a resurrection of the 'Kurdish problem'. Fears of a strengthened Kurdish minority in northern Iraq, or, even worse, the establishment of a Kurdish state, heightened concerns about Kurdish separatist movements within Turkey. In this national security domain, then, negativity towards the war due to fear of enhanced Kurdish strength was weighed against the benefits of US-reinforced military strength in and political influence over northern Iraq. The third dimension, public opinion, is related to both of the above. Acute memories of both economic and human losses resulting from the 1991 Gulf War and the much longer struggle against Kurdish separatism culminated in overwhelming anti-war sentiment among the Turkish population.[23]

Erdoğan's initial line on the US request to deploy troops through Turkey to northern Iraq was reserved: he declared that Turkey would not support military action against Iraq without a Security Council resolution, and emphasised the need for a peaceful solution to the crisis (Çalışkan and Taşkın, 2003). But when the issue reached Parliament, Erdoğan encouraged parliamentary approval of the US requests. The first vote on the matter, on 1 March 2003, yielded a dramatic result: three votes short of approval of the US plans.[24] The delicate political cost for Erdoğan of another negative result in Parliament – which could have been considered a vote of no confidence for the government he was not yet officially leading – led to the delaying of a second parliamentary vote (Smith and Watt, 2003). This delay severely frustrated the United States, and its final result (on 20 March) bred major tension in Turkey–US relations: only US over-flights through Turkey would be allowed, as would the entry of Turkish troops into northern Iraq.

The decision was problematic on several counts. First, it significantly hindered initial US war strategies and thus exacerbated US disappointment with Turkey. Second, the United States strongly opposed the deployment of Turkish troops in the area, particularly because of its strategically important relationship with the pro-US Kurds of northern Iraq, a relationship that could be threatened by US support of a Turkish troop presence in the area. Furthermore, the decision disturbed the Turkish markets, which felt the results immediately as hopes for the US multi-billion-dollar aid package seemed to fade.

Finally, and most important for our purposes, the Turkish vote also upset Turkey–EU relations. Following a two-day meeting in Brussels for discussion of policy on Iraq, EU leaders issued a clear statement that Turkey should not cause further complications by dispatching troops to northern Iraq: 'We call on all countries of the region to refrain from actions that could lead to further instability' (*Turkish Daily News*, 22 March 2003). Likewise, EU Commissioner Günter Verheugen declared that 'any crossing of Turkish troops into northern Iraq is undesirable and will have to be taken into account in the final assessment of whether Turkey is ready to accede [to the EU]' (quoted in Lobjakas, 2003). Individual EU countries also issued their own warning statements to Turkey. The Belgian Foreign Minister declared that it would be 'unthinkable' for Turkey to join the EU if Turkish troops entered northern Iraq, and both he and his German counterpart threatened to withdraw their country's personnel from NATO surveillance planes in Turkey (*Dünya Gazetisi*, 24 March 2003). Belgium issued an even more severe threat to block Turkey's EU membership application (Dymond, 2003).[25]

Conclusions

These 'litmus tests' for the AKP – policy on the EU, Cyprus and Iraq – are still under way at the time of this chapter's drafting. But on the basis of this skeletal overview of the AKP's experiences thus far and in comparison with earlier post-1980 political Islamist formations such as the *Refah* Party, we can draw some preliminary conclusions with regard to the 'vicious cycle' of secularist–Islamist tensions and, by extension, the role of the Islamist movement in Turkey–EU relations. Examining the AKP in the light of our theoretical discussion on religious mobilisations, we see certain critical differences as well as similarities. The most important difference is that the AKP does not represent an anti-system party, as did *Refah*. Like *Refah*, though, it amassed a great number of protest votes against the other leading parties, marked by coalition deadlock, corruption charges and failure to redress the consequences of an especially severe economic crisis. Thus, the party also enjoys cross-class appeal. Religious ideology is a poor predictor of the AKP's behaviour, regardless of any electoral or non-electoral constraints faced directly by the party. From the outset, the AKP's platform reflected considerable moderation. But this of course may be seen as the direct effect of the non-electoral constraints faced by the *Refah* Party: the fact that much of the AKP's leadership base derives from *Refah*, and the stark consequences of the February 28 process, surely go a long way towards explaining the AKP's moderation.

Perhaps the most critical difference in the AKP is the fact that it is the first party since 1991 to enjoy single-party government (Çarkoglu, 2002). Its large mandate in the legislature – just five votes short of the two-thirds parliamentary majority needed to amend the Constitution – is a significant factor in the party's ability to overcome such non-electoral constraints as Court of Cassation cases brought against its leader. More importantly, this mandate also frees the AKP from the coalition deadlock of recent years and enhances its potential to push through much-needed reforms, such as those required for EU membership.

However, as we see in the cases of the Cyprus question and the war in Iraq, this mandate has not led to clear and decisive policies – a fact which, in both cases, carries repercussions for Turkey–EU relations. International observers are quick to assume a large role here played by the Turkish military. Two facts may be considered to support this view: first, that Cyprus has always been an especially sensitive issue for the Turkish military, together with the fact that Erdoğan's rhetoric on Cyprus changed drastically the closer he came to direct contact with the military as Prime Minister; second, the fact that the military remained relatively silent on policy on Iraq prior to the first parliamentary vote (by not issuing a formal opinion on the matter following the NSC meeting before the vote), but were less silent prior to the second vote, the result of which clearly reflects the military's perspective on national security. Other commentators consider the AKP's shortcomings in making best of its mandate a mere fact of political inexperience, particularly in foreign policy terms.

The challenges that the AKP faced in its first months in power would have been daunting for any government. In any case, far more important than any assessments made with regard to such still-developing issues is what I take to be the real test for a European Turkey: an end to the cycle of secularist–Islamist tensions. Quite notably, the words of Richard Tapper (1994) cited on p. 147 on the role of the 'fear of Islam' in Turkey–EU relations were echoed in a draft report prepared by the European Parliament Committee on Foreign Affairs: 'the underlying philosophy of the Turkish state, "Kemalism", implies an exaggerated fear ... an important role for the army, and a very rigid attitude to religion, which means that this underlying philosophy is itself a barrier to EU membership' (EP, 2003).[26]

It is difficult to assess the responsibility of secularists and Islamists respectively in the continued tensions between them. According to Heper and Toktaş (2003), the AKP project aims at political Islam, but does not clash with the concept of a liberal democratic state; and indeed, the Islamist movement in general has directly challenged neither the secular state nor democratic principles. Yet perceptions of indirect challenges, such as appointments of 'pro-Islamic' figures to key state posts, have been enough to spark rumours of a military coup.[27] Accordingly, as with *Refah*, the constraints faced by the contemporary Islamist movement preclude sound assessments of Islamists' 'true' intentions. And with the Islamist movement thus constrained, neither is it possible to know the extent to which secularists are justified in their fears with regard to the Islamist movement.

A further complication arises when one tries to ascertain the European Union's true intentions *vis-à-vis* Turkey too. For example, to what extent is the EU willing to accommodate an Islamic-oriented regime and a predominantly Muslim country? In Turkey, answers to this question are marked with an evident degree of pessimism. In fact, Islamists' age-old complaints that the EU is an exclusive Christian club are now being voiced within Turkey's secularist circles as well. There is a marked tendency, even among the pro-Western elite, to view with suspicion even the 'constructive criticism' that the EU may have to offer. Part of the solution to this problem will depend on future EU policies towards Turkey – which must be consistent towards both secularist and Islamist trends, and set a clear and viable path for Turkish membership of the EU.

The other, and perhaps more significant, part of the solution to the problem depends on the extent to which secularist and Islamist circles in Turkey will prove capable of discussing their differences in a way that would be compatible with the principle of accommodation that characterises the EU system. In other words, what is important is not only whether Turkey can fulfil a Copenhagen criteria 'checklist'; equally important is the extent to which domestic politics and political debate in Turkey can be conducted in a manner consistent with the standards that the Copenhagen criteria represent.

Appendix: note on interviews

The research for this study includes just over 100 interviews conducted in Istanbul and Ankara during four weeks in June/July and two weeks in September 2000; and in Istanbul over ten days in May 2001. The interviews were semi-structured, and generally lasted between one and one and a half hours. The questions asked centred on the perceived role of religion in relations between Turkey and Europe/the EU. The fact that the scholarly nature of this inquiry was fully explained, enhanced the likelihood that the respondent would express his or her genuine views.

The sample for this study is non-random, as my intent was to compile a sample of potentially knowledgeable and influential leaders. I concentrated on the following groups: political, mass media, diplomatic, intellectual, religious, civil service and business elites. Hence, the sample does not mirror overall population characteristics in terms of sex, education, social background, age or region of origin. The sample was designed to be representative not of the mass of Turkish voters, but of the leadership community in Turkey. However, the sample does cover a broad range of ideological perspective – from hard-line Kemalist to Marxist and to socially and/or politically conservative Islamist.

The methodology for this elite survey is modelled in part on the work of Karl Deutsch, Roy Macridis, Lewis Edinger and Richard Merritt for *France, Germany and the Western Alliance: A Study of Elite Attitudes on European Integration and World Politics* (New York: Charles Scribner's Sons, 1967), I use the term 'elites' to indicate both formal and informal decision-makers, interested and/or involved in decisions important for the politics of Turkish society. Elite surveys are valuable for three reasons. First, elites play a crucial role in a state's political process. Second, although other elite groupings (e.g. in business or the media) may play a less direct role in politics, they are important in terms of their actions as interest groups lobbying to secure certain goals; as veto groups who must be appeased before a given policy may be implemented; or as shapers of public opinion. Third, and as a less manifest source of policy, the values, beliefs and attitudes of the broad stratum of elites may be indicative of those that go into the making of policy.

To identify the leaders to be interviewed, I began with a basic list of contact details for a number of Turkish elites, provided to me by ELIAMEP (Hellenic and Foreign Policy Research Organisation). I added to this list names from my readings on the subject of my research, and sought their contact details once I was in Turkey. My sample further expanded through the suggestions of those interviewees on the original list. The sample thus also reflects the reputational and positional characteristics of the respondents.

Of course, self-selection was an important element shaping the panel of respondents. I contacted potential interviewees via e-mail or telephone, and depended upon the individuals' willingness or ability to meet me. In the case of some politicians and some 'religious figures', I relied on other contacts to secure my interviews with them. No one declined, and few never responded to my letters (only two journalists, whom I had tried to contact via their newspapers' e-mail addresses).

The number of interviewees is equally divided between those who identify themselves as secular or religious respectively. The group of secular interviewees includes university professors, diplomats, journalists, and business figures. The group of religious interviewees includes bureaucrats, Muslim intellectuals, university professors, politicians, business figures and journalists. This group also reflects a spectrum of Turkish Islamism, including representatives of Nurçu, Nakşibendi, Fethullahçı, and Alevi groups.

Notes

1 On 2 November 2002, 14 September 2002 and 5 November 2003 respectively.

2 The following four points regarding religious mobilisation are drawn from Kalyvas (2003).

3 This was also the case, to a certain extent, for ANAP in the 1980s and a number of centre-right parties earlier. See Yıldız (2003) for a discussion of the specific determinants of *Refah*'s use of religious discourse in its focus on centre-periphery cleavages, as compared with that of other centre-right parties. Most interesting is his explanation of how *Refah* inserted religious themes into its discourse without conveying their sources (e.g. the Koran); the party thus managed to communicate with religiously oriented voters who would recognise the sources, but without drawing the attention of the secularist elites.

4 Following *Fazilet*'s closure in June 2001, this division took institutional form with the Justice and Development Party, formed under the leadership of Tayyip Erdoğan, and the Felicity Party, led by Recai Kutan.

5 The US-led force stationed, from July 1991, in south-eastern Turkey to protect the Kurds of northern Iraq against the Iraqi leader, Saddam Hussein. The operation ended in December 1996. See Dorsey (1996).

6 In fact, a heated debate broke out in January 2001 when retired general Erol Özkasnak (the former General Staff Secretary-General) made a statement – which he later retracted – referring to February 28 as a 'post-modern coup'. See *Turkish Daily News*, 16 January 2001.

7 *Refah* was brought to court in May 1997 and was outlawed by the Constitutional Court in January 1998, on the grounds that it violated the principles of secularism and the law of the political parties. Erbakan was charged under article 312 of the Turkish Penal Code and was banned from politics. See Narlı (1999a). In February 2003, the European Court of Human Rights produced a unanimous judgment in favour of Turkey in the *Refah Party and others v. Turkey* case (application nos. 41340/98, 41342/98, 41343/98 and 41344/98). See the court's Internet site for further details (http://www.echr.coe.int).

8 The party was formed by Kutan in December 1997, but was considered to be effectively led by Erbakan.

9 The debate over the article's reform became a major sticking point for the governing coalition in 2001–2002, with the Nationalist Action Party resisting proposed changes. Amendments to the article were approved in February 2002, but the changes to the article were considered by many to be simply tactical.

10 The bill became the centre of a heated debate as the then new President, Ahmet Sezer, refused – three times – to sign it. It was finally passed by Parliament in June 2001. See *Turkish Daily News*, 29 June 2001.

11 It is significant to note that several of the 'Islamists' I interviewed objected to the question 'Would you classify yourself as religious or secular?', most often stating that a *person* cannot be secular, only institutions. Furthermore, these respondents, typically, declared that they were both religious, and in support of *secular* institutions, including their national government.

12 It must be noted, however, that this interview research was conducted before the final break-up of the *Fazilet* Party; a small number of interviewees did indicate that the modernising faction of *Fazilet* might reflect a gradual, sincere transformation of political Islam.

13 At the time of the interview, the active 'religion-oriented party' (to which the interviewee refers) was the *Fazilet* Party.

14 The term 'Muslim intellectual', as per Meeker's (1997: 189) definition, refers to elite figures who, mainly as columnists and essayists, criticise Republican

political and cultural institutions and call for re-Islamization of the way of life of Turkish believers.

15 For a history of tensions between the Alevi Muslims and the Sunni majority in Turkey, see Özdemır and Frank (2000) and Shankland (1999).

16 The Directorate of Religious Affairs, a state institution that administers mosques, religious education, and religious foundations and charities in accordance with the dictates of Sunni Islam.

17 Because of space limitations, I focus below on the AKP specifically and not on the *Saadet Partisi* ('Felicity Party') or on Islamism beyond political Islam.

18 It is significant to note, however, an ANAR report revealing that in terms of grassroots support of Turkish membership of the EU, the AKP (with 69 per cent) ranks second to last, above only *Saadet*'s grassroots support (56 per cent). See Akyol (2002). But more important to the present analysis is the interaction between a strongly pro-EU political Islamist structure and the Turkish state structure.

19 See *Turkish Daily News*, 25 March, 19 September, 15 September and 24 October 2002 respectively. Limitations on Erdoğan also came from President Ahmet Necdet Sezer, through his initial refusal to allow constitutional amendments that would pave the way for Erdoğan's official leadership of the party.

20 See also Çağatay (2002) for his discussion on Erdoğan's efforts towards consensus building.

21 Üktü cites here Hasan Koni, Professor of International Relations, Ankara University.

22 The US offer of grants and loan guarantees amounted to some $30 billion, and Turkey has a $16 billion loan pact with the IMF linked to economic reforms. The military claimed that it would be a shorter, less costly conflict if Turkey were to cooperate with the United States. See Göktaş (2003).

23 An Ankara Social Research Centre poll reported that 94 per cent of the population opposed the use of Turkish bases and troops to attack Iraq, and 87 per cent opposed any US military intervention in Iraq. See Çalışkan and Taşkın (2003).

24 The vote was 264–251 with 19 abstentions; 267 votes were required for its approval.

25 Of course, the fact that the entry of British troops into Iraq led to no comparable statements from the EU against the UK government raised serious questions of fairness in Turkey.

26 The Committee's full title is 'European Parliamentary Committee on Foreign Affairs, Human Rights, Common Security and Defence Policy'. The 'Draft Report on Turkey's application for membership of the EU' was issued on 12 March 2003. Quite notably, after many complaints on the matter, references to Kemalism were removed in the final report (issued in May 2003). The final text does, however, refer to the army as an obstacle to Turkish democratisation. See http://www.abhaber.com/pdf2/oostlanderrapor.pdf, and *Turkish Daily News*, 14 May 2003 respectively.

27 Rumours which, notably, the Chief of Staff, General Özkök, himself has contested. See the Turkish press coverage of 28 and 29 May 2003.

References

Akyol, T. (2000), 'For the love of Europe!', *Milliyet*, 11 June.

Bekdil, B. (2002), 'Turkish president clashes with Erdoğan in "silent war"', *Kathimerini*, 24 December.

Berger, P. (2000), 'Secularism in retreat', in J. Esposito and A. Tamimi (eds), *Islam and Secularism in the Middle East*, New York: New York University Press, pp. 38–51.

Boulton, L. (2002), 'Erdoğan refuses to rise to anti-Turkish bait', *Financial Times*, 11 November.

Bourcier, N. (2002), 'Islamiste, démocrate, conservateur, comment qualifier l'AKP?', *Le Monde*, 9 November.

Bowcott, O. (2002), 'Islamic party wins in Turkey', *Guardian*, 7 November.

Briefing (2000), issue 1305, 14 August, p. 3.

Çağatay, S. (2002), 'The November 2002 elections and Turkey's new political era', *Meria Journal*, vol. 6, no. 4, available at http://meria.idc.ac.il/journal/2002/issue4/jv6n4a6.html (accessed 2 February 2003).

Çakır, R. (1990), 'Les Mouvements islamistes turcs et l'Europe', *Cemoti*, vol. 10, pp. 15–23.

Çalışkan, K. and Y. Taşkın (2003), 'Litmus test: Turkey's neo-Islamists weigh war and peace', *Middle East Report Online*, available at http://www.merip.org/mero/mero013003.html (accessed 2 February 2003).

Çarkoglu, A. (2002), 'Turkey's November 2002 elections: a new beginning?', *Meria Journal*, vol. 6, no. 4, pp. 30–41, available at http://meria.idc.ac.il/journal/2002/issue4/jv6n4a4.html (accessed 2 February 2003).

Dorsey, J. (1996), 'Erbakan striking a balance between Islamic neighbors and secular Army', *Washington Report*, October.

Dorsey, J. (1997), 'Turkish military advice', *Washington Report*, June/July.

Dünya Gazetesi Online (2003), available at: http://www.dunyagazetesi.com.tr/lobby_eng.asp?dept_id=87&menu_htl=on (accessed 24 March 2003).

Dymond, J. (2003), 'Analysis: Turkey's border tensions', *BBC News*, 23 March, available at http://news.bbc.co.uk/1/hi/world/2878803.stm (accessed 23 March 2003).

EP (2003), *European Parliament Committee on Foreign Affairs, Human Rights, Common Defence and Security Policy Draft Report*, available at http://www.abhaber.com/pdf2/oostlanderrapor.pdf (accessed 30 April 2003).

Finkel, A. (1995), 'Çiller stays as caretaker amid search for coalition', *The Times*, 26 December.

Georgiou, T. (2002), 'Main obstacles of Turkey on the path to EU', *Turkish Daily News*, 13 November.

Göksel, M. (undated), 'Islamic fundamentalism in Turkey', http://www.stanford.edu/class/e297c/war_peace/europe/hturkey.html (accessed 3 March 2001).

Göktaş, H. (2003), 'Turkey's Erdoğan set for power, faces Iraq dilemma'. *Reuters*, 11 March, available at www.reuters.com/newsArticle.jhtml (accessed 11 March 2003).

Gülalp, H. (undated), 'Globalization and political Islam: the social bases of Turkey's Welfare Party', unpublished paper.

Heper, M. (1981), 'Islam, polity and society in Turkey: a Middle Eastern perspective', *Middle East Journal*, vol. 35, no. 3, pp. 345–363.

Heper, M. and Ş. Toktaş, (2003), 'Islam, modernity, and democracy in contemporary Turkey: the case of Recep Tayyip Erdogan', *The Muslim World*, vol. 93, pp. 157–185.

Kalyvas, S. (2003), 'Religious mobilisation and unsecular politics', in T. Kselman and J. Buttigieg (eds), *European Christian Democracy: Historical Legacies and Comparative Perspectives*, Notre Dame, IN: University of Notre Dame Press.

Lobjakas, A. (2003), 'Union doubles aid to Turkey, warns against Iraq incursions', Radio Free Europe, 26 March, available at http://www.rferl.org/nca/features/2003/03/26032003153957.asp (accessed 26 March 2003).

Meeker, M. (1997), 'The new Muslim intellectuals in the Republic of Turkey', in R. Tapper (ed.), *Islam in Modern Turkey*. London: I. B. Tauris, pp. 189–222.

Le Monde (2002), 'En Turquie, l'arrivée au pouvoir des islamistes modérés de l'AKP est accueillie dans le calme', 6 November, p. 4.

Narlı, N. (1999a), 'The rise of the Islamist movement in Turkey', *MERIA Journal*, vol. 3, no. 3, available at http://www.biu.ac.il/SOC/besa/meria/journal/1999/issue3/jv3n3a4.html (accessed 8 January 2000).

Narlı, N. (1999b), 'The tension between the centre and peripheral economy and the rise of a counter business elite in Turkey', *Les Annales de l'autre Islam*, no. 6, pp. 50–72.

Narlı, N. (1999c), 'Urbanisation, structural change, and the rise of the Islamist movement in Turkey', paper presented at the International Symposium 'Beyond the Border: A New Framework for Understanding the Dynamism of Muslim Societies', Kyoto.

Osman, K. (1997), 'Turkish army dictates policy over role of Islam in society', *Muslimedia*, 16–31 May.

Özdemır, A. and K. Frank (2000), *Visible Islam in Modern Turkey*, Basingstoke, UK: Macmillan.

Pope, N. (2003), 'Le Pouvoir turc', *Le Monde*, 10 March.

Sayarı, S. (1996), 'Turkey's Islamist Challenge', *Middle East Quarterly*, September.

Shankland, D. (1999), *Islam and Society in Turkey*, Cambridge: Eothen Press.

Smith, H. (2003), 'New Turkish leader seeks deal in Cyprus', *Guardian*, 3 January.

Smith, H. and N. Watt (2003), 'Turkey delays US troop decision', *Guardian*, 3 March.

Tapper, R. (1994), 'Introduction', in R. Tapper (ed.), *Islam in Modern Turkey*, London: I. B. Tauris, pp. 1–30.

Turkish Daily News (2002), 'PM candidate Erdoğan rejects Islamist mantle', 14 September.

Turkish Daily News (2003), 'Doors not closed in Cyprus', 12 March.

Turkish Daily News (2003), 'EU warns Turkey on plans to enter northern Iraq', 22 March.

Ütkü, S. (2003), 'Turkey faces tough decision on Cyprus, its EU future', AFP report published by *EU Business*, 27 February, available at http://www.eubusiness.com/cgi-bin/item.cgi?id=104386&d=101&h=&f=&dateformat=%o%20%B%20%Y (accessed 28 February 2002).

Vick, K. (2002), 'How Islamic is Turkey's new political star?', *Washington Post*, 11 November.

Woollacott, M. (2002), 'Is it in Turkey's interests to join this Christian club?', *Guardian*, 13 December.

Yıldız, A. (2003), 'Politico-religious discourse of political Islam in Turkey: the parties of National Outlook', *Muslim World*, vol. 93, pp. 187–209.

Zubaida, S. (2000), 'Trajectories of political Islam: Egypt, Iran and Turkey', in D. Marquand and R. L. Nettler (eds), *Religion and Democracy*, Oxford: Blackwell.

Part IV

International–domestic interactions

8 Helsinki, Copenhagen and beyond

Challenges to the New Europe and the Turkish state

E. Fuat Keyman and Ziya Öniş

Introduction

A quick glance at recent literature on Turkish democracy and its consolidation reveals that the dominant tendency has been to emphasize the significance of internal or domestic factors, which include both political actors and state institutions (Keyman, 2000; Özbudun, 1999). Thus, the literature refers to the clientelistic and populist centre-right or centre-left political parties and their increasing detachment from Turkish society, as well as to institutional problems stemming from the increasingly ineffective and undemocratic characteristic of the strong-state tradition in Turkey. Although this literature provides us with a set of important insights into Turkish politics and its democratic deficit, it remains partial and limited because it overlooks factors in the international context – that is, international organizations and actors – that also exert powerful pressures on Turkey. For example, recent international developments such as enlargement of the European Union (EU) and the war on Iraq have affected Turkish politics directly and demonstrated that it is no longer possible to separate the national from the international, and vice versa.

Therefore, we propose to analyse the consolidation of Turkish democracy by focusing on what we call 'the international/domestic interactions' (Keyman, 2000; Öniş, 2003). We put forward the argument that the process of Turkey's full accession into the EU has to be taken into account in any analysis of Turkish democracy and its possible consolidation, in so far as this process has been yielding system-transforming effects on Turkish politics. In substantiating our argument, we will first focus on the 'post-Helsinki' period (from 2000 to the present), in which the accession process has been generating significant challenges that confront the state-centric nature of Turkish politics and its increasingly ineffective and undemocratic structure. Second, we will argue that in analysing Turkey–EU relations, we should also take into account important developments that have been taking place in the 'New Europe'. These developments have revealed that the 'New Europe' is not a monolithic idea, nor does it signify an entity immune to contradictory and dialectical developments. Not only individual states (such as the United Kingdom, Germany and France as well as the new Eastern European members) but also broad political movements (such as Christian democrats or social democrats of the Third Way variety) hold rather contrasting visions of the future of Europe. These differences and the tensions associated with them have influenced and will continue to influence the future trajectory of Turkey–Europe relations. Therefore, it is important and methodologically necessary that we look at Turkey's democratization and Turkey–EU relations in a multi-dimensional and reciprocal manner, paying attention to how both domestic and international contexts have impacted on Turkey, Europe and their historical association.

In order to develop and substantiate these arguments, we will first examine recent developments in Turkey and the need to make it an economically stable and democratic society. Then, we focus on the contradictions and tensions that the idea of the New Europe involves, especially in relation to the question of security and war. Third, we will delineate the ways in which the Helsinki summit of December 1999 and the Copenhagen summit of December 2002 have confronted the state-centric structure of Turkish politics and its democratic deficit. Finally, we will conclude our analysis with a suggestion that in the post-September 11 world, where US hegemonic unilateralism privileges security issues over democracy and economic development, the incorporation of a democratic and economically stable Turkey into the New Europe is beneficial to and necessary for both Europe and Turkey.

8.1 Turkey at crossroads

At the beginning of the twenty-first century, Turkey has found itself at a critical juncture. As a country whose economy has been going through a severe crisis and whose state-centric politics has been facing a strong legitimacy crisis, and whose social and cultural life has been generating a number of identity-based conflicts, Turkey has to make a crucial decision about its future. These recent economic, political and cultural developments have been pushing Turkey forcefully into a situation in which it has to decide either to shake itself radically and restructure its state–society relations in a democratic and liberal mode; or to hide once again behind the illusionary walls of state-centricism and nationalism. Although the second choice has always been privileged during the 1990s in the name of stability and security, today there is a strong societal will and demand to make Turkey an economically stable, democratically governed and culturally pluralist society.

The possibility of creating a different, strong and democratic Turkey is no longer naïve optimism; on the contrary, it constitutes an achievable reality. Three historical events, namely those of the November 2002 elections, the Copenhagen summit of December 2002, and the US-led war on

Iraq have played a significant role in this context. These events have indicated that the possibility of creating a democratic and economically strong Turkey can be achieved if the strong societal demand for democratization and economic stability can be transformed into a political will to restructure the state in a way that would make it efficient, accountable and transparent. These historical events also indicated that there should in fact be a strong political will to make Turkey economically strong and democratic. Given that international relations are steadily being reshaped through war in the post-September 11 world, it has become clear that Turkey's strength in dealing effectively with world affairs derives not only from its geopolitical location, but more importantly from its ability to overcome its own internal problems of economic instability and democratic deficit. It will be useful at this point to delineate briefly the ways in which these historical events have forced Turkey to make a crucial decision about its possible future.

On the evening of 3 November 2002, as the final vote count came in, an electoral earthquake shook Turkish politics. The three parties that had formed the coalition government after the 1999 elections, as well as two opposition parties, failed to pass the 10 per cent national threshold and found themselves left outside Parliament. This electoral punishment was so dramatic, but at the same time so deserved, that the winner of the 1999 elections, the Democratic Left Party (DSP), lost almost its entire constituency. Other parties found themselves thrown out of Parliament by losing more than half their electoral support. These results reflected Turkish people's deep anger towards the existing political system and its constituent political parties, characterized by economic populism, clientelism, corruption and democratic deficiencies (Heper and Keyman, 1998). In addition, the November 2002 elections have given rise to the possibility of overcoming these problems of Turkish politics by creating strong, single-party majority rule. The winner of the election, the Justice and Development Party (AKP), received 34.2 per cent of the popular vote, gained 66 per cent of the parliamentary seats and formed a single-party majority government. The Republican People's Party (CHP), with 19.4 per cent of the popular vote and 34 per cent of the parliamentary seats, became the main, and single, opposition party.

At a time when Turkey was going through its deepest economic crisis, with tragic consequences in terms of poverty, insecurity and unemployment, the national elections brought hope and optimism to Turkey. These positive feelings were based on the expectation that the ineffective and undemocratic state-centric governing structure had run its course and that a strong government with institutional and societal support could make Turkey a democratic and economically stable country (Keyman, 2003: 1–2).

After the elections, the first challenge to the AKP government was the Copenhagen summit of December 2002, where the boundaries of the New

Europe were to be determined and in which Turkey aimed to obtain a definite date for the start of accession negotiations. The Copenhagen summit declared that the accession negotiations between the EU and Turkey will start after December 2004 without delay on condition that Turkey fulfils what are known as 'the Copenhagen political criteria'. This decision represents a strong external pressure on Turkey to achieve democratization and economic stability within a given period.

In this sense, the Copenhagen summit was an historical event in two significant respects. First, after the Helsinki summit of 1999, in which Turkey had been finally granted candidate status, the Copenhagen summit has created a sense of 'certainty' in EU–Turkey relations by giving a specific date for the beginning of the accession negotiations (Öniş and Keyman, 2003). Even though 2004 was a conditional date, it was nevertheless an important move forward, in so far as it has provided Turkey with the prospect that full EU membership is a real possibility. Second, the Copenhagen summit has created a historical moment in Turkey, in that the AKP, even though it has failed to achieve its main goal (i.e. obtaining a definite date for the start of accession negotiations), has learned an important lesson: as a country ridden with economic and political crises, Turkey would always face serious problems in its relations with the EU, even though it remains a geopolitically important force. In contrast, a Turkey that had solved its economic and political problems (i.e. a Turkey that had achieved democratization and economic stability) would be better placed to begin accession negotiations.

Yet the Copenhagen summit has also demonstrated that creating an economically stable and fully democratic Turkey is not an easy process. This outcome cannot be achieved only through the legal and constitutional changes that Turkey initiated in August 2002 – that is, the abolition of capital punishment, the protection of human rights and the recognition of minority rights. Although these changes play a critical role in securing a conditional date for the start of accession negotiations, they do not yet constitute proof that democracy has become the defining aspect of state–society relations in Turkey. What is needed is the full application of the Copenhagen political criteria in such a way that substantial democracy (with emphasis placed on the normative primacy of individual rights and freedoms) becomes the defining feature of Turkish politics (Müftüler-Baç, 2002).

Whereas both the November 2002 elections and the Copenhagen summit of December 2002 have played a positive role in the process of overcoming the crisis-ridden nature of Turkish politics, the US-led war on Iraq so far has had highly negative effects. As a country that borders Iraq, Turkey found itself forced to decide either to ally with the United States by allowing the deployment of US troops in its own territory or to refuse to be directly involved in the war by acting in accordance with the strong anti-war will of its people. At a time when its economic policy was framed to a large extent by the IMF structural adjustment programme and when its historical association with Europe had gained a certain degree of momentum after the Copenhagen summit of December 2002, Turkey could hardly afford to be torn between strong US military demands on the one hand and the strong international and national civil resistance to the war on the other.

When the Bush administration declared at the end of 2002 that the use of military force was the only option to disarm Iraq of weapons of mass destruction, it directed its attention to Turkey, the so-called strategic partner. The reason for this attention was the geopolitical importance of Turkey in the creation of what has come to be known as 'the Northern front', which would give easy passage to US troops to enable them to reach Baghdad in a speedy fashion. Negotiations between the Bush administration and the AKP government involved a set of economic, military and political issues. Economically, what was at stake was the necessary financial assistance to compensate Turkey for its economic losses during the war. Militarily, they concerned the deployment of US troops. Politically, they concerned serious reservations that the Turkish state had on the post-war reconstruction of Iraq and the status of the Kurds in northern Iraq.

Confronted by deep economic insecurity, the AKP government gave primacy to the financial aid that it would receive from the United States and announced that it was ready to accept the US military demands. However, by the small margin of three votes, the Turkish Parliament decided against the government's bill and disallowed the deployment of US troops through south-eastern Turkey. Although this decision was right, and reflected the will of the Turkish people, it has created a serious political crisis in Turkey. That was because the AKP government has thus become subject to serious criticism initiated by both national and international economic/financial actors supporting the US-led war against Iraq. The AKP has been criticized for lacking the political will to govern Turkey powerfully, and has been charged with misleading the Bush administration, thereby creating a serious crisis in the strategic alliance between the United States and Turkey. It has also been criticized for creating unnecessary turmoil in the Turkish economy, which has been going through its deepest crisis yet.

Although these criticisms could be justified on the grounds that the AKP government did mislead the Bush administration and did not present its position on the war clearly, Parliament's decision to reject the enabling bill was an internationally significant stance. It demonstrated to the international community that Turkey could act morally irrespective of what its economic interests dictate and that it could say no to the hegemonic power even though its ability to overcome the economic crisis depends largely on its alliance with that power. However, Turkey's relations with the Bush administration in the pre-war period made it clear that without solving its economic problems and its democratic deficiencies, Turkey cannot be strong in its relations with powerful national or international actors, nor can it take autonomous decisions concerning its future. Only an economically strong and democratic Turkey can be powerful as a middle-ranking power in international relations. In that sense, the war on Iraq has demonstrated to Turkey that in the post-September 11 world, security, economic stability and democracy should be considered intertwined processes – especially for those countries within the reach of US influence. It is therefore necessary for Turkey not to ignore or defer its economic and political problems under the pretext of prioritizing its security and/or geopolitical interests. On the contrary, it has to come to terms with the fact that Turkey can ensure its security and maintain its geopolitical importance only to the extent that it can resolve its economic and political problems.

Turkey is not the only country that has been affected negatively by the US-led war against Iraq. The EU too found itself entering perhaps the worst political crisis since its inception. The unconditional support that Britain and Spain have given to the Bush administration in its unilateral decision to declare war (which had no international support or legitimacy) and the alliance between Germany and France to seek a political solution to the problem of disarming Iraq have created a deep split in the EU. In this process, the EU has realized that its exclusive focus on democracy and economic prosperity, without internalizing the importance of security, does not constitute a sufficient basis for making Europe a powerful actor in rapidly changing world affairs and against US hegemony (Anderson, 2002). In what follows, we will examine the political crisis that Europe is faced with, a crisis that must be overcome not only if Europe is to provide any credible alternative to the US view of world politics but also if it is to continue playing a positive role in Turkey's democratization process.

8.2 The 'New Europe' and its contradictions

In his important study on the process of European enlargement, Christopher Hill (2002: 104) has argued as follows:

> Ultimately the citizens of the European Union have to decide whether they need collectively to be a major *actor* in world politics like the United States, with all the advantages and disadvantages that implies, or whether they are willing to settle for an EU near the centre of a *network* of international processes but without the ability to have a decisive impact on matters affecting security and the pattern of international order. It is not mere chance that this potentially explosive issue has barely surfaced thus far. The progress of enlargement, however, will bring it inexorably into the open. [emphasis in original]

Hill's prediction came true long before he expected, as the United States' unilateral actions to impose the 'new American century' reached an apogee with its declaration of war on Iraq. Just after the 'New Europe' was announced in the closing ceremony of the Copenhagen summit of December 2002, the declaration of war on Iraq had a devastating impact on the EU. As the unconditional support of the British government for the war was followed first by Spain, then by some other members of the EU (including the most of the Eastern European entrants), and as Germany and France allied themselves with Russia and China in the United Nations Security Council to oppose the war on Iraq, the EU has found itself in a very serious political crisis.

Although the split in the EU has emerged as a result of different member-state reactions to the Unites States' unilateralist decision, the difference constituted a political crisis for two important reasons. First, it has become clear that European states did not act as unified members of the New Europe, but rather as separate and autonomous nation-states pursuing their own national interests within the hegemonic space to be created by US unilateralism. This development indicates that when security and war rather than economic prosperity and cultural identity are at stake, some European states would prefer hegemonic power to economic union for formulating and pursuing national interests. While the individual stance of Britain in this direction was not too surprising, what was surprising was the pronounced divisions that the impending Iraq war created within the broad ranks of the New Europe itself. In a rather paradoxical manner, the core Franco-German alliance was subjected to a growing challenge by a number of EU members, including Spain, Portugal and the new Eastern European entrants, which adopted a strongly pro-US position in relation to terrorism and the necessity of a war in Iraq. Thus, in the post-Copenhagen context, the EU appeared to be a fragmented entity faced with a serious identity crisis.

Second, and more generally, the political crisis in the EU indicates that the idea of the New Europe, constructed by the discourses of economic prosperity and advanced democracy, is not powerful enough to constitute a solid alternative to the 'security-based thinking' initiated by the Bush administration. In that sense, the New Europe and the process of enlargement on which it has been founded have to take seriously the questions of security and geopolitics. Otherwise, Europe can become neither an economically and democratically prosperous space of integration, nor a major global actor powerful enough to influence the process of shaping and reshaping international politics.

However, to understand the EU's failure to generate a common foreign and security policy, it is important also to question the theoretical and normative grounds on which the idea of the New Europe has been founded. The New Europe of the 1990s can be distinguished with reference to the two separate yet interrelated theoretical arguments. The first argument is that the New Europe is a post-Westphalian formation (Rumford, 2002). This argument suggests that the post-Cold War world is increasingly framed by globalization, a process that makes states, societies and individuals interdependent in a complex way. This results in the decline of nation-states' role in international relations, the increasing importance of international organizations, and the possibility of deep and complex cooperation among nation-states, especially in the interest of economic prosperity and democratization. As a result, the basic units and principles of the Westphalian international relations have lost their privileged positions, as the world is becoming more and more global. It has become more difficult, the argument goes, to think of international relations as mainly inter-state relations, to assign primacy to the principle of state sovereignty, and to overlook the importance of economic prosperity and democracy in the production and reproduction of order and stability in world affairs.

On this view, the post-Westphalian world involves cooperation, democratization and economic prosperity, and the New Europe operates as a post-Westphalian formation (Held, 1995; Linklater, 1998; Beck, 1997). Although significant progress in the EU has been achieved in terms of pooling sovereignty around a supra-national project notably in the areas of economic integration and in terms of establishing common standards of democracy and human rights, the EU has failed to see the continuing importance of security issues in the post-Westphalian world – especially in the post-September 11 world. It is clear today that the future of the New Europe and its place in international relations, framed increasingly by the United States' unilateralist mode of operation and its quest for hegemony, will be determined by its ability to forge strong cooperation in the fields of foreign and security policies. The ability to do so depends upon thinking theoretically of security, economic prosperity and democracy not as separate but as intertwined dimensions of the European identity.

The second argument concerning the theoretical and philosophical foundation of the New Europe is that it is a post-national state. For some, the New Europe represents a transition from the nation-state to the post-national state (Curtin, 1997; Habermas, 2001; van Ham, 2001). This transition involves 'the emergence of a legally constituted quasi-transnational state and the resulting loss in national sovereignty', both of which together have 'clearly undermined the territorial nation-state as the primary unit in the making of European history' (Delanty, 2003: 8–9). The post-national state, in this view, constitutes a move towards political integration in which the New Europe defines itself mainly as a space of economic prosperity and democracy rather than security. However, what we are observing today is the fact that the move from the nation-state to the post-national state is not, in fact has not been, a linear and unproblematic process. Considerable tensions have existed in the past and continue to exist in certain key domains. Countries are clearly reluctant to lose sovereignty over key areas of national security and foreign policy in a world where the nation-state remains an important political actor in its own right. The war on Iraq has made this role of the nation-state very clear – so much so that the hegemon, in its unilateralist mode of operation, is acting as a nation-state privileging its own national interest over global problems and attempting to impose its security-based thinking on international relations through force rather than consent (Anderson, 2002).

Having briefly delineated the crucial problems with which the EU and its idea of the New Europe are faced, we can now argue that the EU and its enlargement strategy can no longer ignore the question of security and geopolitics. It is true that international relations today are post-Westphalian and post-national, and that economic prosperity and democracy are crucial areas for cooperation among the units of the international system. It is also true that the world is increasingly global, in that the EU, with its emphasis on post-national norms and values, is an important actor that constitutes a crucial point of reference for the creation of democratic global governance. However, it is equally true that we are living in a post-September 11 world, in which force enjoys primacy over consent, security matters and national interest remain important, and geopolitics maintains its importance in the determination of power, influence and domination. In this context, the New Europe, to achieve further progress in the direction of a post-Westphalian and post-national formation, should take into account the importance of security and geopolitics in thinking about its political place and role in world affairs and in discussing its cultural identity.

Given the importance of security and cultural identity, Turkey (with its geopolitical importance and its pivotal position at the EU's borders) constitutes an important and challenging test case for the New Europe (Delanty, 2003; Larrabee and Lesser, 2003). Therefore, Turkey's place in the New Europe would depend not only upon its democratization and economic stability, but also upon the decisions that the New Europe will make about its power and role in the post-September 11 world. To appreciate the relevance of analysing Turkey–EU relations in a multidimensional and reciprocal manner, it is necessary to focus on the increasingly complex nature of these relations and their impacts on the consolidation of Turkish democracy since the Helsinki summit of December 1999, where Turkey was granted candidate country status. It is to this question that we will direct our attention in what follows.

8.3 Democratization and challenges to the Turkish state in the post-Helsinki era

By offering Turkey the possibility of full membership, the Helsinki decision of December 1999 provided a powerful impetus for change in

Turkey's domestic politics and helped to instigate a series of radical reforms on the democratization front. The comparative literature on democratization suggests that external influences *per se* cannot generate democratic transition or consolidation within a single national space (Whitehead, 1996). Nevertheless, the literature also suggests that external dynamics can play a significantly positive role, provided that the underlying conditions for such transformation are also favourable (ibid.). Hence, to establish a balanced perspective on the impact of the Helsinki summit, we need to take into account that parliamentary democracy constituted the norm in Turkey in the post-1945 period in spite of its inherent limitations and frequent, though short-lived, interruptions (Özbudun, 1999). Furthermore, Turkey enjoyed the beginnings of a vibrant civil society during the 1990s. Finally, we should recognize that the end of the armed conflict with the Kurdistan Workers' Party (PKK) in the early part of 1999 also helped to provide a more congenial environment within which democratization reforms could proceed.

Given this background, the Helsinki decision was a crucial catalyst in Turkey's democratization trajectory. Previously, the major locus of interaction between Turkey and the New Europe in the 1990s involved the signing of the customs union agreement (Balkır, 1998). In the absence of firm prospects for full membership, however, the customs union provided few incentives for the Turkish political elites to undertake the reforms that would satisfy the Copenhagen criteria. Following the Helsinki decision, Turkey was confronted with a more balanced set of conditions and incentives to undertake the kind of reforms demanded by the EU for full membership. Admittedly, the mix of conditions and incentives provided by the EU continued to be less favourable than those offered to Eastern European candidate countries. Financial assistance by the EU was extremely limited. Furthermore, Turkey was faced with asymmetric incentives in terms of its ability to resolve the Cyprus dispute. The fact that the EU was willing to admit (Southern) Cyprus as a full member without any conditions concerning the resolution of the conflict with the North provided few incentives for an equitable solution to the dispute (Öniş, 2001). It was only with the announcement of the UN plan shortly before the Copenhagen summit that there was a serious possibility of a peaceful resolution to the dispute, with the prospect of eliminating a major hurdle on the path to Turkey's full membership.

In retrospect, the process of institutionalized interaction with the EU initiated at Helsinki represented a powerful stimulus for change in Turkish politics. Post-Helsinki dynamics clearly facilitated the development of a powerful 'pro-EU coalition' in Turkey. This coalition not only was committed to EU membership as a general ideal, but also was prepared to push for the kinds of reforms needed to satisfy the conditions specified by the EU. Business-based civil society organizations, notably the organization that represented the community of big business in Turkey, the Turkish Industrialists' and Businessmen's Association (TUSIAD), emerged as the dominant components of this pro-EU coalition (Öniş, 2003; and see Chapter 5 of this book). This coalition, in turn, presented a major challenge to the Turkish state, and notably the security and the foreign policy establishment. To be fair, the Turkish state elites were also committed to the notion of EU membership, mainly because membership has been considered a natural step in Turkey's modernization drive, which was synonymous with steady integration with the West. Nevertheless, such groups were not willing to relinquish autonomy and sovereignty on issues that they considered of vital importance for national security (Cizre, 1997). The mindset of the security-conscious state elites could not comprehend the kind of post-national state and the notion of pooling of sovereignty that had been associated with the emergence of the New Europe in the 1980s and the 1990s. In other words, the so called 'anti-EU coalition' in Turkey was characterized by its unwillingness to undertake the kinds of reforms necessary to graduate to EU membership, on the grounds that such reforms would undermine the autonomy and sovereignty of the nation-state.

A powerful bloc represented not only by the security and foreign policy establishments but also by the political parties of the right and the left continued to provide serious resistance to EU-related reforms in the post-Helsinki era. It is fair to say that the two dominant parties of the coalition government formed in 1999, namely the left-wing DSP and the right-wing Nationalist Action Party (MHP), were both characterized by a heavily nationalistic outlook (Kınıkoğlu, 2002; Çınar and Arıkan, 2002). Both parties resisted the kind of sensitive political reforms demanded by the EU such as the abolition of the death penalty and the extension of cultural rights for minority groups. Only the Motherland Party (ANAP), a centre-right party and a minor member of the coalition government, appeared to be more supportive of the EU-related reform agenda. Even in the case of ANAP, a considerable rift could be identified between the leader and the rank and file of the party in terms of commitment to EU-related reforms. In retrospect, political parties in Turkey lagged behind civil society organizations in terms of the degree of support they provided for EU membership. Rather paradoxically, the AKP, in spite of its Islamist roots, emerged as the political party that appeared to display the type of commitment towards EU membership that was not visible in the case of any other political party on either the right or the left of the political spectrum. The AKP, with a claim to establish itself as a moderate, centre-right party distinct from its predecessors (the Welfare and the Virtue Parties), proved to be particularly vigorous in its push for EU membership in the two months leading up to the Copenhagen summit of December 2002.

In a joint article published in 1999, Buzan and Diez had claimed that EU membership would be detrimental for Turkey because it would help to repress or undermine its essentially Islamic identity. Five years after the publication of this article, it was quite a paradox that a political party with explicit Islamist roots should emerge as the most vocal element of support for EU membership in Turkey. The underlying motive for the party's active support for EU membership involved not only the material benefits associated with full membership, but also the extension of religious freedoms that challenged the authoritarian secularism of the Turkish state. What Buzan and Diez had failed to see at the time was that the EU could provide a degree of protection for Islamists in Turkey and enable them to be more vocal in their identity claims, admittedly within well-defined limits. In that sense, the EU clearly posed a challenge to the boundaries of democratic politics set by the Turkish state.

In spite of considerable resistance from various segments of the state and the party political spectrum, EU-related reforms gained considerable momentum during the course of 2002. Clearly, the pro-EU coalitions led by civil society organizations performed an instrumental role in this respect. The pressures emanating from civil society have not been confined to TUSIAD alone. Other organizations, primarily those with certain links to the private sector – notably the Economic Development Foundation (IKV) and a liberal think-tank organization, the Turkish Economic and Social Studies Foundation (TESEV) – have also been quite active in this context. Indeed, the IKV has been instrumental in the creation of an unprecedentedly broad-based civil movement in Turkey under the umbrella of Movement for Europe 2002, which constituted a broad platform that mobilized 175 civil society organizations to take collective action in June 2002 in favour of Turkey's accession to the EU. We should also be careful in treating the Turkish state as a monolithic entity in this respect. Certainly, important segments of Turkey's state bureaucracy adopted a liberal approach towards EU-related reforms and consequently constituted an important segment of the emerging pro-EU coalition. Elements of the pro-EU coalition within the Turkish state included elements within the Ministry of Foreign Affairs, the newly created Secretariat for EU Affairs as well as constituencies in key segments of the economic bureaucracy such as the Central Bank, the Treasury and the State Planning Organization among others. Looking back, one could argue that one of the important repercussions of the Helsinki decision was the creation of a rift not only between the state and civil society, but also between different components of the Turkish state itself.

The deep economic crisis that Turkey experienced in late 2000 and early 2001 was another important force that accelerated the reform momentum. The potential material benefits associated with EU membership looked all the more attractive at a time when the country was experiencing its deepest economic crisis of the post-war period. The economic crisis also had the effect of breaking down the resistance of the anti-EU coalition, a process that would have been far more difficult under normal circumstances. No doubt the impending Copenhagen summit placed additional pressures on the domestic political actors in terms of accelerating the pace of legislative changes required by the EU. The way that the reform process picked up in the latter half of 2002 after a slow start in the immediate post-Helsinki phase clearly illustrates the power of the EU anchor.

To the surprise of most observers, Turkey experienced a series of rather path-breaking legislative changes on the democratization front in August 2002. A number of important reforms that would have been unimaginable only a few years ago (abolition of the death penalty altogether and a radical extension of cultural rights for minority groups) became a reality by the end of summer 2002, with direct implications for the Kurdish segments of the population. Given the pace with which the reform process was accomplished, the impending Copenhagen summit was anticipated with considerable enthusiasm by wide segments of the Turkish public. Expectations concerning a favourable decision emerging at the Copenhagen summit were raised considerably at a time when the anti-EU coalition clearly found itself in a defensive position. The United Nations Plan for Cyprus – the so-called Annan Plan – was announced during November 2002, shortly after the general elections, and raised hopes concerning the possibility that the long-standing dispute over Cyprus could be resolved in a peaceful manner. The resolution of the Cyprus problem would have removed yet another major obstacle on the path to Turkey's EU membership.

A sober assessment, however, would indicate that the progress achieved fell rather short of EU expectations in several key respects in spite of path-breaking legislative changes. From the EU point of view, a vital consideration involved the ability to translate major legislative changes into effective implementation. The privileged position of the army and the nature of civil–military relations continued to be a cause of serious concern. Political changes were not in themselves sufficient if they accompanied by fundamental economic reforms that would help to overcome the low-growth, high-inequality syndrome in which the Turkish economy has appeared to be trapped in recent years. In the presence of limited economic progress, the task of accommodating Turkey from the EU standpoint would appear to be insurmountable. Finally, the Cyprus dispute, in spite of some rapprochement between the key actors involved, had not been resolved. Clearly, a balanced assessment of all these considerations rendered an exceptionally favourable decision rather unlikely in spite of the high hopes generated in the immediate prelude to the Copenhagen summit.

8.4 The Copenhagen summit from a Turkish perspective

Considerable pressure was brought to bear upon the EU authorities to generate a favourable outcome from the Copenhagen summit not only by the Turkish government and civil society organizations but also by the

United States. A favourable outcome essentially meant an early date to start accession negotiations. Considerable pressure placed by the United States on the EU leadership reflected an underlying strategic concern to tie Turkey firmly to the Western camp. In immediate terms, however, the overriding concern was to secure Turkey's cooperation in the context of the impending war on Iraq. The Copenhagen summit was also interesting in the sense that the question of how to deal with Turkey appeared to produce a considerable rift among EU members themselves. The core of the EU represented by the Franco-German alliance was not receptive to idea of early negotiations with Turkey. Britain and Southern European countries such as Spain, Italy and Greece, on the other hand, displayed greater readiness to accommodate Turkey by offering the possibility of an early date to initiate the negotiation process. At the end of the day, the position of the core alliance dominated and Turkey was offered a conditional date of December 2004, where progress with respect to reform implementation would be subjected to a comprehensive review. In retrospect, the Copenhagen summit was also significant in terms of illustrating the limits of US power and influence on the EU – particularly over decisions concerning the internal accession process.

The decision reached at Copenhagen could be interpreted as a double-edged decision from the Turkish point of view. In certain respects, it represented a definitive step forward. At Helsinki, Turkey had been offered the possibility of full membership but no date had been specified. Three years later, in the aftermath of the Copenhagen summit, Turkey was now faced with a clear timetable and a firm commitment on the EU's part that substantial progress in terms of satisfying EU conditionality would be rewarded by the opening of accession negotiations. A formal assessment would suggest that the position adapted by the EU was understandable, considering the remaining deficiencies of Turkish democracy emphasized earlier. The fact that significant progress was made over the interim period did not mean that reforms were complete. The EU clearly wanted to monitor the implementation of the key legislative changes before committing itself fully to the start of accession negotiations.

In addition to concerns indicated earlier, EU officials were also apprehensive about the true meaning of the November 2002 elections that brought the AKP to power. Although the AKP presented itself as a moderate political force, the EU elites were clearly concerned about the possibility of future clashes between the governing party and the state establishment over basic constitutional issues such as the secular character of the Turkish state. At this point, we need to indicate that a fundamental feature of EU's approach to democratization is its fundamental dislike of religious fundamentalism. Given this background, it was not surprising that the EU approached the AKP's electoral success with a certain degree of ambivalence. At one level, it was critical of the decision that, just before the elections, banned the party's leader (Tayyip Erdoğan) from active political participation. Yet at the same time, the EU was also uncertain of the party's moderate credentials, given its Islamist heritage. The EU authorities clearly feared the possibility, although they were careful not to state this openly, that the AKP's position would sooner or later assume a radical stance on religious or identity issues (such as the headscarf dispute) and could find itself in a head-on clash with the Turkish state. Taking into consideration the uncertainty surrounding the state–AKP relationship, it made sense to postpone negotiations with Turkey in order to be able to determine the ability of the Turkish state to accommodate an apparently moderate Islamic party that promised to remain within the boundaries of a secular constitutional order and yet would sooner or later push for the extension of what it considered to be essential religious freedoms.

Under normal times, and given the need for further progress in Turkey's reform process, the Copenhagen decision would have been an understandable outcome. What is critical for our purposes, however, is that the Copenhagen decision was not reached under normal circumstances. Indeed, it was reached in an extraordinary period when several important developments were taking place simultaneously. One ought to remember that the Copenhagen summit was also the occasion at which the decision to admit the Republic of Cyprus as well as several Eastern European states was approved. The ten new members could influence Turkey's accession negatively, given the potential veto power at their disposal. In addition, the early incorporation of the Republic of Cyprus into the Union, with no conditions attached in terms of resolving the dispute with the North, has created asymmetric incentives and reduced the feasibility of a solution that would comply with the broad contours of the UN initiative. Finally, the Copenhagen decision was taken at a time when the United States was preparing to wage a war on Iraq.

Given the extraordinary global context in which the Copenhagen summit was concluded, we argue that the decision was somewhat shortsighted and displayed a certain lack of vision on the part of the EU policymaking elites. A more favourable signal provided by the EU at a time of massive uncertainty concerning the future of the international society would have been of crucial significance. The decision itself has clearly been interpreted as unfavourable by wide segments of Turkish society. Therefore, the Copenhagen decision resulted in a certain loss of enthusiasm for the implementation of EU-related reforms and a revitalization of the anti-EU coalition which manifested itself, in particular, in the form of vigorous opposition to the Annan Plan.

Although it would be too early to make a prediction, the resolution of the Cyprus dispute along the lines of the Annan Plan (which provides for the re-unification of the island on the basis of two essentially sovereign states) suffered a major setback at the Copenhagen summit. Arguably, a better mix of conditions and incentives, meaning concrete terms and an earlier starting date for accession negotiations of December 2003, would have helped to strengthen the position of the pro-EU coalition considerably. The optimistic mood that such a decision would have generated would have sustained the momentum of the reform process and strengthened the hand of the AKP government to proceed with the resolution of the Cyprus dispute in line with the UN plan. The AKP clearly wanted an early date to strengthen its hand against the anti-EU coalition. After Copenhagen, the AKP became increasingly passive, was unable to meet the challenge regarding the Cyprus conflict and failed dramatically to distinguish itself from anti-EU forces. Hence, the AKP lost on two fronts in the immediate aftermath of the Copenhagen summit. On the one hand, it lost against the military and the Turkish Cypriot leader, Rauf Denktaş. It also lost against the EU because it became obvious that, at least up to the beginning of 2004, it was not prepared or able to take its fight with the anti-EU coalition to its logical conclusion. Currently, there is a possibility of solving the Cyprus problem as a result of the AKP government's recent effort to reinitiate negotiations along the lines of the Annan Plan.

Finally, the Copenhagen decision embodied two additional negative ramifications from a Turkish perspective. First, Turkey was effectively pushed into a state of isolation at a time when the country faced a crucial decision on the impending war on Iraq. Arguably, more powerful signals transmitted by the EU in a positive direction would have enhanced Turkey's ability to reduce its security dependence on the United States. This, in turn, would have enabled Turkey to tie itself explicitly to the core EU position in opposing the war and US unilateralism at the same time. Second, the Copenhagen decision helped to bring into the open the rift between the majority of the Turkish Cypriots and key segments of the Turkish state regarding the future of the island. The former appeared to favour a peaceful resolution of the Cyprus dispute along the lines of the UN plan, hoping to capitalize on the benefits of future EU membership for the island as a whole. Key elements of the Turkish state, however, voiced concerns about the plan on the grounds that it would not be consistent with Turkey's security interests. Possibly if the Copenhagen decision had been more favourable to Turkey, a rift of this nature would not have materialized, or at least, the military and the state elite would have found themselves less able to cling on to their heavily exaggerated and increasingly irrelevant security concerns.

At a deeper level, the Copenhagen summit raised some fundamental questions concerning the nature of European identity and the very meaning of the notion of 'Europeanization' itself. Turkey's aspirations to become a full EU member had raised questions concerning the precise boundaries of Europe right from the outset. Indeed, a clear dividing line had emerged between the social democrat and Christian democrat perspectives. The former, with its broad vision of a multicultural Europe, proved more receptive to Turkey's eventual accession provided that the country undertook the reforms necessary to satisfy the Copenhagen criteria. Christian democrats, in contrast, found it more difficult to come to terms with Turkey's eventual membership, given their narrow conception of European identity (EUobserver, 2002). The problems posed by Turkey for the EU on identity grounds have no doubt influenced EU policy towards Turkey over time and clearly constitute one of the important influences that might account for the relatively unfavourable mix of conditions and incentives faced by Turkey in comparison with other candidate countries.

Although the EU made a firm commitment towards Turkey at the Helsinki summit, Turkish membership had usually hitherto appeared to be an issue that could be safely relegated to a distant future (Uğur, 1999). Perhaps what the European elites implicitly hoped for was that Turkey would fail to satisfy a number of key conditions and that the difficult decision concerning Turkey's incorporation could be postponed indefinitely. The hope that Turkey could be kept on the sidelines for a long time, however, experienced a major setback with the unexpected pace of reforms in the months leading to the Copenhagen summit. Clearly, the radical step taken in August 2002 and the AKP's ability to transform itself into a moderate political force were developments that have generated considerable unease among EU and national policy-makers. In retrospect, it is fair to say that most Europeans did not expect progress on this scale in the immediate aftermath of the Helsinki summit.

Hence, the fact that Turkey had accomplished considerable progress in terms of satisfying EU conditions meant that the question of accommodating a large country such as Turkey with a predominantly Muslim population became a serious practical question that could no longer be pushed into the background. In this respect, the Copenhagen summit, effectively for the first time, initiated a serious debate within Europe itself concerning the future of what Europe would look like in the future with a country like Turkey included. It also highlighted the limitations of the project that was intrinsically concerned with integration as an inward-oriented process. We propose that the inward-oriented nature of the EU has clearly limited its prospects of playing the role of a genuinely global actor, the kind of actor seriously interested in pursuing a multilateral agenda and providing a counterweight to the role of the increasingly unilateralist United States.

Given that the inward-oriented nature of the integration project was broadly shared (or at least not seriously challenged) by political parties on either side of the European political spectrum, the eventual incorporation of Turkey clearly posed serious problems. In this inward-looking vision, Turkey would be more of a security liability than an asset, mainly owing to its location in a problematic region of the world. The vision also implied that incorporation of a large entity such as Turkey would pose special problems for the EU – especially in the decision-making process and the EU labour market. The Copenhagen summit clearly represented the start of a rethinking process within Europe on how Turkey could be effectively accommodated within the framework of existing EU institutions and orientations.

Stated somewhat differently, the EU's ability to accommodate Turkey, or a relatively large Eastern European country such as Poland for that matter, rests on the vision of what 'Europeanization' actually means. Clearly, if the EU is seriously interested in becoming a genuinely global actor with a multicultural orientation, the incorporation of a genuinely democratic Turkey makes considerable sense. If, on the other hand, Europeanization essentially meant an inward-oriented integration project that is insensitive to broader regional or global issues, the incorporation of a country like Turkey would constitute more of a liability. At the present stage of its evolution, the EU has accomplished significant steps towards economic integration, democratization and establishing peace within its boundaries. Nevertheless, it falls considerably short of assuming the role of a genuinely proactive global actor. This deficit, in turn, is clearly influencing the direction of EU policy towards Turkey.

Looking back, a striking contrast may be identified between the Helsinki and the Copenhagen summits. The principal issue at stake at Helsinki concerned the ability of Turkey to transform its own state and democratic institutions in line with the European norms, on the assumption that the norms of the New Europe and its future direction had been firmly established. At Copenhagen, however, there was a realization that the issue at stake involved not only Turkey's ability to transform itself, but also the future direction of the European project itself.

Conclusion: future prospects

Future progress in Turkey–EU relations will depend heavily on the ability of the key actors involved to come to terms with the principles of multi-dimensionality and reciprocity. In the post-Helsinki period, the EU has played a crucial role by inducing Turkey to transform its state-centric polity into a more democratic, economically stable and pluralist one. This role, we argue, has affected positively the process of consolidating Turkish democracy. Recent improvements in Turkey's democratic order would have not been conceivable, at least at such a rapid pace, without a strong EU anchor. Of course, one should not neglect the fact that strong societal calls for democratization in Turkey had already been building up in recent years. The Copenhagen political criteria have nevertheless constituted the main point of reference for the concrete steps that have to be taken to transform Turkish politics into a more transparent, accountable form. Moreover, the EU anchor has also contributed to the development of civil society and its impact on the process of remaking Turkish democracy.

The recent global conjuncture, however, indicated that Turkey too has a significant role to play in shaping the future of the New Europe. Today,

Turkey clearly constitutes an important test case for the New Europe and its future. It must be added that the test case does not involve cultural variables alone. In other words, Turkey's membership can no longer be assessed with reference to the cultural foundations of the 'New Europe' or to the domain of cultural essentialism versus multiculturalism (Delanty, 2003). Turkey also constitutes a test case in terms of its geopolitical importance and its pivotal status in the Balkans, Caucasia and, more importantly, in the Middle East. Therefore, the decision to include or exclude Turkey from the New Europe is a decision that the EU should take in reference not only to an essentially inward-oriented integration project but also to its role in the drastically changing international order. If Europe is to acquire a common identity and foreign policy, and if it is to emerge as an influential global power against US unilateralism, Turkey definitely has a significant role to perform in this process.

Certainly, the realization of such a benign scenario depends critically on Turkey's own ability to transform itself into a genuinely democratic and economically advanced country as well as Europe's ability to overcome its inherent inward-looking bias. Historically, Turkey–EU relations have been characterized by cycles. Yet these cycles have proceeded in the context of an underlying trend that indicates the gradual achievement of closer integration between Turkey and Europe. We expect the developments in the post-Helsinki era to constitute another significant intermediate step in that direction. We are also of the view that the idea of the New Europe is more likely to contribute to a much-desired world order that is based on a balance between democratization, economic development and security if Turkey–EU relations can be constituted on the principles of reciprocity and mutual gain.

Note

An earlier version of the chapter was presented as a paper at the Conference on 'Cyprus's Accession and the Greek–Turkish Rivalry' held at Yale University, New Haven, Connecticut, USA, on 5–6 April 2003. That paper was also presented at the ISA Conference, Budapest, Hungary, 24–28 June, 2003. Valuable comments by Mehmet Uğur on an earlier version of the paper and the able assistance of Gamze Sezer are gratefully acknowledged.

References

Anderson, Perry (2002), 'Force and consent', *New Left Review*, no. 17 (September/October), pp. 5–30.

Balkır, Canan (1998), 'The customs union and beyond', in Libby Rittenberg (ed.), *The Political Economy of Turkey in the Post-Soviet Era: Going West and Looking East?*, Westport, CT: Praeger, pp. 51–79.

Beck, Ulrich (1997), *The Reinvention of Politics: Rethinking Modernity in the Global Social Order*, Cambridge: Polity Press.

Buzan, Barry and Thomas Diez (1999), 'Turkey and the European Union: where to from here?', *Survival*, vol. 41, no. 1, pp. 41–57.

Cizre, Ümit (1997), 'The anatomy of the Turkish military's political economy', *Comparative Politics*, vol. 29, no. 2, pp. 57–74.

Curtin, Deirdre M. (1997), *Postnational Democracy: The European Union in Search of a Political Philosophy*, The Hague: Kluwer Law International.

Çınar, Alev and Burak Arıkan (2002), 'The Nationalist Action Party: representing the state, the nation or the nationalists?', *Turkish Studies*, vol. 3, no. 1, pp. 25–40.

Delanty, Gerard (2003), 'The making of a post-western Europe: a civilizational analysis', *Thesis Eleven*, no. 72 (February), pp. 8–25.

EUobserver (2002), 'Turkey is not a European country says Giscard' [based on a statement by Valéry Giscard d'Estaing]. Article published on 8 November 2002, available at http://www.EUobserver.com/index.phtml?aid=8315&sid=9.

Habermas, Jürgen (2001), *The Postnational Constellation*, Cambridge, MA: MIT Press.

Held, David (1995), *Democracy and the Global Order: From the Modern State to Cosmopolitan Governance*, Stanford, CA: Stanford University Press.

Heper, Metin and Fuat Keyman (1998), 'Double-faced state: political patronage and the consolidation of democracy in Turkey', *Middle Eastern Studies*, vol. 34, no. 4, pp. 259–277.

Hill, Christopher (2002), 'The geopolitical implications of EU enlargement', in Jan Zielonka (ed.), *Europe Unbound: Enlarging and Reshaping the Boundaries of the European Union*, London: Routledge, pp. 95–117.

Keyman, E. Fuat (2000), *Türkiye ve Radikal Demokrasi* (Turkey and Radical Democracy), Istanbul: Alfa Publishing.

Keyman, E. Fuat (2003), 'A political earthquake in Turkey: an analysis of the prospects of the JDP government in Turkey', 8 January 2003, available at http://www.eurozine.com/article/2003-01-08-keyman-en.html (accessed 10 April 2003).

Kınıkoğlu, Suat (2002), 'The Democratic Left Party: Kapıkulu politics *Par Excellence*', *Turkish Studies*, vol. 3, no. 1, pp. 4–24.

Larrabee, F. Stephen and Ian Lesser (2003), *Turkish Foreign Policy in an Age of Uncertainty*, Santa Monica, CA: Rand.

Linklater, Andrew (1998), *The Transformation of Political Community*, Cambridge: Polity Press.

Müftüler-Baç, Meltem (2002), *Enlarging the European Union: Where Does Turkey Stand?*, Istanbul: Tesev Publications.

Öniş, Ziya (2001), 'Greek–Turkish relations and the European Union: a critical perspective', *Mediterranean Politics*, vol. 6, no. 3, pp. 31–45.

Öniş, Ziya (2003), 'Domestic politics, international norms and challenges to the state: Turkey–EU relations in the post-Helsinki era', *Turkish Studies*, vol. 4, no. 1, pp. 9–35.

Öniş, Ziya and E. Fuat Keyman (2003), 'Turkey at the polls: a new path emerges', *Journal of Democracy*, vol. 14, no. 2, pp. 95–107.

Özbudun, Ergun (1999), *Contemporary Turkish Politics: Challenges to Democratic Consolidation*, Boulder, CO: Lynne Rienner.

Rumford, Chris (2002), *The European Union: A Political Sociology*, Malden, UK: Blackwell.

Uğur, Mehmet (1999), *The European Union and Turkey: An Anchor/Credibility Dilemma*, Aldershot, UK: Ashgate.

van Ham, Peter (2001), *European Integration and the Postmodern Condition*, London: Routledge.

Whitehead, Laurence (ed.) (1996), *The International Dimensions of Democratization: Europe and the Americas*, Oxford: Oxford University Press.

9 Turkish political parties and the EU discourse in the post-Helsinki period

A case of Europeanization

Gamze Avcı

Introduction

Turkey's EU candidacy has been studied at great length from the perspective of international relations. The main focus of such studies is how international factors such as the Cyprus issue, relations with Greece, security, and regional balances have influenced the relationship.[1] Internal factors and processes have been largely neglected. In the main theories of European integration, however, domestic politics rather than international relations have become increasingly important. First, domestic politics matters, because 'national' preferences of member states are influential in the evolution of European integration. Second, more recently, it appears that 'Europeanization' has a considerable impact on national political systems. The latter is also relevant for candidate countries and is studied in the context of Central and East European countries (CEECs), focusing particularly on the responses of political parties to Europeanization as well as 'Euro-scepticism' and its impact on party systems. Turkey has rarely been studied in this particular context.

This chapter presents an account and analysis of the positions that political parties have taken *vis-à-vis* EU issues since Turkey was admitted as a candidate at the Helsinki summit in 1999 up until May 2003. The goal is to explore the role political parties have played in Turkey's recent European trajectory. Helsinki is taken as a turning point because the political and economic criteria for membership have become much more pressing since then. As EU candidacy and reforms have become contentious issues in Turkey, they have provoked and created divisions among Turkish political parties. Frequently, parties have perceived and used 'Europeanization' as an 'opportunity structure' for developing their own interests (Ladrech, 2001; Goetz and Hix, 2001). The consequent choices and responses of political parties have influenced inter-party conflicts, the ongoing reform process in Turkey and, ultimately, relations between the EU and Turkey. In other words, party political choices have – depending on the choices made – constrained, accelerated or hampered the Turkish accession process.

From a methodological point of view, the research is guided by the question of *when, how* and *why do parties of government move towards or away from Euro-scepticism* (Szczerbiak and Taggart, 2001). The empirical dimension is based on the four Turkish parties that have been in government since 1999. The chapter is divided into three sections. In the first section, I will take a brief look at the existing literature on European integration and political parties and present an analytical framework. The second and main section entails an analysis of trends in party attitudes since the beginning of Turkey's EU candidacy in 1999. To this end, I will analyse the coalition period when Bülent Ecevit was Prime Minister and the period under the Justice and Development Party (*Adalet ve Kalkınma Partisi*, AKP). The analysis is informed by party positions and related domestic debates based on statements of party leaders, party Web sites and newspapers. The chapter concludes with a summary of the significant findings.

9.1 Analytical framework: political parties and Europeanization

The process of European enlargement is increasingly understood as one involving Europeanization in candidate countries.[2] Europeanization, broadly speaking, refers to responses by actors to the impact of European integration. In candidate countries, this is affected by EU membership conditionality, notably the adoption of the *acquis communautaire*. The Europeanization process is broad and impacts the national context as a whole. For the purposes of this chapter, Europeanization[3] will be defined as 'an incremental process re-orienting the direction and shape of politics to the degree that EC political and economic dynamics becomes part of the organizational logic of national politics and policy-making' (Ladrech, 1994: 69).

Within this growing literature of Europeanization, more and more emphasis is placed upon political parties. Research in this field concentrates on how European issues are incorporated into the national political debate and whether and, if so, how party opinions on Europe can be related to their established ideologies (Marks and Wilson, 1999, 2000). Evidence of Europeanization can be manifested in different ways. One of the prime areas of investigation is in patterns of party competition.[4] In the context of party competition, the argument is that as the EU issue becomes politicized, parties may act 'opportunistically' by adopting a pro- or anti- EU position in order to gain new votes. Furthermore, parties may change tactics and strategies in order to make the most of the 'EU issue' (Ladrech, 2001).

A related area of investigation is the presence of 'Euro-scepticism'. Euro-scepticism relates opposition to European integration to characteristics of the party system. Scholars in this field distinguish between 'hard' and 'soft' forms of Euro-scepticism (Taggart, 1998; Szczerbiak and

Taggart, 2000). Hard Euro-scepticism is the 'outright rejection of the entire European project and EU membership' (Szczerbiak and Taggart, 2000). Soft Euro-scepticism is 'qualified and contingent opposition, which does not imply the rejection of membership itself' (ibid.) These two forms of Euro-scepticism are viewed as poles on a spectrum, with parties moving between them.

There are a number of important propositions that emerge from research in the Euro-sceptic field. It is argued that a party's position on the left–right spectrum is not correlated with whether it is Euro-sceptical or not. Yet it is proposed that the position of parties in their party system is related to the expression of Euro-scepticism. The position of a party relates to whether that party is situated at the core or periphery of a party system. Ultimately, Euro-scepticism matters because it can influence the prospects, timing and nature of an eventual accession. In order to answer the question of whether and what kind of Euro-sceptic behaviour is seen among Turkish political parties, the next sections will give a detailed account of the main debates between and within government parties on EU issues since 1999.

9.2 The DSP–ANAP–MHP coalition: April 1999–November 2002[5]

Keeping in mind that this chapter seeks to answer how party responses to European integration have varied, it is necessary to provide a background to the period before 1999. Until the Helsinki summit of December 1999, Turkish political discourse on the issue of EU membership was relatively straightforward. Since the late 1980s there was some kind of consensus among the major political parties, groups and elites that Turkey should seek EU membership. Even though there were clearly varying degrees of enthusiasm and fine distinctions in their different approaches, no major Turkish political group or actor significantly doubted the benefits of EU membership. At the core of the objective of joining the EU was Turkey's European vocation – one of the major pillars of Turkish foreign policy since the 1960s.

However, this often meant there was no deliberate and conscious assertion of support or public backing for EU membership. In other words, the belief in joining the EU was almost self-understood among the political elite. There was little serious public debate about what EU membership actually entailed – especially the kinds of changes required and the costs and benefits involved. Therefore, the issue of EU membership had little if any effect on the daily lives of individual Turkish citizens. The Turkey–EU debate was couched in broad, abstract geopolitical or historical terms, relating to general notions such as 'becoming part of Europe' or 'becoming European'. This superficial consensus on EU membership was critically shaken by the initiation of the required reform process in Turkey.

The process received its official start when Turkey was formally accepted as a candidate at the Helsinki summit of December 1999.

Before the Helsinki summit, Turkey focused on how to become an official candidate without strings attached and 'on an equal footing with the other 12 candidates'.[6] After the Helsinki summit, with the granting of candidacy, the salience of the EU membership issue increased suddenly – at least in political party discourses. Pending short- and medium-term deadlines began to divide the political spectrum, and the issue of EU membership moved up the political agenda as the deadline for reforms drew nearer. Increasingly, some politicians and the media presented the 'homework' needed for EU membership in a negative manner, and EU membership emerged as a central point for controversy and opposition. The sheer scale of Turkey's problems added to the tensions. To a great extent, politicians began to appear less inclined to state their full commitment to the reform process. This situation was aggravated by suspicions that the EU will never admit Turkey.[7]

Given that the fulfilment of membership criteria was bound to require painful political, economic and social change, it was inevitable that there would be some questioning of Turkey's EU vocation. Difficult issues that needed to be tackled, not surprisingly, included the concessions that Turkey will have to make. Thus, as negotiations became a real prospect, discussions within Turkish politics were increasingly polarized. This was also a reflection of the fact that the Turkish public and politicians became increasingly aware that EU accession is a costly process and will generate losers as well as winners. At the same time, the EU became a convenient scapegoat for Turkish politicians, enabling them to shift the blame for the negative consequences of reform by claiming that these were forced upon Turkey by EU membership requirements. Thus, the beginning of the candidacy status marked a politicization of the debate on Turkey's EU membership. The consequent debate was not so much about whether the country should join *per se*, but more about the actual terms of accession. This politicization set the scene for the beginning of diverging choices among political parties and other political actors.

The focal point in party political discussions during Ecevit's coalition government was the details of what the government was ready to concede to the EU.[8] These discussions very often turned into ideological confrontations between the nationalists and the rest of the parties. The Nationalist Action Party (*Milliyetçi Hareket Partisi*, MHP) became the primary source of the nationalist opposition. However, the military elite and left-wing nationalists have also repeatedly voiced their concern about or opposition to certain EU-related issues. It must nonetheless be noted that, despite its reservations, the Turkish military elite has always been careful to distance itself from an 'anti-EU' label overall as it believes that Turkey's economic and political destiny lies in Europe.

On the other hand, support for EU membership continued to come more from business circles, liberals and, somewhat inconsistently, from the mainstream right-wing parties: the True Path Party (*Doğru Yol Partisi*, DYP) and the Motherland Party (*Anavatan Partisi*, ANAP).[9] Occasionally, pro-Islamists[10] voiced support for EU membership, but there were widespread doubts about the extent to which that support was genuine. At this point, it should also be mentioned that nationalist overtones have been heard occasionally from all parties.[11] Finally, NGOs have been outspoken and generally very supportive of Turkey's EU membership.[12]

From 1999 to November 2002, the MHP's role became more noticeable as a coalition partner and a key factor in passing (or blocking) reforms required under the Copenhagen criteria. The MHP was in the coalition government led by Ecevit, together with the ANAP. Ecevit's Democratic Left Party (*Demokratik Sol Parti*, DSP) received 22.3 per cent of the votes in 1999, and his coalition partners the MHP and ANAP received 18.1 per cent and 13.3 per cent respectively.[13] The election itself also demonstrated the decline of the secular centre-right in Turkey. The coalition that emerged was widely seen as the only plausible alternative, given Ecevit's known desire to work with Yılmaz, Yılmaz's objection to working with Çiller (DYP), and the pro-Islamist Virtue Party's (*Fazilet Partisi*, FP) unacceptability to the military.

On 18 March 2000, the new government announced that the three coalition partners had finally reached a compromise on the commitments Turkey would make in the context of the EU accession process. The National Programme for Adoption of the *Acquis* (NPAA) listed the short- and medium-term reforms, which required 89 new laws, amendments to 94 existing laws and a significant overhaul in Turkish politics. This occurred only after long deliberations and much struggle in Parliament. The NPAA appeared to be a joint declaration by the three coalition partners but also, in a way, was a symbol of all the difficulties the coalition partners had faced when trying to agree on sensitive issues. Many of the reforms required by the EU's Accession Partnership were either watered down or dealt with in a vague manner.

Despite the commitment made in the NPAA, progress was inconsistent, particularly in some of the substantial areas. Most of the delay was due to protracted discussions concerning the 'national interest'. Although nationalist tendencies existed in all three coalition parties, they tended to be more pronounced in the MHP. Consequently, the MHP acquired a critical role in the coalition when it came to EU reforms. Parties either responded to the the MHP's objections or compromised despite some degree of internal protest. Frequently, the MHP's attitude led to deadlocks within the frail coalition. This situation may have been predictable, given the MHP's ideological standing. However, recognition of this eventuality was delayed because of the 'mainstreaming' effect of being in government.[14]

The MHP cadres had had a highly reserved attitude towards the EU until the early 1990s, but they adopted a more cool-headed and multi-dimensional approach thereafter.[15] Yet when referring to the (then) upcoming Accession Partnership Agreement, which set out the reforms needed in order to join the Union, the leader of the MHP and then Deputy Prime Minister, Devlet Bahçeli, stated that it was the party's right to expect the interests of the Turkish nation and people to be taken into account.[16] When the EU membership plan was first proposed in November 2000, it angered the MHP cadres as well as the military,[17] particularly with reference to national security issues such as Cyprus and Kurdish separatism. In all these critical issues, the MHP accused the EU of being inconsistent and indeterminate.[18] The progress reports were also perceived as problematic. Responding to the then Deputy Prime Minister Mesut Yılmaz's statements that the EU progress report is objective, Bahçeli said, 'supporting the EU's stance or calling it "objective" ignores the EU's insincerity in its policies towards Turkey' (Cumhuriyet, 21 November 2001). Bahçeli also maintained that in the past, the MHP had been falsely portrayed as an EU enemy while the journey towards joining the EU had been overly beautified (ibid).

As the deadline for meeting the short-term EU requirements approached, the MHP became even more resentful of the EU. Yet, EU membership was not totally rejected. For instance, Bahçeli stated that 'we want to take part in this Union'. In the same breath, he also stated that 'this participation should be in compliance with the magnitude, history and potential of our country'. Moreover, he said that 'it is hard to claim that EU administration is quite aware of Turkey's efforts and contributions to the Union so far' (*Anadolu Agency*, 18 June 2002). In his evaluation of the post-Helsinki period, Bahçeli observed that since Helsinki there had been some positive developments but that the relationship was not sufficiently transparent and comprehensible. He pointed to the geopolitical and geo-economic nature of the partnership and noted that there are factors that are way beyond (and more powerful than) the EU's apparent attitude, which suggested that one has to do one's homework to become a member.[19]

A key issue for the MHP was Cyprus's bid to join the Union. The bid itself and its implications were considered problematic.[20] Bahçeli believed that the EU would like to create a *fait accompli* in Cyprus through its support for the Greek and Greek Cypriot positions. He made it known that no concessions will be made concerning Cyprus and that the MHP will support Denktaş until the end.[21] It must be indicated here that there is little difference between the MHP and other Turkish parties on this issue. Cyprus appears as a 'national' priority. For example, Mesut Yılmaz, the ANAP's leader, accuses the EU of giving guarantees to the Greek Cypriot side and putting pressure on Turkey (*Anadolu Agency*, 21 March 2002). Similarly, Ecevit asserted that 'it would be hardly possible that the EU would follow a conciliatory path' with respect to the Cyprus issue (*Turkish Daily News*, 22 March 2002).

Another important issue of contention for MHP was the abolition of the death penalty, as this had direct implications for the Öcalan case. Abdullah Öcalan, the former leader of the now-defunct Kurdistan Workers Party (*Partiya Karkaren Kurdistan*, PKK), was found responsible for the death of an estimated 35,000 people in the guerrilla warfare between 1984 and 1999. He was sentenced to death for high treason after his capture in 1999 – even though Turkey had maintained a moratorium on executions since 1984. The MHP and other nationalists within the Ecevit government coalition wished to retain the right to order the execution of Öcalan. In October 2001, an amendment to the Constitution abolished capital punishment except in time of war, under the imminent threat of war and for terrorist crimes. The first two exceptions are permitted under Protocol 6 of the European Convention on Human Rights, but the third one, concerning terrorist crimes, is not. It is this third exception that is particularly important for those who wish to retain the right to order the execution of Öcalan. Yet by refraining from executing Öcalan, Turkey could advance its EU candidacy. Addressing this controversy, Bahçeli stated that Turkey wants to unite with Europe in an honourable, fair and full membership. In order for it to do that, there should be 'no bargaining concerning Öcalan' (*Türkiye*, 1 December 1999).

Bahçeli's view has been in direct contrast with the then Prime Minister Ecevit's position, which was very much in favour of abolishing the death penalty.[22] Ecevit claimed that it is not in Ankara's interests to execute Öcalan (*Guardian*, 13 January 2000). He argued that Turkey is bound by international obligations to obey the European Court of Human Rights' call to put on hold the Kurdish leader's execution until an appeal lodged by his lawyers is given consideration.

Meanwhile, the MHP leadership was being pressured by the grassroots because of its acceptance that the Öcalan file should be held at the Prime Ministry and rather than send it to Parliament for debate. MHP leaders were worried that if the party accepted the lifting of the death penalty while in government as a coalition partner, it would be very harmful for the party. Indeed, one of the MHP's election pledges in 1999 was that if it came to power, it would ensure the execution of Öcalan (*Sabah*, 6 December 1999). This pledge explains why the MHP changed its position during the course of discussion despite the fact that it initially suggested that it would not oppose abolition of the death penalty if the DSP and ANAP legislated the measure through Parliament with the support of the opposition (*Turkish Daily News*, 24 May 2002).

The DSP and ANAP asserted their shared position that the death penalty should be replaced with lifetime imprisonment with no chance of parole.[23] The pro-Islamist parties, the AKP and the Felicity Party (*Saadet Partisi*, SP), stated that the death penalty should be lifted through a constitutional change because decree-related legal changes are susceptible to being reversed in the future.[24] However, their views on this issue changed frequently (*Zaman Gazetesi*, 25 June 2002). In effect, Turkish political parties' dilemmas on this issue were best summed up in the DYP's attitude, which stated that the party would not oppose the lifting of the death penalty, but only after Öcalan had been executed. By taking such a stand, the DYP also tried to lure voter support away from the MHP.

The use of Kurdish in education and on television constituted another dilemma for the coalition government. The problem with extending rights to the Kurdish minority had much to do with the violent struggle between the PKK and the Turkish army. Quite often, the enlarged package of 'cultural rights' is seen as rewarding terrorism or approving violence. In that context, Bahçeli called the EU's attitude concerning terrorism 'double-faced and not serious'.[25] He argued that 'most European countries continue to embrace terrorists who are the enemies of Turkey'. This demonstrates that Turkey is justified in its concerns (*Cumhuriyet*, 21 November 2001). Yılmaz did not sound much different when he stated that 'the EU has always been egoistical on the issue of terrorism'. The EU tolerates terrorist organizations targeting Turkey unless they cause any damage to the EU itself (*Anadolu Agency*, 21 March 2002).

Bahçeli's view was that allowing teaching, broadcasting or publication in Kurdish would help separatism – a view shared by the military establishment. The military, however, were open to some changes, given that they would be under strict governmental/state control (Peuch, 2002a). The MHP, on the other hand, was strictly against allowing education in Kurdish even as an optional course and claimed that it was a new strategy of separatism devised by the outlawed PKK (*Turkish Daily News*, 27 January 2002). In contrast, the ANAP leader, Yılmaz, urged tolerance for demands related to education in Kurdish while adding that making such a move would be impossible under current laws (ibid.). Consequently, Yılmaz's attitude caused an open rift between the ANAP and the Euro-sceptic MHP (Peuch, 2002b).

Finally, the MHP opposed the amendment of article 312 of the Turkish Penal Code, which bans the inciting of hatred on religious or ethnic grounds. Speaking at the MHP's parliamentary group meeting, Bahçeli stated that the proposed amendments to article 312 would neither save nor punish anyone. He said that his party was against total lifting of the article or making radical amendments to it in a manner that would 'make it an empty shell' (*Sabah* and *Hürriyet*, 23 January 2002). He maintained that exempting provocative speech or behaviour from punishment could not be reconciled with either democracy or freedom of speech (*Hürriyet* and *Cumhuriyet*, 23 January 2002).

Similarly, the European Security and Defence Identity (ESDI) became an intractable problem.[26] Turkey has made it known that it would like to participate in the decision-making process of the ESDI. The problem is that, for many, the ESDI 'cannot be without Turkey as Turkey is Europe's strategic partner'.[27] Successive US governments have made it no secret that the United States believes Turkey should be included in the emerging EU defence structure (Akşam, 2 December 1999). Meanwhile, Turkey, with the second largest army in the Atlantic alliance, does not want to give its approval to this force, because of its fears that it may eventually operate in Turkey's immediate neighbourhood and interfere with Turkish national interests.

Until the latest Iraq crisis, EU governments could not go ahead without NATO's approval, partly to avoid undermining it, and partly because they will need to use its weapons and equipment. Ankara has traditionally refused to drop its opposition to the EU's Rapid Reaction Force (RRF) – intended to mount limited operations when NATO is not involved. An agreement (the so-called Ankara document) concerning the ESDI was reached between the United States, Britain and Turkey in December 2001 but was vetoed by Greece. At the time, MHP indicated that leaving Turkey outside the ESDI sheds an interesting light on the EU's true intentions.[28] The ESDI issue was eventually resolved at the EU Copenhagen summit on 12 December 2002, and permanent arrangements for NATO support of EU-led operations were put in place.

The final issue dividing the coalition parties in the EU debate was early elections (at some point in conjunction with the EU reform package). Bahçeli wanted to call for early elections to end the political uncertainty that had grown in recent months as Ecevit's illness kept him from work while coalition members clashed over EU reforms. Ecevit's DSP, which saw its parliamentary presence halved in July 2002 after defections, feared that it could suffer at the polls. The third coalition partner, the ANAP, also backed a November 2002 election, but wanted to complete the EU reforms first to strengthen its hand in the election campaign. Meanwhile, the SP supported ANAP's bid,[29] whereas the DYP exhibited a mixed attitude and remained non-committal.[30]

The New Turkey Party (*Yeni Türkiye Partisi*, YTP), a new party established by former Foreign Minister İsmail Cem – the most prominent member of the government to abandon Ecevit – said that it would support the EU reforms.[31] During these discussions, another important development was that Kemal Derviş, the Economy Minister and architect of the government's economic recovery programme, resigned and joined the Republican People's Party (*Cumhuriyet Halk Partisi*, CHP). Both Derviş and the CHP were seen as supportive of Turkey's EU bid. Finally, the AKP supported early elections and appeared supportive of EU reforms.

The debate on early elections overlapped with a final attempt to pass a number of necessary EU reforms. As Parliament finally approved elections to be held on 3 November 2002, it also approved, on 3 August 2002, a package (the third package) of human rights reforms that it hoped would clear the way for EU membership. This package was adopted after an overnight marathon session. It included the abolition of the death penalty in peacetime, to be replaced with life imprisonment with no possibility of parole. It also legalized broadcasting and education in languages other than Turkish, notably Kurdish. Furthermore, the package did away with penalties for criticizing state institutions, including the military; eased restrictions on demonstrations and associations; and allowed non-Muslim religious foundations to buy and sell real estate. The package was presented by Yılmaz's ANAP and was passed despite the opposition of the MHP, with the support of the DSP, ANAP and opposition parties. The MHP voted 'no' *en bloc.* The other parties – despite their various prior statements – supported the package. There were defections from all parties (government and opposition) but there was no consistent resistance to the package as a party line. In remarks made on 4 August 2002, Bahçeli stated that the MHP would appeal to the Constitutional Court in a bid to force Parliament to reverse its decision regarding the death penalty and minority rights. The Constitutional Court eventually rejected this petition in December 2002.

9.3 The AKP government: November 2002–May 2003

The 2002 elections proved to be a massive electoral reaction to the established political parties' inability to master the economic crisis or to deliver on their promises. The ANAP, MHP and DSP lost all their seats in Parliament. In conjunction with the decline in the economy and the constant quarrelling, the coalition government's inability to use EU integration as an election-winning issue rendered that government obsolete. The AKP, which had pro-Islamic roots and had been formed only 18 months before the elections, won a landslide victory. The AKP was established by Recep Tayyip Erdoğan, the former Mayor of Istanbul. Erdoğan had split with the more conventionally Islamist leftovers of the old Welfare and Virtue parties, and campaigned on a liberal Islamist platform. The AKP captured 362 of the 550 parliamentary seats, only a few seats short of the two-thirds absolute majority that would have allowed it to amend the Constitution without a referendum. The Republican People's Party (*Cumhuriyet Halk Partisi*, CHP) won 177 seats. The remaining eight seats went to independent candidates. Elections were declared void in three districts of the eastern Anatolian Siirt Province. The victory made the AKP the first party in recent years to be able to govern without coalition partners. Yet it should also be mentioned that the AKP gained 80.4 per cent of the seats in Parliament while it won only 34.2 per cent of the votes cast. This was a peculiarity of the 10 per cent electoral threshold rule, which in effect rendered 46 per cent of the votes cast irrelevant.

The AKP victory arrived 38 days before the crucial Copenhagen summit at which the EU leaders were to decide about a potential negotiation date for Turkey. The AKP leader, Erdoğan, moved quickly to assure the West that he does not have an Islamic agenda and is committed to the secular principles that govern Muslim Turkey. Immediately after the first unofficial results were in Erdoğan also promised support for Turkey's bid to join the EU. Once the government was sworn into office in late November, Erdoğan embarked upon a series of trips to European capitals. He outlined an ambitious programme of EU-oriented reforms and lobbied leaders to gain their support for Turkey's bid for membership. He subsequently went to the United States to try to mobilize support for a date for the start of accession negotiations. He made his trips as the *de facto* leader of the AKP government since he did not hold office officially; he had been barred from running for Parliament on account of a previous conviction for reading a poem 'inciting religious hatred'.

The AKP has pro-Islamist roots. However, unlike the Welfare Party under Necmettin Erbakan, it is publicly committed to pushing for membership of the European Union. AKP cadres have repeatedly stated that, regardless of the EU, they are fully committed to securing freedom of expression and thought, transparent government, and the strengthening of local government. The AKP has presented itself consistently and credibly as a new type of pro-Islamic party. The profiles of AKP members are mixed. Some hanker after radical Islamism while others are merely Islamic conservatives who would like to see their religion gain official recognition. The party itself insists that it is committed to the secularism of the Turkish state, while opposing the exclusion of religious symbolism from public life, such as the ban on women wearing headscarves in public facilities (which includes universities). It insists that it is Islamic in the same sense that Christian democratic parties in Western Europe are Christian.[32]

More to the point, the AKP's pro-EU stance represents a radical break with its predecessors and the early generation of Islamists who had always used an anti-Western or anti-EU rhetoric. The EU issue was critical for the AKP in many ways. First, it was important as a 'protection' against those who would prefer the AKP to have a hidden Islamic fundamentalist agenda, or who suspect that it has. A reform programme that is geared towards EU membership could keep both the radical secularists and any radical Islamist fringe in the AKP in check. Second, the AKP could use a positive signal from the EU to kick-start the economic stabilization that previous governments had so consistently mismanaged. Third, the prospect of EU membership could also underpin Turkey's fragile democracy, just as it did in Southern European member states such as Greece, Spain and Portugal in the 1970s, and help the AKP push through more religious freedoms too.

In its election manifesto, it stated that 'obligations and all other criteria that are also required of the other candidates will be met; the [political] agenda will not be unnecessarily preoccupied with artificial issues'. Addressing Parliament on 23 November 2003, the Prime Minister, Abdullah Gül, reiterated his commitment to continue with much-needed political and economic reforms. He stated that the time had come to replace the 20-year-old restrictive constitution adopted in the wake of the 1980 military coup.

> We are going to prepare a new constitution, which will promote freedom and participation [of all members of society] to replace the one that is now in force and constrains our country. Our new constitution will have a strong social legacy. It will conform to international standards, first of all those of the EU. Holding individual rights and freedoms as superior principles and being based on pluralist and participatory democracy, it will convey the idea of a state built on democracy and the rule of law.[33]

Later, the government's programme announced 'full membership of the EU' as the priority 'aim for ensuring economic and democratic development'. On the other hand, regardless of the full membership condition, support will be given to economic and democratic standards, legal and institutional regulations offered by the EU.[34] The party's leader proclaims that they

> believe that it is insufficient to just be a member of the EU and believe that this process should be accelerated. We foresaw this also during the establishment period of our party. We wrote in our party program that EU membership is the biggest project after the establishment of the Republic, and we believe in that.[35]

They add that 'there is a proportional balance and strong tie between Turkey's 'national interests' and being a full member of the EU.[36]

9.3.1 Striving for a date for accession negotiations

Around the time the AKP came into office, fears were mounting in Turkey that unless negotiations with the EU began in 2003, Turkey's accession talks could be stalled indefinitely, as ten new countries are expected to join the EU in 2004. The worry was that Turkey would need to convince 25 members – including a possibly opposed Cyprus – instead of the current 15. Thus, the AKP took over at a time that was considered yet another critical juncture for EU–Turkey relations.

However, despite the efforts of the AKP government, European leaders decided to reject Turkey's demands for early accession negotiations. Instead, the EU reminded Turkey of its 'homework' and stated that

> The Union acknowledges the determination of the new Turkish government to take further steps on the path of reform and urges in particular the government to address swiftly all remaining shortcomings in the field of the political criteria, not only with regard to legislation but also in particular with regard to implementation. The

Union recalls that, according to the political criteria decided in Copenhagen in 1993, membership requires that a candidate country has achieved stability of institutions guaranteeing democracy, the rule of law, human rights and respect for and protection of minorities.[37]

The final decision therefore was that

The Union encourages Turkey to pursue energetically its reform process. If the European Council in December 2004, on the basis of a report and a recommendation from the Commission, decides that Turkey fulfils the Copenhagen political criteria, the European Union will open accession negotiations with Turkey without delay.[38]

In other words, the EU offered to review Turkey's candidacy in late 2004 with an eye to opening accession talks the following year. The response from the Turkish side was mixed. Speaking to reporters at the end of the summit, Turkey's new Prime Minister, Abdullah Gül, claimed that reforms were being carried out for the sake of the people, not for the sole purpose of joining the EU:

Our path, the path of Turkey, is clear. These [reform] packages – be they pertaining to human rights, aimed at raising the level of democratic standards, or those regarding the economy – are being implemented for the sake of the Turkish people. This is what really matters. Had there not been the issue of Turkish–EU relations, these [reform] packages would have been implemented anyway because the Turkish people deserve them.

(*Milliyet*, 28 January 2003)

But the disappointment could be sensed when he stated that 'We have done what we were supposed to do ... but it seems this negotiation date will come at a later date than we expected, namely, at the end of 2004.' Later, this statement was 'rephrased' in the AKP's government programme submitted to Parliament, which stated that the AKP 'worked seriously on EU matters after the November 3 elections and *succeeded* in reaching the stage of receiving a negotiation date for negotiations' (emphasis added). The AKP's then Foreign Affairs Minister, Yaşar Yakış, also vowed that Turkey would meet the criteria a year earlier than expected, stating that 'the government takes 2003 as a target date for the compliance with the Copenhagen criteria'.[39]

9.3.2 Reforms

The reform process that has accompanied the candidacy will obviously remain a measuring stick in Turkey–EU relations. The EU accession process has been an important catalyst in Turkey's human rights progress, especially in 2002.[40] As already mentioned, achievements include abolition of the death penalty, the easing of restrictions on broadcasting and education in minority languages, shortened police detention periods, and lifting of the state of emergency in the formerly troubled south-east Turkey. Since its election in November 2002, the AKP has maintained the flow of reform. It also vowed that in 2003 'there will be no instances of torture, no misbehaving of policemen and no violations of human rights' in Turkey.[41]

Parliament passed the so-called fourth harmonization package on 4 December 2002. The package included 32 articles and envisaged amendments to 16 different laws.[42] The legislation abolished a law stating that police superiors must authorize the prosecution of officers accused of torture. Prisoners will have immediate access to lawyers, and courts are barred from suspending the sentences of convicted torturers. The reforms also seek to strengthen civil and political liberties, including the lifting of restrictions on freedom of association. Similarly, journalists will no longer be required to disclose their sources to authorities. According to the package, non-Muslim religious foundations will be allowed to acquire properties. Associations will be able to stage international activities to reach their targets explained in their regulations. They will be able to open offices abroad, and become members of international associations or organizations (*Anadolu Agency*, 4 December 2002).

The fifth reform package, the second under the AKP, became effective on 23 January 2003. This package paved the way for a retrial of imprisoned Democracy Party (DEP) deputies. Accordingly, former DEP deputies who were granted a retrial by the European Court will have the right to apply to Turkish courts for a retrial within a year. However, the imprisoned leader of the outlawed PKK, Abdullah Öcalan, will be excluded from this right. Meanwhile, the Parliamentary Commission responsible for this law removed an article from the reform package which would have pardoned university students suspended for disciplinary infractions, including female students who insisted on wearing headscarves at universities (*Turkish Daily News*, 23 January 2003). The latter was seen as related to the addressing of the AKP's core voters' demands, but it was removed following public criticism and pressures. The AKP fought off criticism by stating that it would work to lift the ban on women wearing headscarves in universities and state offices, yet it was not a top priority for the new administration. Currently, the AKP is working on pushing through the sixth reform package (*Hürriyet, Dünya, Sabah*, 10 June 2003). The package includes major reforms such as abolishing article 8 of the Anti-Terror Law and extending freedom of broadcasting in Kurdish.

There have been setbacks for the AKP after the elections. When the Constitutional Court banned the pro-Kurdish People's Democracy Party (*Halkın Demokrasi Partisi*, HADEP) on charges of aiding the terrorist organization PKK, and carrying out activities challenging the state, the EU

called this a troubling departure from the country's political and democratic reform efforts in recent years. Furthermore, the AKP has been
unable to make any advances concerning a new procurement law.
Although included in the party's so-called emergency plan, the AKP has
been unable to pass the necessary law. The EU reminded the Party that
'[This] law is very important for fighting against corruption and for a
transparent society' (*Sabah,* 28 December 2002).

9.3.3 Cyprus and Iraq

Two critical international issues coincided with the AKP's first year in
office: Cyprus and Iraq. The impending accession of Cyprus, with or
without an end to the division, caused a major headache for Turkey.
Erdoğan, by taking the issue to the public sphere and trying to create a
national debate on the Cyprus problem, pledged to revise Turkey's traditional policy towards Cyprus. The Cyprus problem is generally considered
a 'national cause' (*Turkish Daily News,* 28 January 2003). Erdoğan stated
that he is 'not in favour of the continuation of the policy that has been
maintained in Cyprus over the past 30–40 years'.[43] He also stated that the
AKP was neither supporting a view in line with the hardliners who have
been defending a 'no settlement is a settlement' policy, nor pursuing a
defeatist sell-out policy: 'Our policy is a "Solve it and let it live" policy.' He
also stressed that a Cyprus settlement must be built on compromises from
both sides and must be found acceptable by both peoples of the island.
He assured the Turkish public and the international circles that he still
believed a settlement in Cyprus was possible. He reiterated the strong will
of his party to bring about an end to the almost four-decade-old problem
on the island. The change of heart in the Turkish government was not
well received by the pro-status quo segments of the Turkish Cypriots
(especially Denktaş) and among various groups within the Turkish political establishment. As a result, the peace talks on Cyprus collapsed.[44]

Turkey's military and political role in the US-led intervention in Iraq
has been on the agenda throughout the AKP period. Erdoğan broke away
from other political leaders who openly opposed a war with Iraq by saying
that a US-led operation against Turkey's southern neighbour 'aimed at
liberating the Iraqi people' might not be so bad after all. He indicated
that the AKP is unlikely to voice dissent against such an operation or
oppose Turkey's participation in it. Eventually, however, the Turkish Parliament, including some of the AKP representatives, rejected the deployment of US troops through Turkey. In the context of EU affairs, Erdoğan
asserted that 'The United States is our friend.' 'But', he said,

> if Turkey had received a date, if Turkey was strong in its relations with
> Europe, knew it was a part of Europe and could act with Europe to
> eliminate the presence of weapons of mass destruction, a better road

map could be prepared for the rest of the world regarding a solution to this crisis.

(Smith, 2003)

9.3.4 The AKP's opposition: the CHP

The centre-left CHP was the only party other than the AKP to win seats in the November 2002 elections. The CHP is considered to be the more committed to secularism of the two. Yet despite their differing philosophies on the issue of religion in politics, the CHP's leader, Deniz Baykal, agreed to act in unison when it comes to the EU. Both Baykal and Erdoğan said that the Copenhagen summit should give Turkey a date for the start of accession negotiations. They also announced that the United Nations' proposal for solving the Cyprus question is to be debated in the Turkish Parliament. Baykal also backed the constitutional changes sought by the AKP government to open the way for its leader, Erdoğan, to stand for election (the CHP's condition was limiting parliamentary immunities in return).

Conclusions

This chapter has provided an initial mapping of Euro-scepticism in Turkey. Some preliminary findings can be offered. First of all, it appears that the fate of Turkey's candidacy depends, at least partially, on the dynamics of competition inherent in the domestic party system. The two parties that critically stand out are the MHP and the AKP.

The MHP frequently acted as a brake when it came to passing necessary reform legislation. It used what is referred to as 'national interest Euro-scepticism' and employed the rhetoric of defending or standing up for 'the national interest' in the context of the debates on the EU. Moreover, the MHP hardened its stance towards the end of the coalition years, despite the initial lip-service paid to EU membership. It stuck to its anti-EU platform during the most critical discussions on EU reforms in August 2002. This confirms that Euro-scepticism is most likely to be stronger when accession is perceived as a more immediate prospect than when it seems more distant (Szczarbiak and Taggart, 2001). It also confirms that smaller, more extreme nationalist parties have become unacceptable coalition parties for governments dealing with EU accession, as their position of power would free them up to take 'hard' Euro-sceptic positions (ibid.).

Bahçeli has chosen to portray the MHP as the 'logical address' for nationalist, anti-EU sentiments, despite the party's low standing in the polls and his own 'official' commitment to EU accession. This reinforces the party's 'outsider' status, given that the Turkish public is broadly supportive of the European project.[45] Yet it appears that the MHP has selected this strategy to emphasize the distinctiveness of the party and enhance its competitive advantage. Nonetheless, this also highlights the MHP's more 'peripheral status' in the party system. Currently, in opposition, the MHP is voicing an increasingly hard Euro-sceptical line.[46]

The AKP, on the other hand, has preferred to 'decouple' the EU issue from ideology politics. If ideology were sufficient to predict party positions, the AKP probably should be more opposed to the EU. Yet despite its ideological heritage, the AKP prefers a more Europhile stance. Utility rather than ideology has come to the forefront when approaching or framing the issue of EU membership. This of course does not mean that ideological tendencies are irrelevant, but rather that opportunity structures offered by European integration have lured the AKP away from Euro-scepticism. The AKP's case shows that even in cases of a potential 'misfit', opportunities to advance your own cause may facilitate political strategies that may lead to acceptable outcomes for all parties involved at the national, domestic and EU levels.

The AKP cadres committed themselves to a more contemporary model of political Islam with strong undercurrents of free-market ideology and Turkish nationalism. The party came to power promising that it would redefine 'the political centre' and create a new, unprecedented global model of democratic Muslim politics – much like an Islamic version of the Christian democrats of Europe. It was clear that the AKP had to act 'strategically' in order to 'deliver' its promises, sustain public support and, ultimately, avoid confrontation with the country's military. It had to develop something like a 'catch-all' strategy that was somewhat contrary to the party's original ideology.

The AKP found itself having to contrast itself with the more traditionalist Islamist worldview of its predecessors, which were more interested in the concept of serving the *ummah*, the global Muslim community. In other words, the AKP eschewed an Islamist platform in favour of a moderate, pro-EU platform in order to allay concerns of the establishment. This shows that, if necessary, political actors, depending on their positions within a party and in the party system, behave strategically and manipulate the EU issue to gain public attention and potential support. It also demonstrates that the dynamics and opportunity structures within the Turkish party system, and potentially at the EU level, tend to increase the strategic incentives for 'consensual' behaviour. In the AKP's case, this led – under the given institutional constraints – to a re-evaluation of interests, reformulation of conflicting issues and adoption of new perspectives and knowledge.

This situation can be summarized as an adaptation independent of the initial compatibility or incompatibility of the AKP with the EU membership project. Thus, the key issue becomes not the perceived or potential fit or misfit of a political party. Rather, it concerns the willingness of the political actors involved to pursue strategies that eventually facilitate political success via compromise. Finally, we can also confirm that a party's position on the left–right spectrum is not correlated with whether it is Euro-sceptical or not. Euro-scepticism in Turkey is not confined strictly to a particular side of the political spectrum. The AKP, given its strength and proximity to power, situates itself at the core of the Turkish party system. This has had clear implications for the EU strategies that this party has pursued so far, as it has shied away from Euro-scepticism.

Notes

1 See Apostolou (1999), Lesser (1999), Roper (1999), Park (2000) and Van Westerling (2000). On the other hand, for a good selection of analysis on Turkish–EU relations from the domestic perspective, see the special issue of *Turkish Studies* (2003), 4.
2 For a thorough discussion of the term 'Europeanization', see Ladrech (2001).
3 Different definitions of the concept exist, and the literature repeatedly notes that the concept of Europeanization is very broad and somewhat fuzzy; see also Radaelli (2000).
4 Ladrech (2001) identifies a total of five different areas of investigation. Most of them are more relevant for member or already negotiating candidate countries. For the purposes of this chapter, I will focus on 'patterns of party competition'.
5 For an earlier version of this period's analysis, see Avcı (2002a).
6 For a discussion of Turkey's candidacy and its characteristics, see Avcı (2002b).
7 House of Commons, *Select Committee on Foreign Affairs, 6th Report: Turkey*, available at http://www.parliament.the-stationery-office.co.uk/pa/cm200102/cms-elect/cmfaff/606/60602.htm (prepared 30 April 2002, accessed 7 June 2003).
8 For a discussion of the various 'turbulences' caused by the democratization process after Helsinki, see Tsakonas (2001).
9 For example, see the statements of Mesut Yılmaz, the ANAP party leader, published in *Hürriyet* on 19 July 2000; *Turkish Daily News*, 11 September 2000; *Cumhuriyet*, 10 October 2000.
10 Past and present Islamist parties include *Refah Partisi* (RP) (Welfare Party), banned by the Constitutional Court in 1998, *Fazilet Partisi* (FP) (Virtue Party), banned in 2000, *Saadet Partisi* (SP) (Felicity Party) and *Adalet ve Kalkınma Partisi* (AKP) (Justice and Development Party).
11 See, for example, Eder (1999) for discussions surrounding the customs agreement between Turkey and the EU.
12 TUSIAD (*Türk Sanayicileri ve İşadamları Derneği*, the Turkish Industrialists' and Businessmen's Association) and IKV (*İktisadi Kalkınma Vakfı*, the Economic Development Foundation) are the leading organizations favouring Turkey's membership of the EU. The IKV frequently acted as an umbrella organization for other NGOs when gathering support for the EU movement. It garnered the support of as many as 200 NGOs when appealing to the government to focus on and speed up EU affairs. TESEV (*Türkiye Ekonomik ve Sosyal Etüdler Vakfı*, the Turkish Economic and Social Studies Foundation), as well as the European Movement 2002, also played a critical role, with their activities geared towards educating the public and mobilizing EU supporters.
13 For more detailed discussions of the 1999 election, see Çarkoğlu and Avcı (2002) and Çarkoğlu and Eren (2002).
14 For recent discussions of the MHP's nationalism, see Çınar and Arıkan (2002) and Bora and Canefe (2002).

15 Devlet Bahçeli's speech at the MHP's Sixth Regular Congress, 6 October 2000, available at http://www.mhp.org (accessed 2 June 2003).

16 Ibid.

17 For a sample of the Turkish armed forces' reaction, see *Sabah*, 27 November 2000.

18 Devlet Bahçeli's group speech at the National Assembly, 11 June 2002, available at http://www.mhp.org.tr (accessed 2 June 2003).

19 Devlet Bahçeli, '21. Yüzyılın zorlukları ve fırsatları karşısında Türkiye ve Türk dünyası gerçeği' (The reality of Turkey and the Turkic world *vis-à-vis* the difficulties and opportunities of the twenty-first century), *Türkiye ve Siyaset*, July–August 2002, available at http://www.turkiyevesiyaset.com (accessed 2 June 2003).

20 Devlet Bahçeli's group speech at the National Assembly, 13 November 2001, available at http://www.mhp.org.tr (accessed 2 June 2003).

21 NTV News, 21 July 2002, available at http://www.ntvmsnbc.com/news/165061.asp (accessed 1 May 2003).

22 See, for example, the mention in J. Naegele, 'Turkey: party leaders agree to postpone Ocalan's execution', Radio Free Europe, 13 January 2000, available at http://www.rferl.org (accessed 5 June 2003).

23 http://www.abhaber.com (accessed 26 June 2002).

24 Ibid.

25 Bahçeli, July-August 2002, available at http://www.turkiyevesiyaset.com (accessed 1 June 2003).

26 For a more detailed discussion, see Brewin (2002: 17–19). The MHP accuses the EU of being inconsistent and indeterminate concerning each of these important issues.

27 Italian Minister of Foreign Affairs Lamberto Dini, quoted in *Türkiye*, 8 December 1999.

28 Devlet Bahçeli, 'Dış ilişkilerimizde yeni gelişmeler, sorunlar ve temel yaklaşım biçimimiz' (New developments, problems and our main approach to our foreign relations), *Türkiye ve Siyaset*, January–February 2002, available at http://www.turkiyevesiyaset.com (accessed 1 May 2003).

29 'ANAP-SP'den "önce AB" önergesi' (ANAP and SP propose to put EU first), available at http://www.ntvmsnbc.com.tr (accessed 25 July 2002).

30 'DYP: Yılmaz'ın sözleri esef verici' (DYP: Yılmaz's statement is appalling), available at http://www.ntvmsnbc.com.tr (accessed 25 July 2002); 'Çiller: AB konusunda elimizden geleni yaparız' (Çiller: We will do whatever we can about the EU), available at http://www.ntvmsnbc.com.tr (accessed 26 July 2002).

31 'Cem'den AB'ye koşulsuz destek' (Cem's unconditional support for the EU), available at http://www.ntvmsnbc.com.tr (accessed 25 July 2002).

32 The AKP also refers to itself as a conservative democratic party. See http://www.akparti.org.tr/istanbul/beyanname.doc (accessed 10 June 2003). For a recent discussion on this issue, see NPQ (2003), available at http://www.npq.org/archive/2003_spring/erdogan.html (accessed 10 June 2003).

33 Election manifesto of the AKP, 'Herşey Türkiye için' (Everything for Turkey), available at http://www.akparti.org.tr (accessed 30 July 2002).

34 The 58th Government Programme, available at http://www.akparti.org.tr, accessed 1 December 2002.

35 Speech of AKP leader Erdoğan, 7 June 2002, available at http://www.akparti.org.tr (accessed 1 July 2002).

36 Speech of AKP leader Erdoğan, 2 March 2002, available at http://www.akparti.org.tr (accessed 1 April 2002).

37 Paragraph 18, EU Presidency Conclusions, Copenhagen European Council, 12 and 13 December 2002.
38 Paragraph 19, EU Presidency Conclusions, Copenhagen European Council, 12 and 13 December 2002.
39 EU Ministerial (Troika) Meeting in Turkey, 31 January 2003.
40 Human Rights Watch, 'Curbing torture top EU–Turkey priority', available at http://www.hrw.org/press/2003/01/turky013003.htm (accessed 2 June 2003).
41 Statement by Murat Mercan, vice-chairman and founding member of the AKP, *EU Observer*, 20 January 2003.
42 From http://www.belgenet.com/yasa/ab_uyum4-2.html (accessed 2 June 2003).
43 BBC News, 2 January 2003, 'Turkey pushes for Cyprus deal'.
44 BBC News, 11 March 2003 'Cyprus peace process collapses'.
45 For recent public opinion data concerning Turkish support for EU membership, see Eurobarometer for Candidate Countries, available at http://europa.eu.int/comm.public_opinion/cceb_en.htm (accessed 21 June 2003).
46 See generally the MHP Web site. In particular, the most recent anti-EU statements came from Devlet Bahçeli in the form of a press statement on 12 March 2003. See http://www.mhp.org.tr (accessed 27 March 2003).

References

Apostolou, A. (1999), 'Turkey, the European Union, and Cyprus', *Mediterranean Quarterly*, vol. 10, pp. 104–121.
Avcı, G. (2002a), 'Turkey's slow EU candidacy: insurmountable hurdles or simple Euro-scepticism?', *Turkish Studies*, vol. 4, pp. 149–170.
Avcı, G. (2002b), 'Putting the Turkish EU candidacy into context', *European Foreign Affairs Review*, vol. 7, pp. 91–110.
Bora, T. and N. Canefe (2002), 'Intellectual roots of anti-European sentiments in Turkish politics: the case of nationalist-conservative tradition and radical Turkish nationalism', *Turkish Studies*, vol. 4, pp. 121–141.
Brewin, C. (2002), *Turkey and Europe after the Nice Summit*, Istanbul: TESEV Publications.
Cowles, M. G., J. A. Caporaso and T. Risse (eds) (2001), *Transforming Europe: Europeanization and Domestic Change*, Ithaca, NY: Cornell University Press.
Çarkoğlu, A. and G. Avcı, (2002), 'An analysis of the Turkish electorate from a geographical perspective', in Yılmaz Esmer and Sabri Sayarı (eds), *Politics, Parties and Elections in Turkey*, Boulder, CO: Lynne Rienner, pp. 115–136.
Çarkoğlu, A. and I. Eren (2002), 'The rise of right-of-centre parties and the nationalisation of electoral forces in Turkey', *New Perspectives on Turkey*, vol. 26, pp. 95–137.
Çınar, A. and B. Arıkan (2002), 'The Nationalist Action Party: representing the state, the nation or the nationalists?', *Turkish Studies*, vol. 3, pp. 25–40.
Eder, M. (1999), 'Becoming Western: Turkey and the European Union', in Jean Rugel and Will Hout (eds), *Regionalism across the North–South Divide: State Strategies and Globalization*, London: Routledge, pp. 79–95.
Goetz, K. H. and S. Hix (eds) (2001), *Europeanised Politics: European Integration and National Political Systems*, London: Frank Cass.

Ladrech, R. (1994), 'Europeanization of domestic politics and institutions: the case of France', *Journal of Common Market Studies*, vol. 32, pp. 69–88.

Ladrech, R. (2001), 'Europeanization and political parties: towards a framework for analysis', Institute of European Studies, The Queen's University of Belfast, Queen's Papers on Europeanization no. 2/2001, available at http://www.qub.ac.uk/ies/onlinepapers/poe2-01.pdf (accessed 7 June 2002).

Lesser, I. O. (1999), 'Turkey's strategic options', *The International Spectator*, vol. 34, pp. 79–88.

Marks, G. and C. J. Wilson (1999), 'National parties and the contestation of Europe', in Th. F. Banchoff and M. P. Smith (eds), *Legitimacy and the European Union: The Contested Polity*, London: Routledge, pp. 113–133.

Marks, G. and C. J. Wilson (2000), 'The past in the present: a cleavage theory of party response to European integration', *British Journal of Political Science*, vol. 30, pp. 433–459.

Park, W. (2000), 'Turkey's European Union candidacy: from Luxembourg to Helsinki – to Ankara?', *Mediterranean Politics*, vol. 5, pp. 31–53.

Peuch, J. C. (2002a) 'Turkey: frustration mounting over EU demands for reform', Radio Free Europe, 15 March, available at http://www.rferl.org (accessed 6 June 2003).

Peuch, J. C. (2002b) 'Turkey: coalition partners cross swords over EU reforms – but is it all about human rights?', Radio Free Europe, 12 September, available at http://www.rferl.org (accessed 2 June 2003).

Radaelli, C. (2000), 'Whither Europeanization? Concept stretching and substantive change', European Integration online Papers (EIoP) 4, available at http://eiop.or.at/eiop/texte/2000-008a.htm (accessed 2 June 2002).

Roper, J. (1999), 'The West and Turkey: varying roles, common interests', *The International Spectator*, vol. 34, pp. 89–102.

Smith, H. (2003) 'Turkey's leader blames EU for failing to give political support in crisis', *Guardian*, 21 February.

Szczerbiak, A. and P. Taggart (2000), 'Opposing Europe: party systems and opposition to the Union, the Euro and Europeanisation', SEI Working Paper 36, available at http://www.sussex.ac.uk/Units/SEI/papers/papers.html (accessed 5 June 2002).

Taggart, P. (1998), 'A touchstone of dissent: Euroscepticism in contemporary Western European party systems', *European Journal of Political Research*, vol. 33, pp. 363–388.

Tsakonas, P. J. (2001), 'Turkey's post-Helsinki turbulence: implications for Greece and the Cyprus issue', *Turkish Studies*, vol. 2, pp. 1–40.

Van Westerling, J. (2000), 'Conditionality and EU membership: the cases of Turkey and Cyprus', *European Foreign Affairs Review*, vol. 5, pp. 95–118.

10 The Turkish contract of citizenship and the Union model

Limits of convergence

Nergis Canefe

Introduction

Citizenship in the supranational context of the European Union (EU) has been hotly debated since the early 1990s (Meehan, 1993). In particular, the post-Copenhagen developments brought forward new questions and concerns in the area of Union citizenship. One of the most widely debated issues in this context is the applicability of this relatively novel form of legal(ised) belonging in settings other than the EU. Union citizenship guarantees only a select group of rights in terms of democratic participation and representation, and it is directly linked with the possession of member state nationality. In this context, who has a legitimate right to claim member state nationality, and what is to happen to those who habitually reside and work within the EU's borders but do not possess 'European' passports, remain as problems yet to be addressed (Wiener, 1997). The main discomfort here is about the European practices of exclusivist cultural politics, continent-wide emergence of new forms of xenophobia, and the imposition of the 'European identity' as a superior form in terms of its civilisational qualities. However, what is even more important for comparative analysis is to determine whether the EU model has produced radical changes in the way we understand citizenship. A related issue is whether it could be used as a panacea for many ills of nation-state politics in terms of state–society relations (Bauböck, 1994; Soysal, 1994; Hammar, 1990). This latter set of questions constitutes the core of the theoretical debate presented in this chapter.

Legal approaches to Union citizenship traditionally characterise it as a compilation of previously existing rights and norms, and remain rather silent about the possibility of the emergence of novel types of belonging in bordered political units (Sommers, 1994, 1999). Surely, the historical context of this new form of citizenship gives us clues about its defining characteristics. However, the current formulation and applications of 'European citizenship' also reflect significant changes in the discourse concerning what the EU stands for and what kinds of interventions have taken place at the supra-national level over the past twenty years. As increasing number of citizens and non-citizens share the European social, political and cultural spheres, membership defined via nationality has become more of a problem than a solution for emergent tensions. In this vein, the sociological literature on citizenship rightly points out the out-moded qualities of the perception of citizenship as state membership. As an alternative, it characterises the EU-level conception of citizenship as a novel formulation. Accordingly, the European geography of [national] cit-izenship should be disentangled from Union-based model of rights and duties, which are defined in terms of human rights codes, workers' rights, local and regional principles of democratic participation, etc.

In this chapter, I accept the argument that the difference between Union citizenship and the canonised definition of [national] citizenship is that of the altered – but not altogether missing – dimension of national belonging and nationality for setting the terms of the citizenship contract. This difference requires the questioning of the absolutist definition of national identity as the primary site of collective identity. Indeed, since the 1960s, social movements have emphasised the marking of 'internal bound-aries' within the national polity, such as class, race, gender, communal identities (Turner, 1999; Wiener, 1997: 531). As a result, national borders are no longer seen as the final venue of inclusion and/or exclusion. The emergent geography of citizenship is more supra-, sub- or trans-national than national. Union citizenship constitutes a prime example of this phe-nomenon (Caporaso, 1996).

However, in this chapter, I also argue that there remains a unique and substantive core endemic to Union citizenship. In other words, despite its pragmatic and ever-changing nature, it reflects a contractual agreement that is circumscribed by the historical developments in member states' relations with their own citizens. In many ways, Union citizenship reflects an ongoing tension between post-national and state-based conceptions of citizenship. Within Europe, post-Maastricht debates on citizenship acquired the form of constitutional politics. Yet the notion of citizenship is regarded as constitutive of a new form of political community only to the extent that it adds to or generalises nationality-based rights already enjoyed by the citizenry of the member states of the Union. As such, it forms a second circle or pillar of rights to be enjoyed within the EU built upon a prior set of engagements. I identify the intersection between national and supra-national pillars of rights as the normative core of the Union model of post- or trans-national citizenship. My central question is not whether or not the Union model embodies principles that enable its practical adaptation in contexts outside the EU. Rather, it concerns the issue of whether its successful adaptation is possible in the absence of an identifiable normative core determined by specific histories in other con-texts. The case I observe to substantiate my arguments is that of the crisis of Republican Turkish model of citizenship. This chapter does examine European citizenship as a 'fragmented' and continuous practice composed of separate yet interrelated components (Wiener, 1997: 536). However, its central concern is about the degree of success that may be expected in this model's applications if relations between the fragments are not given due consideration.

In its broadest terms, citizenship is a relationship between the individual and a defined political community (Carens, 2000; Kymlicka and Norman, 1994; Young, 1990; Ben Habib, 1996). In between lie the institutions representing political authority such as the state, which mediate and regulate this particular kind of relationship. In the EU context, the role of mediation and regulation lies with the EU Parliament, while the boundaries of its actions are set by the *acquis communautaire* (henceforth *acquis*). Therefore, the Union model of citizenship cannot be discussed independent of the evolution of the *acquis*, a process structuring Union politics *in toto*. This frame of analysis leads us to evaluate citizenship in the EU as part and parcel of normative convictions, state traditions, policy paradigm shifts, opportunity structures, social movements, and formulation and expression of societal demands and expectations at large. In order to assess the possibilities and limits of the model's application, we must attend to the historical and community-specific dimensions of the Union model. It is only then that we can make an extrapolation concerning what uses it could be put to and what kinds of remedial promises it embodies. Although at first this may sound like a gesture of an anti-globalisation kind, the present intellectual undertaking is not about undermining the consequences of globalisation but rather about paying due attention to local dimensions of global dynamics.

In the following pages, I first outline the basic institutional trajectory pertaining to the development of a European ideal type in the area of citizenship. In the second section, I underline the historical background and normative basis upon which the European model finds justification and legitimation. In the last two sections of the chapter, I examine the potential areas of promise for Turkish adaptation of this model as well as blind spots, gaps and projections that may need further qualification.

10.1 Genealogy of an emergent paradigm: Union citizenship

> Europe should be personalised.
>
> (Commissioner Davignon[1])

The key turning points in the 'making of Union citizenship' are the Paris summit meetings of 1973 and 1974, the Fontainebleau summit of 1984, the Maastricht summit of 1991, the 1993 Treaty of Union, and the Copenhagen summit of 2002. During this lengthy process, the objectives of establishing special rights for European citizens (including a common passport) and confirming the boundaries of the Union as a privileged

political, cultural and economic area converged. The resultant transformation was a complex process of deliberations, mediations and arbitra-
tions. As I will posit in the later part of this chapter, it is in this particular
field that the expected convergence between Republican Turkish and
Union models of citizenship is prone to be most problem laden.

The idea of Union citizenship found its first clear articulations during
the early 1970s when Community politicians expressed their desire for the
formulation of a common European identity. European Community political discourse at the time reveals that the main debate was not about what
this identity should be, but about how it was to be achieved. The
expressed longing, then, was the creation of a feeling of distinct identity
and belonging. The adoption of the 1976 Council decision to implement
universal (i.e. European Community-wide) suffrage and the first European Parliament elections of 1979, followed by the 1981 Council resolution for the creation of a single European passport, are to be counted as
firm steps taken towards the fulfilment of this desire. In conjunction, the
formulation of a common European identity was put on the agenda as
one of the overarching goals of the *acquis*.

Although these developments appear like the beginnings of an effort to
create a nation-state-like entity, it soon became evident that what was
sought was categorically different. By the late 1980s, Community politicians and bureaucrats alike became well aware of the 'dynamic nature' of
European unification and were wise enough not to impose a rigid format
upon this rather complex process. What the citizenship debate of the
1970s achieved, in this regard, could best be described as the formal identification of citizens of member states as active participants of an emergent
European political community. This recognition was accompanied by the
attribution of political rights at the Community-cum-Union level, such as
the right to vote, to stand for elections and to hold public office. Different
from the criteria for 'national citizenship', this system-level citizenship was
never perceived as requiring naturalisation and/or loss of previous nationality. Instead, what later became EU citizenship is more of an 'additional
package of rights', which is nonetheless not accessible by foreigners habitually residing in member states.

Within this special-rights package, one of the main points of anchorage
for the nurturing of a common – yet loosely defined – political identity
was the item of the issuance of a uniform European passport. This document was clearly expected to develop ties between the legal-bureaucratic
structure of the Community/Union and citizens of its member states. In
other words, its effect was not to be limited to the procedural erasure of
nation-state borders for Europeans. The 'policy objectives' of the European passport were stated as 'to contribute to represent the Community as
an entity vis-à-vis the rest of the world' and, 'to revive the feeling of
belonging among citizens of the Community.' (Wiener, 1997: 541) When
the EU passport was put into practice in 1981, however, the burgundy-

coloured document brought with it problems as well as privileges. The main concern was the maintenance of security between the borders of member states as well as between Europe and the 'outside world'. The Schengen Agreement of 1995 was the next step taken to address these concerns while solidifying the legal structure behind the practice of a common Union citizenship. In this context, one of the most critical questions about Union citizenship became what kind of a common understanding it elicits in terms of who belongs in Europe and who does not. A related one was about where Europe begins and where it ends, and how much and what kinds of force it should, and could, use to protect its conglomerate of borders.

At this point, it is necessary to have a closer look at the construct of 'Fortress Europe', or 'Schengenland'. With the coming into existence of Schengenland on 26 March 1995, this area, comprising seven of the EU states,[2] became something of a 'first'. Schengenland is not a new nation-state or a federative structure. It is closest to a regional, supra-national conglomeration. There were two direct effects of the Schengen Agreement in terms of perception and treatment of national citizenship. While the qualified Europeans benefited from the new 'category' of EU-level belonging, external border controls and rights of resident non-European aliens, refugees and migrants became highly controversial.[3] One of the most noticeable results of these developments was the orchestrated revival of the xenophobic characteristics of individual European nationalisms at a time of regional unification (Mitten, 1994). It is indeed disappointing to witness that the Union model of citizenship, which was imagined to be an arena for creating something new and unique, in certain ways led to a legalised and Unionised repeat of old mistakes endemic to national citizenship contracts across the continent. However, this is not the only commonality it embodies.

At this point, it is important to attend to the details of individual European countries. A comparison between British and French senses of nationality and national citizenship is most illuminating in this regard. While the former entertains a flexible and composite formula (including applications of both *jus soli* and *jus sanguinis*) reflecting its long imperial history, the latter embraces 'active citizenship', calling upon each and every citizen to accept the set principles of the Revolution and the Republic. Against these two examples, there is the German case: citizenship in Germany, until the mid-1990s, was primarily a matter of *jus sanguinis* and thus defined Germanness on the basis of ethnic descent and blood ties. In the light of these differences, how is it possible to talk about a Europe-wide trend pointing to an orchestrated redefinition of the relationship between rights, national belonging and cultural identity? As Yasemin Soysal (1994) has been arguing since the mid-1990s, within the European context a person's identity can be and has been eventually uncoupled from their rights. Supra-national associations, international human rights organisations and local political rights discourse rendered the demanding and obtaining of entitlements that may only have been regarded as just and obtainable for the citizens of a given European country, possible for 'others'. The emergence of this formula is linked with three related developments: implications of decolonisation for the European empires as they began to live with their 'others' at home; the Marshallian enlargement of rights in the national polity; and post-1945 in-migratory flows that created millions of 'guests' who stayed. The combined effect of these developments was a substantial and continent-wide change in the political culture of Europe in terms of defining the individual and his or her relations with the state as well as with the society at large. This change resulted in a move from the liberal, unencumbered model of individual membership to an embedded and rights-based understanding of the self – European or otherwise. It also formalised the right to life, to welfare, to political freedom, to cultural preservation, to demand gender-specific corrections to the existing set of rights, to decent working conditions and hours, to universal education and health care, to a reliable pension system, to a just and working judiciary system, etc. In other words, differences between European countries' specific histories in terms of their understanding of citizenship were amalgamated within the common story of the self-sustenance of historical capitalism as it was experienced at the core. At the very top layer appears to lie the rights discourse, recognising group-specific differences and demands. However, on its own it does not characterise the Union model and its nation-state-specific foundations.

10.2　The Union model: historical background and normative foundations

> Europe cannot be a panacea, a remedy for all ailments afflicting our economies and societies. Rather, it provides a framework within which solutions can be explored.
>
> > (Robert Toulemon, 1998: 128)

Lack of democracy, or 'democratic deficit', has been an important issue in European Union-related debates for almost two decades. It has been frequently suggested that the Union itself does not meet the criteria that it imposes upon member or candidate states. The increasing involvement of the European Parliament in the EU legislative work is one kind of remedy devised to tackle the problems of 'democratisation' and 'accountability' in the EU. The other, albeit less discussed, device is that of Union citizenship, which includes a range of measures to encourage *and* consolidate a sense of belonging and a separate identity among the 'citizens' of Europe.

I have already identified the institutional trajectory providing the context within which this new formulation came into existence. What is now needed is a closer look at what Europeans agree is uniquely European and therefore should be protected. In other words, attention must be paid to the historical and normative foundations upon which the edifice of Union citizenship was built. Notions such as democracy, human rights, civility, etc. are not useful in this context, although they do form part of the meta-discourse of being 'Western' (Delanty, 1985). Instead, here I will attend to something that may appear much more 'selfish' and 'unedifying'.

In recent years, a relatively new debate has emerged about what it means to be 'European': It is the welfare state and the conduct of social democracy that separates the European socio-political space from those in other 'developed' countries, as well as separating the North from the South. In this perspective, a key concern for the majority of Europeans is the sustenance of guarantees for their general welfare – that is, their 'right to a minimum standard of living' (Toulemon, 1998: 126). Here, political philosophy equips us to read this 'minimum standard' as shorthand for prescriptions of a 'good life'. In this regard, for instance, accession to the European Convention of Human Rights is not to be seen simply as a procedural matter. The ability and desire to seek institutional redress against encroachment of political, economic and civic rights define a specific kind of political culture. The end result that we see today is indebted to generations and genres of contention and negotiation within the hub of capitalism that are marked by the demands and exigencies of liberalism, socialism, egalitarianism, utopianism, fascism, Nazism and, of course, social democracy.

It is upon this heritage that the acceptance of a common and committal framework such as the European Charter of Human Rights took place, both at the discursive level and in the actual conduct of European politics (Alston, 1999). Equally noteworthy are the 'formalised' European expectations of transparency and accountability from those who govern. At the Union level, these expectations led to arrangements for effective cooperation in the fight against corruption and crime, and continual guaranteeing of basic liberties against abuse by the police and home affairs authorities.[4] In a similar vein, the mindset behind the creation of a 'European legal area' in penal matters is that of enabling the EU to guarantee citizens' security at the Union level.

As such, European citizenship legalised by the Maastricht Treaty corresponds to a set of 'common rights' to be enjoyed by all those who are bound by the 'European political community' (Jary, 1999; Markoff, 1999; Preuß, 1998; Delanty, 1997; Roche, 1992; Tassin, 1992; Van der Berghe, 1992). As already mentioned, there are two sets of problems about this convention: the status and treatment of those who are not of European descent and yet who legally reside and work within Europe, and the status and treatment of those who are neither European nor live in Europe. Looked from this angle, European citizenship appears as a matter of protecting the privileges of a select group of individuals living in a closely connected set of rich capitalist countries. Internally speaking, however, it reflects a supra-national extension of a kind of contract corresponding to the historical fights and gains of several political communities joined together not only by their geographical proximity but also by their position in the history of capitalism. The EU model, in this context, is the embodiment of institutional remedies for the humane functioning of the system in the face of the challenges posed by under-classes, migrants, refugees, marginalised regions, etc. Union citizenship has an identifiable societal base as it addresses explicit demands of classes, groups, communities and regions.

Within this context, it is plausible to argue that a successful Turkish application for Union citizenship requires the imminent endorsing consent of Turkish society. In order to achieve this end, it should correspond to the wide-ranging set of problems and issues that ail different sectors of the society. Although it appears to be the primary point of anchorage for those who wish to adopt the post-national model of citizenship, group rights is just one of the items in this agenda. Citizenship, if it is to embody a legitimate contract based on societal conventions, must be desirable and satisfactory for those who will be bound by it. This requires contentious processes of confrontation, negotiation and settlements between classes, factions, groups, communities and even nations. In Turkey, there is a continuing problem of a lack of desire to build consent as well as a lack of understanding regarding the terms of integration/ accession in Turkey–EU relations. Citizenship, in this regard, constitutes one of the many aspects of this systemic problem.

10.3 The Union model and the Turkish context

Turkey's EU membership is an issue that affects diverse interests and aspirations in Turkish society. This situation becomes even more complicated when it comes to introducing and implementing reforms as part of the accession (or, in Turkey's case, pre-accession) process. Meanwhile, it should be noted that the phenomenon of fragmented interests is not unique to Turkey. Effects of EU-related issues in domestic and foreign politics are well documented for both EU member states and candidate countries (Goetz and Hix, 2001). What appears to be rather idiosyncratic about Turkey is that ownership of the Westernisation project has changed hands over time. For instance, the army and the bureaucratic elite of Kemalist inclinations traditionally stood for full-scale Westernisation. Yet it is against them and their fears about Turkey's national sovereignty and unity that rising classes and political factions such as the liberalist Second Republicans (*Ikinci Cumhuriyetciler*), Islamists and Kurdish nationalists have had to fight for the completion of reform packages in alliance with the EU. This current confrontation between those who favour various modes of multiculturalism and pluralism, liberal internationalism or Third Way politics, and guardians of the Republican status quo, finds one of its clearest expressions in the area of citizenship in Turkey.

Both the southern enlargement of the EU in the past and the recent eastern enlargement dictated a set of conventions upon the societies that expressed a wish to join the EU. A major part of these relates to a binding, post-1951 European reading of human rights. In the Turkish case, there are four main areas of reform related to human rights that were declared at the Copenhagen summit to be prerequisites for the country's accession to the EU. These are improvement of the conditions for freedom of expression and association, including political parties; the guaranteeing and implementation of ethnic minority rights; abolition of the death penalty; and limiting the military's role in national politics. In response to the European demands, in March 2001 Turkey presented a National Programme for the Adoption of the *Acquis*, outlining short- and medium-term measures to be implemented by the government. The first amendment package passed was related to the first item on the human rights requirements, followed by a series of other packages.[5] Therefore, the issue at this point is not about government inaction but about the actual application of these legal regulations and reforms in Turkish social, political and economical life. If one leg of the application problem is that of bureaucratic inertia, the other leg is political culture – a large sphere of action and influence including economics, social movements as well as the conduct of politics at both state and civic levels.[6] There is also a third dimension totally lacking in the citizenship-oriented debates on human rights: how to take care of the excesses of the capitalist market economy in a country with a weak tradition of social democracy.

Among those four areas of reform, minority rights and those related to religious freedoms are pointed at as the most urgent ones requiring attention. Since minorities are defined by the Constitution as the 'non-Muslim population' of Turkey, ethnic minorities are not identified as groups that require special rights and/or protection. This constitutional quagmire results in the repeated criticism by the EU that Turkey (the Turkish state and/or Turkish society) has very limited if any commitment to ensuring cultural diversity and guaranteeing rights for all its citizens regardless of their ethno-religious origin. This criticism forms the foundations of the Turkish critical discourse on citizenship, for explainable and justifiable reasons. However, it is lacking as a foundation, and the missing components are related to the aforementioned historical background and normative consent exemplified in the European context.

A case in point is the framing of the guarantees extended to EU citizens by the Maastricht Treaty. Article 8 (2) of the treaty states that citizens of the Union shall enjoy rights conferred by the Treaty and shall be subject to the duties imposed by them (Guild, 1996). Articles 8B (1 and 2), on the other hand, state that citizens of the Union who live in a member state other than the one of which they have national citizenship are entitled to full participation in the political life of their state of residence at two levels: municipal and European. Participation at the national level, in these cases, is not part of the rights conferred by Union citizenship, as it is considered a matter of internal, polity-specific decision-making. This drawing of borders indicating where the national political community begins, in effect corresponds to a large vacuum that applications of supranational formulation of citizenship by the EU have to deal with.

Similarly, symbolic acts such as the determination of a flag, an anthem, design of common history textbooks, and the usage of common passports cover the territory that lies in between and/or above the member nation-states. What happens within them, within certain limits, is their own business. In this rather nebulously defined place, rights that accompany European citizenship are related to four kinds of freedoms: free movement of goods, capital, services and persons. By way of extending these freedoms across the geographical space of the Union, the EU legislatures intended to create a uniform contract that ties citizens of member states directly to the Union. With Maastricht, the Union came to make the claim of being a supranational dispenser of rights and imposer of duties, yet with the proviso that these would not clash with the nation-state-based packages. In the case of accession, the proviso is no longer applicable, as the candidate countries are obliged to follow the Union model of citizenship even if it may conflict with their original, nation-state-based contract. The crucial point here is that there is a common understanding in Europe concerning what can justifiably take place within each polity, and between each nation-state and its citizens.

Procedural adaptation of the Union model outside the EU, in this context, becomes a promise on its own for wholesome societal change that can create such a common understanding *ex nihilo*. What is worse, the receiving end often fails to question this assumed linkage and to engage in a debate about the applicability and desirability of the EU package of norms that come attached to candidacy for membership. In the Turkish case, surely the EU model is far superior to what the Republic has had to offer so far. My concern is whether the application of the Union model – in and of itself – could induce the kinds of societal change in the political culture of Turkey that would lead to the enjoyment of freedom of expression, freedom of conscience, cultural and group-specific rights, as well as rights to welfare, just distribution and redistribution of societal resources and good governance.

Furthermore, one of the key logical conclusions of the resultant separation of citizenship and nationality in the EU context is that groups such as migrants and refugees do not need to qualify for national citizenship in order to benefit from the rights associated with it. Similarly, the expectation is that *jus soli* rather than *jus sanguinis* should constitute the basis upon which individuals are granted citizenship or naturalised. However, the new formulation of 'post-national citizenship' in the European context acts primarily as a remedy for the contrast between the generosity of EU provisions for citizens of the member states, and, the restrictive provisions for non-nationals or, as they are known in Euro-speak, 'third country nationals'. This remedy has only limited value in countries such as Turkey, where settled minority groups with significant population figures rather than immigrants pose the biggest challenge in terms of the legitimation of the existing citizenship contract. It is not all that certain whether solutions proposed for Europe-specific problems would work to produce similar effects in contexts characterised by other sets of problems and concerns. Resort to supra-national organs such as the European Court of Human Rights can act as a buffer against possible damage resulting from unfair acts by the nation-state in countries that are candidates for accession to the EU. Similarly, application to bodies such as the International Labour Organisation to curtail the abuse of workers' rights, or for improvement in national legislation organising labour–capital relations, can act as a corrective solution for regime-specific crises. Yet such mechanisms are 'remedial' rather than constituting frames of reference for governance. If that is the case, 'de-territorialisation of rights' may work well only in a well-defined post-national setting. That is why it is possible to argue that Union citizenship as we know it might not have come into effect without the pre-existence of the EU framework.

One way in which EU-wide conventions can constitute valid and applicable references outside their specific context is the institution of consent in these societies for endorsing the adjustment to their 'citizenship contract' in accordance with the criteria set by the Union. We also need to think further about how the re-contextualisation of the Union model can alleviate problems of representation, unequal treatment, unequal access to opportunities, and systemic practices of exclusion and dis-privileging in non-EU contexts. The EU's package of reforms in the area of human rights is somewhat mechanical in terms of addressing the problems of the variant nature of candidate countries. Why it receives such a degree of internal approval rather than being effectively contextualised, however, is a matter that should be regarded as being above and beyond the desire for EU membership.

10.4 Common answers without common questions? The Turkish debate on the crisis of the Republican model

Coexistence of competing accounts of the 'good life' and the conditions of each individual to have the ability to entertain such an account in Turkish society are as important as the protection of groups and communities. In this section, I will briefly examine the debates that are related to these three specific issues in an effort to understand where the limits of convergence between the Union model and Republican Turkish citizenship lie.

In December 2002, the EU leaders formally agreed to expand the Union in 2004 from 15 to 25 members. They also set a schedule under which two more countries, Bulgaria and Romania, would be brought into the Union in 2007. From this massive enlargement process, Turkey was nominally excluded by way of a promise: if Turkey is to be admitted along with Bulgaria and Romania in 2007, it has to prove by 2004 that it does fully comply with the Copenhagen criteria. However, it is not only the EU leaders and the European public that are divided about the possibility and merits of Turkey's accession in the near future. Turkish politics is also coloured by this issue across the whole spectrum of ideologies and persuasions. Those in favour of accession and wishing for the Europeans to agree with it do so for three main reasons (Teitelbaum and Martin, 2003: 98): bolstering the will and ability of those sectors of the Turkish society that are seeking to create a prosperous, democratic and multicultural state out of the eroding Republican regime; proving that Europe is not a Christian club but a unique civilisational project; and strengthening Turkey's economy, which will have stabilising regional effects and curb out-migratory pressures.

Those who are not so favourable to Turkish membership of the EU, on the other hand, state their reluctance primarily in the language of inequality among nations. Accordingly, if the Europeans want Turkey to join them, they should understand the unique needs, cultural make-up, geopolitical position and national security concerns of the Turkish 'society-cum-state'. Although notable sectors of Turkish society – particularly the political elite – insist that EU norms and regulations are beneficial for Turkey, other influential groups – such as nationalists and ultra-nationalists on both the right and the left of the political spectrum, devoted Kemalists, traditionalists, conservatives, etc. have questions and reservations about their applicability. This is not to deny that sectors traditionally benefiting from the status quo and undemocratic practices of governance would not easily be convinced of the benefits of redefining the Turkish citizenship contract. The crisis of Republican citizenship could not be overcome if the onus were left on the parties who have vested interests in the continuation of the status quo. However, my questions are about the vision entertained by those who want the existing framework to change.

Here, I agree with the supposition that there is a crisis to be addressed and that the voices of civil society should be the main guide for its resolution. There is indeed a multiplicity of voices whose common theme is demanding rights for specific communities, blocks or groups. However, whether wholesome changes in the Republican citizenship model could be induced without creating a common ground where these contentious voices can meet to identify core norms remains to be seen. This form of questioning is not to do with defending the Republican model or trying to find a way in which the state elite can be incorporated into the scheme for radical change. Although it is important to understand the founding premises of the Republican model and not to entertain a vision of totally clearing the 'enemy' – as this is never quite possible or indeed desirable – the scope of the present analysis does not include these issues.

In summary, altering the Republican model of citizenship in line with the premises of the Union model constitutes an attractive idea for a large arsenal of groups and communities, albeit for markedly different reasons. In the remainder of this chapter, I will identify some of the dominant themes that lead to such an across-the-board attraction. I will also indicate the dangers pertaining to group-specific justifications of Turkey's adoption of the Union model. Specifically, I will identify the contexts in which piecemeal adaptation of this model can lead to essentialisation, lack of concern for the rights of those who might entertain different visions for justice, and, in general, the lack of a common agenda for social peace in its full meaning and not just as it is related to cultural rights.

10.5 Perceptions of post-national citizenship in Turkish political culture: Alternative venues

In Turkish politics, neo-Islamists, social and radical democrats, Kurdish nationalists (including those who favour a multiculturalist or a federalist solution to the Kurdish problem), those who are engaged in and/or favour civil society initiatives, as well as those favouring a federative solution to the Cyprus problem are identified as the main protagonists of the Union model of citizenship. The common denominator that brings these sectors together is that each finds the very foundations of the Republican regime highly questionable and its political praxis in need of a major renaissance. If the main façade of the crisis of legitimacy endemic to the Republican regime is that of the 'national security syndrome', next on the list is the 'national unity discourse' (Cizre, 2003). Therefore, the critics of both democratic deficit and illegitimate governance conventions in Turkey identify the promise (if not the actual package) of the EU-prescribed political reforms as a worthy starting point for building something new. The problem arises when the common debate then moves on to what is to follow these reforms, and the extent to which every Turkish citizen is to benefit from them. Therefore, the pro-EU and post-national citizenship discourse intent on the supremacy of rights without added qualifiers as to what sustains them, suffers from an oversight.

The venues for the formulation of this discourse are the media, weeklies, and semi-academic and academic journals.[7] In these venues, the ideas of positionality, community, rights and recognition have taken to the front row since the early 1990s. Most notably, regarding this set of key concepts one finds specific readings of community and rights as main points of anchorage. The idea of community has long been central to the theory of citizenship as it implies membership in a chosen political community (Carens, 2000; MacIntyre, 1988, 1995; Horton and Mendus, 1994; Taylor, 1989; Walzer, 1983; Bell, 1993; Sandel, 1982). The controversy about community is not limited to the absence of a communitarian or group-rights vision. It also problematises the very definition of community tied to a particular discourse of justice. For instance, communitarianism bordering on essentialism tends to impose an organic notion of community, which then leads to the proliferation of problems related to both exclusion and rigid criteria of inclusion. Yet this is not all that normative consent can offer. By and large, the tension between citizenship and political community must be regarded as a foundational one that cannot be wished away. The questioning of this proposition is one of the main tenets of the paradigm of post-national citizenship and the discourse of trans-national identities, which are framed above and beyond the nation-state and the established communal identities. Here, the underlying assumption appears to be the existence of a deterritorialised form of belonging in a global setting. A similar inclination is present in universal human rights and refugee rights discourses. In some contexts, it is necessary to make such an argument; but in others, it can lead to a detrimental oversight. These are essential debates that nonetheless are left largely unaddressed in the Turkish context.

The communitarianism versus liberalism debate teaches us that being a citizen does not *only* mean that one can benefit from and participate in the society that one habitually resides in. It also has the dimension of having a say in the definitions of the common good and/or justice in the society of which one enjoys membership and with awareness of what others may want. Furthermore, the common good is not limited to group-specific rights. Informed and active participation of individuals involves but is not circumscribed by the envisioning of boundaries of communities. Another crucial aspect of this engagement is making choices and favouring decisions that justify the access to resources deemed necessary for individuals who entertain particular visions of community, society, justice and morality, without hindering such access for others.

In this context, citizenship can presuppose the coexistence of particular conceptions of the good with general conceptions of justice and rights. It is possible, and indeed necessary, to talk about these particulars in the larger contexts of regions, societies, national polities, confederations, and various other forms of unions and coexistence that do not pre-empt difference and plurality of perceptions of the good and right. The issue, then, is not only how to come up with a representative formulation of particular goods, but also how to reach some form of reconciliatory stand that supports (not just allows) coexistence. Otherwise, the rights discourse can gradually free the self from commitment to any such set of criteria demanding sacrifices and conciliatory moves to coexist with others who

may not agree with our own particular convictions, or who may systematically suffer from relative deprivation in economic as well as political terms.

In the context of Turkish adaptations of the Union model, what I
identify is that the framework to produce foundations for coexistence and
to define acceptable forms of political conduct has not been adequately
examined or formulated. The fact that the post-national world or even the
'third space' are places where morality exists and that there are orientations towards shared perceptions of the good and the just is overlooked.
In addition, these frames of morality would not easily allow for imposed
reorderings; there is a repertoire of apt choices that a dedicated Muslim
or someone who believed in a separate Kurdish state would make. Finally,
both the implicit and the explicit embodiments of these frameworks are
exposed in the histories of state-society relations, perceptions of the self,
and successive waves of critical takes on the status quo. There are no
sudden breaking points for oppositional groups, factions or communities
to realise that their interests do not coincide with those of the dominant
political culture in a given society. Their critical claims and articulated
desire for change can be traced back in the continuum of intellectual traditions and social movements, institutional as well as those in the culture
of everyday life.

A case in point is that of political Islam in Turkey. Although the stance
taken by proponents of this ideological amorph has changed over the 80-
year history of Republican Turkey, it nonetheless is indebted to, and in
constant dialogue with, both Turkish nationalism and various branches of
conservatism and liberalism in Turkey (Bora, 1998). Current Islamist
demands for a new framework of Turkish citizenship and reformulation of
Turkish democracy are not simply a matter of incorporation of the discourses of critique, autonomy and plurality that have come to the fore in
the age of globalisation. Similar voices of contention have been there
since and even before the foundation of the Republic. Perhaps what
makes them so audible now is that such contentious voices came to the
realisation that none of them was alone in their discomforts with the
status quo. This realisation can and does lead to the mindset of a united
front against those who do not 'listen'. However, united fronts at times of
war do not necessarily lead to peace afterwards. There is no natural
unfolding of the rights discourse that would lead to pluralistic harmony.
The European example should be read in this light and not as a generic
formula. With few exceptions (Göle, 1995, 1997; Bulaç, 1993; Insel, 1992,
1993; Sarıbay, 1993; Akçam, 1992), such concerns are absent in the
Islamist discourse or among the academic debates trying to understand
and reflect upon its demands (Alpay, 2002; Karaman, 2002; Bulaç, 2000,
2001; Emre, 1998; Özdenören, 1998; Gerger, 1989).

Another relevant example is the debate on Kurdish identity and rights
in Turkey. There have been several well-endowed contributions to this
debate since the 1990s in Turkish academic and intellectual circles. Again,

the limits of the interventions are set by the desire to provide cultural and political rights for Kurds in Turkey and perhaps test the conditions for a federalist political solution. The bulk of the energy is thus invested upon understanding the form that silencing, oppression, forced assimilation, and abuse of rights can take (Yeğen, 1994, 2000). Although this focus is absolutely necessary to identify the problem at hand, there is a marked absence of arbitration about how Kurds and non-Kurds do, can and will live together, or the conditions of non-Kurds willingly consenting to the introduction of group-specific rights to Turkish politics. There is a crucial article that reveals the parameters of the contemporary debate on Kurdish nationalism, the Kurdish problem or the Kurdish question in Turkey by Kasaba (1997: 18), which states that the Kemalist, Islamist and Kurdish nationalist ideologies have an ideological common point: strong intolerance for competing nationalist projects. The success of the attacks waged against various practices of the Turkish nation-state reveals that what were once presented and, to a certain degree, accepted as absolute norms of national sovereignty are undergoing a significant degree of erosion. However, very few works on Kurdish nationalism in Turkey make an attempt to envision what could follow this erosion and to identify whether new absolutes are established in its place and, if so, at what cost.

The Kurds have indeed been one of the most persistent and active players in Turkish politics, having challenged the hegemony of the nation-state since its inception. And yet, it would be a mistake to treat Kurdish nationalism as a continuous movement and to overlook the changes in its discourse and organisation since the 1970s. Kemal Kirişçi and Gareth Winrow's jointly penned volume titled *The Kurdish Question and Turkey: An Example of a Trans-state Ethnic Conflict* (1997) makes exactly this point very clear. Notably, the main arguments in Kirişçi and Winrow's work concern the question of whether Turkey could become a genuinely multicultural society. In addition to a detailed analysis of issues concerning minority rights and self-determination within the bounds of Turkish Republican history, the authors tackle the various models related to multicultural governance. For instance, they present the deficits and applicability of the Lipjhartian model of consociationalism in the Turkish context. The aim of consociationalism is to ensure democratic governance in the presence of ethno-religious minorities with diverse needs and demands from the state. However, appealing as it is, there is widespread criticism of consociationalism, and almost all its non-European applications have ended up with civil wars, such as in Malaysia, Lebanon and Cyprus. The authors thus feel forced to move on to present the current debate on different forms of autonomy, federal schemes and provision of group rights. They reach the conclusion that, at least for the time being, none of these models is directly applicable to the Turkish case in terms of addressing the Kurdish question in the country. Kirişçi and Winrow are convinced that it is only through step-by-step and gradual application of norms of good governance in a multi-ethnic society that social and political peace can be achieved. In order for an adapted form of multilateralism to take root in Turkish society, the leaders of what they identify as the dominant Turkish ethnic core must feel the necessity to make concessions for a long-lasting solution to the problems at hand. Another interesting aspect of the debate presented in this volume is the authors' belief that multiple forms of identity (a person feeling Turkish as part of a supra-identity but feeling Kurdish as their ethno-religious identity) may indeed carry the seeds of a wholesale resolution regarding the Kurdish question in Turkey.

In general, the pro-societal solution genre of works on the Kurdish question such as those exemplified above point to the fact that the Kurdish ethno-religious and national identity is a construct in the making, just as the Turkish identity was and still is. When we depart from this kind of self-reflexivity, the risk of essentialising group identities and creating new categories of marginality within the communal framework emerges. Equally importantly, societal oppression cannot be explained solely on the basis of undemocratic conventions of governance. The areas of political culture and hegemonic normative convictions also need examination.

Another examination-based approach focusing on systemic qualities of Turkish political culture and how they could be changed has been produced by feminist critiques of Republican Turkish citizenship. Yeşim Arat's work (1999, 2000) for instance, marked a territory that remained relatively untouched before. She identifies her analytical framework as 'gendered citizenship' in the Turkish context. In particular, she attends to the differences between the legal framework for generic citizenship and women's experiences. Like Kasaba, Arat (1999: 275) is convinced that in Turkey, citizenship evolved as a result of the choices made by an enlightened elite for two main purposes: to promote social integration and to strengthen the state. Meanwhile, although citizenship rights for both men and women were shaped from above, she argues that there are both formal and substantive differences regarding their gender-specific applications. She argues that since the 1980s, feminist critiques of citizenship in Turkey have achieved the formidable task of revealing the exclusionary and gender-biased nature of the liberal model. For our purposes, here the question is whether this genre of critique also envisages a new model that can encompass the differences. It is possible to give an affirmative answer to this question. The resultant formula includes Islamist women's critiques of the secular, Republican citizenship contract, with the caveat that the parameters within which Islamic identities are circumscribed have to be enlarged. This type of examination underlines the need for the systemic recognition of gender-specific needs of individuals *as well as* the implementation of wholesome corrective measures to minimise the continual effects of patriarchal traditions in every corner of social life.

Critiques of Turkish nationalism, particularly in terms of identifying what this ideological enterprise includes and what it excludes, constitute the final branch of literature I would like to discuss for underlining the limited presence and yet crucial importance of systemic inquiries about the Republican Turkish citizenship contract. In Ayşe Kadıoğlu's works (1998, 1999), this inclusion–exclusion dynamic is explained as a matter of the paradoxical qualities of Turkish nationalism. She suggests that Turkish nationalism is engaged in a permanent stock-taking between the benefits of the 'East' and the 'West'. She refers to the double bind of Third World nationalisms in terms of trying to transform the 'national culture' to make it more apt for progress while at the same time protecting its 'authentic' characteristics. A related dimension of this paradox is the constant clash between state elites and other kinds of political and cultural elite in Turkey. Kadıoğlu analyses the consequences of this dilemma in the area of the Republican citizenship contract. Her work finds its counterpart in migration and refugee studies in the publications of Kemal Kirişçi (1994, 1996, 2000) and Ahmet İçduygu and Fuat Keyman (İçduygu, 1996; İçduygu *et al.*, 1999; İçduygu and Keyman, 2000). Kirişçi posits that citizenship is central to the understanding of notions such as national identity, democracy and political participation in Turkey (2000: 2). Like Yeşim Arat, however, he makes a distinction between the formal characteristics of citizenship and its substantive content and related practices. On the basis of this distinction, he provides a detailed analysis of exclusionary practices of the Republic that reveal the substantive aspects of the Republican citizenship contract. İçduygu's analysis, on the other hand, favours paying more attention to the 'position' of the individual as a citizen. He links his concerns about membership with international migration and identifies the latter as a site that can be used to elaborate the relationship between the citizen and the nation-state. In his views, international migration challenges the category of national citizenship by definition, as the migrant no longer lives in his or her home country. İçduygu also attends to the issue of multiple citizenships and diasporic identities, two categories of existence that cannot be explained in terms of nation-state-based definitions of membership or sense of belonging.

These debates positioning citizenship in the larger contexts of patriarchy, nationalism and international migration benefit from the added advantage of treating the issue in the light of system-wide concerns and from a comparative perspective. They manage to move beyond the dilemma of delimiting citizenship to the realm of rights, membership, attachments or legality (Keyman, forthcoming). Turkish scholarship on the benefits and costs of the European model of citizenship needs to incorporate this vision further and to dare question the model as it is presented as an attachment to membership, and hence the limits of its applicability. The debate on post-national citizenship is a rapidly evolving one, although there are certain legacies and acceptances endemic to it. The Turkish engagement in this debate, if it remains locked on specific claims and strategies for challenging the state-centric traditions, will remain weak in terms of identifying the many horizons regarding where one can go from there onwards.

Conclusion

As Gerard Delanty rightly argues (2003), the enlargement of the European Union, if it is eventually to include Turkey as well as the former communist countries, will constitute a major challenge for the traditionalist understanding of Europe as an economic, social and cultural space. More than anything else, Turkey's inclusion seems to signal further introduction of flexibility into the definition of a European identity. At the same time, this inclusion will take place if and only if the limits of closure to make Europe a separate and idiosyncratic entity are not eroded to the degree of being nebulous.

Since the 1990s, one of the main anchors of European identity has become the kind of citizenship convention that the part of the continent included in the European Union offers. Prior to the 'European citizenship' debate, it was French versus German or British models that provided the axes for students of citizenship if they were to discuss the concept and its practice in a comparative context (Brubaker, 1996). In this 'older' paradigm, types of nationalism were coupled with different citizenship contracts, and the resultant amalgam was used as a litmus test for identifying the dominant political culture in a given society. With the introduction of the debate on post-national citizenship, however, national differences were largely put aside, and the focus became a supra-national model of belonging that went above and beyond the constraints imposed by the nation-state. This new paradigm of post-national citizenship was coupled with debates on the rights discourse and re-readings of liberalism, radical democracy, cosmopolitanism, diasporic identities, transnationalism and globalisation (Kymlicka, 2001; Carens, 2000; Young, 2000; Işın and Wood, 1999; Held, 1995).

The Turkish context proves no exception in terms of the recent developments of the debate on citizenship. However, at times it suffers from a lack of understanding of the debates' full references and historical dimensions. During the 1980s, citizenship was hardly a matter that could be addressed independent of the strong state tradition in Turkey (Dodd, 1992; Heper, 1985). Since the 1990s, however, in almost every progressive corner of Turkish politics and academia, citizenship is fast becoming a prize item for contemplation in its own right. The new debate on Turkish citizenship – similarly to those in other contexts – takes place under the banner of membership versus position-taking, conciliatory identity politics, critiques of modernisation and Westernisation as totalitarian discourses, civil society initiatives versus the heavy-handed and top-down state tradition, and communal belonging (Keyman and İçduygu, 2003).

In this chapter, I have tried to illustrate that there is a blind spot in these celebrated exchanges between what the post-national and primarily European model has to offer and what can be done at other locales. This blind spot refers to the historical dimensions and normative contents of the Union model and its derivatives. In the Turkish case, I identify a rather problem-laden Habermasian (1996) reading of 'correct' political conduct as a remedy for the ills of the relations in Turkish society and politics. The model is associated with a 'new' way of doing things according to the dictates of multiculturalism, rights discourse, pluralism, and supranationalism/transnationalism. Meanwhile, there are relatively few contributions that address, for instance, the Canadian and British questioning of both the merits and the failings of multiculturalism, and critiques of communitarian revisions of liberalism. Consequently, in the inspiring body of work on the possibilities of creating a new citizenship convention in contemporary Turkey that can move beyond the dictates of the Republican model, debates such as those between liberalism and communitarianism are referred to mainly for the purpose of addressing rights-related problems. Furthermore, issues of critical importance such as inclusion/exclusion of refugees in the national polity, or the links between class conflict, gender inequalities and disenfranchised citizenship, are put on the table rather tangentially. There is little concerted effort to link these together (Özbudun, 2000). These gaps, in addition to the lack of sufficient exploration of what normative foundations the post-national, Union model rest upon, render Turkish readings of post-national citizenship problem laden. In the case of further enlargement of the European Union, then, will the Turkish adaptation of the European conduct in the area of citizenship be just that, an adaptation? If that is to be the case, again the older debate on citizenship indicates that without a strong societal base and an articulated political will, the desired new convention of citizenship may not take root (Turner, 1992, 1999).

The strongest counter-argument for such a sceptical look at the Turkish understanding of the European model of post-national citizenship indicates that there are already-formed interest groups, communities and fractions that have a vested interest in the altering of the Republican citizenship contract. Their calls for change would indeed be served well by the supra-national model promised by the European Union. This is no doubt at least partly due to the required reforms that come with the model. If the human rights record of Turkey is straightened, if the death penalty is removed, if crimes of conscience are annulled, if expression of one's communal and religious identity is allowed as a matter of right rather than as a state-given permission, in no small measure *de facto* steps forward towards building a new convention will have been taken. The 'fragmented politics' argument further posits that the sum total of the parties involved in desiring substantive changes in the governing conventions of Turkish society – including, but not limited to, citizenship – makes them 'internal' rather than imposed from outside. The still lingering concern is whether the parties united in their desire for change are equally united in their vision for sustaining a new covenant of citizenship.

There is indeed an interesting, if annoying, relation between ignorance and injustice. Shifting the gaze away *from* locations where we have to make decisions together *to* those sites where we each can form an oppositional force against those who oppress us, try to mould us or silence us is a pragmatic solution, albeit one with restricted application. The delicate balance between respecting alterity and providing justice for all despite their differences cannot be maintained if all attention is placed upon the former part of this dual enterprise. The dedication to address singularity of wills and rightfulness of rights needs to be incorporated in an idiom that can accommodate many singularities and claims for rights.

Community without unity is possible. The appeal of community (not in the form of a binding totality but in the form of transient commons and continually fought-over agreements) is not necessarily a yearning for pre-modern (or modern) human conglomerations with identifiable bonds such as ethnicity, religion or an admirable moral core. There is space for redefining community as a bridge between the embedded individual and the society and institutions at large. Even then, an active political community cannot be defined as a sum total of miniature self-contained communities. Similarly, justice is not the sum total of rights that accrue to those who have specific claims. As much as meta-discourses are out of fashion, they are still needed if we are to talk about living together in addition to working on why we cannot do so in the way we each would like to, or who and what stops us from achieving such ends.

Looked at from this vantage point, the Union model of citizenship offers more than a road map to follow to reach a desired point of destination for particular groups. It is a historically specific experience, which is then translated into a meta-language of coexistence. The conceptual richness of its terminology is no doubt alluring. Similarly, the multi-faceted phenomenon of globalisation gives us enough of a reason to assume that the same or a similar language can be spoken in other localities. The troubling issue is that of translation to mother tongues. Unless such a translation is achieved, we each take part of a meta-discourse, that which is most suitable for the intuitions and moral frames we entertain, without troubling ourselves much about what the totality of the narrative has to say.

To conclude, more work has to be done in the area of citizenship in Turkey. So far, there is some degree of societal support for passing legislation that adjusts the Turkish civil and penal codes to those of the EU. There is also a well-endowed debate on the merits of the rights discourse as a remedy for the ills of Republican citizenship. What is missing is the concern for ensuring an informed consent for the Union model of citizenship as an umbrella formulation for the self-conduct of contemporary Turkish society. This umbrella formulation, however, cannot be limited to cultural rights and political participation. Turkey has a real democracy deficit in the areas of social democracy and welfare, too. In the absence of a multi-faceted engagement that covers these issues and derivative normative convictions, adjustments to the EU conduct in the name of the long-term goal of accession, or short- to mid-term goals of political gains, could render citizenship relatively obsolete and devoid of substantive content. What one has to keep in mind about the Union model of citizenship is that, among other things, it reflects an agreement about what the Europeans want for themselves and what they see as their right, as well as the price they paid to issue and protect these rights. Therefore, in the Turkish context, reforms at the level of legislature and introduction of the rights discourse constitute only the beginning of the convergence process.

Notes

I would like to thank Mehmet Uğur, Ferhunde Özbay and Kenan Çayır for their most helpful critical comments on an earlier version of this chapter.

1 *Agence Europe*, no. 713, 5 January 1973, p. 4; also cited in Wiener (1997: 539).
2 Greece, Italy and Austria later joined the Schengen deal while successive British governments have resolutely remained outside.
3 In David Cesarani and Mary Fulbrook's words, this new sort of Eurocentricism corresponded to 'a sort of higher xenophobia directed against Muslims and the modern version of the Mongol hordes – East Europeans attempting to escape the economic rubble of communism' (1996: 3).
4 Note here that the military are not mentioned as a significant or possible actor that can encroach on basic human rights. This is a crucial difference between *current* Turkish and European politics (Cizre, 2003).
5 These include 34 constitutional amendments, adopted in October 2001, in order to meet the Copenhagen criteria (including the partial abolition of the death penalty and authorisation of greater use of languages other than Turkish in public life); further amendments to the Penal Code, passed between January and March 2002, which concern freedom of expression and press, the activities of associations, closure of political parties and prevention of torture; the EU Adaptation Law of August 2002 to meet the requirements of accession in the human rights field; and current legislative activity to curb the powers of Turkish military in terms of its involvements in Turkish politics and economy. For a full chronology, see Erdemli (2003).
6 For instance, with amendments made to the 1982 Turkish Constitution, Turkey came close to full compliance with articles 10 and 11 of the European Convention of Human Rights (Hale, 2003: 110–111). However, the steps to be taken for the full enjoyment of these newly issued rights are yet to be realised. Similarly, amendments on articles related to political parties and terrorism – articles 69, 159 and 312 of the Turkish Constitution – are claimed to be a legal success, although the consequences of their practice are yet to be observed.
7 The newspapers *Zaman*, (*Yedinci*) *Özgür Gündem*, *Özgür Halk*, *Yeni Şafak* and *Radikal*, and the academic and semi-academic journals *Doğu-Batı*, *Cogito*, *Sivil Toplum*, *Toplum ve Bilim*, *Türkiye Günlüğü*, Birikim, *Gerçek Hayat* (*Özgür-Der* publication) are the main venues where these debates take place. In contradistinction, the newspapers *Akit* (*Vakit*), *Türkiye*, *Cumhuriyet* and *Hürriyet* take a negative stance on the issue of group-rights. The dailies *Milliyet* and *Vatan*, with the largest distribution in Turkey, take a middle-of-the-road attitude and do not encourage confrontational engagements in this debate.

References

Akçam, Taner (1992), 'Türkiye için yeni bir toplumsal projeye doğru (Towards a new social project for Turkey)', *Birikim*, no. 42, pp. 7–17.

Alpay, K. (ed.) (2002), *Avrupa Birliği Süreci ve Müslümanlar* (The Process of European Integration and Turkey), İstanbul: Özgür-der.

Alston, Philip (1999), *The EU and Human Rights*, Oxford: Oxford University Press.

Arat, Yeşim (1999), 'Gender and citizenship in Turkey', in Suad Joseph (ed.), *Gender and Citizenship in the Middle East*, Syracuse, NY: Syracuse University Press, pp. 275–286.

Arat, Yeşim (2000), 'From emancipation to liberation: the changing role of women in Turkey's public realm', *Journal of International Affairs*, vol. 54, no. 1, pp. 107–125.

Bauböck, Rainner (1994), *Transnational Citizenship. Membership and Rights in International Migration*, Aldershot, UK: Edward Elgar.

Bell, D. (1993), *Communitarianism and Its Critics*, Oxford: Clarendon Press.

Ben Habib, Seyla (1996), *Democracy and Difference*, Princeton, NJ: Princeton University Press.

Bora, Taril (1998), *Milliyetçiliğin Kara Baharı* (The Dark Spring of Nationalism), Istanbul: Iletişim Yayınları.

Brubaker, Rogers (1996), *Nationalism Reframed: Nationhood and the National Question in the New Europe*, Cambridge: Cambridge University Press.

Bulaç, A. (1993), 'Medine Vesikası üzerine tartışmalar (Debates on the Medine Vesikası)', *Birikim*, vol. 47, pp. 40–46.

Bulaç, A. (2000), 'AB süreci: kimlik ve Gelecek (The process of European integration: identity and future)', *Islami Araştırmalar*, vol. 13, no. 2, pp. 143–153.

Bulaç, Ali (2001), *Avrupa Birliği ve Türkiye* (European Union and Turkey), Istanbul: Zaman.

Caporaso, James (1996), 'The European Union and forms of state: Westphalian, regulatory or post-modern?', *Journal of Common Market Studies*, vol. 34, no. 1, pp. 29–52.

Carens, Joseph (2000), *Culture, Citizenship and the Community*, New York: Oxford University Press.

Cesarani, David and Mary Fulbrook (eds) (1996), *Citizenship, Nationality amd Migration in Europe*, London: Routledge.

Cizre, Ümit (2003), 'Demythologizing the national security concept: the case of Turkey', *Middle East Journal*, vol. 57, no. 2, pp. 213–225.

Delanty, Gerard (1985), *Inventing Europe: Idea, Identity, Reality*, London: Macmillan.

Delanty, Gerard (1997), 'Models of democracy: defining European identity and citizenship', *Citizenship Studies*, vol. 1, no. 3, pp. 285–303.

Delanty, Gerard (2003), 'The makings of a post-western Europe: a civilisational analysis', *Thesis Eleven*, vol. 72, no. 1, pp. 8–26.

Dodd, Clement (1992), *The Crisis of Turkish Democracy*, Huntingdon, UK: Eothen Press.

Emre, A. (1998), 'Alkışla Cumhuriyet olmaz (You can't have a Republic with clapping and cheering)', *Yenişafak*, 28 October.

Erdemli, Özgül (2003), 'Chronology: Turkey's relations with the EU', in Ali Çarkoğlu and Barry Rubin (eds), *Turkey and the European Union: Domestic Politics, Economic Integration and International Dynamics*, London: Frank Cass, pp. 4–9.

Gerger, M. E. (ed.) (1989), *Tanzimat'tan Avrupa Topluluğu'na Türkiye* (Turkey from the Ottoman Reform Movement Tanzimat to the European Union), Istanbul: İnkilab.

Goetz, Klaus H. and Simon Hix (eds) (2001), *Europeanised Politics? European Integration and National Political Systems*, London: Frank Cass.

Göle, Nilüfer (1995), 'Authoritarian secularism and Islamist politics: the case of Turkey', In A. R. Norton (ed.), *Civil Society in the Middle East*, Leiden: E. J. Brill, pp. 17–43.

Göle, Nilüfer (1997) 'The quest for the Islamic self within the context of modernity', in Sibel Bozdoğan and Reşat Kasaba (eds), *Rethinking Modernity and National Identity in Turkey*, Seattle: University of Washington Press, pp. 81–94.

Guild, Elspeth (1996), 'The legal framework for citizenship of the European Union', in David Cesarini and Mary Fulbrook (eds), *Citizenship, Nationality and Migration in Europe*, London and New York: Routledge, pp. 26–47.

Habermas, Jürgen (1996), *Between Facts and Norms: Contributions to a Discourse Theory of Law and Democracy*, Cambridge: Polity Press.

Hale, William (2003), 'Human rights, the European Union and the Turkish accession process', in Ali Çarkoğlu and Barry Rubin (eds), *Turkey and the European Union: Domestic Politics, Economic Integration and International Dynamics*, London: Frank Cass, pp. 107–126.

Hammar, Thomas (1990), *Democracy and the Nation-State: Aliens, Denizens and Citizens in a World of International Migration*, Aldershot, UK: Avebury.

Held, David (1995), *Democracy and the Global Order: From the Modern State to Cosmopolitan Governance*, Cambridge: Polity Press.

Heper, Metin (1985), *The State Tradition in Turkey*, Beverley, UK: Eothen Press.

Horton, J. and S. Mendus (eds) (1994), *After MacIntyre: Critical Perspectives on the Work of Alasdair MacIntyre*, Cambridge: Polity Press.

Işın, Engin and P. K. Wood (1999), *Citizenship and Identity*, London: Sage.

İçduygu, Ahmet (1996), 'Transit migration and Turkey', *Bogazici Journal*, vol. 10, nos. 1–2, pp. 127–142.

İçduygu, Ahmet and Fuat Keyman (2000), 'Globalisation, security, and migration: the case of Turkey', *Global Governance*, vol. 1, no. 6, pp. 383–398.

İçduygu, Ahmet, Y. Çolak and N. Soyarık (1999), 'What is the matter with citizenship?', *Middle Eastern Studies*, vol. 35, no. 4, pp. 187–208.

İnsel, Ahmet (1992), 'Totalitarizm, Medine Vesikası ve özgürlük (Totalitarianism, the Medine Vesikası and freedom)', *Birikim*, no. 37, pp. 29–32.

İnsel, Ahmet (1993), 'Toplumsal beraberlik ve ortak anlama olan ihtiyaç (Social unity and the need for a common understanding)', *Birikim*, no. 47, pp. 10–13.

Jary, David (1999), 'Citizenship and human rights: particular and universal worlds and the prospects for European citizenship', in Dennis Smith and Sue Wright (eds), *Whose Europe?*, Oxford: Blackwell, pp. 207–231.

Kadıoğlu, Ayşe (1998), 'The paradox of Turkish nationalism and the construction of official identity', in Sylvia Kedourie (ed.), *Turkey: Identity, Democracy, Politics*, London: Frank Cass, pp. 177–193.

Kadıoğlu, Ayşe (1999), *Cumhuriyet İradesi Demokrasi Muhakemesi* (The Will of Republicanism and Democratic Deliberation), Istanbul: Metis Yayınları.

Karaman, H. (2002), 'AB ve İslamcılar (The European Union and Turkish Islamists)', *Yenişafak*, 15 March.

Kasaba, Resat (1997), 'Kemalist certainties and modern ambiguities', in Resat

Kasaba and Sibel Bozdogan (eds), *Rethinking Modernity and National Identity in Turkey*, Seattle: University of Washington Press, pp. 15–37.

Keyman, Fuat (forthcoming) 'Articulating citizenship and identity: the "Kurdish Question" in Turkey', in Fuat Keyman and Ahmet İçduygu (eds), *Challenges to Citizenship in a Globalising World: European Questions and Turkish Experiences*, London: Routledge.

Keyman, Fuat and Ahmet İçduygu (2003), 'Globalisation, civil society and citizenship in Turkey: actors, boundaries and discourses', *Citizenship Studies*, vol. 7, no. 2, pp. 203–219.

Kirişçi, Kemal (1994), 'Refugees and Turkey since 1945', *Bogazici Research Papers*, ISS/POLS (September), pp. 94–103.

Kirişçi, Kemal (1996), 'Refugees of Turkish origin since 1945', *International Migration*, vol. 34, no. 3, pp. 385–412.

Kirişçi, Kemal (2000), 'Disaggregating Turkish citizenship and immigration practices', *Middle Eastern Studies*, vol. 36, no. 3, pp. 1–22.

Kirişçi, Kemal and Gareth M. Winrow (1997), *The Kurdish Question and Turkey: An Example of a Trans-state Ethnic Conflict*, London: Frank Cass.

Kymlicka, Will (2001), *Politics in the Vernacular: Nationalism, Multiculturalism and Citizenship*, Oxford: Oxford University Press.

Kymlicka, Will and Wayne Norman (1994), 'Return of the citizen: a survey of recent work on citizenship theory', *Ethics*, no. 1, pp. 352–381.

MacIntyre, Alastair (1995), 'The spectre of communitarianism', *Radical Philosophy*, vol. 70, no. 1, pp. 34–35.

MacIntyre, Alastair (1988), *Whose Justice? Which Rationality?*, London: Duckworth.

Markoff, John (1999) 'Our "common European home" – but who owns the house?', in Dennis Smith and Sue Wright (eds), *Whose Europe?*, Oxford: Blackwell, pp. 21–47.

Meehan, Elizabeth (1993), *Citizenship and the European Community*, London: Sage.

Mitten, Richard (1994), 'Jörg Haider, the anti-immigrant petition and immigration policy in Austria', *Patterns of Prejudice*, vol. 28, no. 2, pp. 27–47.

Özbudun, Ergun (2000), *Contemporary Turkish Politics: Challenges to Democratic Consolidation*, Boulder, CO: Lynne Rienner.

Özdenören, R. (1998), *İki Dünya* (Two Worlds), Istanbul: İz.

Preuß, Ulrich (1998), 'Citizenship in the European Union: a paradigm for transnational democracy?', in Daniele Archibugi, David Held and Martin Köhler (eds), *Re-imagining Political Community: Studies in Cosmopolitan Democracy*, Cambridge: Polity Press, pp. 138–152.

Roche, Maurice (1992), *Rethinking Citizenship: Welfare, Ideology and Change in Modern Society*, Cambridge: Polity Press.

Sandel, Michael (1982), *Liberalism and the Limits of Justice*, Cambridge: Cambridge University Press.

Sarıbay, Ali Yaşar (1993), 'İslami populizm ve sivil toplum arayışı (Popular Islam and the search for civil society)', *Birikim*, no. 47, pp. 14–20.

Sommers, Margaret (1994), 'Rights, relationality and membership: rethinking the making and meaning of citizenship', *Law and Social Inquiry*, vol. 19, no. 2, pp. 63–112.

Sommers, Margaret (1999), 'Privatization of Citizenship', in Lynn Hunt and Victoria Bonnell (eds), *Beyond the Cultural Turn*, Berkeley: University of California Press, pp. 121–161.

Soysal, Yasemin (1994), *Limits of Citizenship: Migrants and Post-national Membership in Europe*, Chicago: University of Chicago Press.

Tassin, Etienne (1992), 'Europe: a political community?', in Chantal Mouffe (ed.), *Dimensions of Radical Democracy. Pluralism, Citizenship, Community*, London: Verso, pp. 169–192.

Taylor, Charles (1989), *Sources of the Self: The Making of a Modern Identity*, Cambridge: Cambridge University Press.

Teitelbaum, Michael S. and Philip Martin (2003), 'Is Turkey ready for Europe?', *Foreign Affairs*, vol. 82, no. 3, pp. 97–110.

Toulemon, Robert (1998), 'For a democratic Europe', in Martin Westlake (ed.), *The European Union beyond Amsterdam: New Concepts of European Integration*, London: Routledge, pp. 116–130.

Turner, Bryan (1992), 'Outline of a theory of citizenship', in Chantal Mouffe (ed.), *Dimensions of Radical Democracy: Pluralism, Citizenship, Community*, London: Verso, pp. 33–62.

Turner, Bryan (1999), 'The Sociology of Citizenship', in Bryan Turner, *Classical Sociology*, London: Sage, pp. 262–275.

Van der Berghe, G. (1982), *Political Rights for European Citizens*, Aldershot, UK: Gower.

Walzer, Michael (1983), *Spheres of Justice*, New York: Basic Books.

Wiener, Antje (1997), 'Making sense of the new geography of citizenship: fragmented citizenship in the European Union', *Theory and Society*, vol. 26, no. 1, pp. 529–560.

Yeğen, Mesut (1994), 'The archeology of Republican Turkish state discourse', unpublished PhD thesis, University of Essex, Colchester, UK.

Yeğen, Mesut (2000), 'The Turkish state discourse and the exclusion of Kurdish identity', in Sylvia Kedourie (ed.), *Turkey: Identity, Democracy, Politics*, London: Frank Cass, pp. 216–230.

Young, Iris M. (1990), 'Polity and group difference: a critique of the ideal of universal citizenship', in Cass Sustein (ed.), *Feminism and Political Theory*, Chicago: University of Chicago Press, pp. 117–142.

Young, Iris M. (2000), *Inclusion and Democracy*, Oxford: Oxford University Press, pp. 81–195.

11 Leverage in theory and practice

Human rights and Turkey's EU candidacy

Jonathan Sugden

Introduction

Throughout the 1990s, any reporter collecting information on the latest human rights scandal in Turkey would ask, in a puzzled tone, why the government permitted security forces to burn villagers from their homes or beat a trade unionist to death: 'After all, Turkey wants to get into the European Union, doesn't it?'

Turkey had applied for membership, and it was clear that its long record of serious human rights violations was perhaps the most obvious obstacle to that membership, so it was a plausible assumption that this would provide effective leverage for reform. Journalistically, that leverage was often presented as a straightforward swap of economic advantage for human rights reform and the enhanced political stability that human rights reform can bring (Ertan, 1995). The European Commissioner for Enlargement, Günter Verheugen, avoids such a blunt formulation, but he also acknowledges that membership is conditional, and that existing members are prepared to support the integration of the applicants on the understanding that the latter are prepared to take steps towards establishing democracy, human rights, the rule of law and respect for minorities (see, for example, Verheugen, 2000).

The human rights lobby is constantly seeking ways in which to bring international influence to bear on problem states, and therefore had high hopes of the leverage that Turkey's accession aspiration would provide (Cohen, 1999). But in practice, the aspiration of European Union (EU) membership has been far from consistent as an incentive for reform. From 1987, when Turgut Özal submitted his application, until 1995, human rights violations were not decreasing in response to the bait of EU membership – they were increasing fast.

The EU process has produced less than the human rights lobby expected, because for most of the period in question there was insufficient confidence and commitment on either side to provide effective leverage. On the one hand, the EU was deeply sceptical about Turkey's application, and on the other, the actors in the Turkish state apparatus that drive security and human rights policy probably did not find the promised benefits of EU membership particularly appealing.

It is no secret that many within the EU are lukewarm about admitting a large, developing, predominantly Muslim country (albeit with a secular regime) bordering unstable neighbours. Some argue that if it had not been for Turkey's strategic position (a NATO member and a buffer against militant Islam), the EU might have turned down Özal's application and shut the door for good in 1990. Strategic importance kept the door ajar, but it also reduced the chance of tough talking on human rights from the EU or, for that matter, the United States. As a valuable front-line ally, Turkey always merited 'special understanding', which included turning a blind eye to gross violations.

The perceived benefits of EU membership (economic security, freedom of movement) were attractive to ordinary Turkish people and, at certain times, for Turkish business.[1] But if the Turkish state – that inward-looking network of generals, Interior and Justice Ministry officials, local governors, police chiefs, gendarmerie officers, judges, prosecutors and village guard chiefs – thought about Europe at all, they must have seen that the European way of going on, with its emphases on transparency in government, and multiculturalism, for example, was a potential threat to their interests. The most dramatic contrast is how the state is viewed within the EU as compared with how it is viewed by the Turkish state elite, which is 'reluctant to give up its tutelage of the masses' (Kramer, 2000). In Turkey, politicians and governors maintain a hedge of inscrutability and impunity around the state, fencing it with laws that have been used to punish criticism of state policy, and even describing the state as 'sacred'. In Europe, however, the expectation is that the state should be account-able to the public, and that the security forces should be firmly and unam-biguously under civilian control. European armies do not gulp nearly a fifth of the national budget or bully the government over matters of social policy. Therefore, it would be hardly surprising if Turkish generals, gover-nors and judges were essentially Euro-sceptic and ever ready to view Euro-pean pressure for reforms as threats to Turkey's 'unity' and 'integrity'. As a whole, Turkey has been torn between the desire to be part of Europe and the reluctance to see its hands tied by the rules of the game that govern the accession process.

Certainly, a comparison of annual reports from the major human rights organizations indicate that after 1995 there was a reduction in almost every category of human rights violation,[2] but the chief factor was not the EU or the accession process. The improvement was due to internal demand for change in the context of receding political violence. If inter-national pressure played a role, it was rather through the Council of Europe, which, on balance, exerted more consistent and effective influ-ence than the EU. There was one moment, however, in the spring of 2002, when the EU process did gain serious traction and helped Turkey to abolish the death penalty, and recognize minority language rights. The push the EU process supplied at that moment empowered those who made up the 'reform coalition' – civil society, the business community and the Foreign Ministry side of the government – to overcome what might have been insurmountable opposition from the state.

This chapter examines the interactions between Turkey's human rights record and its European orientation from the early 1990s in order to assess the extent to which European pressure has been influential in engendering change. The first section analyses the background to the EU–Turkey customs union agreement, and demonstrates that the link that the EU and others sought to establish between the customs union and improvements in Turkey's human rights standards did not deliver the expected outcomes. The second section describes the effectiveness of the Council of Europe, as compared to the EU, in influencing Turkey's human rights record until the end of the 1990s. Improvements were mainly due to widespread domestic outrage against human rights violations, and, in parallel, the Council of Europe exercising its special powers to investigate, publicly criticize and in some cases punish human rights violations. The third section returns to examine the EU's inputs after the Helsinki summit decision of 1999, which granted candidate status to Turkey. The EU's influence on Turkey's human rights performance remained severely limited until long after the publication of the accession partnership and Turkey's National Programme for the Adoption of the *Acquis* (NPAA). Section 11.4 examines the brief and dynamic period in 2002 when the EU's influence was decisive in bringing about change as the prospect of membership strengthened the hands of the reform coalition. The conclusion summarizes the main findings and evaluates the potential for intergovernmental pressure in achieving human rights reform.

11.1 A customs union conditionality that failed to deliver

Turkey and the EU were negotiating their customs union at a moment when the pace of violations was intense. On 26 March 1994, Turkish air force jets and helicopters bombed the villages of Kumçatı and Sapanca in Şırnak province, killing 36 villagers, including 17 children. The previous week, gendarmes had threatened the villages because they refused to join the corps of village guards, armed and paid by the government to fight the Kurdistan Workers' Party (PKK).[3]

From 1991 onwards, the army was experimenting with new methods of combating the PKK. In Mardin province, a death squad began to murder anyone known locally as a 'Kurdish patriot' and therefore suspected of being a member of the PKK (Amnesty International, 1994: 55–67). By 1992, political murders were running at nearly one a day, and over the following two years, more than a thousand people were shot dead by 'unknown assassins', who often appeared to be guided by the security forces. Gendarmes also killed hundreds of civilians while putting down demonstrations, or in reprisal attacks following PKK raids.[4] 'Disappearances' increased until 1994, when there were more than 50 documented cases (see Amnesty International, 1995a: 3–18).

In rural areas, gendarmes conducted a programme of village destruction, often with extreme violence, emptying and destroying any village that was not prepared to put up a squad of village guards. Official figures are probably an underestimate but still convey the scale of the crime: 378,335 villagers displaced from 820 villages and 2,345 smaller settlements from 1987 to 1995.[5]

Torture also reached a peak in 1994 with 34 deaths in custody in that year. Journalists, politicians and trade unionists were regularly serving time in prison, and prosecutors were confiscating newspapers and books for 'separatism', and insulting state institutions or Kemal Atatürk, the founder of the Turkish Republic. By the mid-1990s, it seemed that a ruthless and lawless group had seized control of the security apparatus. Turkish law-and-order forces were moving away from their authoritarian tradition of 'sharp discipline' into a Latin American style of state criminality where hired killers, drug smugglers and local chieftains worked hand-in-glove with gendarmerie commanders.

The EU was not doing much to arrest the Turkish government and military's slide down this slippery slope. While aircraft (possibly supplied by Italy, Germany and France) bombed the villages Kumçatı and Sapanca, the EU was actually getting ready to reward Turkey with a long-promised customs union.

The EU had grown from a strictly economic arrangement into a vast political project, but it was not a human rights organization, and had never worked systematically on human rights issues. It had no formal monitoring mechanisms, or any defined system of standards or sanctions. In the early and mid-1990s, when Amnesty International lobbyists approached foreign ministries at their European capitals, civil servants frequently responded that their government preferred to raise these concerns through the Council of Europe.

Yet, in late 1992, the Council of Europe seemed like a hopelessly quiet backwater. Its last firm action on Turkey had been in 1983, when Denmark, France, the Netherlands, Norway and Sweden initiated state complaints; but these were dropped when Turkey signed the European Convention against Torture and recognized Turkish citizens' right to make individual petitions to the European Court of Human Rights. The right of petition was almost unknown in Turkey, and no cases had reached the verdict stage. The European Committee for the Prevention of Torture (CPT) had visited Turkey several times, but the Turkish government had not given permission for publication of the delegations' findings. In fact, more was happening than appeared on the surface, and, as we shall see later on, the Council of Europe was soon to make important contributions.

Back at the EU, only the European Parliament (EP) regularly examined human rights issues and voiced its concern. Members of the European Parliament (MEPs) often visited Turkey, and the parliament passed a series of strongly critical resolutions. But rightly or wrongly, the Turkish government seemed to view the EP as little more than an overexcitable talking shop, and judged that real power was concentrated in the Commission. The Commission probably thought the same. The EP's heart was in the right place, but its resolutions were not particularly effective in communicating concern to the Turkish public or government. For one thing, they could easily be presented as partial. Greek MEPs were known to lobby and vote *en bloc* for resolutions critical of Turkey's treatments of its Kurdish minority, while all Turks knew that the Turkish minority in western Thrace were subject to similar discrimination. EP resolutions on Turkey repeatedly conflated concerns about fundamental human rights issues with the Cyprus question, and this did not help convey the idea that human rights were a set of objective standards, independent of partisan politics. It was easy for the Turkish government and media to dismiss EP resolutions as shrill, ill-informed outbursts by hypocritical politicians seeking to further Greek aims, or the aims of a selfish, rich Christian club who wanted to exclude Muslim Turks but were too politically correct to admit their motives.

Consequently, it was better for a Turkish politician's career to be seen to be 'standing up to the Europeans' rather than listening to their human rights concerns. In June 1995, State Minister Ayvaz Gökdemir referred to three women members of the European Parliament who came to Turkey to investigate human rights violations as 'these prostitutes coming from Europe'. He was not asked to resign and was reappointed to the cabinet of the new coalition government in March 1996. Turkish politicians were actively seeking integration with Europe, but when it came to human rights they still felt entitled to tell Europe to keep its interfering nose out of domestic business. In May 1995, the Foreign Minister, Erdal İnönü, deprecated 'the fashion to scrutinize the level of democracy in each country. The principle of human rights has taken precedence over another important principle – that of not interfering in the internal affairs of other states.' He went on to describe the EP's attitude as 'offensive and separatist'.[6] The sharp and unapologetic tone of such statements shows that members of the Turkish political class were confident that they could tell Europe to back off on human rights without paying a heavy price.

The customs union showed that they were right. In the year prior to the customs union agreement, Amnesty International and other human rights organizations were providing the EU with a wealth of information about patterns of abuse, together with clear recommendations about the measures that would signify political will for change. There was an appearance of tough bargaining and close scrutiny. The EU Commissioner Hans van den Broek announced that 'progress in the field of human rights was even more important than the technical measures'.[7] In an interim report, the Commission stated, 'The European Union strongly supports constitutional and legal reform in Turkey and the Commission will continue to follow developments closely and will keep Parliament informed.'[8] In theory, if Turkey did not pull its socks up, the EU would withhold the customs union. Yet as it turned out, the customs union came into force in January 1996 without a single brick of reform being put in place, despite a year of intense diplomatic traffic.

It looked as if the Turkish government had got something for nothing. But when Prime Minister Tansu Çiller put on a firework display in Ankara to celebrate the customs union agreement, she was actually making the most of a rather meagre prize. The customs union was only a substitute for an accession process, and may actually have imposed burdens rather than benefits on the Turkish economy (Uğur, 1996). For the human rights movement, the nothing-for-nothing exchange of the customs union was emblematic of the ineffectiveness of EU leverage in producing reform.

11.2 Domestic protests and European pressure – from Strasbourg

From 1995 onwards, the rate of human rights violations began to slow down. But this was a consequence of the decline in political violence rather than a product of EU influence. The PKK, presumably exhausted after years of intense fighting, made less frequent strikes against gendarmerie posts and village guards. Fewer fatal attacks on security forces meant fewer punitive security force raids involving torture and extrajudicial killing, and fewer reprisal raids on the civilian population.

At the same time, a series of events had alerted the Turkish public to the ruthlessness and criminality at the heart of the state. A parliamentary inquiry into political killings eventually revealed (to anyone prepared to read between the lines) that the state had indeed resorted to murder as a tactic for combating insurgency.[9] After the 'disappearance' of Hasan Ocak in Istanbul in January 1995, his parents began a vigil on Saturday mornings in Istiklal Street in the centre of Istanbul. They were soon joined by the mothers of other victims of 'disappearance'. The police harassed, detained, ill-treated and prosecuted the mothers, but were forced to do so under the full glare of media attention. Although the Turkish authorities had made a habit of gagging human rights defenders by branding them sympathizers of terrorism, this was not so easy to do with elderly women who told television journalists in simple, eloquent and resolutely unpolitical words how their children had been taken from them by gendarmes, police officers or village guards.

In January 1996, Sabri Ergül, Member of Parliament for Manisa, near Izmir, received a phone call that the sons and daughters of several constituents had been detained and were being held in detention, incommunicado. He made an unannounced visit to Manisa police headquarters: 'I heard a cry and opened the door of the next room to find out what was going on. The young people were there. They were blindfolded and some of them were naked' (Amnesty International, 1996: 44). Ergül immediately notified the media, and several television channels showed news footage of him hanging notices outside the police station saying, 'There is torture here'.[10]

If the Turkish public needed graphic images to alert it to the state's wrongdoing, then the Susurluk crash on 4 November 1996 was the conclusive snap-shot: a village guard chief and a police chief touring holiday spots with a drug smuggler who was also a death-squad leader wanted for carrying out a multiple political killing. The boot of the car was stuffed with cash and weapons, some apparently intended for murder, as they were equipped with silencers. Added to this, the death-squad leader, Abdullah Çatlı, had been travelling on a 'green passport' – a document strictly reserved for high-ranking civil servants.

The Turkish media act under considerable legal and informal constraints, but even these were not sufficient to keep news of such events suppressed. For weeks, the media boiled with rage at what had happened in Manisa, and the Susurluk scandal fuelled months of journalistic inquiry and fierce debate in late-night television programmes. The Turkish public expressed its exasperation in a mass protest that lasted for six weeks in February and the first part of March 1997. The 'minute of darkness' spread across the country as citizens flashed the lights in their households every evening to protest corruption in general and the Susurluk incident in particular. The protest frightened the authorities enough to trigger an inquiry into the circumstances surrounding the Susurluk incident. The inquiry was little short of a whitewash, but it did confirm that the state had been involved in political killing.[11]

By the mid-1990s, meanwhile, Europe was applying new and effective pressure on human rights in Turkey – not through the EU, but through Council of Europe mechanisms, which included the CPT and the European Court of Human Rights (ECHR). The CPT had been visiting police stations and gendarmeries in 1990, 1991 and 1992, and, predictably, the Turkish government had refused to allow publication of the reports. But in December 1992, the CPT took the unprecedented step of making a public statement without government approval. It stated that torture was 'widespread ... a deeply-rooted problem'.[12] Until then, the Turkish authorities were still denying that the police really were torturing people. The CPT's statement brought the debate to an end, and the existence of a pattern of torture became a matter of record. In December 1996, responding to the Turkish government's persistent failure to implement safeguards for detainees, the CPT made a further statement confirming that torture was continuing.[13] The Council of Europe watchdog had started to bite.

The first ECHR judgments against Turkey came through in mid-1995, and by mid-1996 they were piling up thick and fast. The judgments happened to come when the Manisa case and the Susurluk incident were hitting the headlines in Turkey. The court found that Turkish courts were imprisoning Turkish citizens for expressing their non-violent opinions, and the security forces were torturing and 'disappearing' Turkish citizens, and burning them out of their homes. One of the earliest judgments was on the case of Zeki Aksoy, who had been tortured while in police custody at Mardin police headquarters.[14] He reported that he had been blindfolded, stripped naked, strung up by the arms, beaten, hosed with cold water and given electric shocks through his genitals. The plaintiff never learned that he had won his case. The police threatened him in order to induce him to withdraw his complaint, and on 16 April 1994 Zeki Aksoy was shot and killed by 'an unknown assailant'.

The ECHR's findings were seen as credible because they were the product of independent investigation. Turkey could not rubbish the court judgments as it had rubbished EP resolutions, because Turkey itself was a long-standing Council of Europe member and an active participant in its processes. There was a Turkish representative on the CPT, and Turkish judges sat on the bench in Strasbourg.

The Council of Europe had unique tools with which it could reach inside the walls surrounding the state and hold state actors accountable for their actions. The importance of this cannot be overstated in the Turkish context. The CPT was able to walk into police stations and gendarmeries that had been closed to the outside world since Ottoman times. The ECHR summoned and cross-questioned gendarme commanders and state security court prosecutors, and demanded to see documentary evidence in a manner that was quite unprecedented in a country where courts tend to treat security forces with extreme deference. The CPT visited only a few score out of thousands of police stations, and the court investigated a relatively small number of the widespread abuses, but the psychological shock of such interventions to the whole security apparatus, which had hitherto enjoyed more or less complete immunity from scrutiny, let alone prosecution, can only be imagined.

The CPT's highly critical December 1996 statement came hot on the heels of the Strasbourg judgments as well as the Manisa and Susurluk scandals, and appears to have contributed decisively to the first substantial reform for several years. In February 1997, the Erbakan government substantially reduced detention periods, abolished incommunicado detention in law for criminal detainees and reduced incommunicado detention to four days for State Security Court detainees.[15] In practice, police and gendarmes persisted (and still persist) in holding both groups of detainees incommunicado, and torturing them. But the shortened detention periods limited the security forces' ability to suppress complaints. Previously, when detention periods were up to 30 days, the final weeks of detention were used to permit the physical signs of torture to heal. After the February 1997 reform, allegations of the severest torture were less common, and the annual rate of death in custody fell almost to zero by 2001.

11.3 The EU blows cold and hot

Domestic outrage and international reproof had forced the Turkish state to take a step back. The rate of 'disappearances', extra-judicial executions, deaths in custody and village-burnings also began to fall. But EU pressure had played little part in turning the tide. In the following four years, as the EU swerved between rejection and acceptance of Turkey's European aspirations, its impact on the human rights picture remained negligible.

At the Luxembourg Council in 1997, the EU put Turkish accession on indefinite hold, listing human rights violations and lack of respect for minorities among its reservations.[16] The Turkish side's response was not to embark on a reform programme but to put its relations with the EU on ice.

Complex factors brought about the EU's 1999 Helsinki Council about-face. Ground-breaking speeches by the presidents of the Turkish Supreme Court and the Constitutional Court had challenged the stale old self-image of the Republic and inspired an atmosphere of optimism.[17] The PKK responded to the arrest of its leader, Abdullah Öcalan, by declaring an indefinite ceasefire, which fuelled hopes for lasting peace and stability in the south-east. After the 'earthquake diplomacy' of summer 1999, Greece was no longer an intransigent enemy of Turkey's European hopes.

But it would have been difficult for Europeans to preach too loudly about human rights at Helsinki. Neither Italy nor Greece had shown sufficient nerve to arrest and indict Abdullah Öcalan, responsible for years of gross human rights abuses as leader of the PKK, when he was their reluctant guest after his expulsion from Syria. The Turkish side, on the other hand, surprised some observers by resisting the temptation to murder, torture or execute Öcalan once they had him in their hands.

In the Helsinki presidency conclusions recognizing Turkey's candidacy, the European Council welcomed 'recent positive developments in Turkey as noted in the Commission's progress report, as well as its intention to continue its reforms towards complying with the Copenhagen criteria'. In fact, the 1999 Regular Report records that there had been hardly any improvements at all during the year. Indeed, there had been no significant legislative steps since February 1997. The presidency conclusions were a diplomatic form of words to avoid the embarrassing admission that Turkey had jumped the next European stepping stone without making any human rights concessions.

The Helsinki decision did not trigger an 'Ankara spring', as some had hoped. The Turkish government did not capitalize on the first extended period of peace and optimism for decades by making some generous gestures towards, for example, respect and protection of the minority in the south-east. Quite the reverse: on 28 February 2000, Ankara State Security Court sentenced the leader of the mainly Kurdish People's Democracy Party (HADEP) and 16 members of his party to three years and nine months' imprisonment on trumped-up charges of 'aiding an armed organization'. The same day, gendarmes roughly arrested three HADEP mayors and charged them with the same offence.

Nonplussed by this unexpected turn of events, the ambassadors of the EU troika and the EU's permanent representative in Ankara went to the Turkish Foreign Ministry to express their concern. They provoked a sharp reaction from the Prime Minister, Bülent Ecevit, who snapped back, 'We are very irritated by the attitude of the members of the E.U. . . . we are very sensitive about our territorial integrity and will, if necessary, warn the European countries'.[18] It appeared that Ecevit was trying to send a strong message to Europe (and to the conservative state forces) that he was not planning to cave in to EU demands concerning the Kurds. Turkey might be a candidate, but it was to be business as usual as far as minorities were concerned. In March, Ecevit defiantly repeated the traditional state view that Kurdish is a dialect of Turkish and not a language in its own right.

After Helsinki, EU officials had assured Human Rights Watch that Turkey was finally locked into a process that required it to conform to the Copenhagen criteria requiring the 'stability of institutions guaranteeing democracy, the rule of law, human rights, and respect for and protection of minorities'. Progress was bound to be swift, they said, because each goal in the Accession Partnership document then being prepared was scheduled as short term (to be accomplished within a year) or medium term (within three years).

Unfortunately, the reality fell short of this ideal. The Turkish government had earned much kudos for winning the prize of candidacy, and was not keen to spend this easy credit on politically expensive reforms. It was a foregone conclusion that the EU was going to demand abolition of the death penalty, for example, so the government might just as well have abolished it in January 2000. But with Abdullah Öcalan under sentence of death, abolition was going to be unpopular with a substantial part of the population as well as with the army. Commuting Öcalan's sentence to life imprisonment might be appreciated by some Kurds, but they were not Ecevit's constituency, much less the constituency of the junior coalition partner, the Nationalist Action Party (MHP). The government preferred to do as little as possible until the EU Commission produced the Accession Partnership, nearly a year later, on 8 November 2000.

The Turkish government's National Programme,[19] which was supposed to 'mirror' the EU's Accession Partnership document, exploited the lack of specificity in the latter and attempted to bargain down the EU's human rights demands. Whereas the Accession Partnership required abolition of the death penalty, the National Programme promised merely to 'consider' it. The Accession Partnership required removal of restrictions to broadcasting and education in minority languages, but the National Programme ignored these goals, merely stating that Turkish citizens were entitled to use languages other than the official language 'in their daily lives'.

Turkey wasted a year and a half dithering on the starting line until the publication of the National Programme, and then squandered a further year passing a series of disappointing 'harmonization' packages.[20] These laws tinkered with freedom of expression issues, detention procedures and the death penalty. They granted some valuable concessions, but were obviously mainly designed to provide the EU with something to put in the Regular Report and give the impression that Turkey was 'busy with reform'. In fact, it was just putting off difficult but inevitable decisions.

By March 2002, one year after the National Programme began, Turkey should have fulfilled the short-term goals of the Accession Partnership. Instead, it had failed to bring the right to freedom of expression in line with article 10 of the European Convention on Human Rights, failed to release all prisoners of conscience, failed to align procedures concerning pre-trial detention with the recommendations of the CPT, and failed to remove legal obstacles to broadcasting in minority languages. Nor had it taken any steps to 'develop a comprehensive approach to reduce regional disparities, and in particular to improve the situation in the South-East, with a view to enhancing economic, social and cultural opportunities for all citizens'. The most pressing problem in the south-east was the continuing displacement of hundreds of thousands of Kurdish villagers, and no genuine steps had been taken to relieve their distress or secure their safe return to their homes.

The Turkish government met only two short-term aims within the required twelve months: intensifying human rights training for judges, prosecutors and security forces; and maintaining the death penalty moratorium.

The EU had begun to notice and criticize Turkey's lacklustre performance in meeting the Copenhagen criteria. The October 2001 Regular Report on Turkey's Progress towards Accession was more frank and detailed than previous reports. Its conclusion was that 'many aspects of the overall human rights situation remain worrying. . . . Freedom of expression as well as freedom of association and assembly are still regularly restricted'. Most importantly, 'compared to last year, the situation on the ground has hardly improved and Turkey still does not meet the Copenhagen political criteria'.

The Commissioner for Enlargement voiced unmistakable disappointment: 'One would expect the country to be more forthcoming. . . . We expect that the next steps will address issues which were not addressed . . . in areas like the death penalty and education.'[21] After the EU–Turkey

Association Council in Luxembourg in April 2002, he reiterated the EU's human rights concerns and said that Ankara had to go further in buttressing the rights of ethnic minorities, concluding, 'We feel deeper, more far-reaching reforms are needed in, for example, the area of freedom of expression and of association'. He urged Turkey to accelerate like a 'racing car'.[22]

Those who had close contact with the EU, such as İsmail Cem (the Foreign Minister) and Mesut Yılmaz (Deputy Prime Minister with special responsibility for European relations), tried to put a bold gloss on the disappointing packages but knew that Turkey was falling badly behind schedule. They also knew that there was a queue of ten other countries already in negotiation for membership, and that as time passed, and the EU began to realize the costs of enlargement, flexibility on deadlines would disappear. Member states could well begin to seek excuses for barring the way for the largest, least developed and most 'different' candidate. Therefore, in January 2002 both Cem and Yılmaz began to raise the temperature of the EU debate, claiming that if Turkey made a strong effort to fulfil the Copenhagen criteria, then it could secure a date for negotiations at the Copenhagen summit. They suggested that if Turkey dawdled, the door might close for good.

> We should start full membership negotiations during Greece's term of presidency [the first half of 2003]. This is our target. If we cannot fulfil our commitments, we cannot reach our target. In that case we will experience many difficulties in our relations. Because the EU will have resolved its enlargement with other countries, and our uncertain candidacy status will continue. If we can succeed in starting full membership negotiations, we will have set up certain relations with the EU.[23]

Verheugen had asked to see progress on the death penalty and minority language restrictions, but these were probably the most politically difficult items on the list. Abolishing the death penalty meant commuting the separatist Öcalan's sentence. The nationalist coalition partner (the MHP) had always opposed this, and throughout the spring of 2002 it attempted to whip up public feeling around the issue. For example, MHP leader and Deputy Prime Minister Devlet Bahçeli protested that 'this murderer has become a condition for Turkey even to be given a date to start membership talks. If that is not injustice and disrespect to our country, then what is it?'[24] The army seemed to take much the same view. Asked about moves to abolish the death penalty, the Chief of General Staff, General Kıvrıkoğlu, responded, 'We are a party [to the prosecution brought against Öcalan], we struggled with this business for many years and sustained many casualties. Our answer is obvious.'[25] The Deputy Chief of General Staff, General Yaşar Büyükanıt, echoed the MHP's threat that abolishing the death penalty could mean that Öcalan would one day walk free (see Berberoğlu, 2002).

The language issue was also a touchy subject, and very much on the agenda at this time. Thousands of students and their parents had been inspired by the removal from the constitution of the concept of 'languages forbidden by law' to submit petitions for optional courses in Kurdish to be added to university curricula. Hundreds were detained and many tortured. Scores were in prison and threatened with seven and a half years' imprisonment for 'supporting an armed gang'. Prosecutors claimed that the petition campaign was organized by the PKK, or the Democratic Congress of Kurdistan (KADEK), as it was now known. The head of the military-founded Higher Education Council, Kemal Gürüz, rejected the possibility of Kurdish-language education out of hand:

> nobody should expect us to give up this basic tenet of the Turkish republic, unity of the language. Everybody can speak any language they want in their daily lives. But, it's obvious that the official, the language of education of this country is Turkish and there'll be no going back on this issue – it is a sina [*sic*] qua non.
>
> (Jones, 2002)

The Deputy Prime Minister, Bahçeli, announced his undying opposition to both abolition of the death penalty and minority language education: 'These things are not to happen and so do not waste time.'[26]

During the period from 1997 to the spring of 2000, there was dramatic ebb and flow in relations between the EU and Turkey. This was accompanied by much talk of human rights, but the warmth or chill from Brussels did not reflect Turkey's performance in this area. The Turkish side, now accustomed to ignoring the formal finger-wagging, continued to resist firm steps in the direction of reform. However, the formula of inaction (to please the military and state forces) and cosmetics (to please the EU) that had sufficed for more than a decade was beginning to look out of date.

11.4 Domestic demands and European pressure – from Brussels

The struggle between those who wanted a push to fulfil the criteria and those who resisted was going on at an awkward time. In January and February 2002, there were ongoing rows with the EU over its failure to put the PKK on a list of terrorist organizations,[27] and the news magazine *Aydınlık* (Enlightenment) had published excerpts of the e-mail traffic of the EU's ambassador to Ankara, Karen Fogg. Chosen selectively, and particularly in translation, the excerpts suggested European high-handedness. These developments played on ancient fears of an arrogant Europe fostering internal enemies to bring Turkey to its knees. All Turks know that several states that are now members of the European Union attempted to partition Turkey at the end of the First World War. Italian, French, British and Greek troops occupied Turkish soil and were expelled only by force of arms or the threat of it. What is more, throughout the nineteenth and early twentieth centuries, European countries pressed what we would now call human rights concerns issues repeatedly in order to amputate chunks of Ottoman territory.

The General Secretary of the National Security Council, General Tuncer Kılıç, expressed unease about the EU process in very strong terms, and put forward the familiar hypothesis of an alternative to Europe:

> Turkey definitely needs to be looking for new opportunities . . . obviously in Russia and the USA, but also if possible with Iran. Turkey has not received the slightest help from the EU. The EU takes an antagonistic view on issues of importance to Turkey.[28]

Until then, the military had not declared any unequivocal position on European integration, and therefore Kılıç's statements raised alarm that the military might be turning against the EU project.

Civil society mounted a strong counter-attack in support of the EU bid. On 29 May, TUSIAD (the Turkish Industrialists' and Businessmen's Association) published full-page advertisements in daily newspapers, reminding the government that 'Turkey is at a crossroads' and calling on the parties to act to facilitate accession: 'Our political parties and Parliament should undertake the necessary responsibility in this vital project, which we believe will enlighten the future of the country, and take immediate action in order to take the steps required for membership.' TUSIAD produced drafts of laws on the death penalty and minority languages that met the EU's requirements while protecting nationalist sensibilities. A TUSIAD delegation personally visited the General Staff Headquarters to deliver their message to the military.[29]

TUSIAD had been arguing since the late 1980s that a stable free-market economy needed a participatory, pluralistic democratic system. It had produced recommendations for legal, administrative and constitutional reform in the early 1990s, and in 1997 added its weight to the human rights lobby with its report *Türkiye'de Demokratikleşme Perspektifleri* (Perspectives on Democratization in Turkey), a finely detailed assessment of constitutional, political and legal shortcomings as measured against international standards, with recommendations for reform that would have been an ideal model for the Accession Partnership. TUSIAD has an office in Brussels, and a glance at its publications and press releases for the past five years shows that it was far better tuned in to the European process than the Turkish Foreign Ministry. Clearly, TUSIAD was keeping the Foreign Ministry and Yılmaz's office briefed, interpreting EU demands and resolving misunderstandings.

On 9 May 2002, another heavyweight of the business community, the IKV (the Economic Development Foundation), had established a civil society platform together with 175 other organizations representing an extraordinary cross section of society from left to right, including secularists, devout Muslims, trade unionists and entrepreneurs. In the same week that TUSIAD put out its advertisements and visited the General Staff, the IKV put out a public statement with the same message: 'Turkey's place is with the European Union. We have no time to lose.'[30] Signatories of a public statement included TOBB (the Turkish Union of Chambers and Exchanges), MUSIAD (the Association of Independent Industrialists and Businessmen – the counterpart to TUSIAD from the devout Muslim sector) and DISK (the Confederation of Progressive Trade Unions). That same week, the anti-Europe lobby produced its own National Alliance Platform against the European Union, led by a group of trade unionists, diplomats and academics, but it had much less firepower than the pro-European camp.[31]

As the media picked up the vivid, anxiety-inducing image that Turkey was about to 'miss the European train', Ahmet Necdet Sezer took the presidential step of calling party leaders to a summit on 7 June. The proceedings of the summit were confidential, but the conclusion was that Parliament should proceed with all speed to enact legal and constitutional reforms to achieve harmonization, within the terms of the European Human Rights Convention.

It soon became clear that the MHP would oppose the abolition of the death penalty and language reforms. MHP State Minister Ramazan Mirzaoğlu expressed his opposition in lurid terms: 'the political criteria coming out the mouth of the PKK and the EU's Copenhagen Criteria are exactly the same. We need to show the same unity as [Atatürk's] National Independence Army against them both.'[32] But the summit also showed that the other parties to the coalition could achieve a majority with the assistance of the opposition parties, and this is how the third legislative package – a package that actually contained something of genuine value – was passed.[33]

That package, passed on 3 August 2002, abolished the death penalty in peacetime, and removed the legal obstacles to education in minority languages. The following day, Mesut Yılmaz challenged the EU to show courage and reward Turkey with a date for negotiations at the Copenhagen summit in December. Allowing for a politician's tendency to hyperbole, his assessment of the significance of the third package is fair:

> It reflects a fundamental change in our concept of identity and Turkish citizenship. It embraces all our citizens with their cultural diversity and undertakes not only to respect but also to promote such

diversity. This reform package eliminates the bondage of fear and replaces it with a confidence in the enriching value of diversity for national unity. In a country that has suffered so much from terrorism ... the elimination of the death penalty for crimes of terror is the most dramatic measure one can imagine. For those who do not face such challenges, this may seem as a simple and straightforward measure to align the Turkish legal system with the European norms. But you will all agree that in the context of Turkey this has been a major achievement.[34]

Yılmaz was right that the European side would not grasp how politically difficult abolition of the death penalty had been to achieve, or give due credit to Turkey's contribution to making the continent an execution-free zone. But the international human rights lobby understood the importance and value of the step very clearly indeed. A predominantly Muslim abolitionist state was a precious new member of the world movement against the death penalty. Before the end of the month, the Turkish Justice Minister, Aysel Çelikel, had taken advantage of Turkey's new status to write to the Nigerian Justice Minister appealing against the execution of Amina Lawal for alleged adultery.[35]

Turkey had been hoping to gain the next stepping stone, a date for negotiations, at the Copenhagen summit in December 2002. The new government[36] expressed disappointment at being told that negotiations could not begin until December 2004, and only then on condition that Turkey had met the political criteria by that time. Surprisingly, the new AKP government maintained the reform momentum and passed a fourth[37] and a fifth[38] harmonization package in January 2003. These at last abolished incommunicado detention in law, and finally opened the way for the four Kurdish parliamentarians – still held at Ankara Central Closed Prison – to seek a fair retrial.

11.5 EU leverage and internal dynamics: an assessment

Despite the reforms, many human rights defenders are left with a nagging feeling of frustration, and a sense that they have not achieved all they had hoped for. Even if the level of violations has fallen and some rights have been granted on paper, there has been no change of heart, and not much change in the day-to-day reality.

The grudging manner in which the reforms were granted, and the fact that several issues (shortcomings in detention procedures; articles 159 and 312 of the Criminal Code and article 8 of the Anti-Terror Law;[39] retrial for plaintiffs at the European Court of Human Rights)[40] had to go back to Parliament repeatedly and in fact are still not fully resolved, contribute to the sense that an authoritarian and unreformed force is still in the driving seat, and leaning on the brakes.

In addition, there has been no reckoning with the past. Since 1980, hundreds of thousands of Turkish citizens have been tortured, imprisoned after unfair trial, stripped of their citizenship, 'disappeared', and extra-judicially executed, but there has been no admission of error, few prosecutions, and only a handful of perpetrators brought to justice. Massacres have gone unpunished, and the state is doggedly unapologetic for the misery it has caused. It is unrealistic to expect the EU process to substitute for a truth commission, or to have the same transformational impact as tearing down the Berlin Wall or the release of Nelson Mandela, but in the absence of such a cathartic milestone to mark the past from the future it is difficult to feel that genuine change has happened.

The EU process did effect change, but the language reforms, for example, have the unconvincing, slightly hollow quality that comes with an 'outside-in' process. The same can be said for improvements the EU secured for Roma in Eastern European candidate states. Progress in protections for Roma would not have been made at the pace and level achieved in the 1990s if the EU had not prioritised protection of Roma in its accession negotiations with those states, but governments were implementing the reforms as a matter of foreign policy, not as measures that had a deeply felt value to national policy-makers. The minorities protection report of the Open Society Institute's EU Accession Monitoring Programme confirms that the Eastern European states in question took significant efforts to comply with the Copenhagen criteria's minority protection component by acceding to key international conventions, modifying laws and adopting minority policies. And yet, it notes that

> No country in the region has yet adopted anti-discrimination legislation in full compliance with the European Union's Racial Equality Directive, a comprehensive prohibition against racial or ethnic discrimination enacted in mid-2000. Public declarations by senior officials underlining the importance of combating racism and discrimination remain rare. And in some cases, political leaders continue to voice, rather than condemn, racist viewpoints. Pervasive prejudice contributes to racially-motivated violence against Roma and to a broad range of more subtle, but equally pernicious, discriminatory practices.[41]

The sense of inconclusiveness that hangs about the Turkish reforms is hardly surprising, given that a good deal remains to be done to meet the Copenhagen criteria: for example, the restrictions on minority language broadcasting and education were lifted, but there is no broadcasting or education in minority languages. It was a bold move to grant these rights, but implementing regulations that were later devised pile on so many restrictions that they look like an attempt to snatch the rights back.

A further example is the abolition of incommunicado detention in law.

This was a prize that intergovernmental human rights bodies, as well as international and domestic human rights non-governmental organizations, had fought for since the time of the military coup. But in practice, police still are not letting lawyers into police stations, and the stream of torture allegations from political and common criminal detainees, adults and children has continued throughout the early months of 2003.

There is also much work to be done with regard to freedom of expression. The changes to the criminal code and other laws that restrict expression did not bring legislation into line with the European Convention, and trials continue. Every week brings more prosecutions so redolent of the 1980s and 1990s that it is very difficult to argue that a new age has dawned. In March 2003, a 14-year-old boy was arraigned for 'inciting racial hatred' at Diyarbakır State Security Court. He faces up to three years' imprisonment for saying, 'Happy is he who says I am a Kurd' during school assembly in Bismil (Cebe, 2003). In April 2003, Ibrahim Güçlü, deputy president of the Rights and Freedoms Party (Hak-Par), was jailed at Ankara Central Closed Prison, sentenced to serve a one-year sentence for 'separatist propaganda' under article 8 of the Anti-Terror Law for non-violent comments made to journalists about the Kurdish minority.

Most of the hundreds of thousands of Kurdish villagers displaced during the conflict with the PKK are still living in hardship in the cities. Government return schemes have been so ineffective that they appear to be deliberately intended to keep the villagers away from their homes, and avoid the expense of assisting reconstruction of the homes and farms the security forces destroyed. Local governors, gendarmes and village guards prevent the displaced villagers from returning to their homes and their livelihoods. In 2002, village guards killed five villagers who did attempt to return and reclaim their land. Other villagers were permitted to return only on condition that they signed documents exculpating the security forces, and releasing the government from all financial liability.[42]

Conclusion

Turkey's accession process has been only partially successful in bringing international economic relations to bear on human rights problems. The difficulty has been that the 'deep state' network that was driving human rights violations was very well insulated against the kinds of pressure that the EU could exert, even at the best of times. The ultimate weapon was suspension of financial assistance, and the European Parliament did wield it sporadically, but the police/security establishment always had first call on state funds, particularly while the armed conflict and emergency continued, and would always be the last to feel a financial squeeze. In fact, the military has arranged independent finance of some of its institutions through its industrial holdings, an issue that the EU has yet to address. To the closed world of the police station, the gendarmerie unit, the village guard corps and the armed forces, European promises of markets and investment were as abstract, distant and uninteresting as European moral outrage.

For the Turkish public, business community and some of the political elite, however, EU membership is the imaginative equivalent of the American Dream: liberation from near-Third World squalor, inefficiency and the second-rate. The dream is clearly a potent one, and this is why so many inside Turkey and abroad had high expectations of what could be achieved by making membership conditional on performance in human rights. But until 1999, the membership target was just too remote, and there were too many reasons for the EU to default on the deal. Even when Turkey's candidacy was (rather serendipitously) recognized in December 1999, governmental indolence and state intransigence combined to block serious reform. It was only in early 2002, when it became clear that there was a chance of permanently losing the trophy, that the various elements came together to force a positive conclusion.

The Council of Europe's critical contribution has been described at some length. One rather imponderable question is the extent to which Turkey felt obliged to comply with CPT probing and ECHR judgments in the interests of its EU aspirations. Certainly, withdrawal from the Council of Europe, or suspension or expulsion from it, would surely have been fatal to all hopes of EU candidacy. If the door to Brussels had been conclusively shut, what incentive would Turkey have to subject itself to regular public humiliations (and expense) at the hands of the Strasbourg institutions? In this connection, it will be interesting to see whether Russia stays the course with the Council of Europe, given the fact that it too has widespread patterns of violations, but no immediate plans or prospects for EU integration. However that may be, it is clear that the existence of a transparent, independent expert human rights mechanisms armed with serious powers to investigate, report and punish is an indispensable companion to the highly politicized and much less transparent operations of the EU.

In the week following the August 2002 reforms, Mehmet Ali Birand, a long-standing commentator on the European process, wrote a formal thank-you to those who had assisted Turkey in taking an important step towards realizing its destiny. It is interesting to spot who he puts at the top of his honours list: 'for the first time cooperation between the nongovernmental organizations (NGOs) and the media came to the foreground and served as a driving force. In the past, politics used to take the initiative while the NGOs watched on' (Birand, 2002). The contribution of TUSIAD and the IKV has already been mentioned, but the whole gamut of nongovernmental organizations in Turkey were also key players in the story. In spite of all the problems with freedom of expression in Turkey, it is a country in which information about human rights moves far and fast. The Human Rights Association, *Mazlum-Der* (the Association for Oppressed Peoples) and the Human Rights Foundation kept all the players (particularly the European Commission) furnished with a huge amount of accurate and detailed information, and the Turkish media, imperfect as they are, were a powerful vehicle for the passionate debate that played out over the spring of 2002.

Turkish civil society and the EU worked together to secure the key August reforms, but civil society alone was the driving force behind most of the expansion of fundamental freedoms and the protection of human rights over the past decade. It is a commonplace that Turkey – pro-Western, cooperative, with a parliamentary democracy and a secular constitution – is the kind of Muslim state that the West likes. But it has been a singularly repressive brand of parliamentary democracy, and a highly authoritarian, manipulative kind of secularism that has long obscured the rich colours and strong tradition of tolerance in Turkey. Burgeoning civil society has set an example in expressing that tolerance. During the course of the accession process, *Mazlum-Der*, for example, played a particularly creditable role: it was one of the main champions of the legal changes to protect the property rights of Armenian, Greek and Jewish foundations, and ran a strong public campaign for the protection of those rights.

The analysis here suggests that the future of Turkey's human rights depends very much on non-state formations, with their direct experience of the value of social solidarity in challenging an overbearing state. Muslims and atheists, Kurds and Turks, have set aside their differences to stand up and defend their opponents' right to express their views as part of the Freedom for Freedom of Expression Initiative.[43] If Turkey follows this road, it could well prove before long to be a standard-setter for human rights in Europe and beyond, as it has already been on the death penalty and in the abolition of incommunicado detention in law.

But this bright picture will be possible only if conditions of peace continue. From the 1970s until the mid-1990s, armed violence from right, left, Kurdish separatist, Islamist and state forces created an environment in which human rights could not find a root and flourish. It was virtually impossible to talk of the rights of the Kurdish minority while body-bags of young soldiers were returning from the south-east every day. The arguments for protections against torture are just as valid in times of internal conflict as they are in peacetime, but experience worldwide shows that they do not get a good hearing while the government is using a terrorist threat to excuse itself from offering proper safeguards. As the story told here illustrates, the EU contribution was rather adventitious to the main story of the past half-decade: the retreat of political violence.

Note

The views expressed in this chapter are those of the author and do not necessarily represent those of Human Rights Watch.

1 See *Türk Halkının Avrupa Birliği Üyeliğine Bakışı* (How Turkish people view European Union membership), Turkish Economic and Social Studies Foundation (TESEV), July 2002.
2 Compare, for example, entries for Turkey in Human Rights Watch (1995) *World Report 1995*, Human Rights Watch, New York, with Human Rights Watch (2003) *World Report 2003*, Human Rights Watch, New York.
3 The illegal armed organization PKK was founded in 1978. In 1984, it began open hostilities with the government by attacking a gendarmerie in Eruh. In the following 15 years there were frequent clashes between PKK militants and the security forces.
4 Illegal armed opposition groups also committed appalling atrocities during the same period. Reliable news reports indicate that PKK members killed at least 400 prisoners and civilians between 1993 and 1995. Organizations such as the Revolutionary People's Liberation Party-Front (DHKP-C), the Turkish Revolutionary Communist Union (TIKB), the Turkish Liberation Army of Peasants and Workers (TIKKO) and the Islamic Raiders of the Big East-Front (IBDA-C) also carried out deliberate and arbitrary killings of prisoners or civilians (Amnesty International, 1996).
5 'Doğu ve güneydoğu Anadolu'da boşaltılan yerleşim birimleri nedeniyle göç eden yurttailarımızın sorunlarının araştırılarak alınması gereken tedbirlerin tespit edilmesi amacıyla kurulan meclis araştırması komisyonu raporu' (Report of the parliamentary commission established for the purpose of identifying remedies to be implemented on the basis of research into the problems of citizens who have migrated as a result of evacuation of settlements in east and south-east Anatolia), submitted to the Grand National Assembly of Turkey 14 January 1998, p. 11.
6 *Cumhuriyet* (Republic), 10 May 1995, quoted in Amnesty International (1996: 100).
7 Agence Europe, 25 April 1995, quoted in Amnesty International (1995b: 1).
8 Interim report by EU Commission entitled *Concerning the Reform Process: The Human Rights Situation and the Consolidation of Democracy in Turkey*, quoted in Amnesty International (1995b: 1).
9 Report of the Turkish Parliamentary Commission for Investigation of Killings by Unknown Perpetrators, published 12 October 1995.
10 The publicity forced the authorities to open a case against the alleged torturers in June 1996, but after passing through a maze of judgments and appeals, that case is still undecided. Police officers and the authorities did all they could to delay final judgment, and the case was due to expire on 25 June 2003.
11 Report by government inspector Kutlu Savaş, submitted to Parliament on 3 April 1997.
12 Public Statement on Turkey, Committee for the Prevention of Torture, CPT/Inf (93) 1 [EN], 15 December 1992.
13 Public Statement on Turkey, Committee for the Prevention of Torture; CPT/Inf (96) 34 [EN], 6 December 1996. In 2001, Turkey gave permission for all CPT reports to be published.
14 ECHR, *Aksoy* v. *Turkey*, 18 December 1996.
15 Law 4229 was published in *Resmi Gazete* (Official Gazette) on 6 March 1997.
16 Luxembourg European Council 1997, Presidency Conclusions, paragraph 35.
17 In a speech in March 1999, Ahmet Necdet Sezer, then president of the

Constitutional Court (but appointed President of the Republic the following year), declared that the Constitution imposed unacceptable restrictions on the basic freedoms of Turkish citizens – including limits on language rights – and called for harmonization of Turkish domestic law with the European Human Rights Convention. In September 1999, at the official opening of the judicial year and in the presence of the President and Prime Minister, the president of the Supreme Court, Dr Sami Selçuk, rated the legitimacy of the Constitution as 'almost zero' and expressed the hope that Turkey would not enter the twenty-first century under a regime that continued to 'crush minds and stifle voices'.

18 *Cumhuriyet* (Republic), quoted in the *Bulletin of the Kurdish Institute*, no. 179, February 2000, Paris.

19 Avrupa Birliği Müktesebatının Üstlenilmesine İlişkin Türkiye Ulusal Programı (Turkey's National Programme for the Adoption of the European Union [Acquis]), March 2001.

20 *Türkiye Cumhuriyeti anayasasının bazı maddelerinin değiştirilmesi hakkında kanun* (Law amending certain articles of the constitution of the Republic of Turkey), Statute 4709, 3 October 2001; *Bazı kanunlarda değişiklik yapılmasına dair kanun* (Law amending certain laws), Statute 4744, 6 February 2002; *Çeşitli kanunlarda değişiklik yapılmasına ilişkin kanun* (Law amending various laws), Statute 4748, 26 March 2002.

21 'EU urges Turkey to speed up reforms on death penalty, Kurdish rights', Associated Press, 15 February 2002.

22 'EU expects more steps to be taken on freedom of expression,' *Turkish Daily News*, 17 April 2002.

23 'Yılmaz holds a press conference in Brussels', Anatolia: News Agency, 21 March 2002.

24 'Deputy PM: Turkey can't join EU for a decade, no hurry for reforms', Associated Press, 11 June 2002.

25 'Asker AB tartışmasını bitirdi' (The soldiers have put an end to the EU debate), *Radikal*, 25 April 2002.

26 'Bahçeli refused to discuss death penalty ban, mother tongue education', NTV/MSNBC, 23 May 2002, available at www.flash-bulletin.de/2002/eMai23.htm.

27 The EU added the PKK to its list in May 2002.

28 'Avrupa kavgası kızıştı' (The Europe row heats up), *Radikal*, 9 March 2002.

29 'TUSIAD ultimatum: urgent reforms', *Turkish Daily News*, 30 May 2002.

30 'Civil society platform created to support EU bid', *Turkish Daily News*, 5 June 2002.

31 'Teslimiyetçiliğe hayır' (No to defeatism), *Cumhuriyet* (Republic), 7 June 2002.

32 'Kopenhag Kriterleri PKK'nın amaçlarıdır' (The Copenhagen criteria are the aims of the PKK), *Yeni Şafak* (New Dawn), 7 July 2002.

33 *Çeşitli kanunlarda değişiklik yapılmasına ilişkin kanun* (Law amending various laws), Statute 4771, 3 August 2002.

34 'Yılmaz asks EU to show same courage Turkey did', Anatolia News Agency, 5 August 2002.

35 At the time of writing, the sentence of execution against Amina Lawal has not been carried out.

36 The new government was established by the Justice and Development Party (*Adalet ve Kalkınma Partisi*, AKP), which has an Islamic legacy and won the national elections held in November 2002.

37 *Çeşitli kanunlarda değişiklik yapılmasına ilişkin kanun* (Law amending various laws), Statute 4793, 2 January 2003.

38 *Çeşitli kanunlarda değişiklik yapılmasına ilişkin kanun* (Law amending various laws), Statute 4778, 23 January 2003.

39 Article 159 of the Criminal Code provides for three years' imprisonment for insulting state institutions. Article 312 of the Criminal Code provides for three years' imprisonment for incitement to religious or racial hatred. In practice, it has been used to imprison those who press a view of ethnicity or religion in politics that challenges the unitary secular nature of the state. Two journalists, Ahmet Ünlü and Mehmet Kutlular, were imprisoned in 2002 for claiming that the 1999 earthquake was a divine punishment of a society that had departed from Islamic principles. The former president of the Human Rights Association, Akın Birdal, was imprisoned under article 312 in 1999 for making a speech referring to 'the Kurdish people'.

40 The August 2002 package contained a measure that provided the automatic right of retrial for anyone who, according to a judgment of the European Court of Human Rights, had suffered a violation under the convention. But the August package did not make this right retrospective, and thereby excluded the four Kurdish parliamentarians imprisoned for their legitimate activities as parliamentary deputies after a trial that was (according to the ECHR) unfair: Hatip Dicle, Orhan Doğan, Selim Sadak and Leyla Zana.

41 'Soros calls on EU to highlight importance of core democratic values in aftermath of September 11 attacks', press release, Open Society Institute, EU Accession Monitoring Programme, 11 October 2001.

42 For further information on this topic, see Human Rights Watch (2002).

43 The Freedom for Freedom of Expression Initiative re-publishes statements, articles, caricatures and songs that do not advocate violence but have nevertheless been subject to prosecution under various articles of the Turkish criminal code. These re-publications are then submitted to the courts, which are obliged to open court actions. The actions embarrass the authorities because the re-publishers are either well-known public figures or huge groups of ordinary citizens. A record-breaking 77,663 defendants were responsible for publishing a book on the trial in this case: 'Freedom of Expression – for All.'

References

Amnesty International (1994), 'Turkey: responses to an emerging pattern of extrajudicial executions', in *'Disappearances' and Political Killings: A Manual for Action*, Amnesty International, Amsterdam.

Amnesty International (1995a), *A Policy of Denial*, Amnesty International, London.

Amnesty International (1995b), *Unfulfilled Promise of Reform*, Amnesty International, London.

Amnesty International (1996), *No security without human rights*, Amnesty International, London.

Berberoğlu, E. (2002), 'TSK [Turkish Armed Forces] and MHP keep quiet at MGK meeting', *Radikal*, 6 June 2002.

Birand, M. A. (2002) 'Let us give everybody their due', *Turkish Daily News*, 9 August.

Cebe, Ö. (2003), 'Kürt demedim, suçsuzum' (I did not say Kurd, I am innocent), *Milliyet* (Nationhood), 5 March 2003.

Cohen, R. (1999), 'Hard cases: internal displacement in Turkey, Burma and Algeria', *Forced Migration Review*, no. 6 (December).

Ertan, N. (1995), 'Turkey and the European Union open a new era', *Turkish Daily News*, 14 December.

Human Rights Watch (2002), *Displaced and Disregarded: Turkey's Failing Village Return Program*, New York: Human Rights Watch.

Jones, Dorian (2002), 'Turkey's "cultural crackdown" may backfire', Radio Netherlands, 25 January, available at www.rnw.nl/hotspots/html/turkey020125.html.

Kramer, H. (2000), *A Changing Turkey*, Washington, DC: Brookings Institution Press.

Uğur, M. (1996) 'Customs union as a substitute for membership? A re-interpretation of EU–Turkey relations', *Cambridge* Review of International Affairs, vol. 10, no. 1, pp. 10–29.

Verheugen, G. (2000), 'A bigger EU will be good for America, too', *European Affairs*, vol. 1, no. 4.

12 Turkey and European integration
Conclusions

Mehmet Uğur and Nergis Canefe

In contrast to usual practice, we begin this concluding chapter with a digression. Instead of going into the book's main findings on the current state of Turkey–EU relations, we will step back to the late 1980s and early 1990s – when the collapse of the Soviet Union prompted speculations on whether Turkey's geo-strategic importance would decline. In response, Turkish policy-makers initiated a campaign asserting the significance of the 'Turkish model' in a post-Soviet world. The argument was simple and, therefore, appealing: Turkey, with the exception of Israel, was the only country in the region that combined parliamentary democracy with a market economy that was able to deliver satisfactory growth rates. Referring to the country's Islamic heritage and its ethnic affinities with many of the post-Soviet countries in the Caucasus and Central Asia, it was argued that Turkey is well placed to act not only as a 'model' for many countries at the periphery of Europe but also as a bridge between the East and the West. Such arguments were in clear abundance – not only in statements envisaged for domestic consumption, but also in those aimed at strengthening Turkey's case in negotiations with Western interlocutors, especially the European Union (EU).

This volume does not attempt to assess the relevance of such arguments or wishes. True, the Turkish economy had become integrated with the world economy and registered satisfactory growth rates from 1981 to 1988. In addition, at the microeconomic level, both large and small to medium-sized companies have proved capable of responding to the incentives provided by the policy of export-led growth as well as withstanding the international competitiveness that comes with liberalisation. Politically, the strength of Turkish civil society, which flourished under the Turkish model, and the challenges it has begun to pose for the legitimacy of the 'strong state' tradition cannot and should not be underestimated.

Yet, and without prejudice to what we have just said, we are of the view that the so-called Turkish model contained significant deficiencies that became apparent from the mid-1990s onwards. Not only has Turkish democracy left too much to be desired, but also the Turkish economy has suffered from inefficiency, macroeconomic instability, and regional as well as social inequality. True, the contributions to this volume cannot and should not be taken as a basis for a comprehensive assessment of the Turkish model, simply because this has not been their remit.[1] Nevertheless, and irrespective of Turkey's achievements in the 1980s and 1990s, the contributions to this volume expose significant weaknesses in the 'Turkish model'. In its political dimension, the 'Turkish model' has been too restrictive to ensure either rule of law or respect for human rights. In terms of economic governance, the model has perpetuated populism and produced graphic examples of economic mismanagement.

More to the point, however, the contributions to this volume demonstrate that the Turkish model has now become dysfunctional for Turkey's long-standing aim of joining the EU as a full member. In fact, the model's staunch proponents (the Kemalist elite, the centre-left and centre-right political parties, and the military establishment) have eventually become a major source of resistance to Turkey's integration with Europe. The only exception in this respect has been some sections of the business elite, which broke ranks with the political elite in the mid-1990s as the latter began to waver in their commitment to integration with Europe. In contrast, the model's ardent critics[2] have emerged as the new 'owners' of the EU membership project.

This volume's somewhat unintended contribution to the debate on Turkey–EU relations can be stated as follows: recent developments in the crisis-prone Turkey–EU relations can be read in the light of the change in the ownership of Turkey's EU membership project. Up to now, many studies on Turkey–EU relations have come up with various explanations for the rejection of Turkey's membership application in 1989, Turkey's exclusion from the eastern enlargement in 1997, and Turkey's evident divergence from European foreign policy objectives, including, but not limited to, the resolution of the Cyprus problem. Explanations on offer vary from systemic changes brought about by the end of the Cold War (Eralp, 1993) through cultural/identity conflicts (Keyder, 1992; Buzan and Diez, 1999) to the perception of Turkey as 'the other' in the construction of European identity (Müftüler-Baç, 2000). Although we do not intend to discuss the relevance of these explanations here, we are of the view that they have overlooked the early signals of the 'ownership change' and, as a consequence, underestimated the negative repercussions of the uncertainty that would be inevitably associated with this change.

What is the evidence concerning the ownership change and what are the implications for Turkey–EU relations? For example, Çarkoğlu's detailed analysis of public opinion on EU membership (Chapter 2) points to an evident reluctance on the part of the political parties to 'own' the European project in their recent election campaigns. In fact, Çarkoğlu draws our attention to an anomaly that is unique to Turkey: the fact that the political elite, instead of building on mass support for EU membership, have tended to manipulate the public debate on Turkey–EU relations by pitching their rhetoric around 'sensitive issues' such as cultural rights for the Kurdish minority and abolition of the death penalty. Even pro-EU forces gave 'the impression of being intimidated by the anti-EU camp'. Çarkoğlu's findings, however, suggest that such a strategy was never likely to pay off in terms of electoral success even though it was likely to harden the stance of those already against EU membership.

The change of heart among the political establishment is also pointed out by Avcı in Chapter 9. According to Avcı, political party leaders had been content with declaring general support for Turkey's EU membership as long as the debate on Turkey–EU relations was couched in 'broad, abstract geopolitical or historical terms'. This 'superficial consensus' broke down dramatically when the extent of necessary reforms became apparent – especially after Turkey had been granted candidate status at the Helsinki summit of December 1999. Indeed, not only has the Nationalist Action Party (*Milliyetçi Hareket Partisi*, MHP) begun to harden its anti-EU stance, but also other parties have shifted towards the MHP's position with a view to either attracting support from potential MHP voters or limiting their losses. Ironically, it was the party with an Islamic background, the Justice and Development Party (*Adalet ve Kalkınma Partisi*, AKP), that emerged as the 'owner' of the EU membership project. The AKP government, established after the November 2002 elections, declared 'full membership of the EU' to be the 'priority aim', and one that would also ensure 'economic and democratic development' in Turkey.

Evidence of ownership change can also be seen in Keyman and Öniş's contribution in Chapter 8. Keyman and Öniş detect ownership change among political parties as well as state bureaucracy. As far as political parties are concerned, they concur with Çarkoğlu and with Avcı. They state that 'political parties in Turkey lagged behind civil society organizations' in terms of their support for EU membership. The AKP, despite its Islamist background, 'emerged as the political party that appeared to display the type of commitment towards EU membership that was not visible in the case of any other political party on either the right or the left of the political spectrum'. As far as the state elite is concerned, they indicate that these groups, despite their long-standing support for integration with the West, have become part of the anti-EU coalition mainly because their 'mindset ... could not comprehend the kind of post-national state and the notion of pooling of sovereignty that had been associated with the emergence of the New Europe in the 1980s and the 1990s'.

Keyman and Öniş also provide some evidence on the composition of the 'new owners' of the integration project. This pro-EU coalition is led by civil society organisations, which include not only business organisations such as TUSIAD (the peak business organisation of the business elite) and the Economic Development Foundation (IKV) (on this, see also Atan's contribution in Chapter 5); but also non-business members of the 'Movement for Europe 2002', which mobilised 175 civil society organisations in favour of Turkey's accession. Keyman and Öniş also draw attention to the fact that the pro-EU coalition included some sections of the state bureaucracy – especially those engaged in the design and implementation of economic policy. Given this composition, one can only agree with Keyman and Öniş that the issue of Turkey's EU membership, especially in the post-Helsinki period, has exposed a significant rift 'not only between the state and civil society, but also between different components of the Turkish state itself'.

The implications of this change for Turkey–EU relations are not difficult to predict. One implication is that the ownership change is highly likely to induce the EU to prioritize the risks and discount the benefits associated with Turkey's accession. Turkey's exclusion from the eastern enlargement in 1997 and the Copenhagen summit's refusal to grant a definite date for the start of accession negotiations can be read in this light. As Keyman and Öniş suggest, however, the EU's approach to Turkey's integration can and should be criticised on the grounds that it is short-sighted and deprives the emergent pro-EU coalition of vital support in its struggle against the stakeholders of the *ancien régime*.[3]

Nevertheless, the uncertainty associated with the change in the ownership of the Europeanisation project cannot be overlooked altogether. On the one hand, the EU will look for signs that the emergent pro-EU coalition can gel, and fill in the vacuum created by the desertion of the traditional owners of the EU membership project. On the other, the EU will also want to see that the AKP government can 'govern' without alienating other stakeholders of the membership project, and, more importantly, without major policy reversals to appease either its religious support base or the anti-EU coalition, especially the military establishment. Therefore, in the short term, Turkey's accession process is highly likely to be marked with tensions emanating from the triangular interactions between the societal sections of the pro-EU coalition, the AKP government itself and the EU's weak commitment to integrate Turkey.

On the positive side, the change of ownership provides some scope for optimism too. Evidence pointing in this direction is generally indirect and related to serious doubts about the sustainability of the Turkish model. Eder's and Uğur's contributions (Chapters 3 and 4) provide theoretical and empirical evidence suggesting that the Turkish model may have run its course. While Eder demonstrates why Turkey's liberalisation reforms have produced 'voodoo politics', Uğur demonstrates the extent to which Turkish macroeconomic policy has been conducive to recurrent crises and pushed Turkey down various 'league tables' of economic performance. On the other hand, Atan's contribution demonstrates how these indicators of 'model failure' have prompted some sections of the business elite to campaign for radical change and elicit societal as well as 'official' commitment to EU membership. As Keyman and Öniş indicate, frustration with past policy failures has been an essential stimulus for civil societal activism in favour of EU membership too. Finally, some of Çarkoğlu's findings suggest that a credible commitment to EU membership by AKP leadership is likely to strengthen the pro-EU constituency. Put together, these findings suggest that there is an emerging consensus that EU membership has become an essential 'operation' to treat the 'ills' of the Turkish model. This emerging consensus, in turn, is likely to induce the EU to revise its essentially short-termist, risk-minimising approach to Turkey's integration.

Having examined the crisis of the Turkish model and the implications of the ownership change, we can now return to the main findings of this volume on a number of issues in Turkey–EU relations. As is well known, one issue concerns cultural compatibilities or incompatibilities between Turkey and Europe. The debate on this issue has always struck us with an evident imbalance between the passion with which it began to be pursued after the Helsinki decision of December 1999 and the inadequacy of the empirical foundations on which it is based. With the exception of a few statements by the centre-right parties in some member states, and by Helmut Kohl and Valéry Giscard d'Estaing in a personal as opposed to an official capacity, we are not aware of any publicly available information that would enable us to gauge the extent to which official EU policy towards Turkey is drawn largely with Turkey's cultural difference in mind. Of course, we do not pretend that this issue is insignificant for understanding the evolution of Turkey–EU relations. Nor do we overlook the possibility that the 'language' of the debate can acquire a force in itself and modify the 'reality' of Turkey–EU relations. Yet on the basis of the findings in this volume, we can argue that there is ample scope for questioning the central role that is being increasingly ascribed to essentialist cultural/identity arguments encountered in the academic study of Turkey–EU relations as well as in the media.

One reason is that Turkish culture and identity are subject to change – and at a faster pace than the current European experience. During a short period after 1998, not only the role of Islam in Turkish politics but also the concept of Turkish citizenship has been under immense pressure for change. The contributions by Duran and Fokas (Chapters 6 and 7) provide significant evidence of the extent as well as the direction of the change concerning the role of Islam in the Turkish polity and Turkish society. The extent of the change is unprecedented because, for the first time in Turkey's post-1980 history, a political party with an Islamist background has formed a government that is committed to representative democracy, the rule of law, secular legitimacy, and integration with Europe. The direction of change, on the other hand, is towards convergence with Europe, because it reflects a gradual move away from essentialist definitions of Islamic and European identities towards relativism and accommodation.

The other reason why we should qualify the significance of the cultural/ identity issues in Turkey–EU relations is the following: Turkey's eventual

EU membership would not pose a 'new' problem for EU and national policy-makers; it would merely force European policy-makers to address a long-standing but conveniently avoided problem that arises out of Europe's relations with Islamic countries in general and its substantial Muslim minority in particular. In other words, Turkey's EU membership would induce European policy-makers to give substance to the concept of 'New Europe' rather than pose an obstacle to its construction. Duran's contribution provides significant evidence of the extent to which at least some Islamists in Turkey are aware of this fine distinction and its implications for European identity. This is a significant development that demonstrates that Turkey's Islamists can be as pragmatic as their 'Christian' counterparts in the EU.

Without prejudice to what we have just said, however, the contributions to this volume also draw attention to difficulties likely to be encountered prior to and after Turkey's EU membership. For example, Fokas, on the basis of a careful analysis of her evidence, identifies two difficulties that would arise prior to Turkey's EU membership: ascertaining the credibility of the AKP's commitment to a secular, republican regime in Turkey; and the extent to which both Islamists and secular/Kemalist forces are prepared to discuss their differences in a manner compatible with basic requirements of democracy. We conjecture that the EU will monitor progress in these areas and decide on the timing of actual accession accordingly. That is why it is not surprising to observe that discussions in Turkey on the role of religion in general and Islam in particular first began when EU membership ceased to be a distant eventuality. In that respect, the issue of religion in Turkey–EU relations is actually not dramatically different from other issues involving convergence, which is a necessary condition for and an inevitable consequence of Turkey's integration within Europe.

Yet it would be naïve not to expect the discussion to continue into the future – embracing not only Turkey but also the EU. The evidence provided by Duran suggests that even non-essentialist Islamists in Turkey are highly likely to push for a redefinition of the European identity. In addition, Canefe in Chapter 10 detects some weaknesses in the concept of European citizenship that may interact with those of the Turkish version. The discussion on these issues may well degenerate into essentialist arguments and counter-arguments, for the resolution of which the EU system is not (and cannot be expected to be) equipped. The chapters by Fokas, Duran and Canefe rightly draw attention to such difficulties, but they do not confuse the probability of such eventualities with *ex ante* assertions about the compatibility or incompatibility of European and Turkish cultures or identities.

The second issue in Turkey–EU relations that this volume can shed light upon is the extent to which Turkey is likely to act as a brake on the deepening of European integration. There are two possible reasons why Turkey could adopt a Euro-sceptic position, similar to that of the United Kingdom, that would resist increased delegation of authority to regional institutions. First, Kemalist/nationalist forces may have relinquished the ownership of the Europeanisation project, but neither their legacy nor their rearguard actions in the future can be disregarded. Second, Islamists may well be in the process of redefining their Islamic identity, but their outlook shares some of the assumptions of the Kemalist tradition and embodies an anti-Western reflex that blames the West not only for the collapse of the Ottoman Empire but also for misfortunes of the Islamic world in general. For these reasons, Turkish governments of all shades may well be inclined to invoke the concepts of 'sovereignty' and 'national interests' either to slow down the decision-making process or to secure significant concessions.

What is the evidence indicating that such outcomes are possible? For example, Eder's chapter demonstrates that populism may well survive economic liberalisation reforms. Although Eder is aware of the fact that the Copenhagen criteria also require political and institutional reforms, she draws attention to the danger that the latter may either remain on paper or fail to go far enough because of the 'bureaucratic-technocratic' aspects of the EU system itself. To the extent that this proves to be the case, populism may continue to haunt Turkish economic policy even within the EU. The implication here is that the discipline of EU membership may increase the premium on discretion as a tool that would enable Turkish policy-makers to satisfy parochial claims in return for political support.

Uğur concurs with Eder that discretion has survived (and, in fact, has been reinforced by) the economic liberalisation programmes of the 1980s and early 1990s – leading to disastrous consequences in terms of economic governance as well as performance. Yet Uğur also draws attention to the possibility that the persistence of discretion may have been due to wrong sequencing – that is, the introduction of economic liberalisation prior to political and institutional reforms. Because EU membership requires a significant change in 'the rules of the game' and imposes discipline on Turkish policy-makers, the scope for discretion and rent-seeking may diminish.[4] Then, the extent to which Turkey could resist deep integration would depend on the balance between two opposing tendencies: (i) an increased premium on discretion as a means of satisfying rent-seeking demands; and (ii) reduced scope for discretion under EU rules and regulations.

Other indications that Turkey could emerge as a significant Euro-sceptic force within the EU can be gleaned from the contributions by Duran and Çarkoğlu. For example, Duran draws the significant conclusion that Islamist discourses in favour of EU membership 'pay much attention to "being in Europe"', but 'they pay far less attention to "being/becoming part of Europe"'. This imbalance is clearly related to unresolved issues in the wider Islamist debate as well as to the anti-Western reflex that the Islamists are inclined to resort to when they are unhappy with European influence. On the other hand, Çarkoğlu's findings on sensitive issues in Turkey–EU relations call for serious attention. Although a clear majority of the respondents agree that some fundamental rights and freedoms should exist in Turkey, the overwhelming support disappears when it comes to reforms for securing the exercise of such rights and freedoms. In addition, the resistance increases even further when such reforms are presented as the last hurdle facing Turkey's EU membership. In other words, the Turkish public tends to be willing to compromise on essential rights and freedoms if the latter imply radical change or are seen as part of EU conditionality. Put together, these findings suggest that there is a substantial basis that fosters civil-societal Euro-scepticism, which Turkish policy-makers can draw upon to align themselves with their Euro-sceptic counterparts within the EU.

The Kemalist legacy and the anti-Western reflex resorted to in times of difficulties will continue to shape Turkey's foreign policy – as can be seen in the approach to the Cyprus problem as well as Greco-Turkish bilateral issues. Avcı's analysis of Turkish political parties demonstrates clearly that the latter either toe the military establishment's line on these issues or, as is seen in the case of the AKP, have had to modify their election manifestos as well as their post-election statements. This finding is supported by those of Fokas, who sees the Cyprus issue as a significant litmus test for the AKP's ability to govern. What is important here is not whether Turkey can join the EU before demonstrating some flexibility on these issues, but the ability of the Kemalist/military elite to act as a 'veto group' when it comes to foreign policy issues equated with Turkish 'national interest'. Taken together with Duran's and Çarkoğlu's findings concerning the civil-societal reflex against concessions involving sensitive issues, the findings by Avcı and Fokas suggest that Turkey is likely to favour loose as opposed to deep integration across a range of domestic and foreign policy issues. Given that Turkey's voting power on the basis of current criteria, will be equivalent to that of Germany, we can conclude that Turkish membership may strengthen the intra-EU arguments in favour of slow integration.

The third issue in Turkey–EU relations that this volume has put under the spotlight is the extent to which the EU has acted as a catalyst for reforms in Turkey. The contributions enable us to formulate two conclusions on this issue. First, and at a general level, the granting of candidate status in the Helsinki summit of December 1999 has led to the acceleration of adjustment reforms. Second, the quality of the reform has been dependent on two factors: the emergence of a pro-reform coalition within Turkey, and the EU's ability to monitor the quality of the reform output. The first conclusion is supported by the findings of Keyman and Öniş and Avcı. While the former observe an increase in the EU's influence following the reduction in the asymmetry between the costs and incentives of the EU–Turkey partnership; Avcı relates the EU's influence to the logic of

Europeanisation, which generates both pro- and anti-EU dynamics in accession countries.

The second conclusion finds its full expression as well as its support in Sugden's contribution. As a well-informed observer of Turkey's human rights record for more than a decade, Sugden demonstrates clearly that EU leverage remained limited until the reform package in the summer of 2002. For Sugden, this outcome was predictable because the EU, despite its conditionality and annual progress reports, is not as effective or experienced as the Council of Europe when it comes to identifying loopholes or making concrete recommendations. The outcome was predictable also because human rights reforms in particular and democratisation in general must be owned domestically if the EU, or any other external actor for that matter, is to have effective leverage.

Having identified the main findings of this volume on Turkey–EU relations, we can now indicate what we, as editors, have learned from this project and what new research avenues can be explored in the future. First of all, we benefited immensely from the critical approach to Turkey–EU relations. Interrogating both Turkish and EU positions is a *sine qua non* condition for understanding not only Turkey's accession prospects, but also the EU's ability to integrate a large and developing country that has been suffering from the fallouts of an increasingly dysfunctional regime. Second, we have discovered that the EU itself, irrespective of the strengths and weaknesses of its policy towards Turkey, can actually serve as a lens that puts the shortcomings of the Turkish polity into sharp relief for everybody to see. Finally, we have become convinced that Turkey–EU relations, despite evident indicators of divergence and tensions, are now beyond the stage of asking essentialist questions about compatibility or incompatibility. On the contrary, Turkey–EU relations are now at a stage where the balance is in favour of innovative and pragmatic problem-solving rather than scholastic contemplation on whether or not Turkey can become part of the EU. Although problem-solving may well involve questions of fundamental significance, it is very different from debating essentialist questions concerning compatibility or incompatibility.

As far as future research is concerned, we identify a number of themes brought to the fore by the contributions to this volume. One such theme involves economic governance in Turkey and its connections with EU governance. This theme is highly relevant for two reasons. First, since 1999 a wide range of reforms have been introduced in Turkey, mainly to satisfy the IMF conditionality. Second, Turkey must achieve growth rates above the EU average on a sustainable basis in order to narrow the development gap, which has been widened by the boom–bust cycles of the post-1994 period. Therefore, it is time to take stock and explore answers to three questions (i) Are the economic reforms adequate for breaking the discretion/rent-seeking vicious circle that has undermined Turkey's economic performance? (ii) How can a new member such as Turkey (or other new members from Central and Eastern Europe, for that matter) comply with the rule-based EU regime? (iii) How can the ongoing debate on EU economic governance (especially the stance of monetary policy and the issue of fiscal discipline) be rephrased in a way that takes into account the development needs of the new member states? Unfortunately, indications emerging from the new member states in Central and Eastern Europe do not foster optimism, as the debate seems to be revolving around old-fashioned and, given the limits to the EU budget, futureless distributional issues. Turkey's accession process may turn out to be the final opportunity to address these questions before they come back to haunt EU economic governance with a vengeance.

The second research theme involves the geographical and substantive widening of the debate on the role of Islam in the Turkish polity as well as European integration. Impressive as it is, the *non-essentialist* version of the Islamist debate in Turkey is still in its infancy and does not address a number of fundamental questions. Therefore, it needs to be extended substantively. It must also be extended geographically so that it becomes part of the European debate too. True, the European literature on Islam has a long history, but it tends to be coloured by orientalism. That is why European questions on Islam tend to reflect the epistemological premise that Islam is external to the European 'reality'. Yet irrespective of whether or not Turkey joins the EU, the globalisation process itself and the existence of a large Muslim population in Europe combine to make Islam a European issue, rather than a merely external 'object' for social-scientific study. Therefore, and given the emerging non-essentialist Turkish interpretations of Islam documented in this volume, there is a strong case for collaborative research by both Turkish and European scholars on questions such as the following: (i) Is Europe a 'civilizational project' that can accommodate different faiths? (ii) Do Islamists in Turkey accept Europe as such a project? (iii) What are the limits to and contradictions of the emerging non-essentialist approach to Islam and Europe? (iv) What are the practical issues that would emerge as a result of integrating Turkey as a Muslim country?

The third research theme concerns the production of public goods or avoidance of public bads at a regional level.[5] This theme is related to the findings of the contributors to Part IV on domestic–international interactions in the context of Turkey–EU relations. The contributions in this part of the book examine the extent to which the membership prospect given at the Helsinki summit of December 1999 has encouraged reform and change in Turkey. The findings may differ in their emphasis on what constitutes the primary stimulus for change, but they are in agreement on the linkage between the pace of reform/change in Turkey and the latter's perceived chance of joining the EU as a full member. Given this correlation, one is encouraged to think that regional integration can act as an arrangement that enables either individual countries or a regional grouping to overcome collective action problems that limit the supply of essential reforms within the country itself or within the region. Research questions within this theme may include, but are not limited to, the following: (i) How does European integration affect the scope for overcoming collective action problems in candidate countries? (ii) What are the connections between intra-country collective action problems and cross-border externalities? (iii) What are the costs and benefits of reforms and how are these distributed between accession countries and the EU? (iv) Can the regional public good approach inform the debate on a multi-speed Europe?

We would like to conclude by thanking our contributors for improving our knowledge of Turkey–EU relations and inspiring us to ask further questions. We hope that our positive experience will be shared by the readers of this volume too.

Notes

1 For a balanced assessment of the 'Turkish model' in the mid-1990s by one of the contributors to this volume, see Öniş (1998).
2 We refer here to intellectuals, revisionist Islamic groups, the Kurds, Alevis, civil society organisations etc. who either had been against integration with Europe in the past or were marginalised in the essentially elite-driven debate.
3 This is similar to Uğur's (1999, 2003) criticism that the EU failed to act as an effective anchor for Turkish policy reform in the 1980s and 1990s. Yet the 'anchor/credibility dilemma' framework also suggests that EU's failure to act as an effective anchor is partly due to frequent policy reversals in Turkey, which made the latter's commitment to EU membership non-credible.
4 We must also note here that fiscal constraints emanating from the IMF conditionality will continue to limit the scope for discretion and patronage distribution. This is due to the fact that Turkey's external debt burden is very high relative to its export earnings or gross national product.
5 There is already a burgeoning literature on regional and global public goods. See, for example, Kaul *et al.* (1999) and Sandler (1998).

References

Buzan, B. and T. Diez (1999), 'The European Union and Turkey', *Survival*, vol. 41, no. 1, pp. 41–57.

Eralp, A. (1993), 'Turkey and the European Union in the changing post-war international system', in C. Balkır and A. M. Williams (eds), *Turkey and Europe*, London: Pinter, pp. 24–44.

Kaul, I., I. Grunberg and M. Stern (eds) (1999), *Global Public Goods: International Cooperation in the 21st Century*, New York: Oxford University Press.

Keyder, Ç. (1992) 'Les Dilemmes de l'occidentalisation en Turquie', in S. Mappa (ed.), *L'Europe de Douze et les autres: intégration ou auto-exclusion?*, Paris: Éditions Karthala, pp. 241–256.

Müftüler-Baç, M. (2000), 'Through the looking glass: Turkey in Europe', *Turkish Studies*, vol. 1, no. 1, pp. 21–35.

Öniş, Z. (1998), 'The state and economic development in contemporary Turkey: étatism to neo-liberalism and beyond', in Z. Öniş (ed.), *State and Market: The Political Economy of Turkey in Comparative Perspective*, Istanbul: Boğaziçi University Press, pp. 455–476.

Sandler, T. (1998), 'Global and regional public goods: a prognosis for collective action', *Fiscal Studies*, vol. 19, no. 3, pp. 221–247.

Uğur, M. (1999), *The European Union and Turkey: An Anchor/Credibility Dilemma*, Aldershot, UK: Ashgate.

Uğur, M. (2003), 'Testing time in EU–Turkey relations: the road to Copenhagen and beyond', *Journal of Southern Europe and the Balkans*, vol. 5, no. 2, pp. 161–178.

Index

Page numbers in *italics* indicate tables and figures.